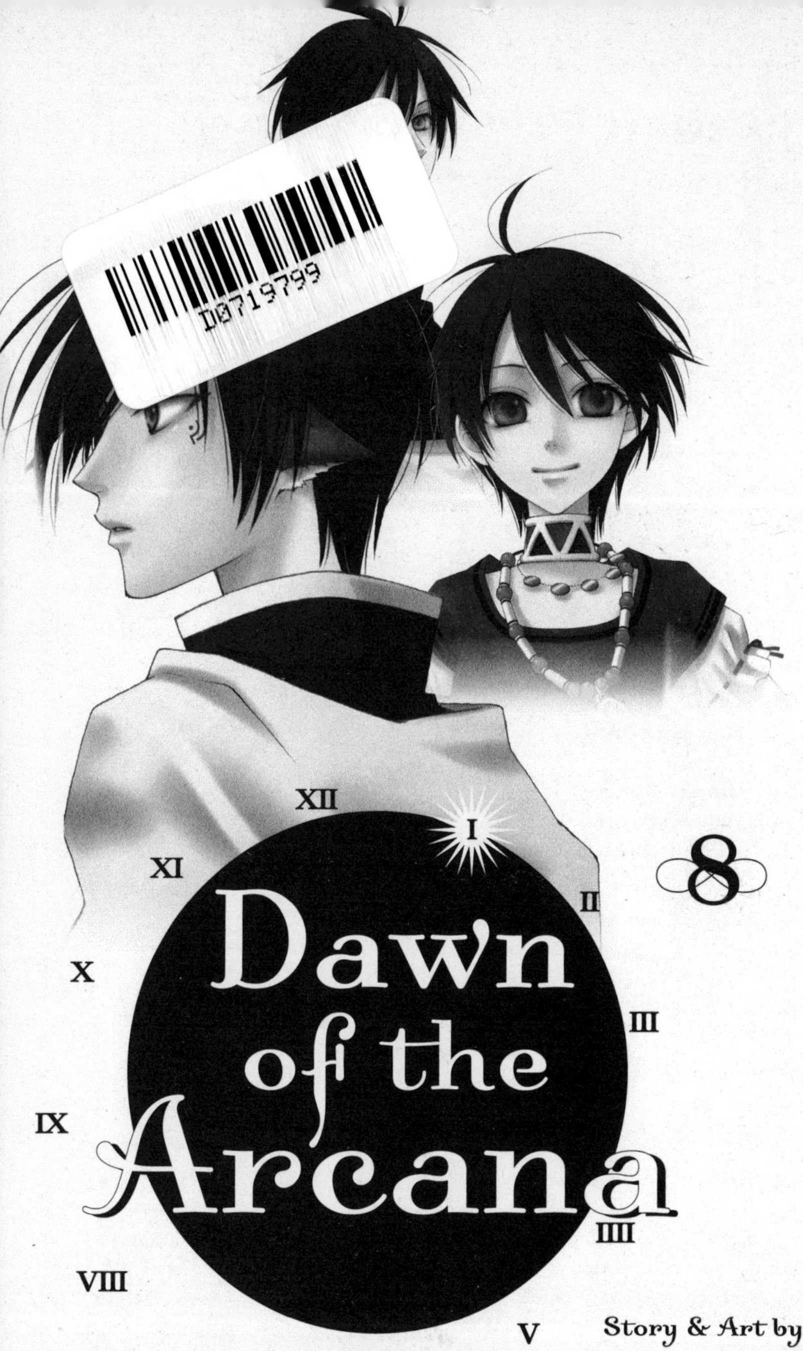

Dawn of the Arcana

8

Story & Art by

Rei Toma

characters

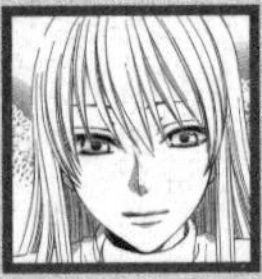

Sara
King Guran's concubine. Deceased.

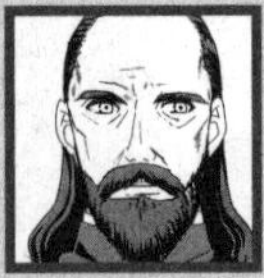

Guran
King of Belquat.

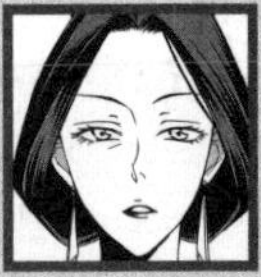

Rosenta
Queen of Belquat.

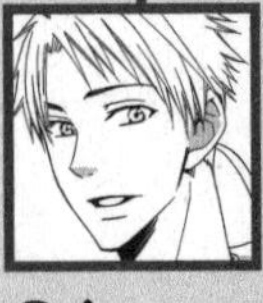

Cain
First-born prince of Belquat. Caesar's brother. He was recently killed by Loki.

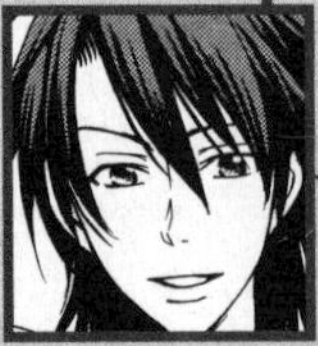

Caesar
The second-born prince of Belquat. Nakaba's husband through a marriage of political convenience. Headstrong and selfish.

Married

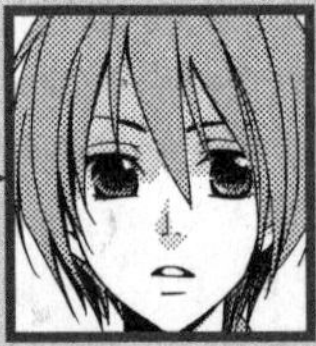

Nakaba
The princess royal of Senan. Strong of will and noble of spirit, she possesses a strange power.

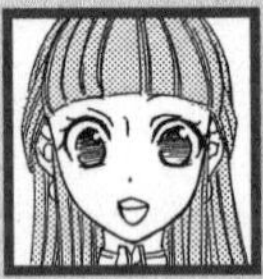

Lemiria
Bellinus's younger sister. Fond of her big brother.

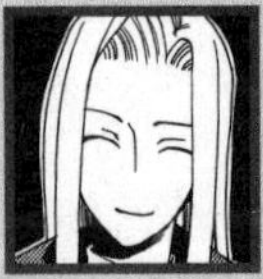

Bellinus
Caesar's attendant. Always cool and collected.

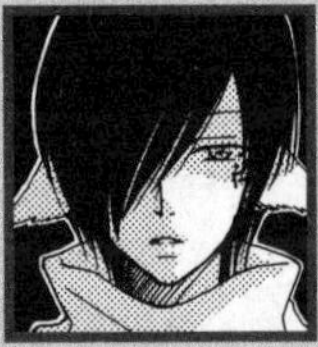

Loki
Nakaba's attendant. His senses of perception are unmatched.

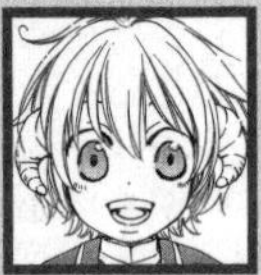

Rito
Nakaba's attendant. Recently arrived from Senan.

story

• Wed to Prince Caesar as a symbol of the peace between their two countries, Nakaba is actually little more than a hostage. Unbeknownst to King Guran, she is a survivor of the race he tried to destroy for fear of their power. Nakaba herself possesses the Arcana of Time, so she can see the past and the future.

Neighboring Kingdoms

Senan
A poor kingdom in the cold north of the island. Militarily weak.

Belquat
A powerful country that thrives thanks to its temperate climate.

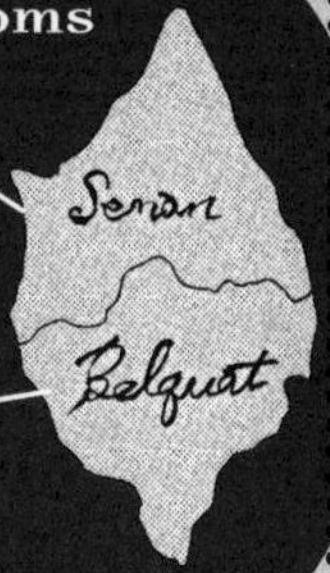
Senan
Belquat

• The political marriage between Nakaba and Caesar gets off to a rocky start, but as they grow to know each other, the gulf between them begins to close. After learning of King Guran's plans to test a devastating new weapon on a demi-human village, Nakaba and her companions try to stop them. But with Caesar's brother Cain in command of the mission, they are unable to avoid a battle. In order to protect Nakaba, Loki kills Cain.

• Nakaba becomes deeply depressed over Cain's death, but Caesar is able to reach her and draw her back. Their growing love for each other deepens.

• Realizing that pursuit from Belquat is inevitable after Cain's death, Nakaba and the others travel to Senan and visit the castle. The king of Senan is eager to form ties with the country Lithuanel, so the group make the journey there on his majesty's orders.

• Being acquainted with Akhil, the fifth prince of Lithuanel, Nakaba and company reach out to him for help upon arrival. He agrees, on the condition that they help capture a group of bandits plaguing the country, thus bolstering support for the second prince, Azhal, in his bid to be crowned king.

• Using the Arcana of Time, Nakaba identifies the bandits' next target and accompanies Akhil's people there...only to find that the bandits include a snake demi-human!

Dawn of the Arcana

Volume 8

CONTENTS

XII

XI

X

IX

VIII

VII   VI

Chapter 28

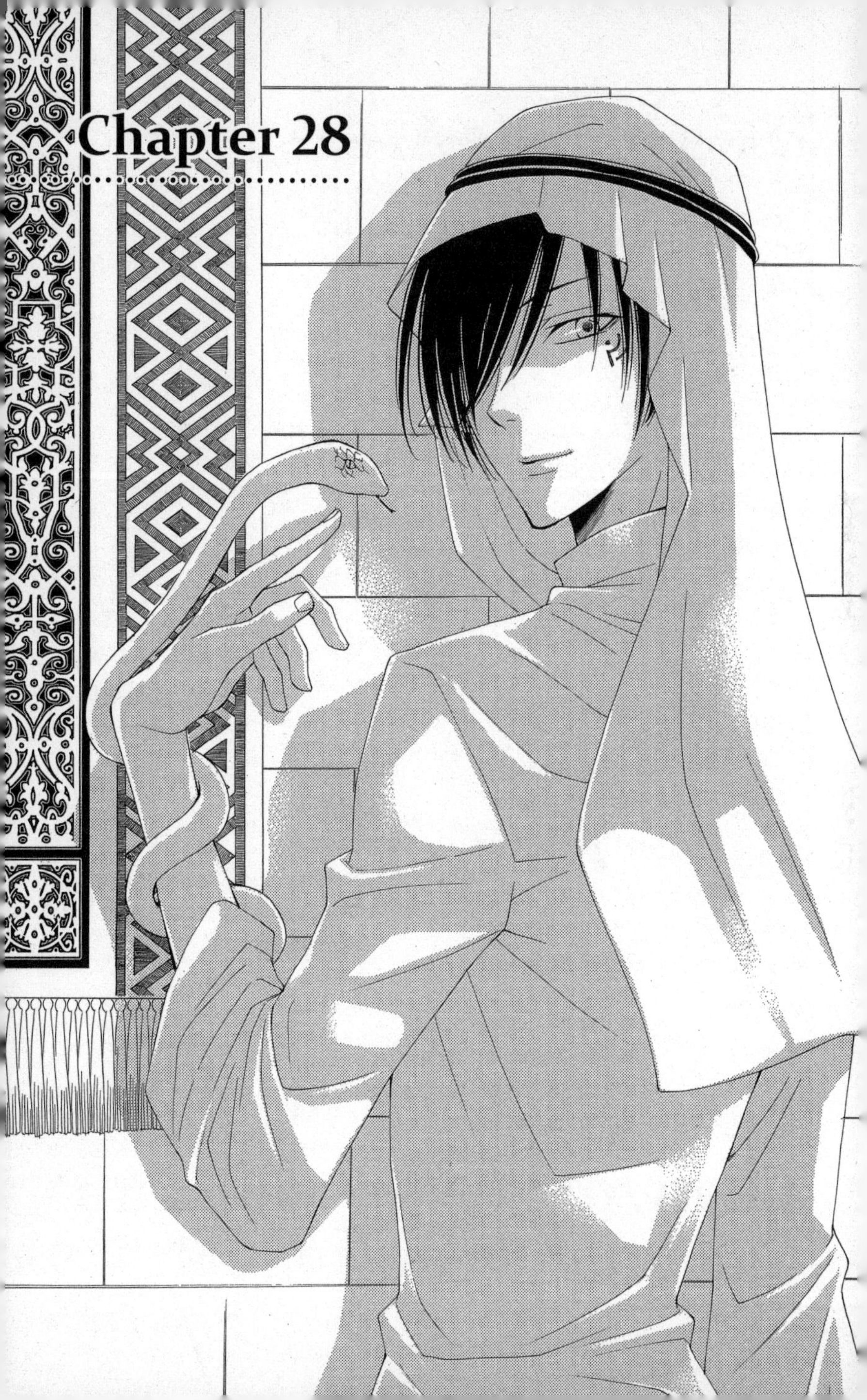

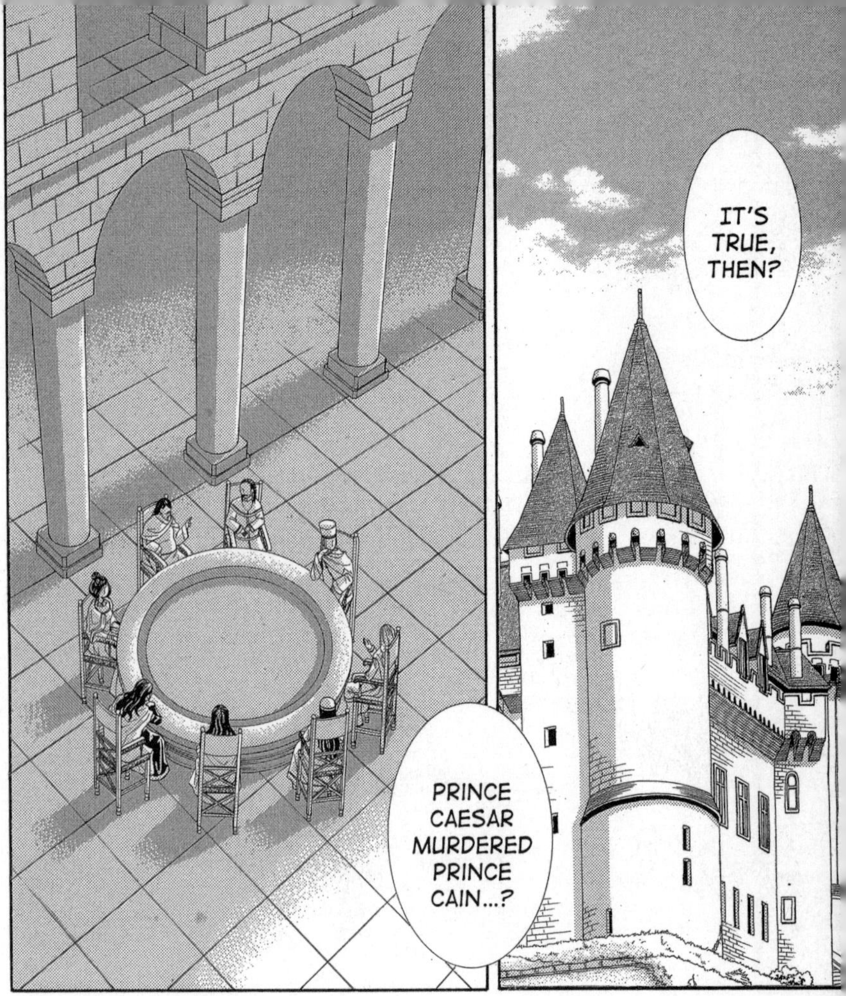
IT'S TRUE, THEN?
PRINCE CAESAR MURDERED PRINCE CAIN...?

Dawn of the Arcana

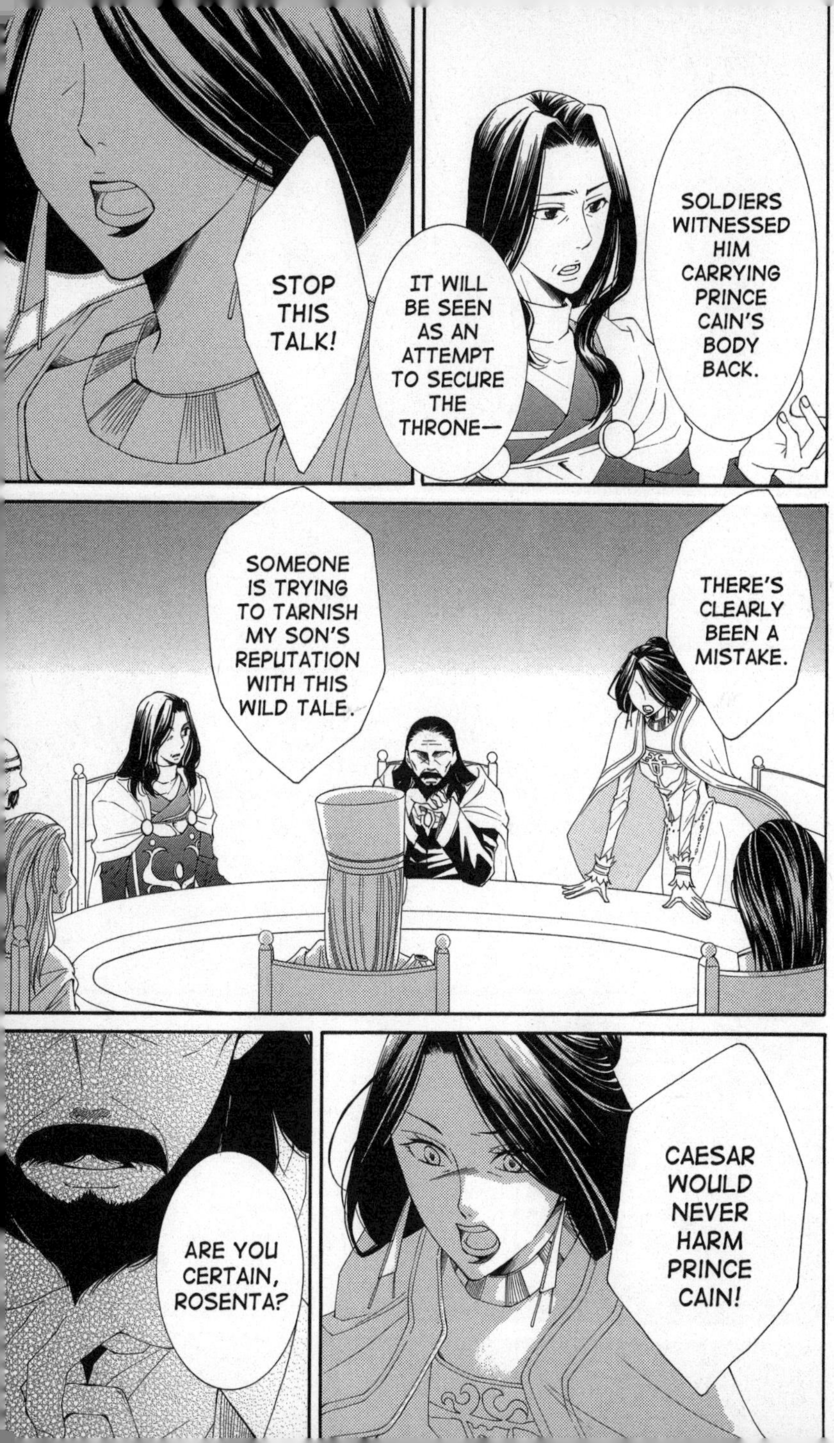
SOLDIERS WITNESSED HIM CARRYING PRINCE CAIN'S BODY BACK.
IT WILL BE SEEN AS AN ATTEMPT TO SECURE THE THRONE—
STOP THIS TALK!
THERE'S CLEARLY BEEN A MISTAKE.
SOMEONE IS TRYING TO TARNISH MY SON'S REPUTATION WITH THIS WILD TALE.
CAESAR WOULD NEVER HARM PRINCE CAIN!
ARE YOU CERTAIN, ROSENTA?

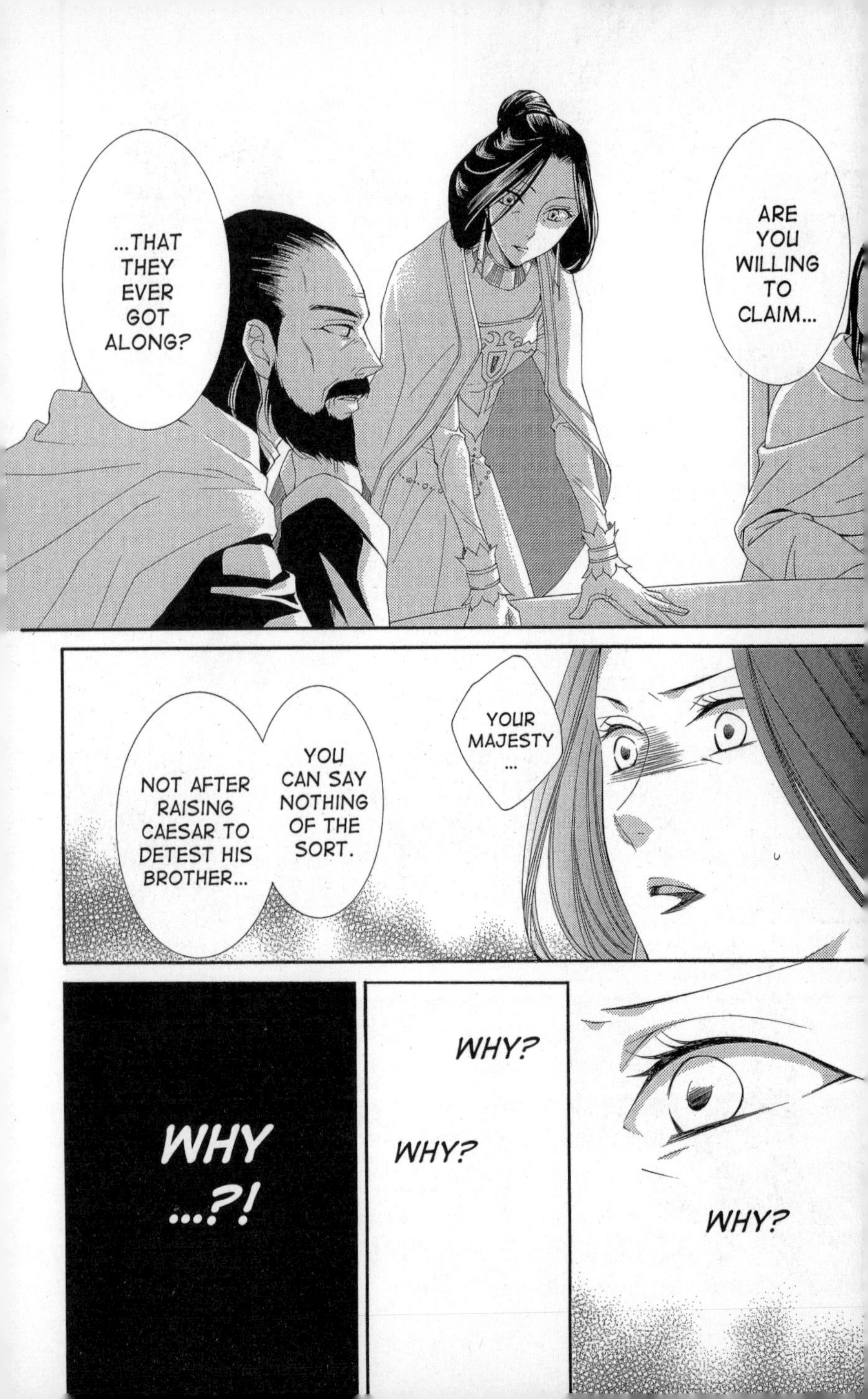
ARE YOU WILLING TO CLAIM...
...THAT THEY EVER GOT ALONG?
YOUR MAJESTY ...
YOU CAN SAY NOTHING OF THE SORT.
NOT AFTER RAISING CAESAR TO DETEST HIS BROTHER...
WHY?
WHY?
WHY?
WHY ...?!

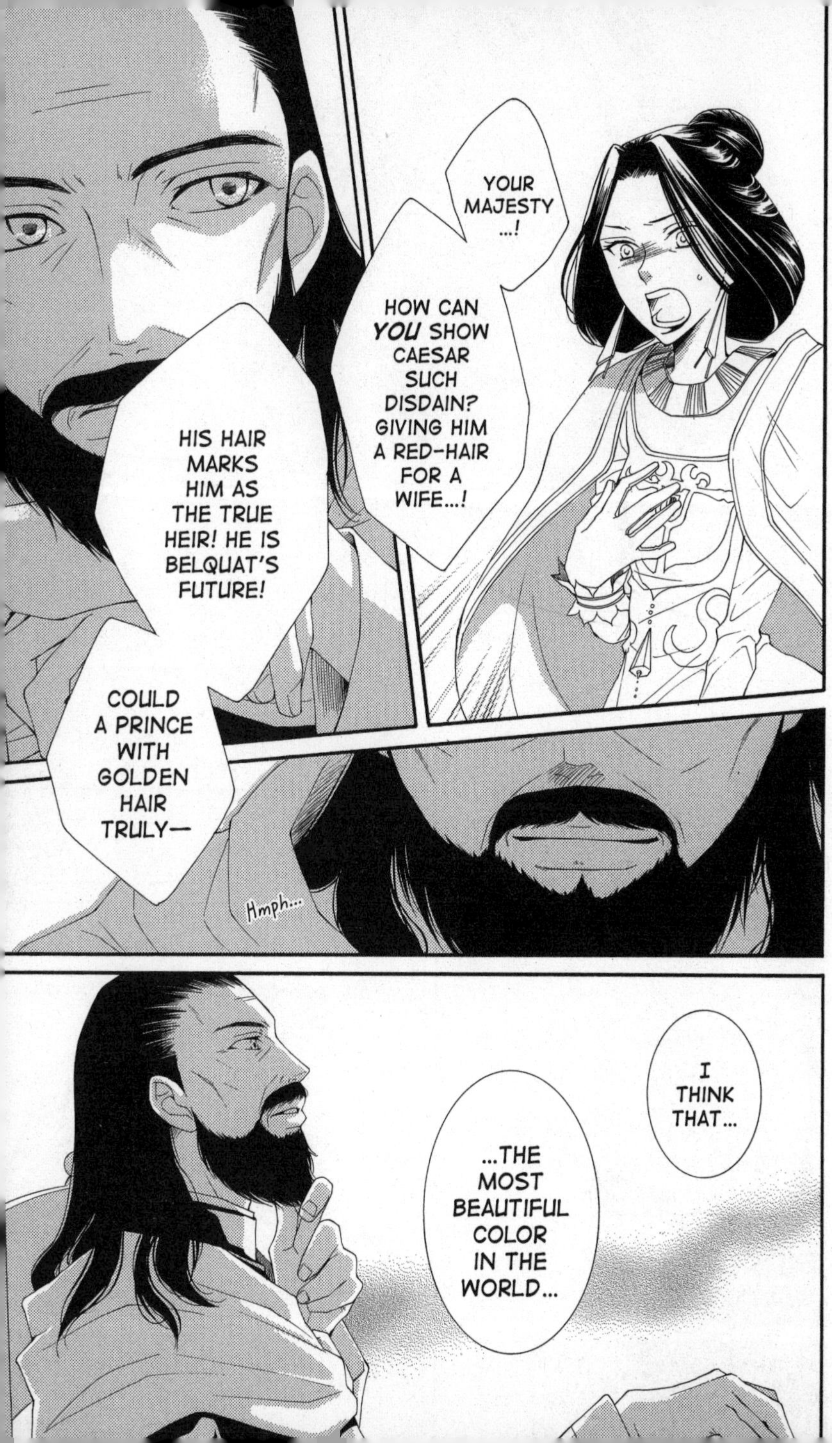
YOUR MAJESTY ...!
HOW CAN *YOU* SHOW CAESAR SUCH DISDAIN? GIVING HIM A RED-HAIR FOR A WIFE...!
HIS HAIR MARKS HIM AS THE TRUE HEIR! HE IS BELQUAT'S FUTURE!
COULD A PRINCE WITH GOLDEN HAIR TRULY—
Hmph...
I THINK THAT...
...THE MOST BEAUTIFUL COLOR IN THE WORLD...

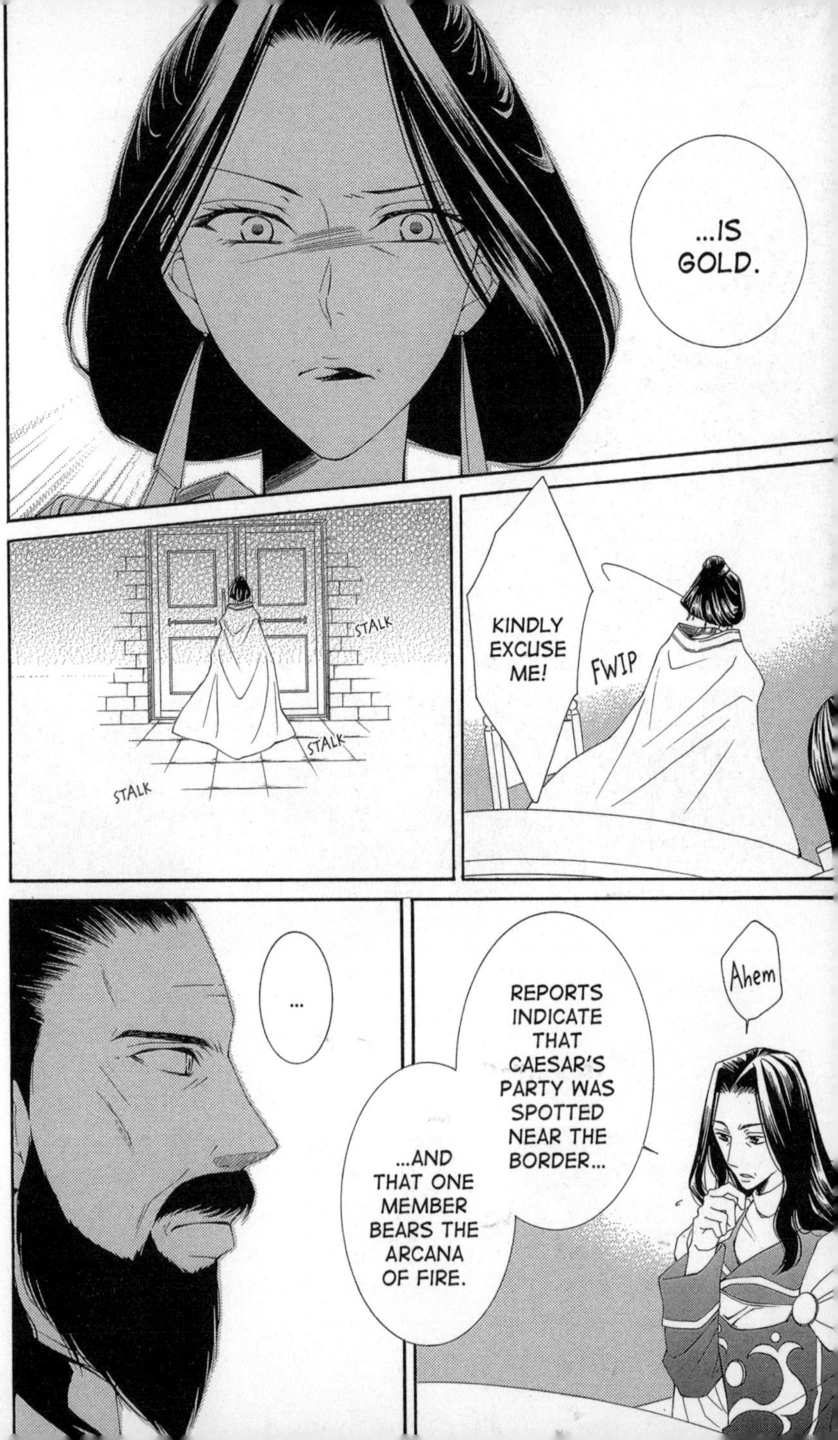
...IS GOLD.
KINDLY EXCUSE ME!
FWIP
STALK
STALK
STALK
Ahem
REPORTS INDICATE THAT CAESAR'S PARTY WAS SPOTTED NEAR THE BORDER...
...AND THAT ONE MEMBER BEARS THE ARCANA OF FIRE.
...

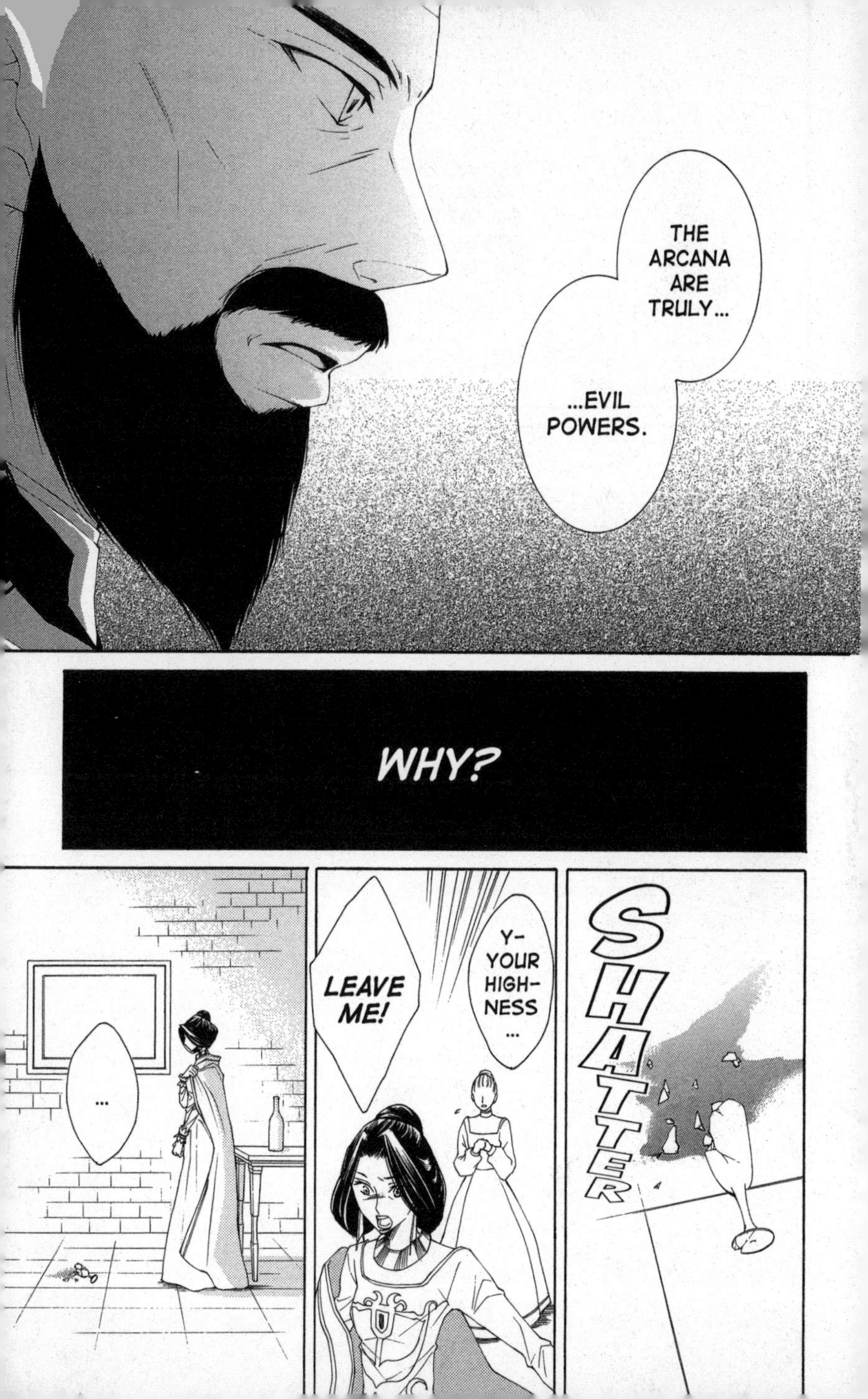
THE ARCANA ARE TRULY...
...EVIL POWERS.
WHY?
SHATTER
Y-YOUR HIGHNESS...
LEAVE ME!
...

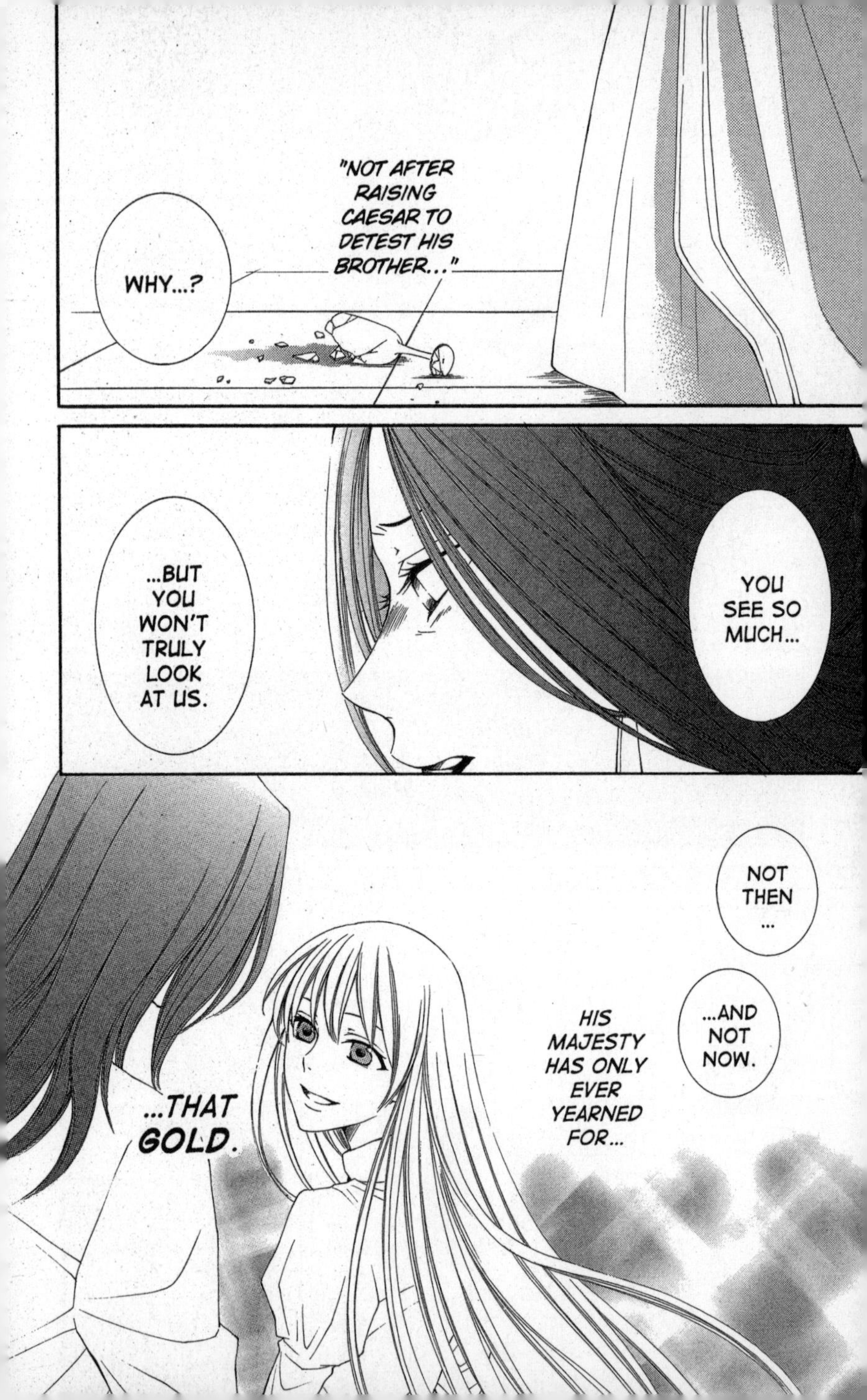
"NOT AFTER RAISING CAESAR TO DETEST HIS BROTHER..."
WHY...?
YOU SEE SO MUCH...
...BUT YOU WON'T TRULY LOOK AT US.
NOT THEN ...
...AND NOT NOW.
HIS MAJESTY HAS ONLY EVER YEARNED FOR...
...THAT GOLD.

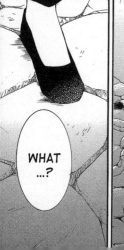

WHAT
...?

Unh
...

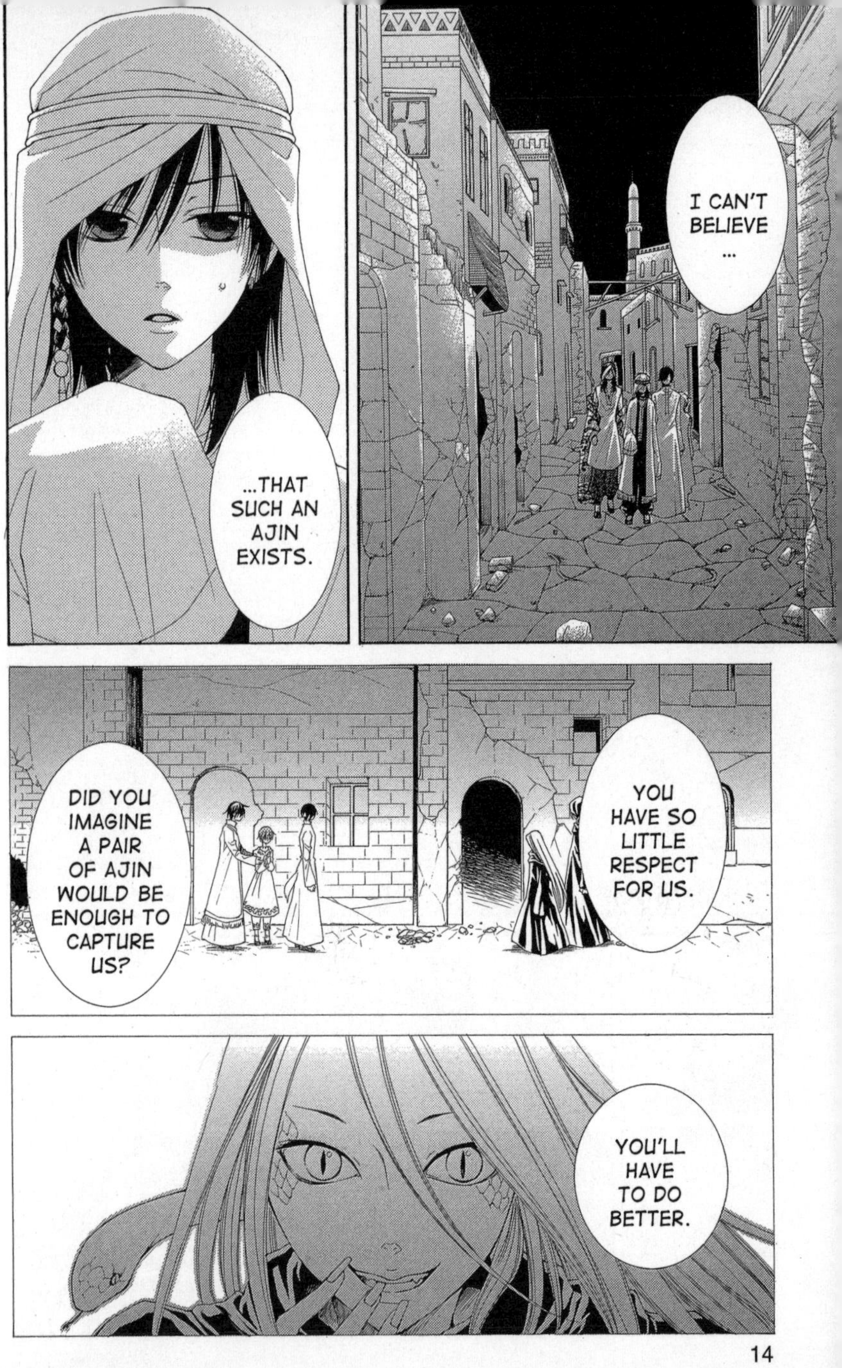
I CAN'T BELIEVE ...
...THAT SUCH AN AJIN EXISTS.
YOU HAVE SO LITTLE RESPECT FOR US.
DID YOU IMAGINE A PAIR OF AJIN WOULD BE ENOUGH TO CAPTURE US?
YOU'LL HAVE TO DO BETTER.

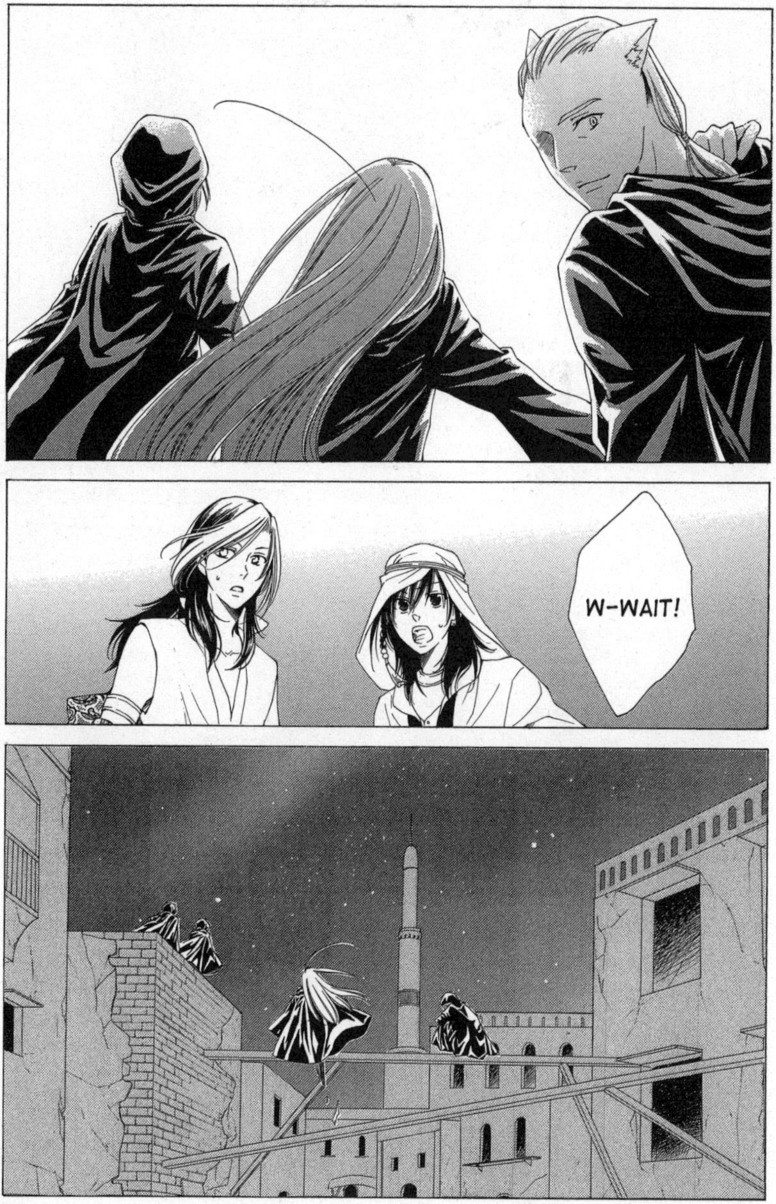
W-WAIT!

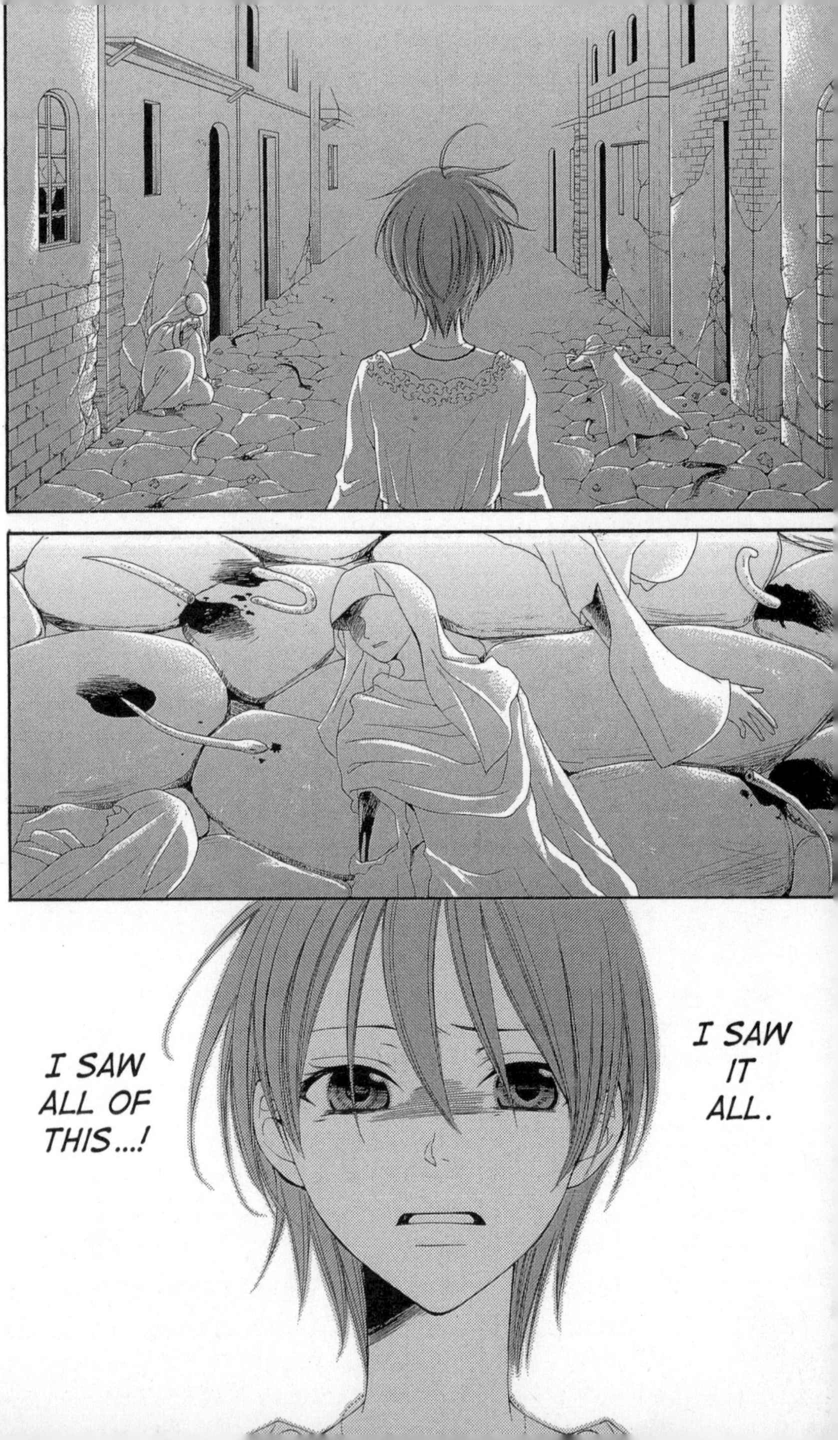
I SAW IT ALL.
I SAW ALL OF THIS...!

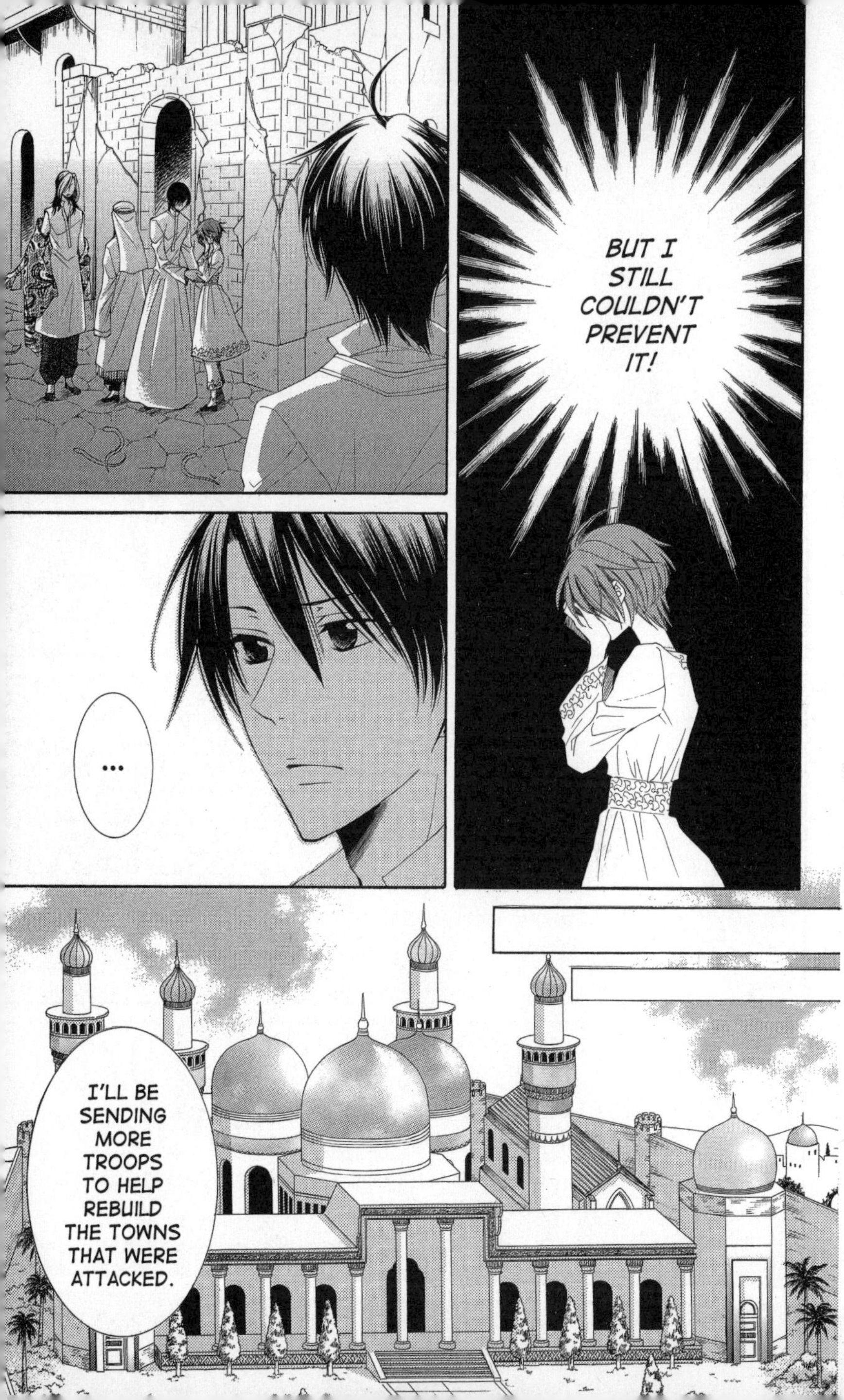
BUT I STILL COULDN'T PREVENT IT!
...
I'LL BE SENDING MORE TROOPS TO HELP REBUILD THE TOWNS THAT WERE ATTACKED.

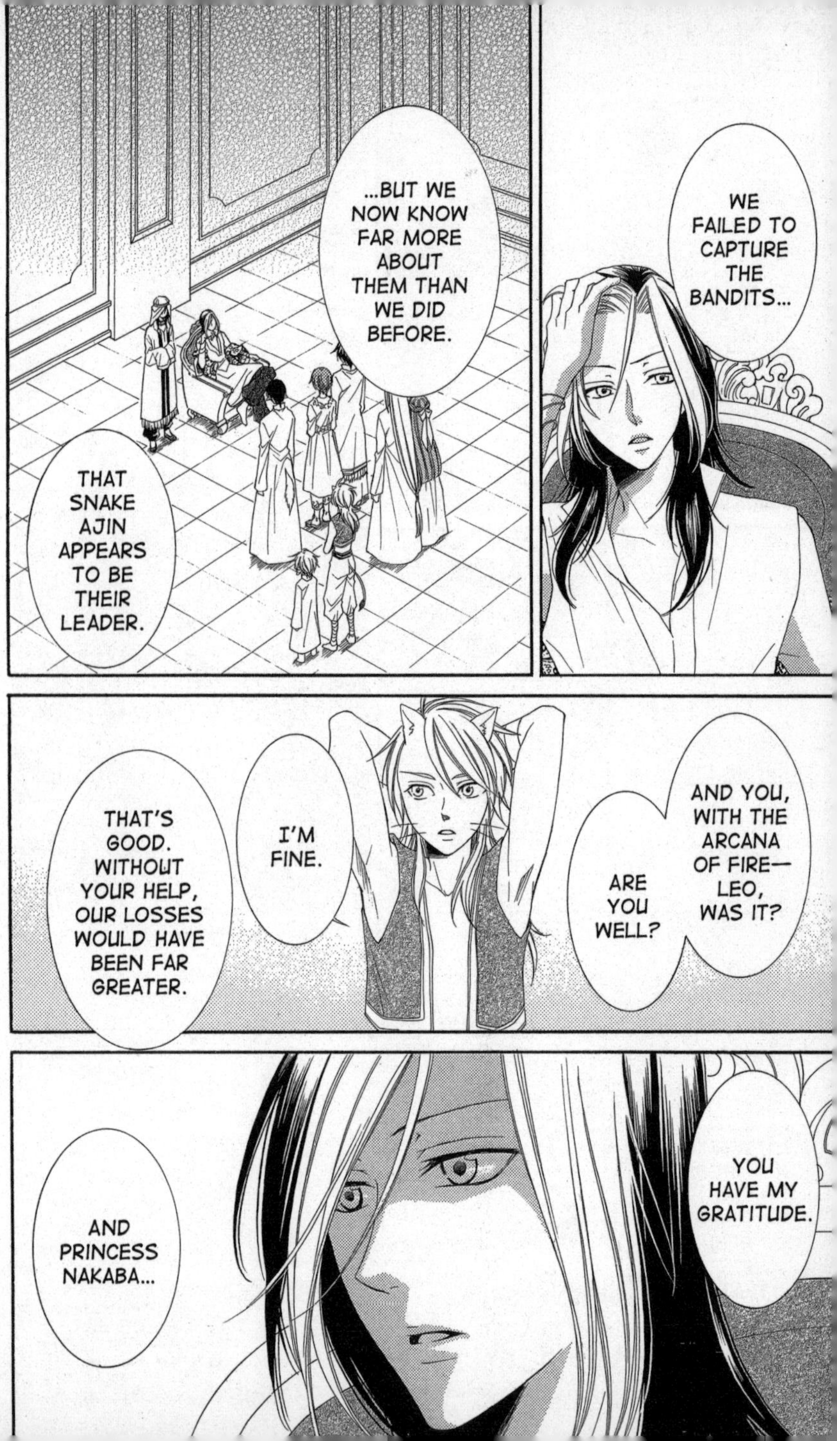
WE FAILED TO CAPTURE THE BANDITS...
...BUT WE NOW KNOW FAR MORE ABOUT THEM THAN WE DID BEFORE.
THAT SNAKE AJIN APPEARS TO BE THEIR LEADER.
AND YOU, WITH THE ARCANA OF FIRE— LEO, WAS IT?
ARE YOU WELL?
I'M FINE.
THAT'S GOOD. WITHOUT YOUR HELP, OUR LOSSES WOULD HAVE BEEN FAR GREATER.
YOU HAVE MY GRATITUDE.
AND PRINCESS NAKABA...

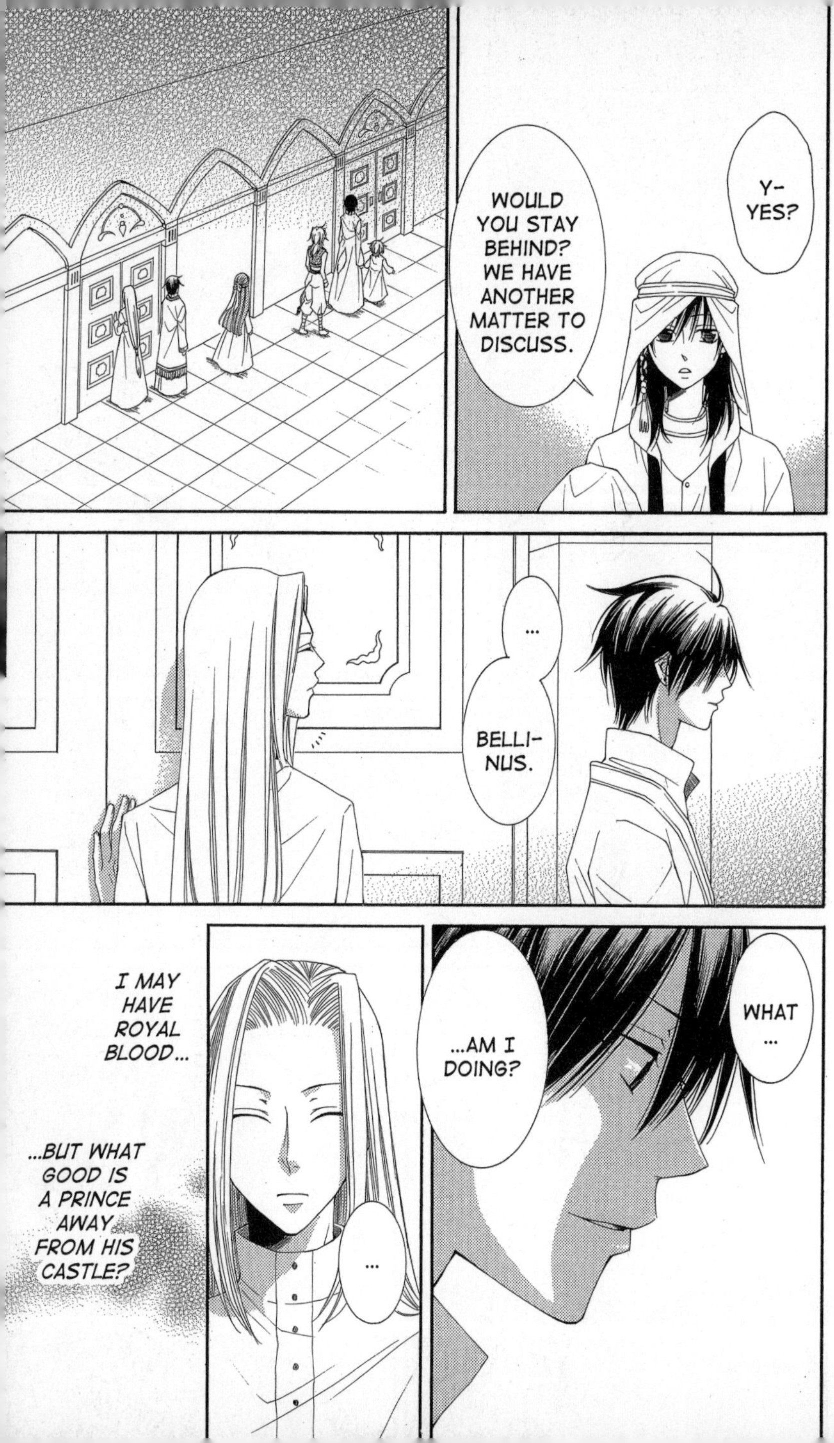
Y- YES?
WOULD YOU STAY BEHIND? WE HAVE ANOTHER MATTER TO DISCUSS.
...
BELLI- NUS.
WHAT ...
...AM I DOING?
I MAY HAVE ROYAL BLOOD...
...BUT WHAT GOOD IS A PRINCE AWAY FROM HIS CASTLE?
...

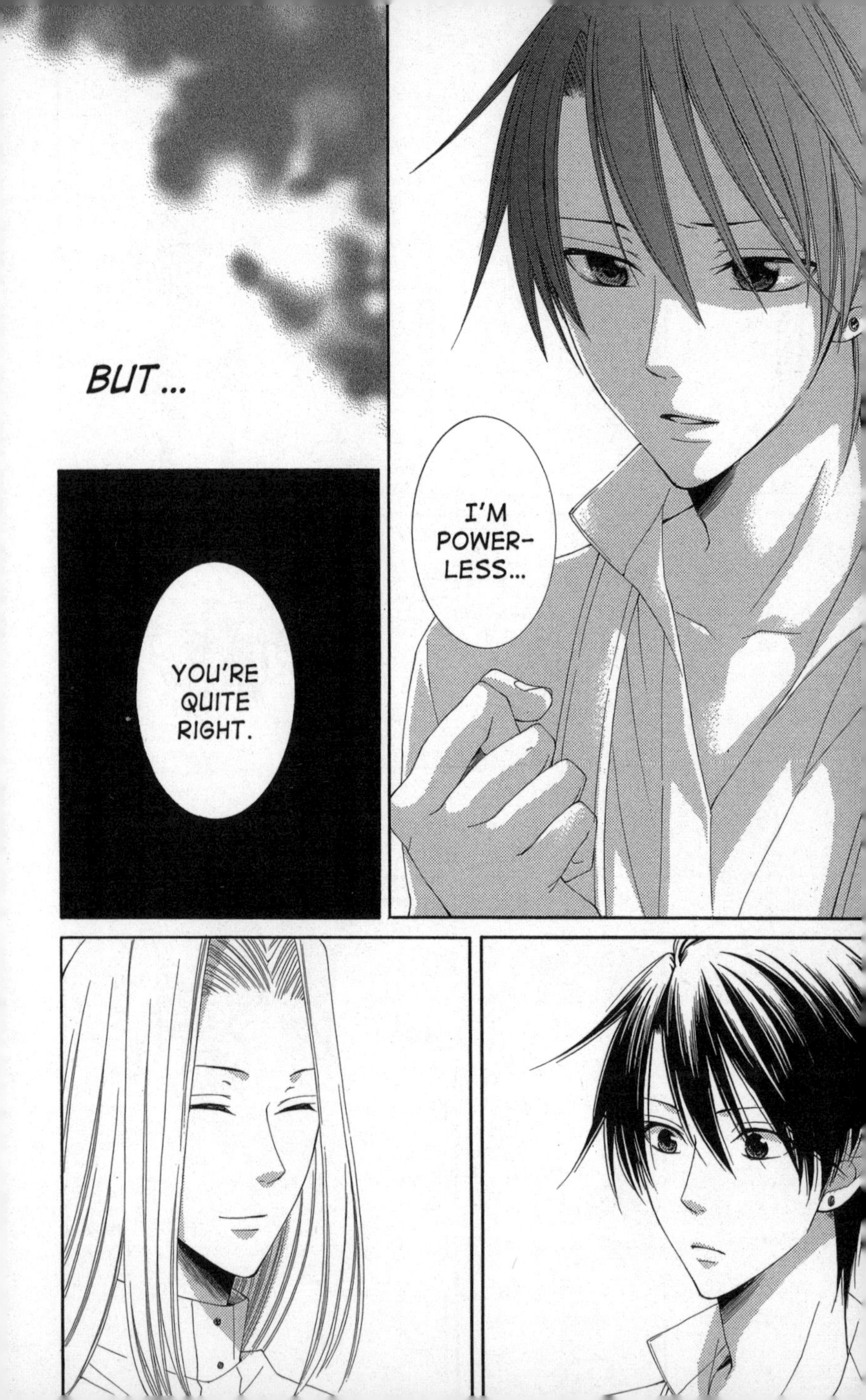
I'M POWER-LESS...
BUT...
YOU'RE QUITE RIGHT.

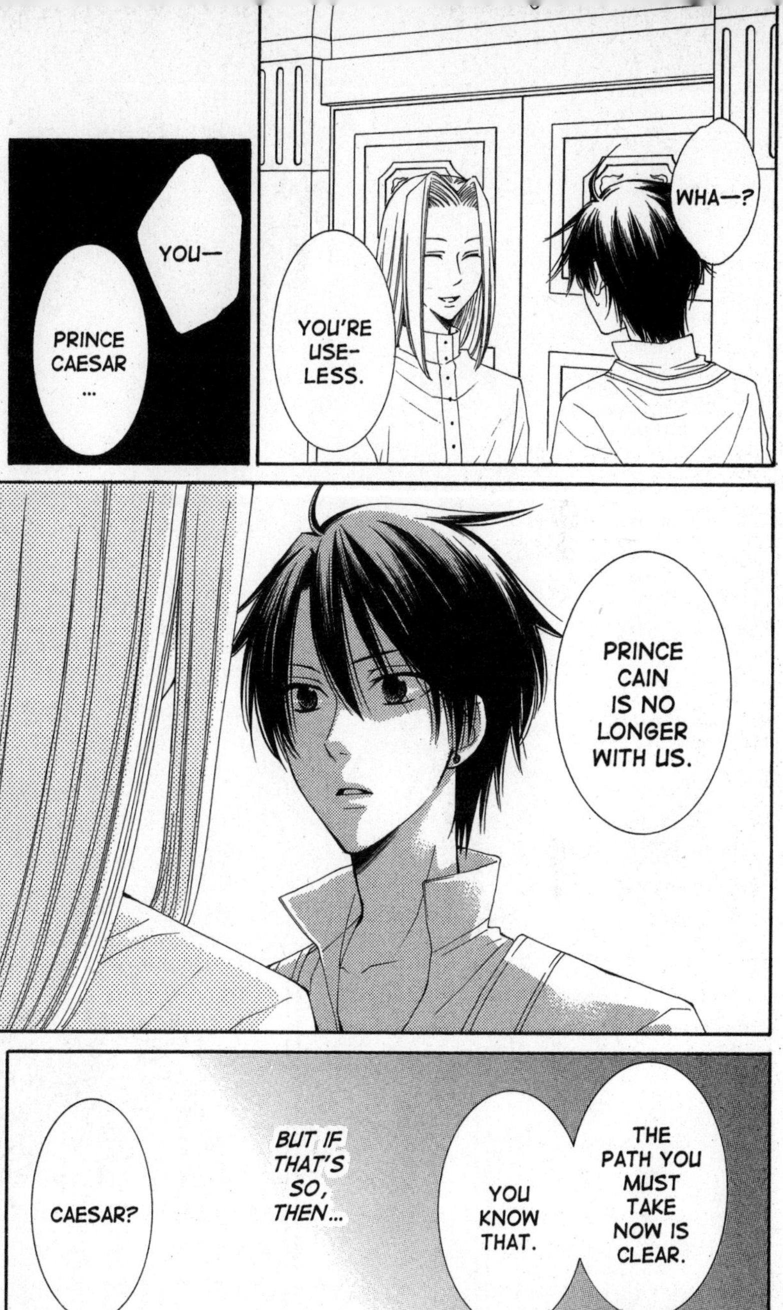
WHA—?
YOU'RE USE-LESS.
YOU—
PRINCE CAESAR ...
PRINCE CAIN IS NO LONGER WITH US.
THE PATH YOU MUST TAKE NOW IS CLEAR.
YOU KNOW THAT.
BUT IF THAT'S SO, THEN...
CAESAR?

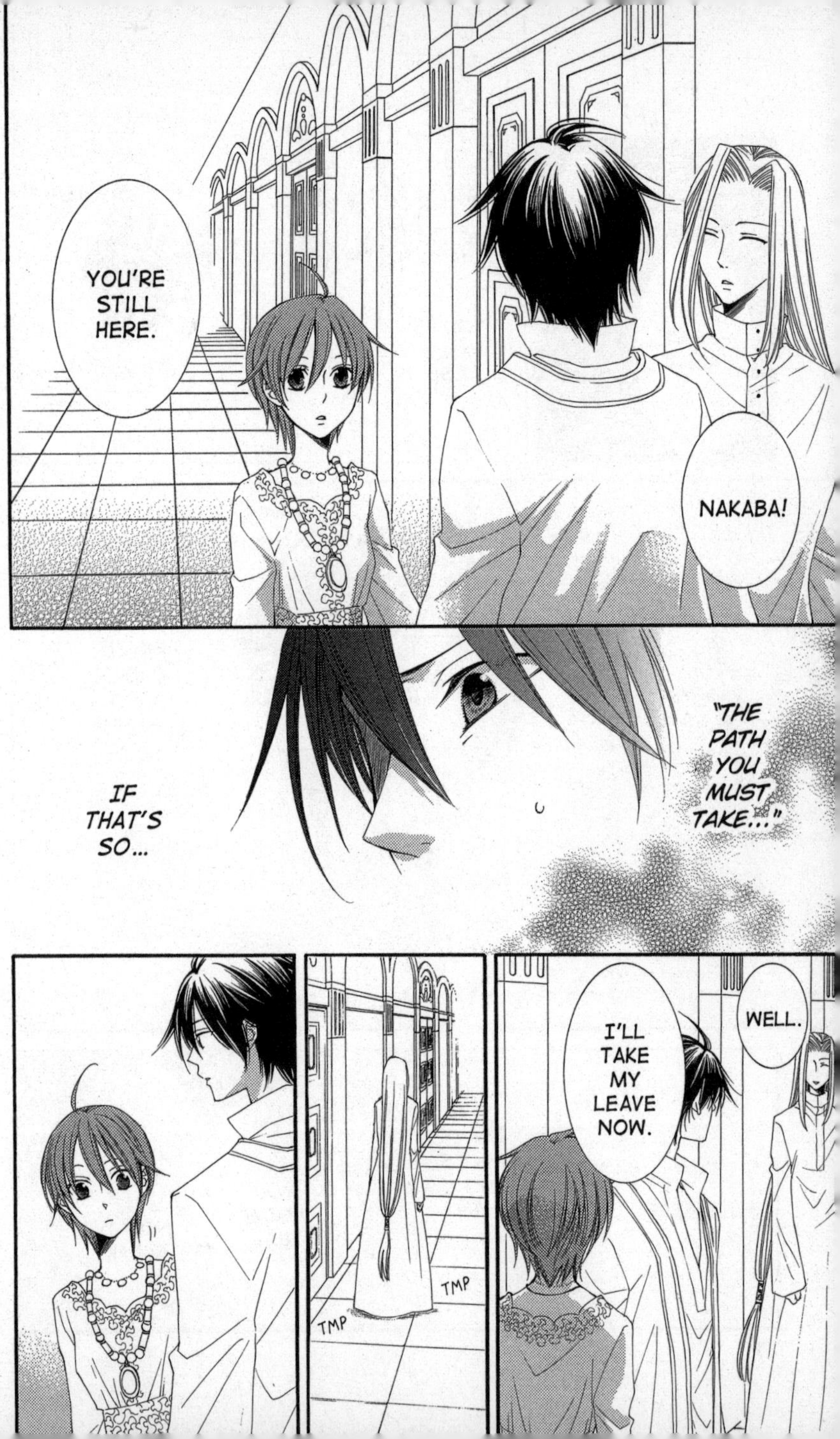
NAKABA!
YOU'RE STILL HERE.
"THE PATH YOU MUST TAKE..."
IF THAT'S SO...
WELL.
I'LL TAKE MY LEAVE NOW.
TMP
TMP

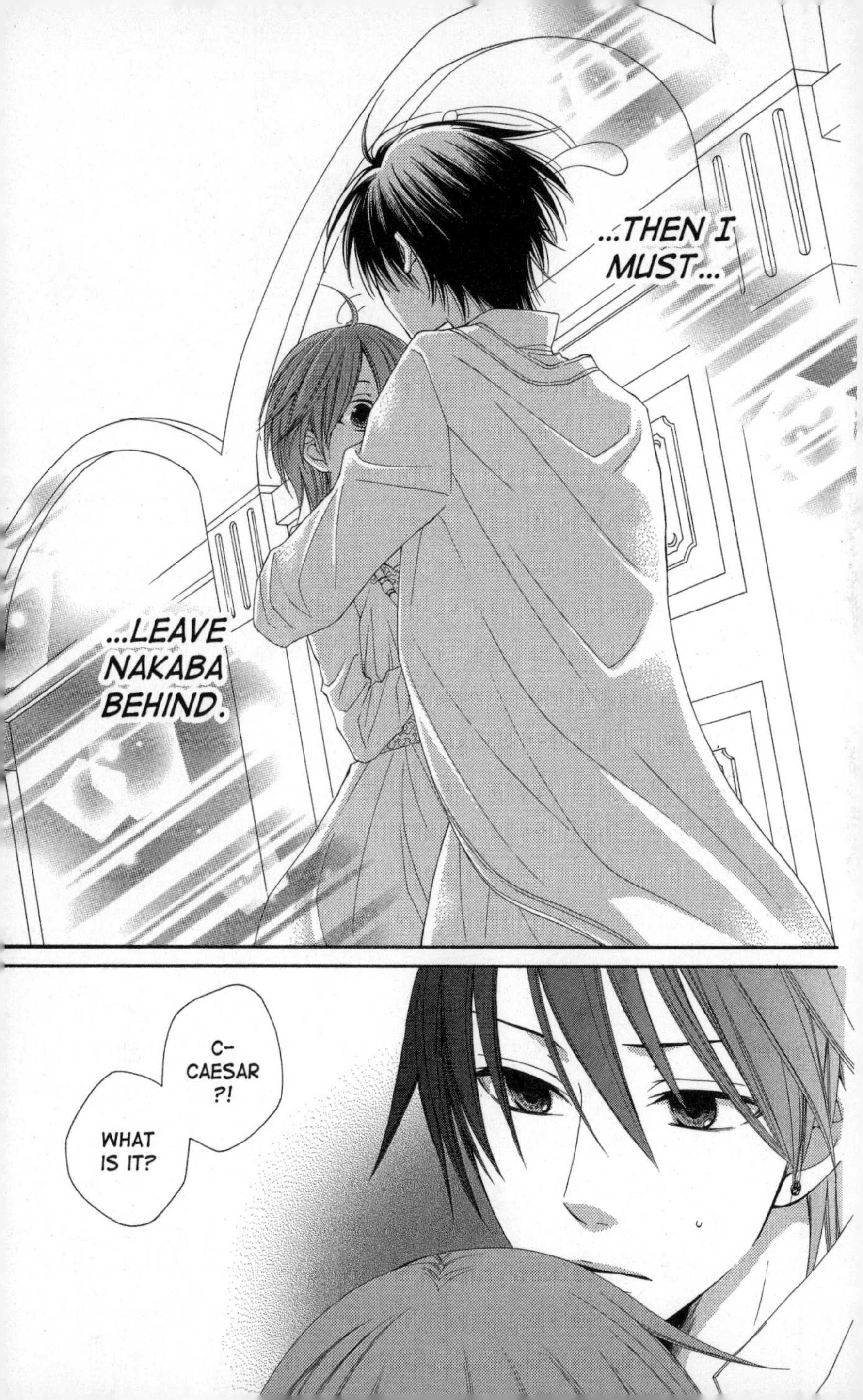
...THEN I MUST...
...LEAVE NAKABA BEHIND.
C-CAESAR?!
WHAT IS IT?

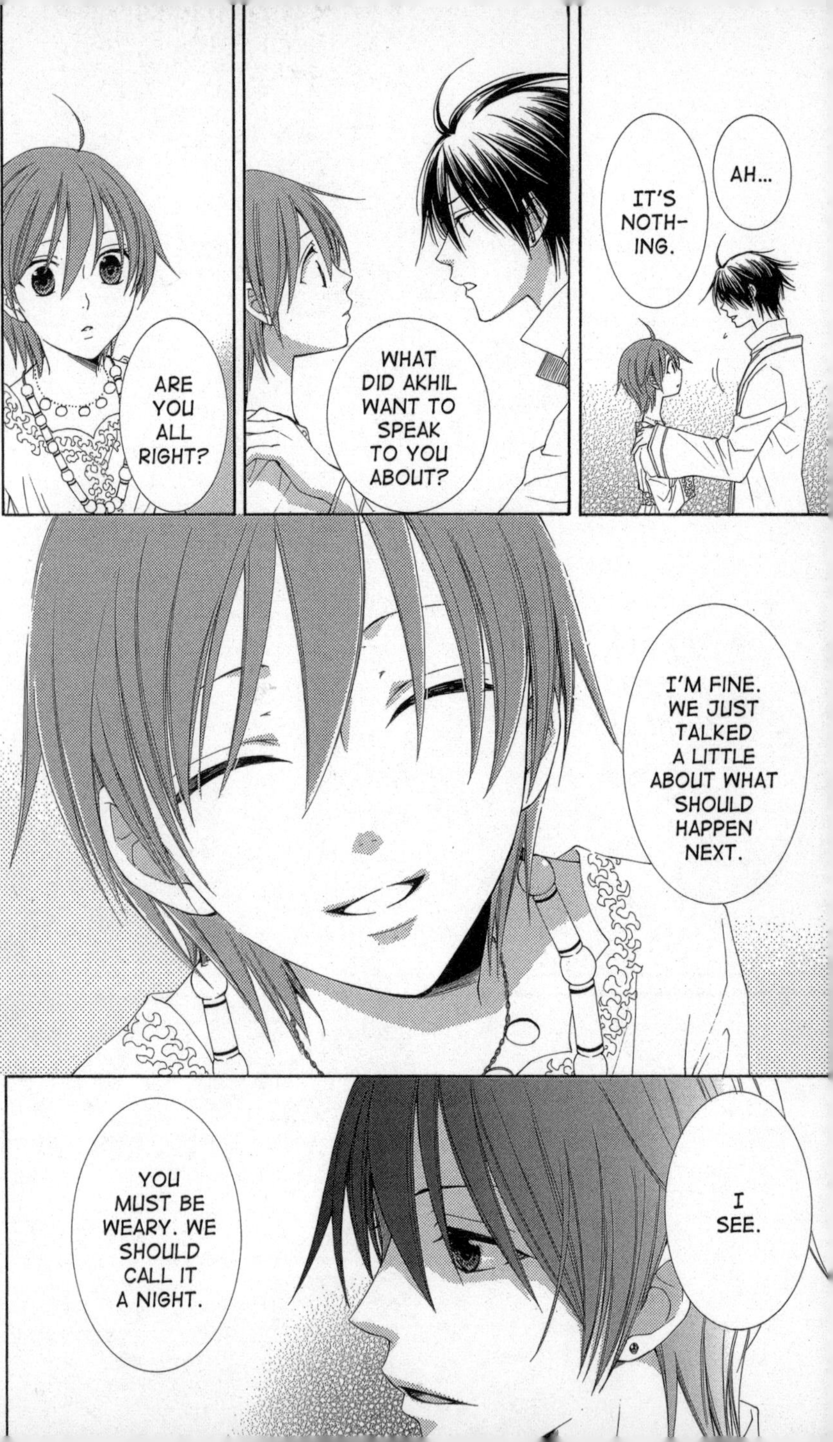
AH...
IT'S NOTH-ING.
WHAT DID AKHIL WANT TO SPEAK TO YOU ABOUT?
ARE YOU ALL RIGHT?
I'M FINE. WE JUST TALKED A LITTLE ABOUT WHAT SHOULD HAPPEN NEXT.
I SEE.
YOU MUST BE WEARY. WE SHOULD CALL IT A NIGHT.

"PRINCE CAIN IS NO LONGER WITH US."

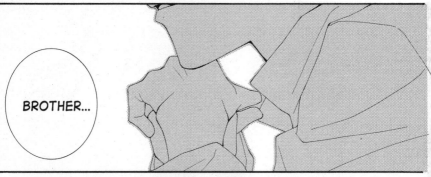

BROTHER...

I SUP-POSE...

CAN YOU GIVE ME A SWORD LESSON?!

CAESAR?

CAIN.

CAIN ...!

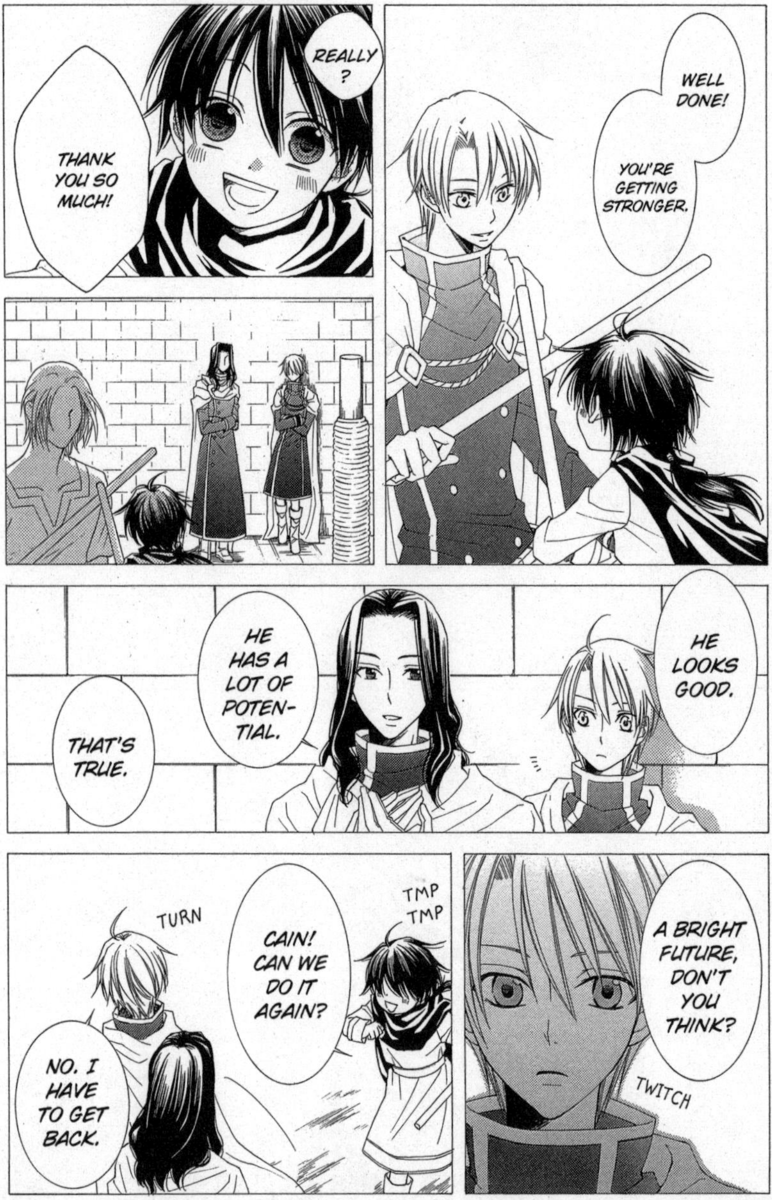
WELL DONE!
YOU'RE GETTING STRONGER.
REALLY?
THANK YOU SO MUCH!
HE LOOKS GOOD.
HE HAS A LOT OF POTENTIAL.
THAT'S TRUE.
A BRIGHT FUTURE, DON'T YOU THINK?
TWITCH
TMP TMP
CAIN! CAN WE DO IT AGAIN?
TURN
NO. I HAVE TO GET BACK.

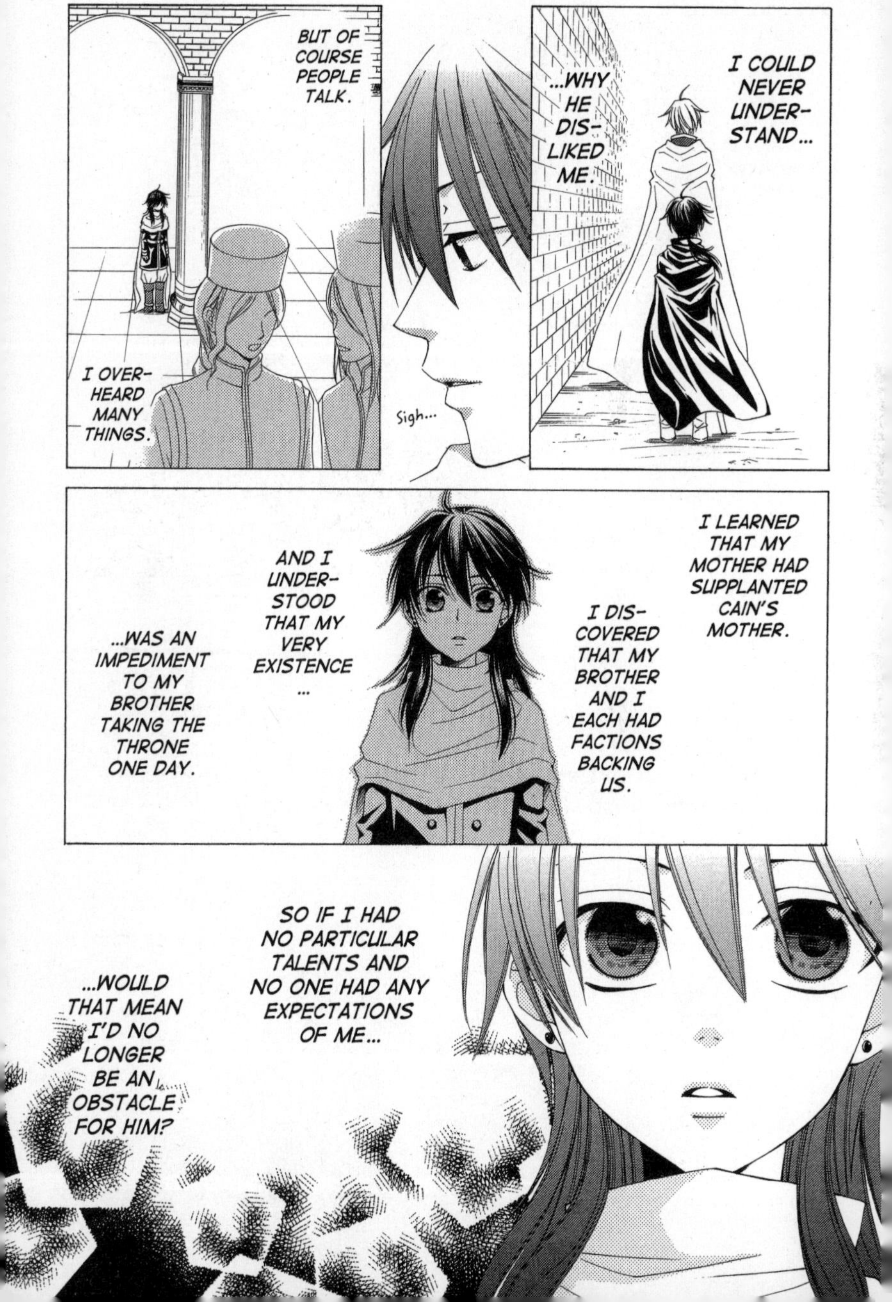
I COULD NEVER UNDER-STAND...
...WHY HE DIS-LIKED ME.
Sigh...
BUT OF COURSE PEOPLE TALK.
I OVER-HEARD MANY THINGS.
I LEARNED THAT MY MOTHER HAD SUPPLANTED CAIN'S MOTHER.
I DIS-COVERED THAT MY BROTHER AND I EACH HAD FACTIONS BACKING US.
AND I UNDER-STOOD THAT MY VERY EXISTENCE ...
...WAS AN IMPEDIMENT TO MY BROTHER TAKING THE THRONE ONE DAY.
SO IF I HAD NO PARTICULAR TALENTS AND NO ONE HAD ANY EXPECTATIONS OF ME...
...WOULD THAT MEAN I'D NO LONGER BE AN OBSTACLE FOR HIM?

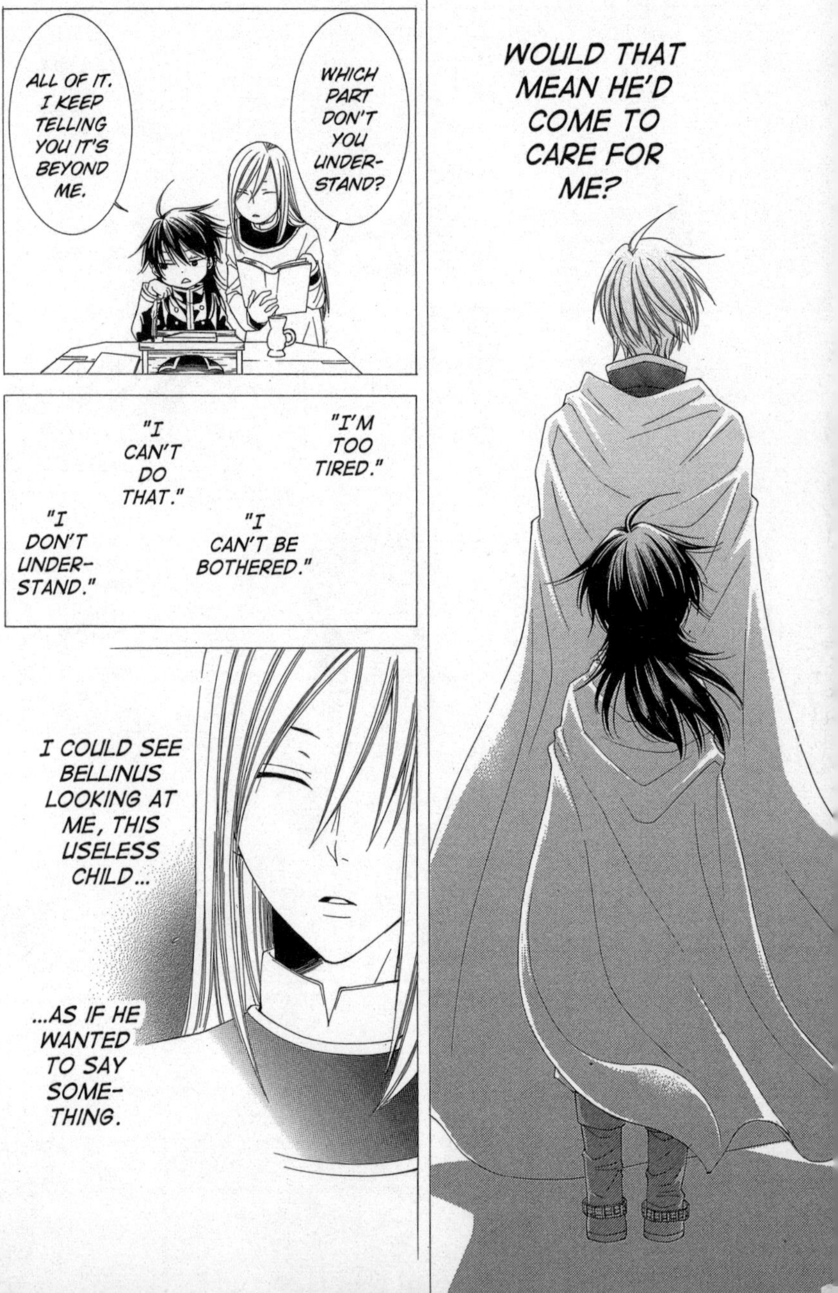
WHICH PART DON'T YOU UNDER-STAND?
ALL OF IT. I KEEP TELLING YOU IT'S BEYOND ME.
"I'M TOO TIRED."
"I CAN'T DO THAT."
"I CAN'T BE BOTHERED."
"I DON'T UNDER-STAND."
I COULD SEE BELLINUS LOOKING AT ME, THIS USELESS CHILD...
...AS IF HE WANTED TO SAY SOME-THING.
WOULD THAT MEAN HE'D COME TO CARE FOR ME?

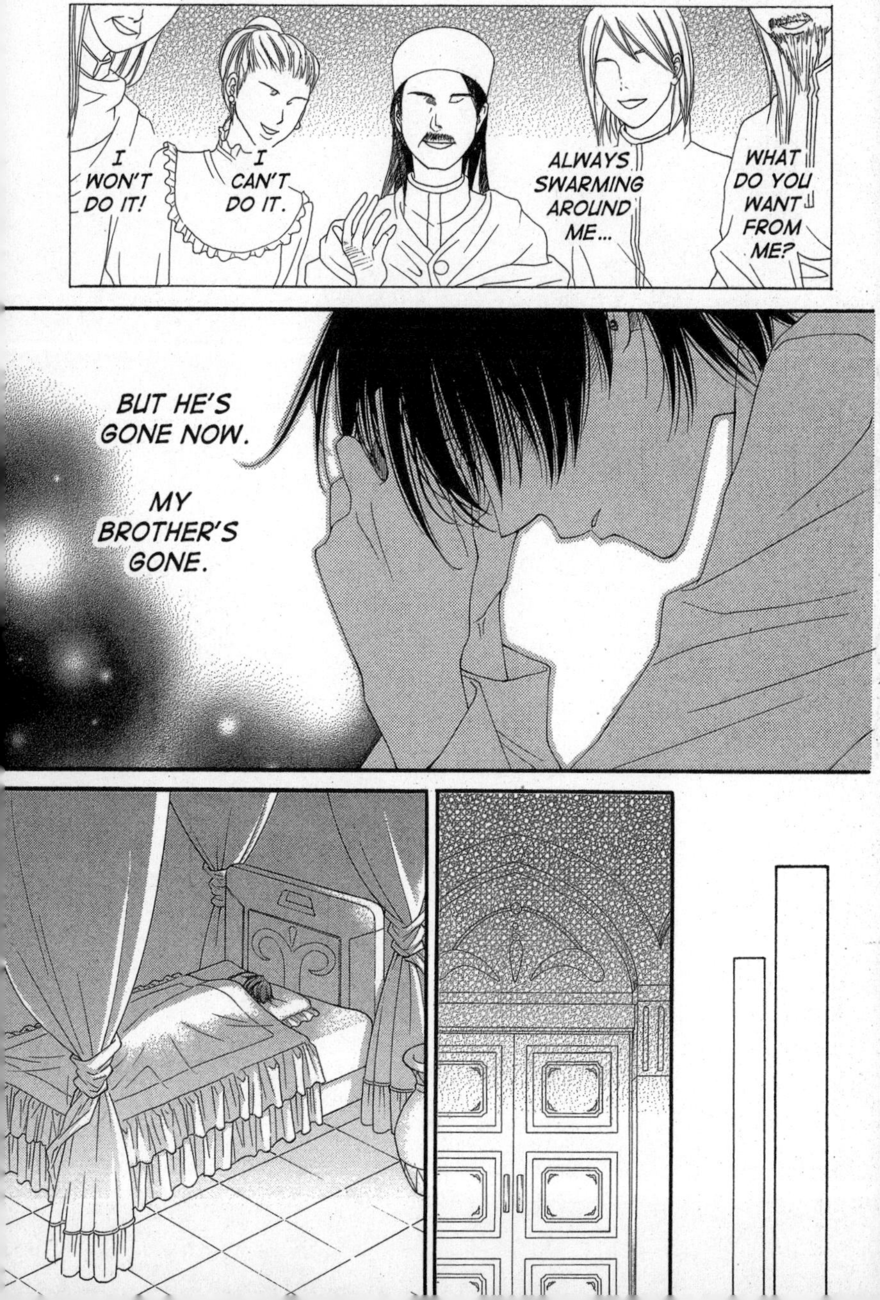
WHAT DO YOU WANT FROM ME?
ALWAYS SWARMING AROUND ME...
I CAN'T DO IT.
I WON'T DO IT!
BUT HE'S GONE NOW.
MY BROTHER'S GONE.

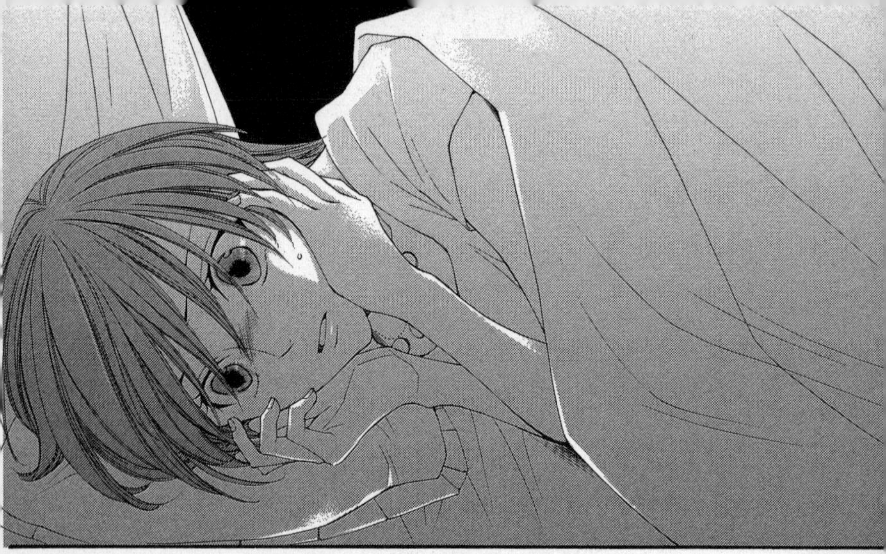

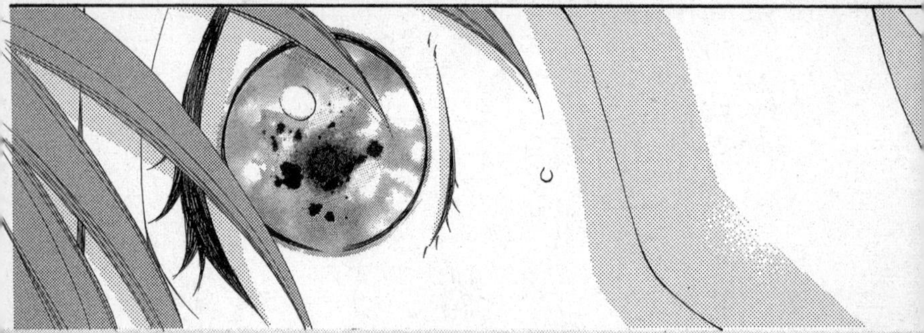

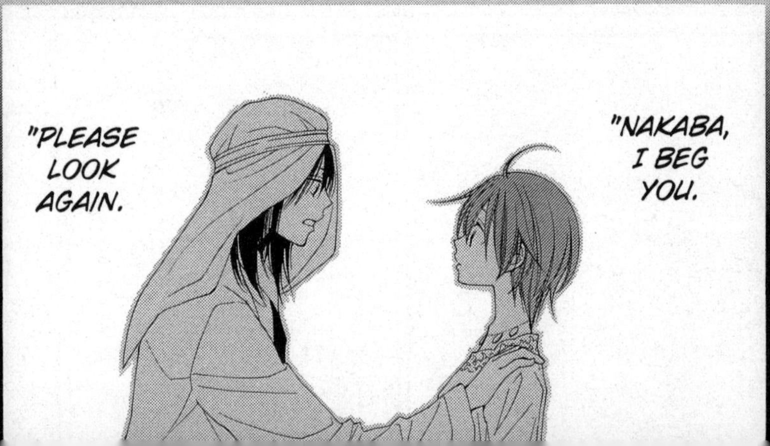
"NAKABA, I BEG YOU.
"PLEASE LOOK AGAIN.

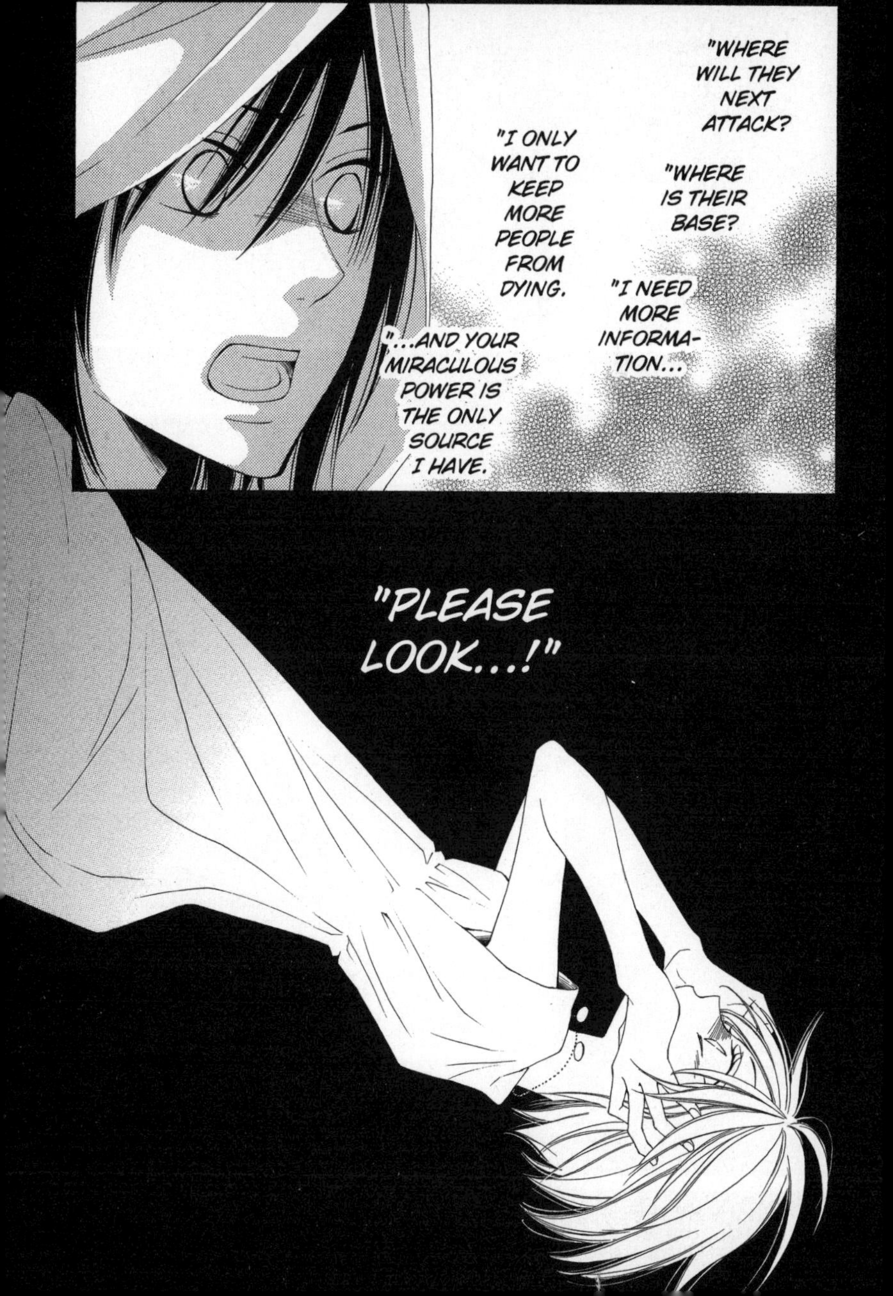
"WHERE WILL THEY NEXT ATTACK?
"WHERE IS THEIR BASE?
"I NEED MORE INFORMATION...
"I ONLY WANT TO KEEP MORE PEOPLE FROM DYING.
"...AND YOUR MIRACULOUS POWER IS THE ONLY SOURCE I HAVE.
"PLEASE LOOK...!"

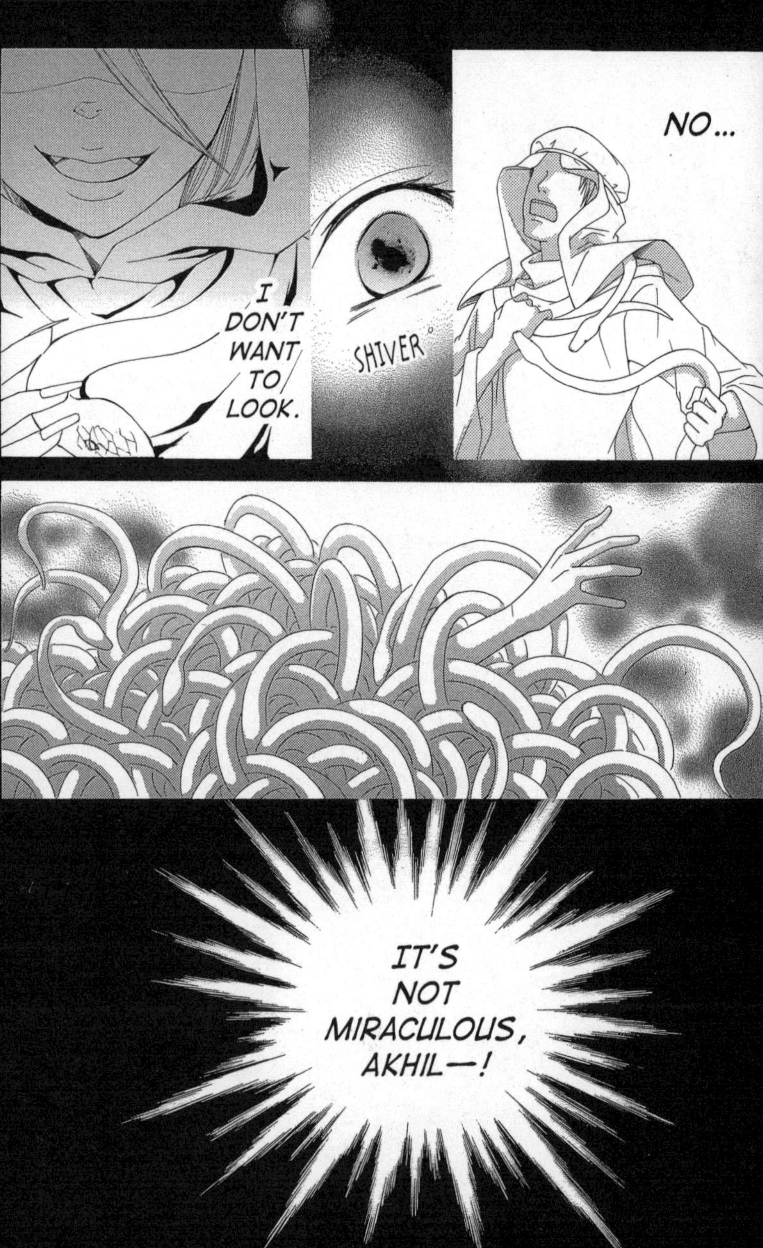
NO...
SHIVER
I DON'T WANT TO LOOK.
IT'S NOT MIRACULOUS, AKHIL—!

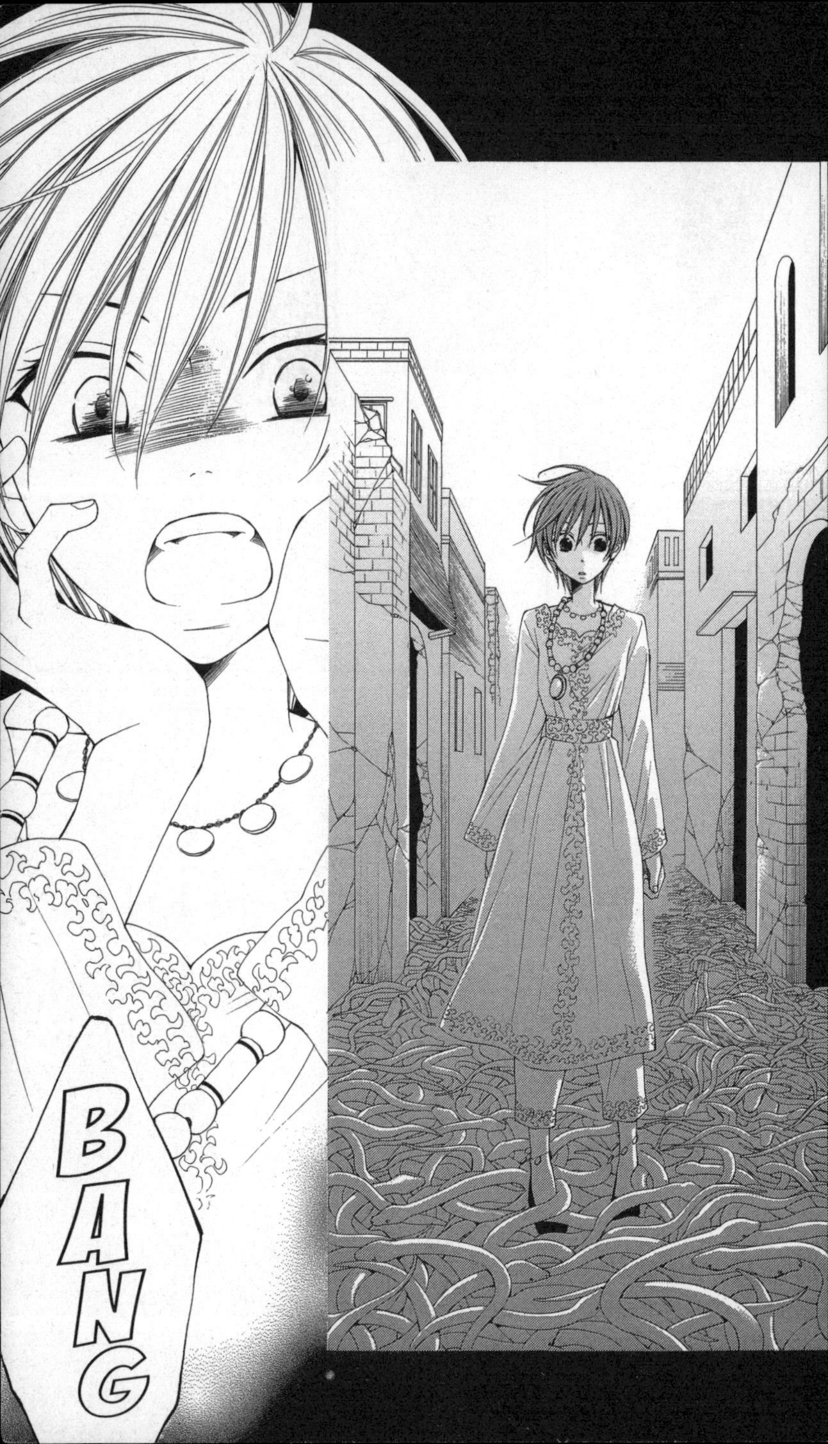
BANG

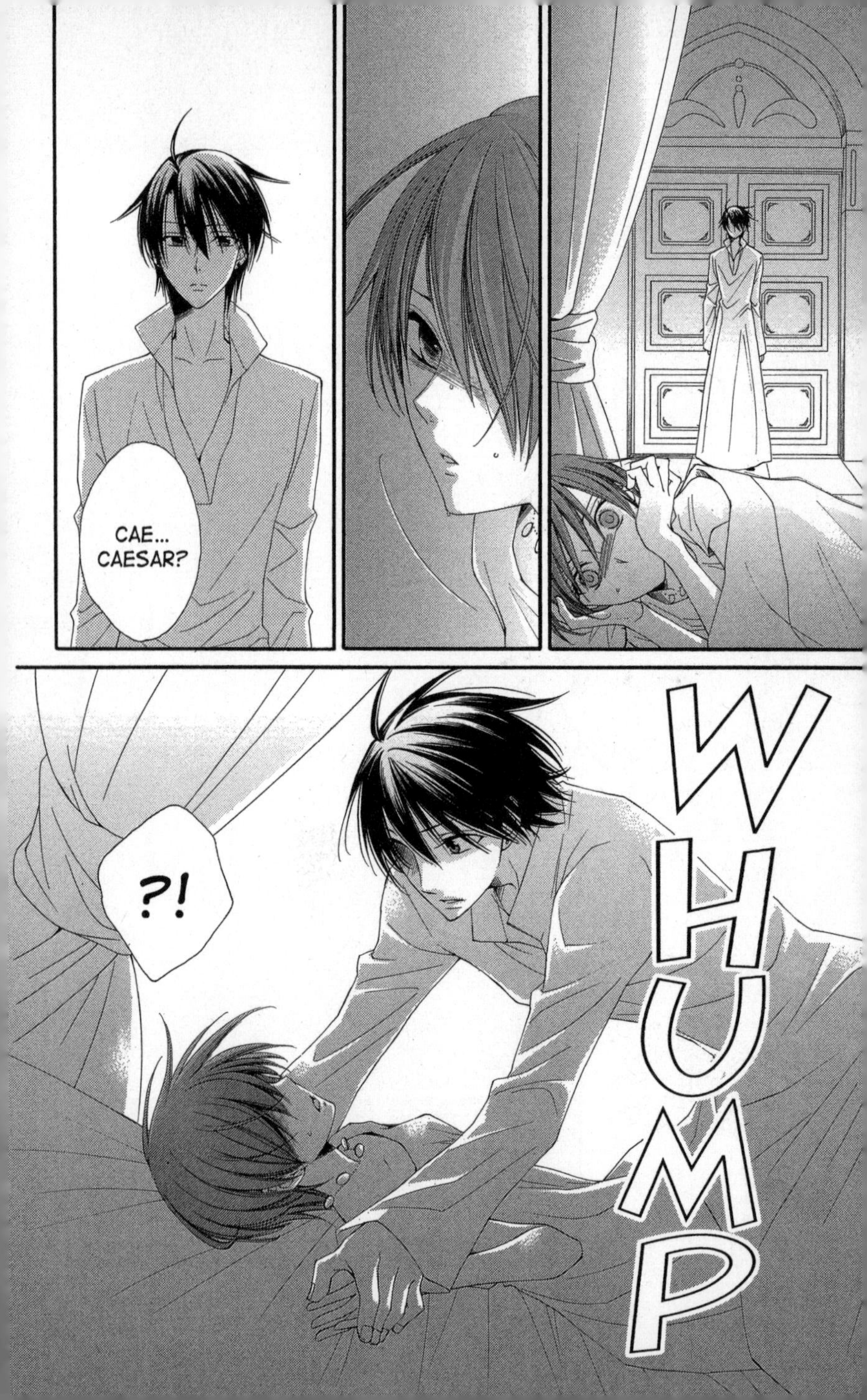
CAE...
CAESAR?
?!
WHUMP

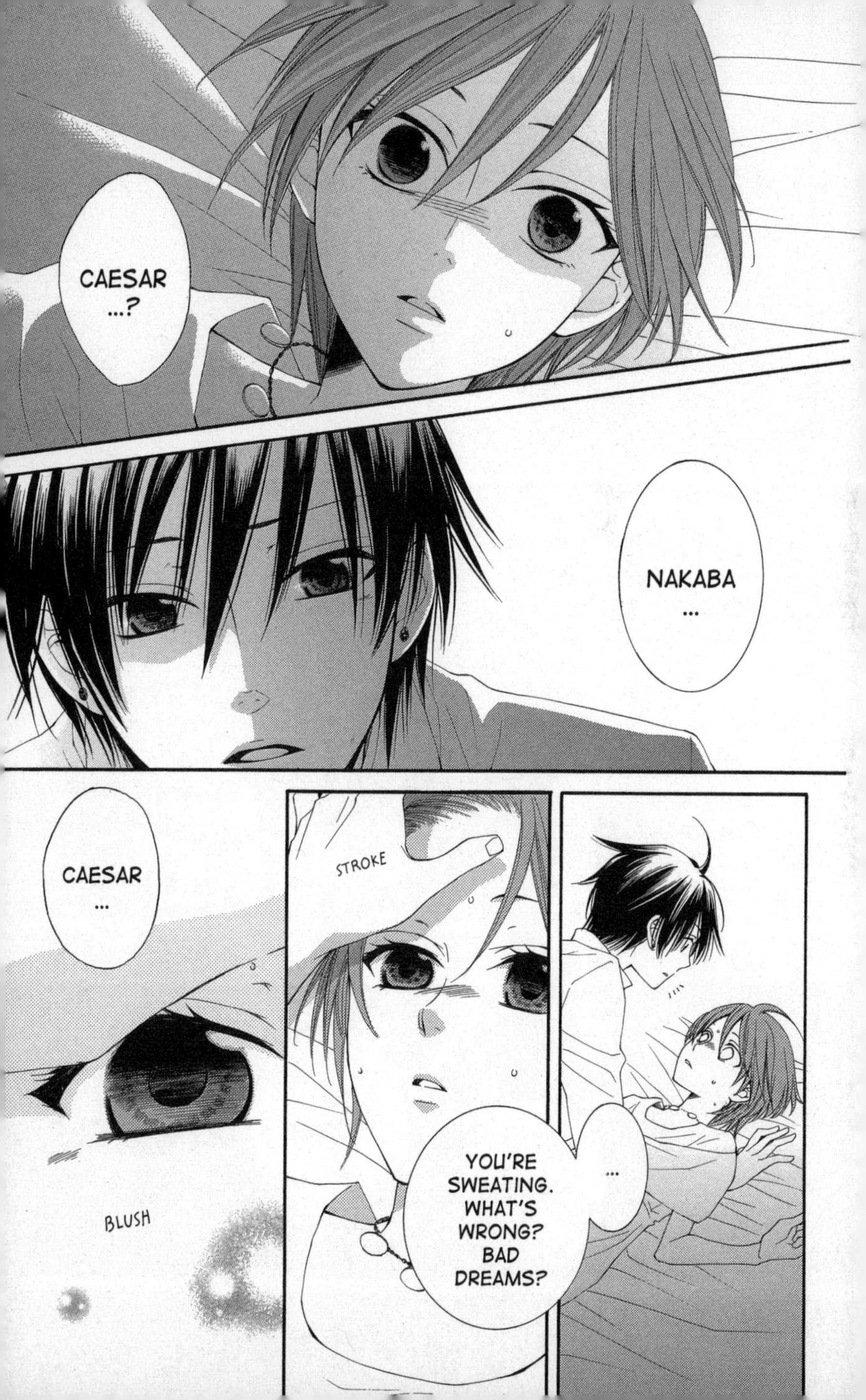
CAESAR ...?
NAKABA ...
...
STROKE
YOU'RE SWEATING. WHAT'S WRONG? BAD DREAMS?
CAESAR ...
BLUSH

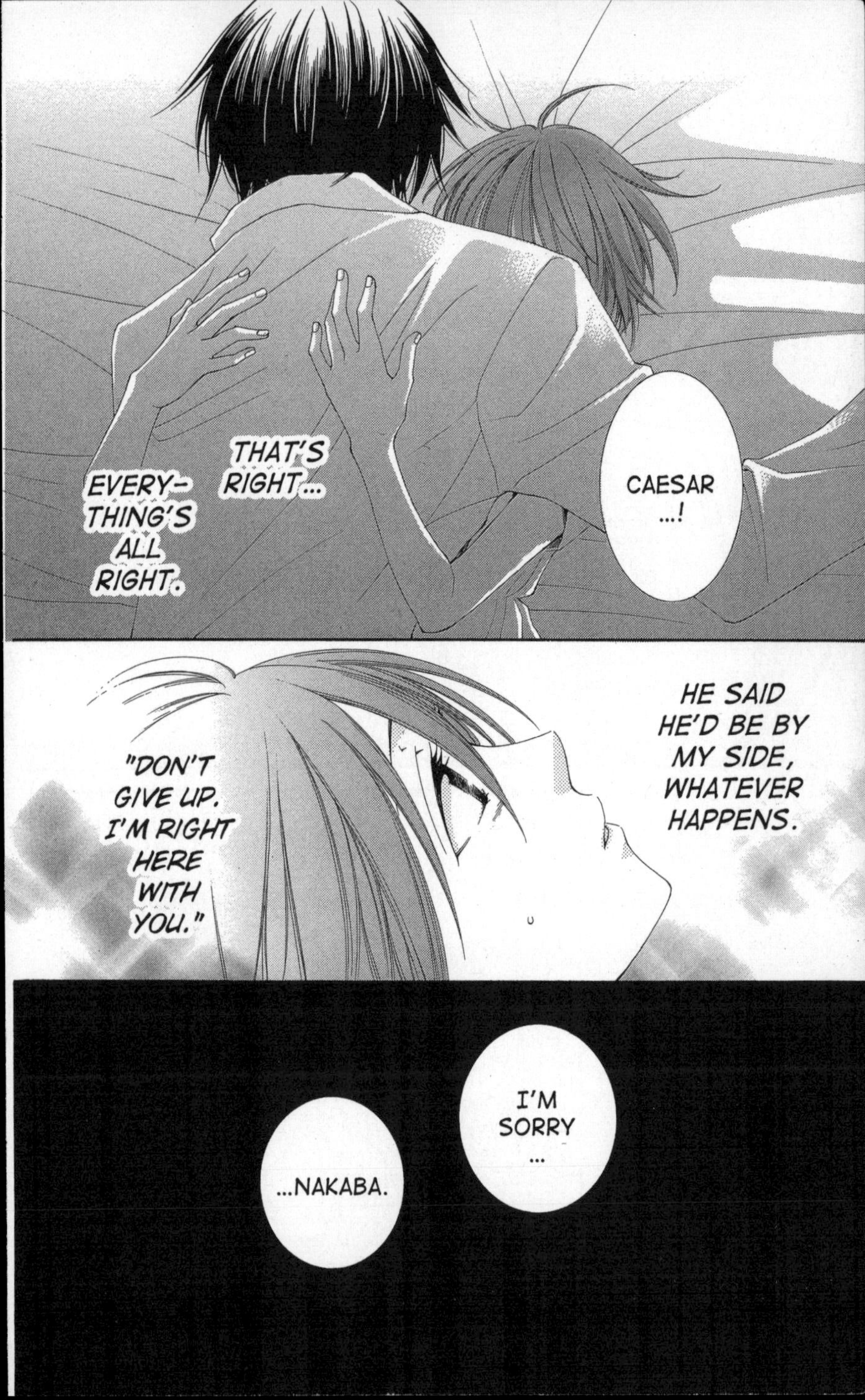
CAESAR ...!
THAT'S RIGHT...
EVERYTHING'S ALL RIGHT.
HE SAID HE'D BE BY MY SIDE, WHATEVER HAPPENS.
"DON'T GIVE UP. I'M RIGHT HERE WITH YOU."
I'M SORRY ...
...NAKABA.

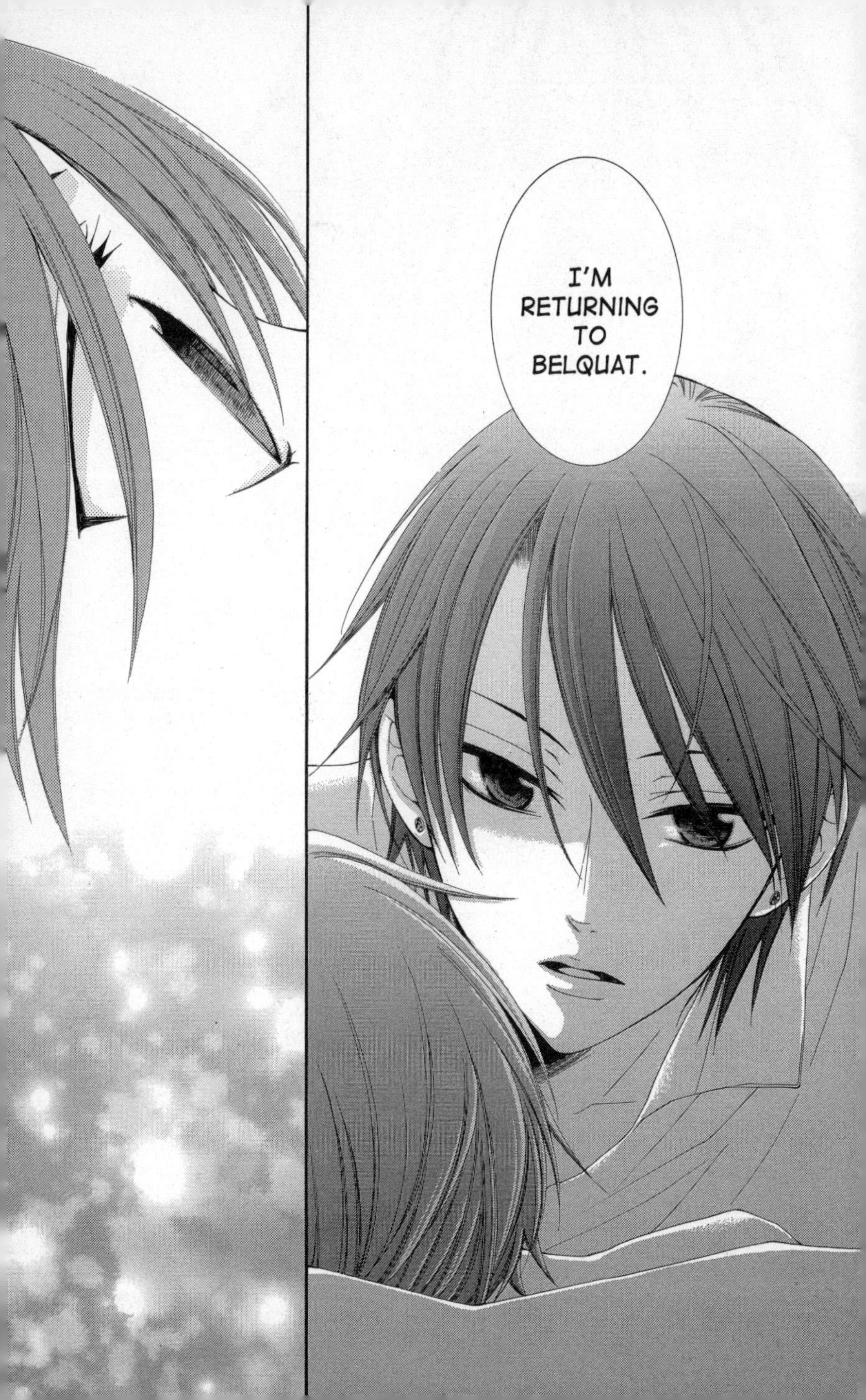
I'M RETURNING TO BELQUAT.

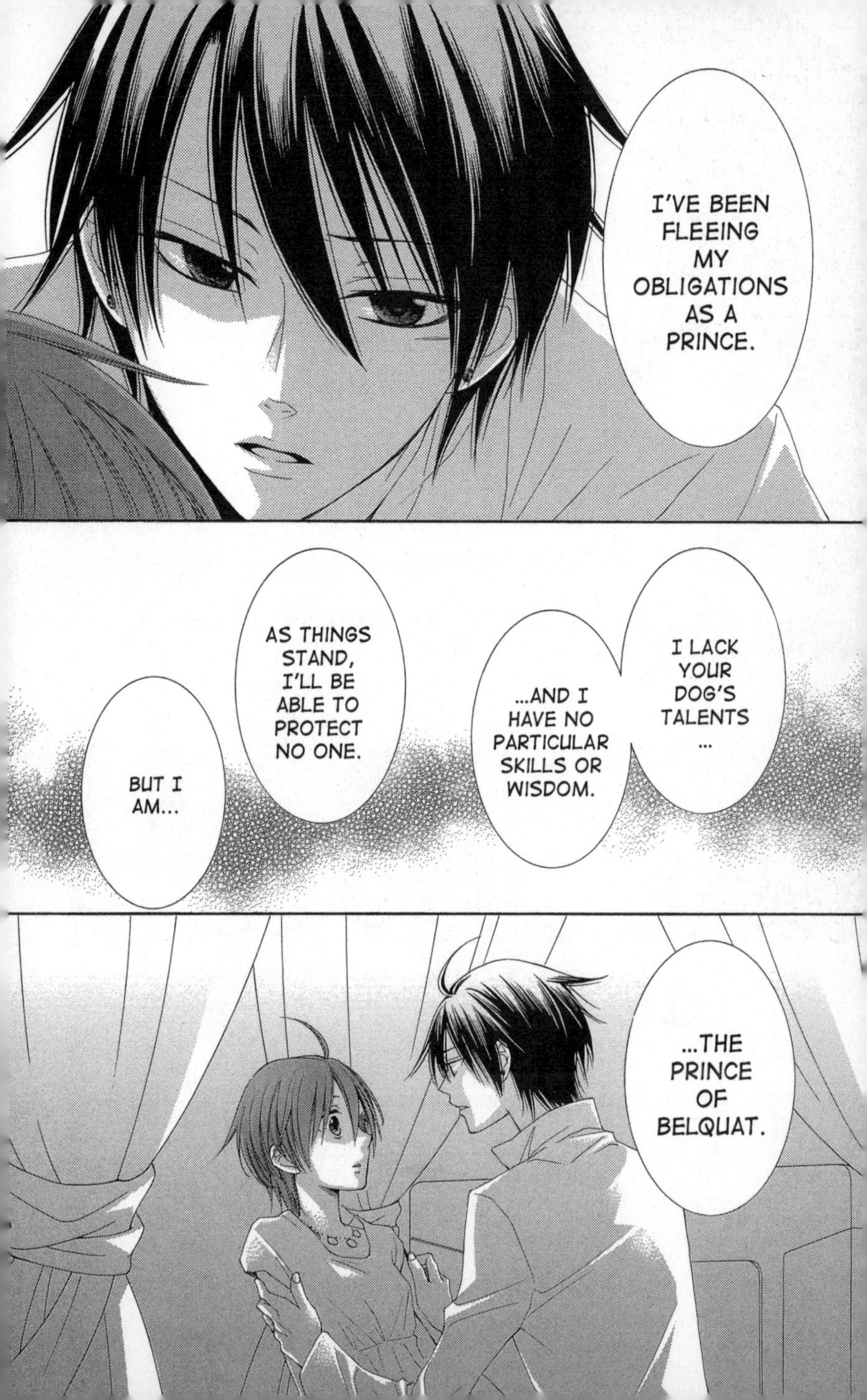
I'VE BEEN FLEEING MY OBLIGATIONS AS A PRINCE.
I LACK YOUR DOG'S TALENTS ...
...AND I HAVE NO PARTICULAR SKILLS OR WISDOM.
AS THINGS STAND, I'LL BE ABLE TO PROTECT NO ONE.
BUT I AM...
...THE PRINCE OF BELQUAT.

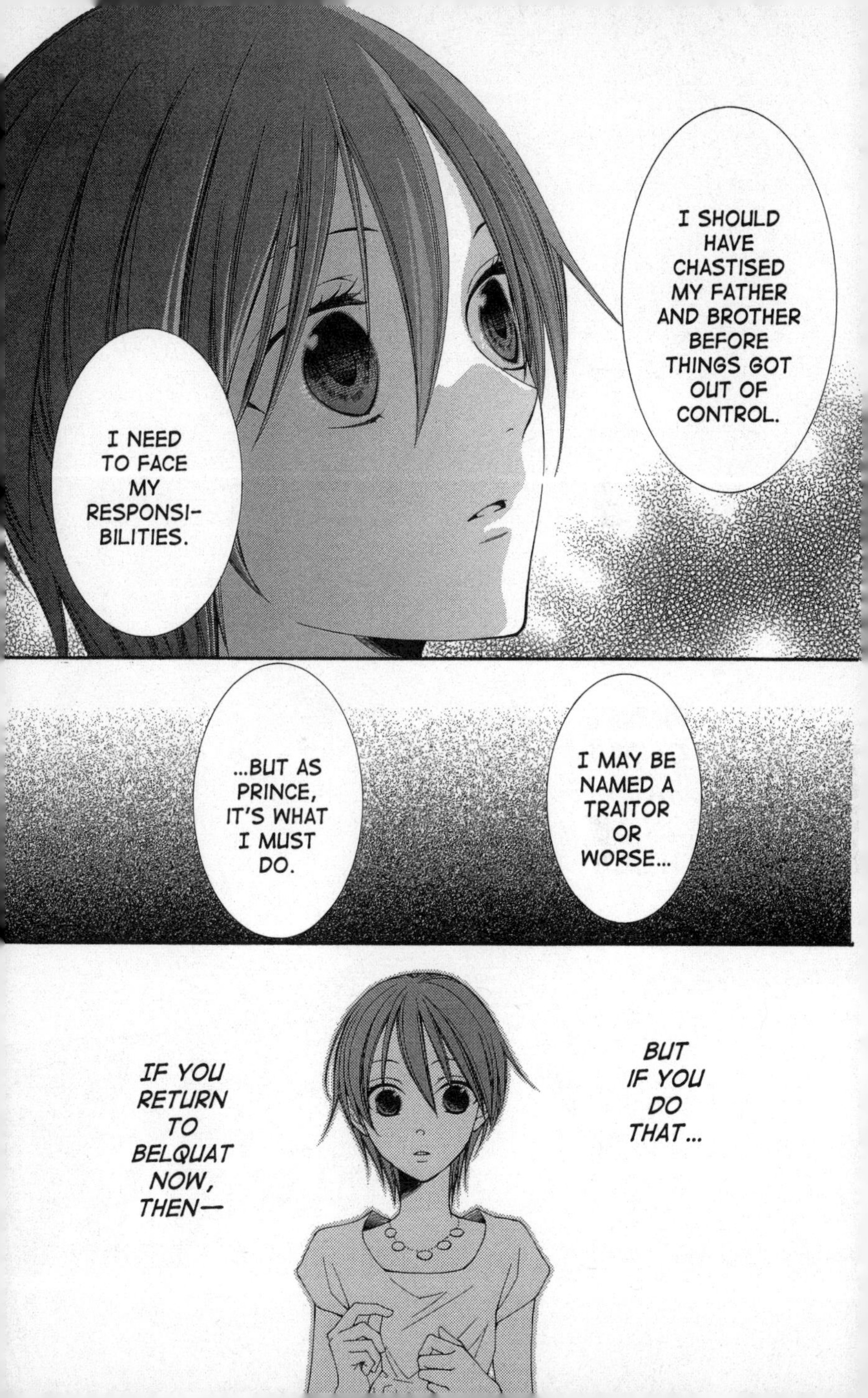
I SHOULD HAVE CHASTISED MY FATHER AND BROTHER BEFORE THINGS GOT OUT OF CONTROL.
I NEED TO FACE MY RESPONSI-BILITIES.
I MAY BE NAMED A TRAITOR OR WORSE...
...BUT AS PRINCE, IT'S WHAT I MUST DO.
BUT IF YOU DO THAT...
IF YOU RETURN TO BELQUAT NOW, THEN—

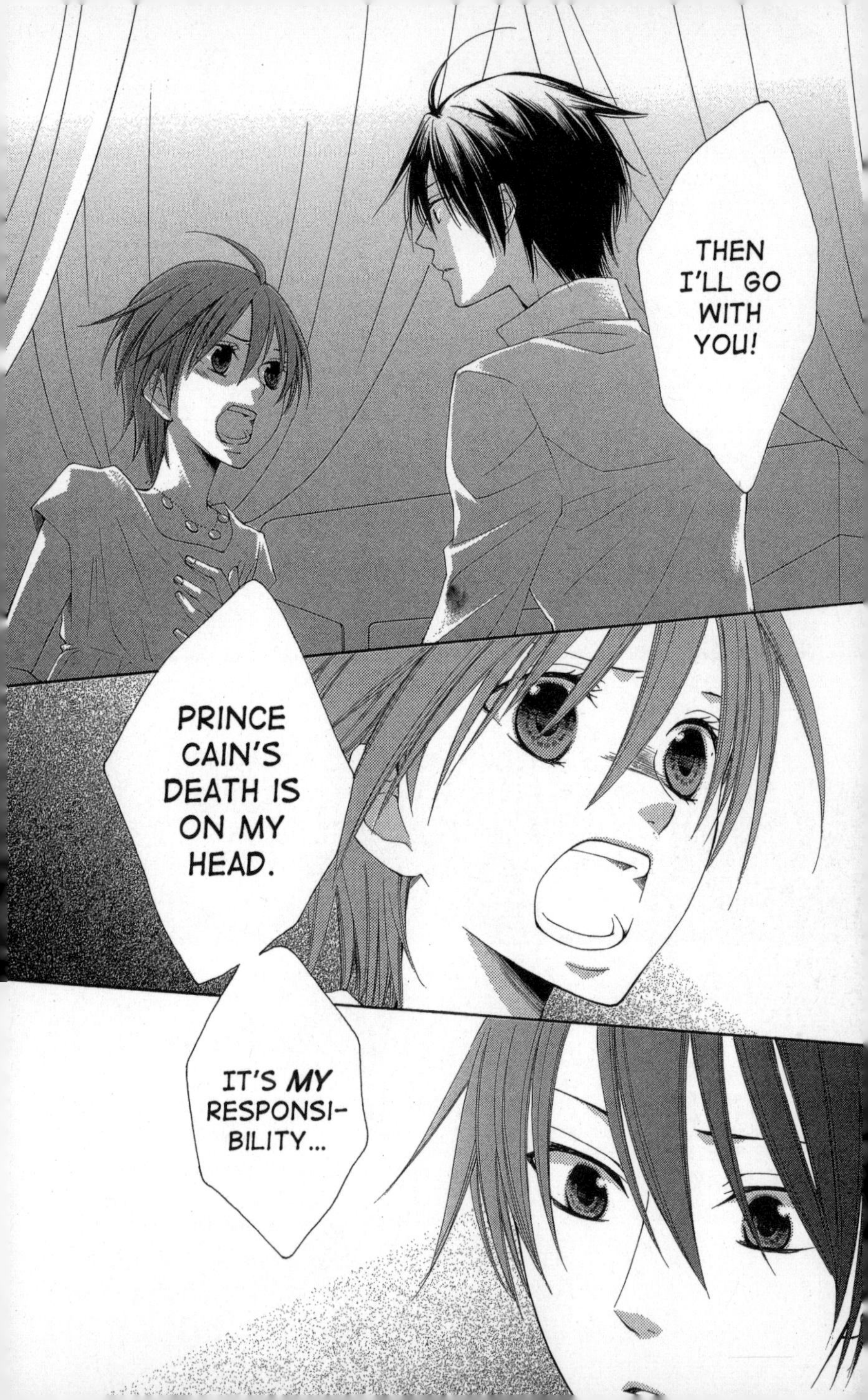
THEN I'LL GO WITH YOU!
PRINCE CAIN'S DEATH IS ON MY HEAD.
IT'S *MY* RESPONSI-BILITY...

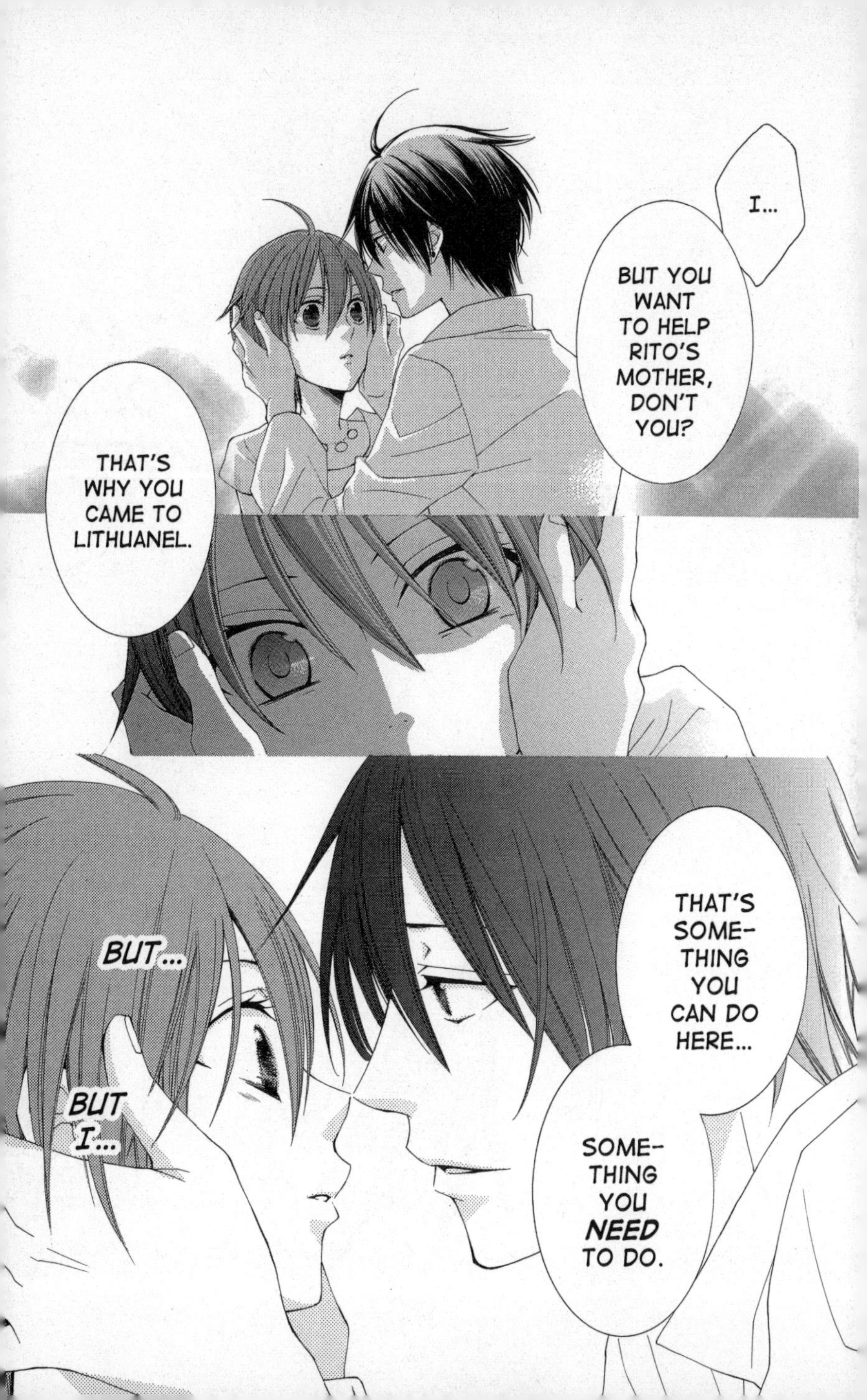
I...
BUT YOU WANT TO HELP RITO'S MOTHER, DON'T YOU?
THAT'S WHY YOU CAME TO LITHUANEL.
THAT'S SOME-THING YOU CAN DO HERE...
SOME-THING YOU *NEED* TO DO.
BUT...
BUT I...

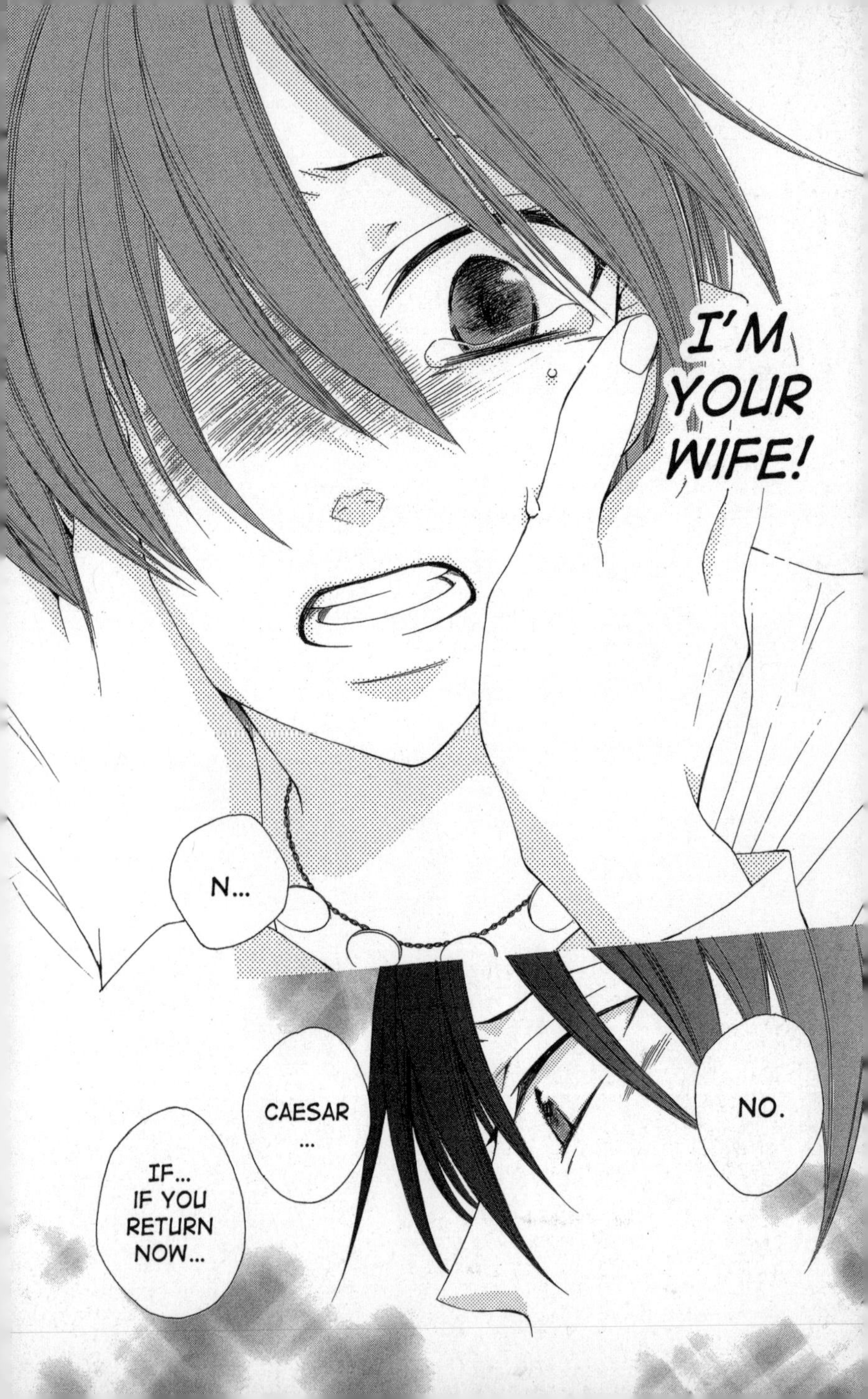
I'M YOUR WIFE!
N...
NO.
CAESAR ...
IF... IF YOU RETURN NOW...

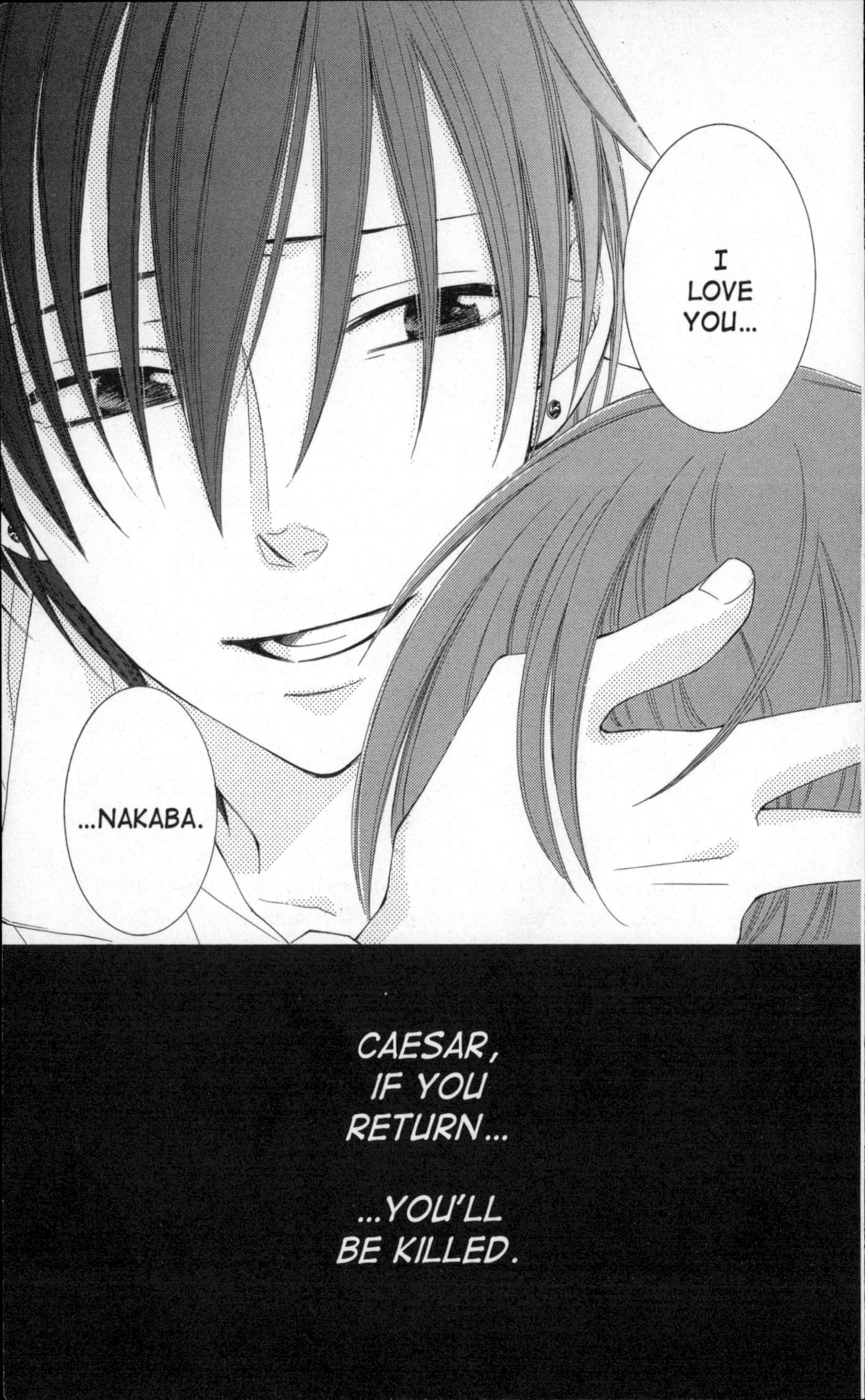
I LOVE YOU...
...NAKABA.
CAESAR, IF YOU RETURN...
...YOU'LL BE KILLED.

A Random Tidbit

Akhil is meant to be 25.
He has such a young face.
He's somewhat more mature
than he appears, though. I was
planning to work that bit of
information in somewhere,
but there just weren't any
opportunities. Anyway, I'd
already done the age thing with
Lemiria, so I decided not to
worry about it. By the way,
Loki and Cain (deceased)
are the same age. They're both
27. Caesar is 19, and Nakaba
is 16. I'm sure Nakaba and
Caesar both believe Akhil
is around 17. (*Ha ha.*)

Chapter 29

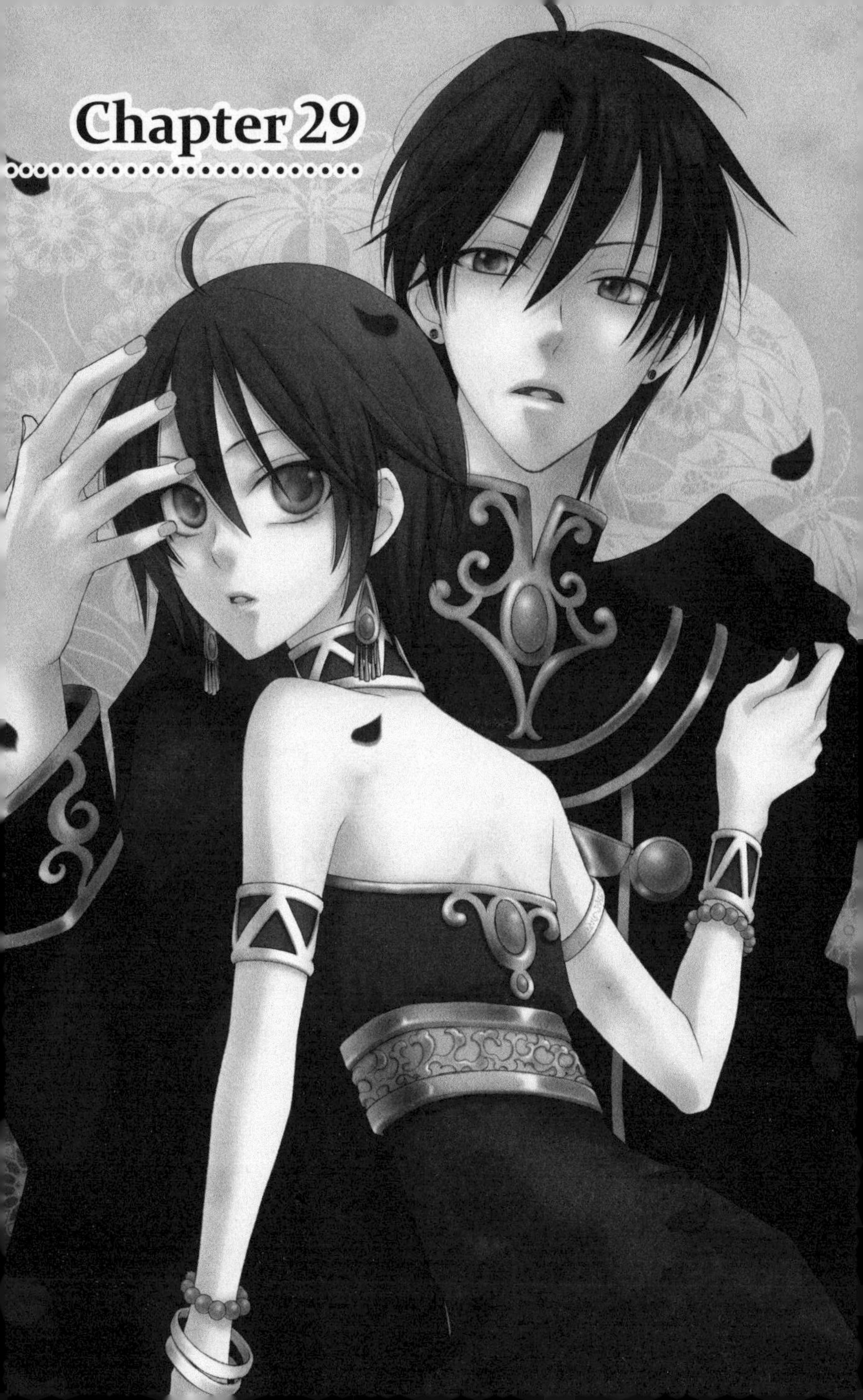

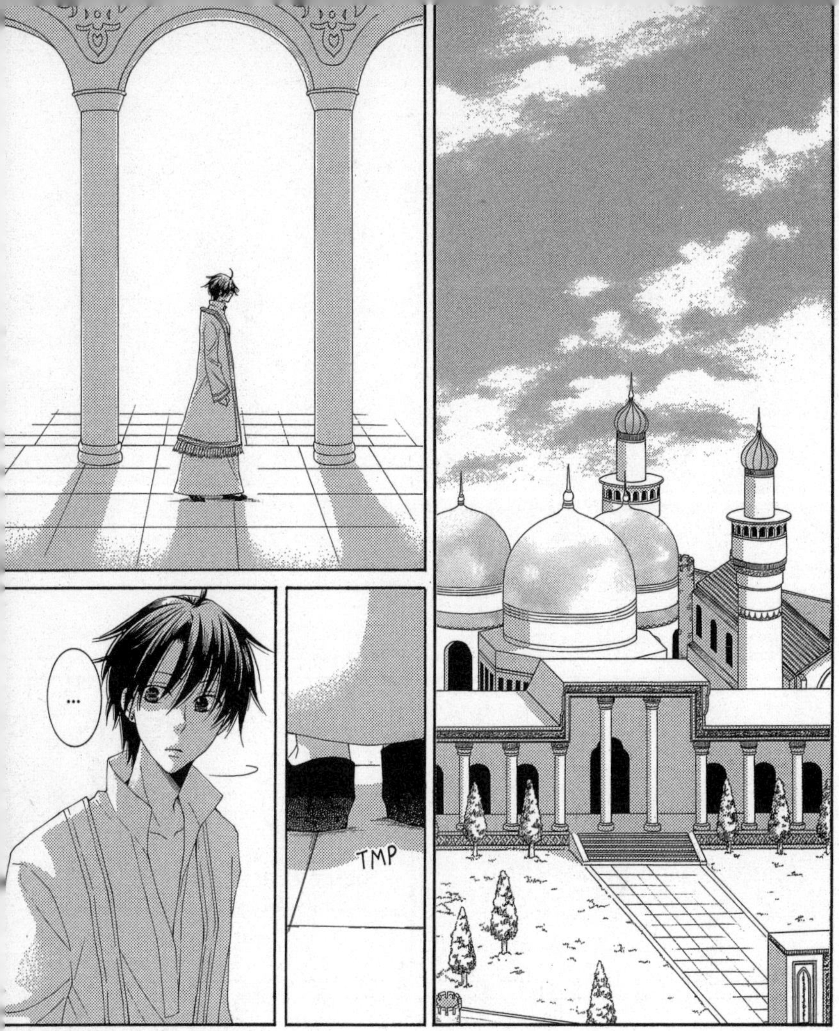
TMP
...

Dawn of the Arcana

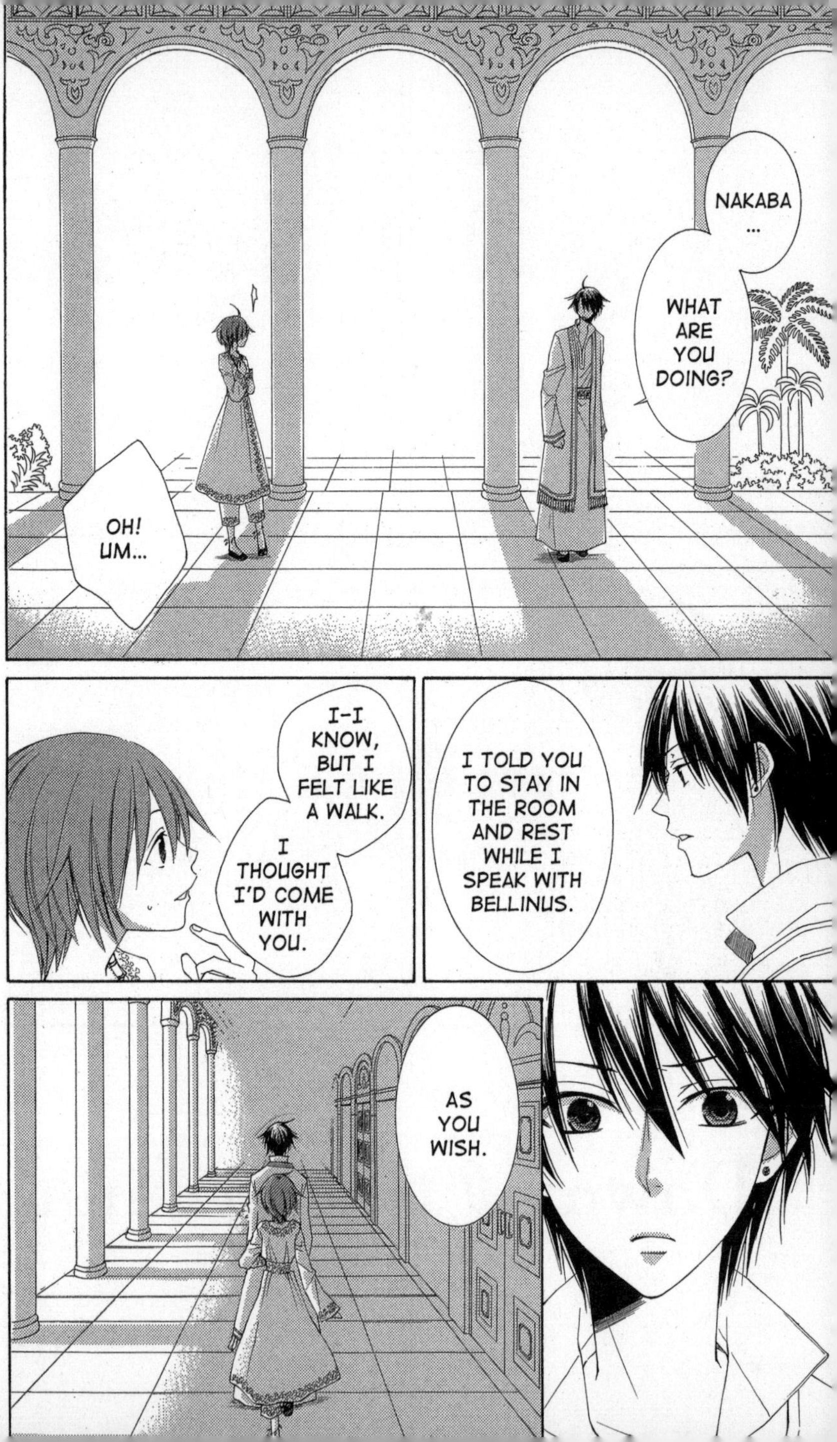
NAKABA...
WHAT ARE YOU DOING?
OH! UM...
I TOLD YOU TO STAY IN THE ROOM AND REST WHILE I SPEAK WITH BELLINUS.
I-I KNOW, BUT I FELT LIKE A WALK.
I THOUGHT I'D COME WITH YOU.
AS YOU WISH.

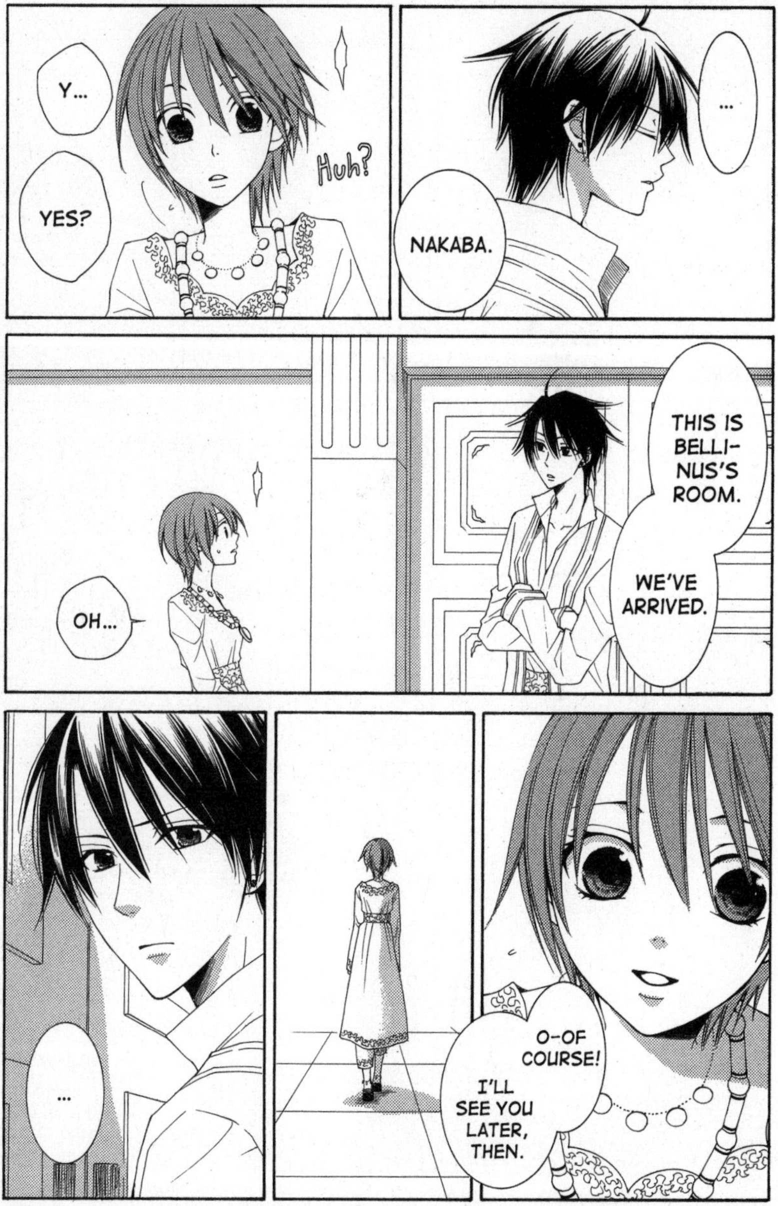
...
NAKABA.
Huh?
Y...
YES?
THIS IS BELLI-NUS'S ROOM.
WE'VE ARRIVED.
OH...
O-OF COURSE!
I'LL SEE YOU LATER, THEN.
...

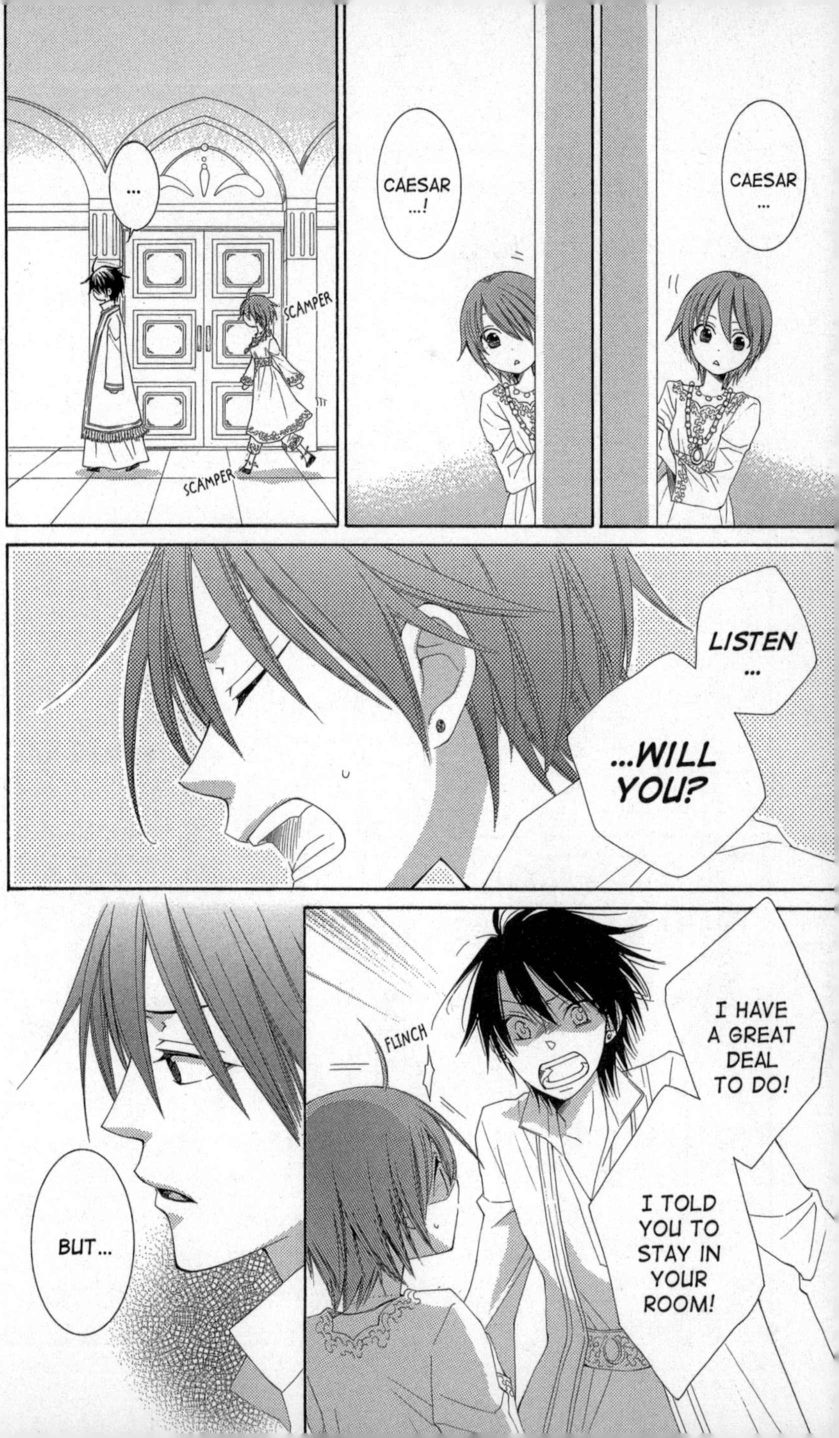
CAESAR ...
CAESAR ...!
...
SCAMPER
SCAMPER
LISTEN ...
...WILL YOU?
I HAVE A GREAT DEAL TO DO!
I TOLD YOU TO STAY IN YOUR ROOM!
FLINCH
BUT...

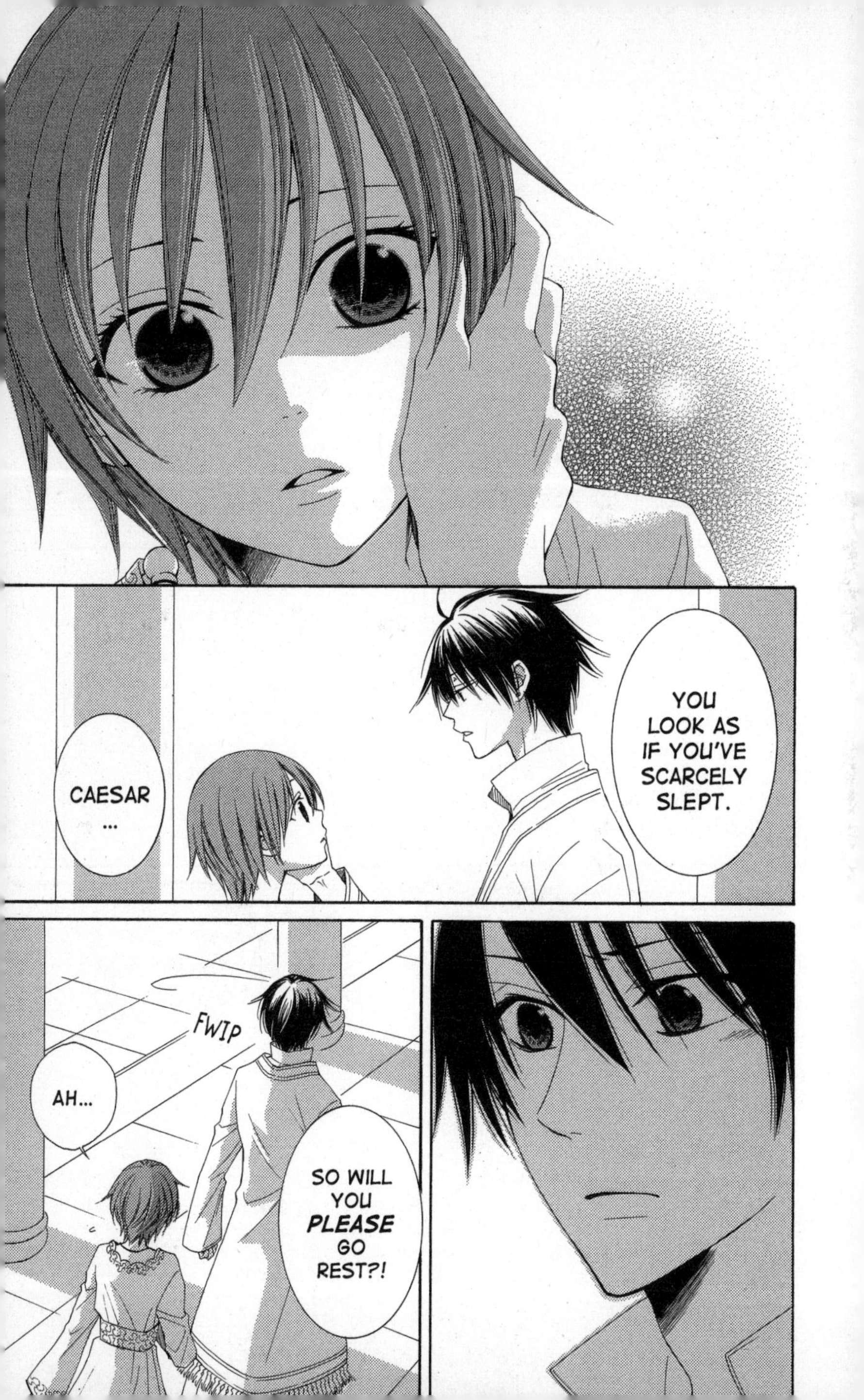
YOU LOOK AS IF YOU'VE SCARCELY SLEPT.
CAESAR ...
SO WILL YOU *PLEASE* GO REST?!
FWIP
AH...

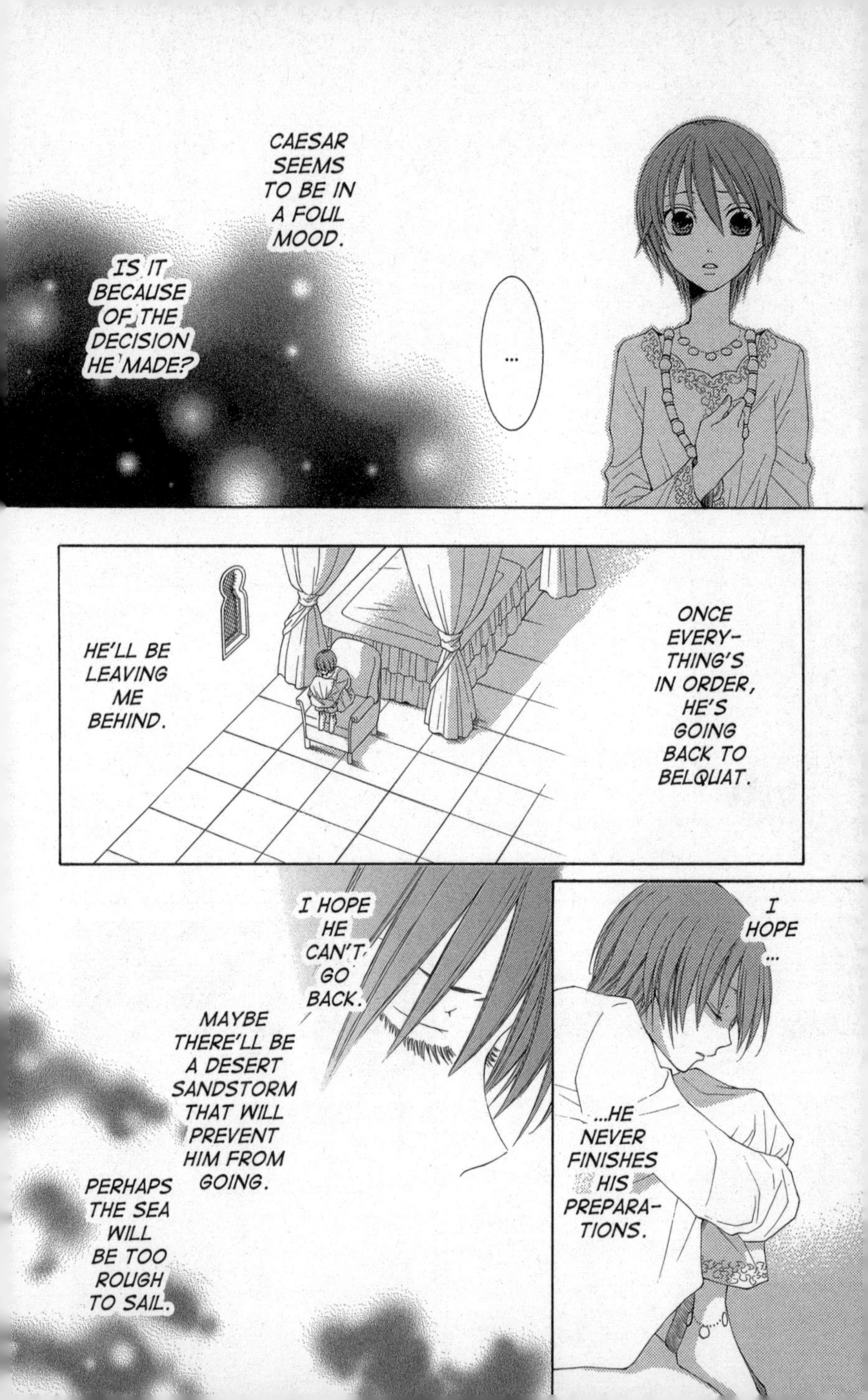
CAESAR SEEMS TO BE IN A FOUL MOOD.
IS IT BECAUSE OF THE DECISION HE MADE?
...
ONCE EVERY-THING'S IN ORDER, HE'S GOING BACK TO BELQUAT.
HE'LL BE LEAVING ME BEHIND.
I HOPE ...
...HE NEVER FINISHES HIS PREPARA-TIONS.
I HOPE HE CAN'T GO BACK.
MAYBE THERE'LL BE A DESERT SANDSTORM THAT WILL PREVENT HIM FROM GOING.
PERHAPS THE SEA WILL BE TOO ROUGH TO SAIL.

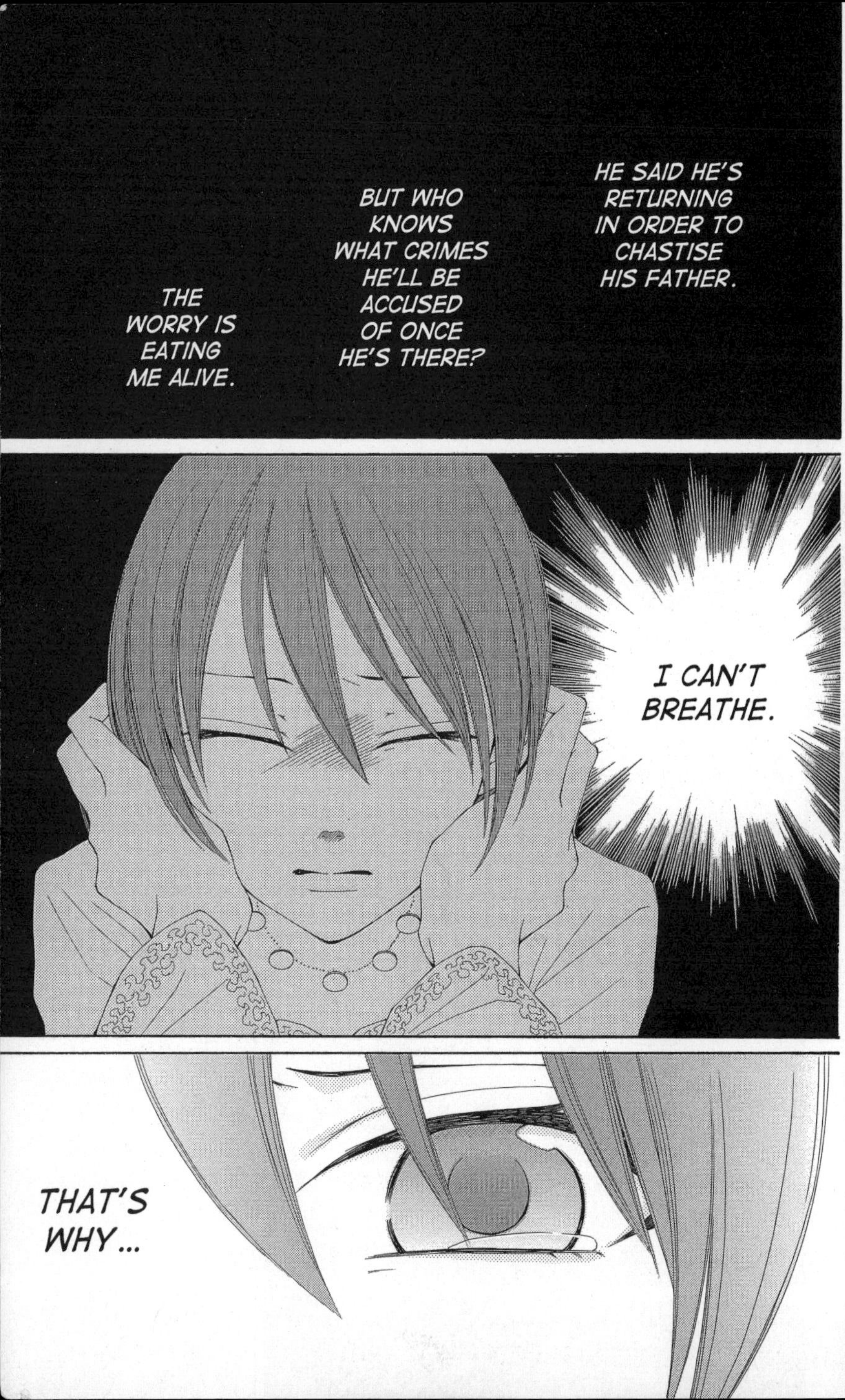
HE SAID HE'S RETURNING IN ORDER TO CHASTISE HIS FATHER.
BUT WHO KNOWS WHAT CRIMES HE'LL BE ACCUSED OF ONCE HE'S THERE?
THE WORRY IS EATING ME ALIVE.
I CAN'T BREATHE.
THAT'S WHY...

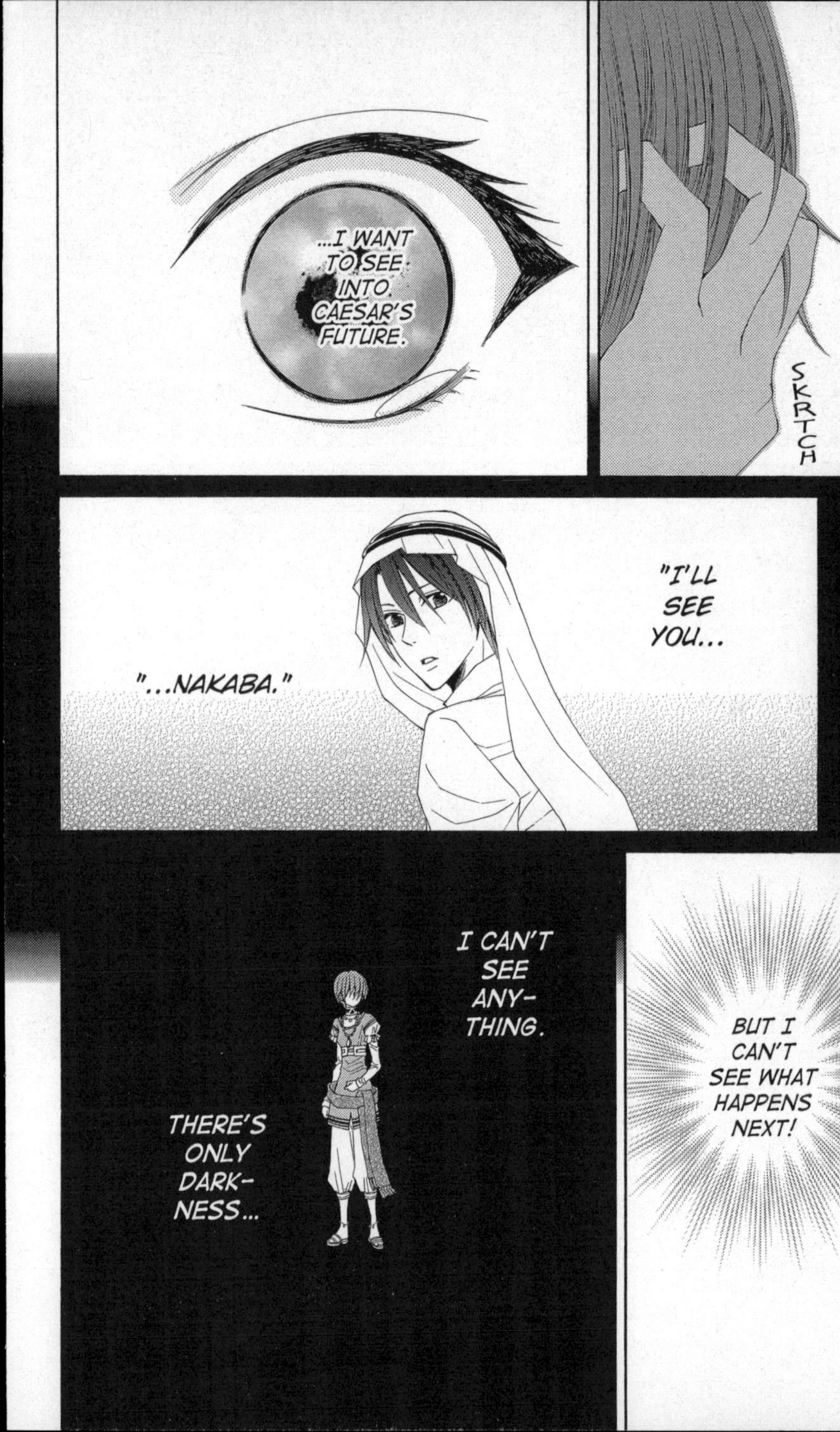
SKRTCH
...I WANT TO SEE INTO CAESAR'S FUTURE.
"I'LL SEE YOU...
"...NAKABA."
BUT I CAN'T SEE WHAT HAPPENS NEXT!
I CAN'T SEE ANY-THING.
THERE'S ONLY DARK-NESS...

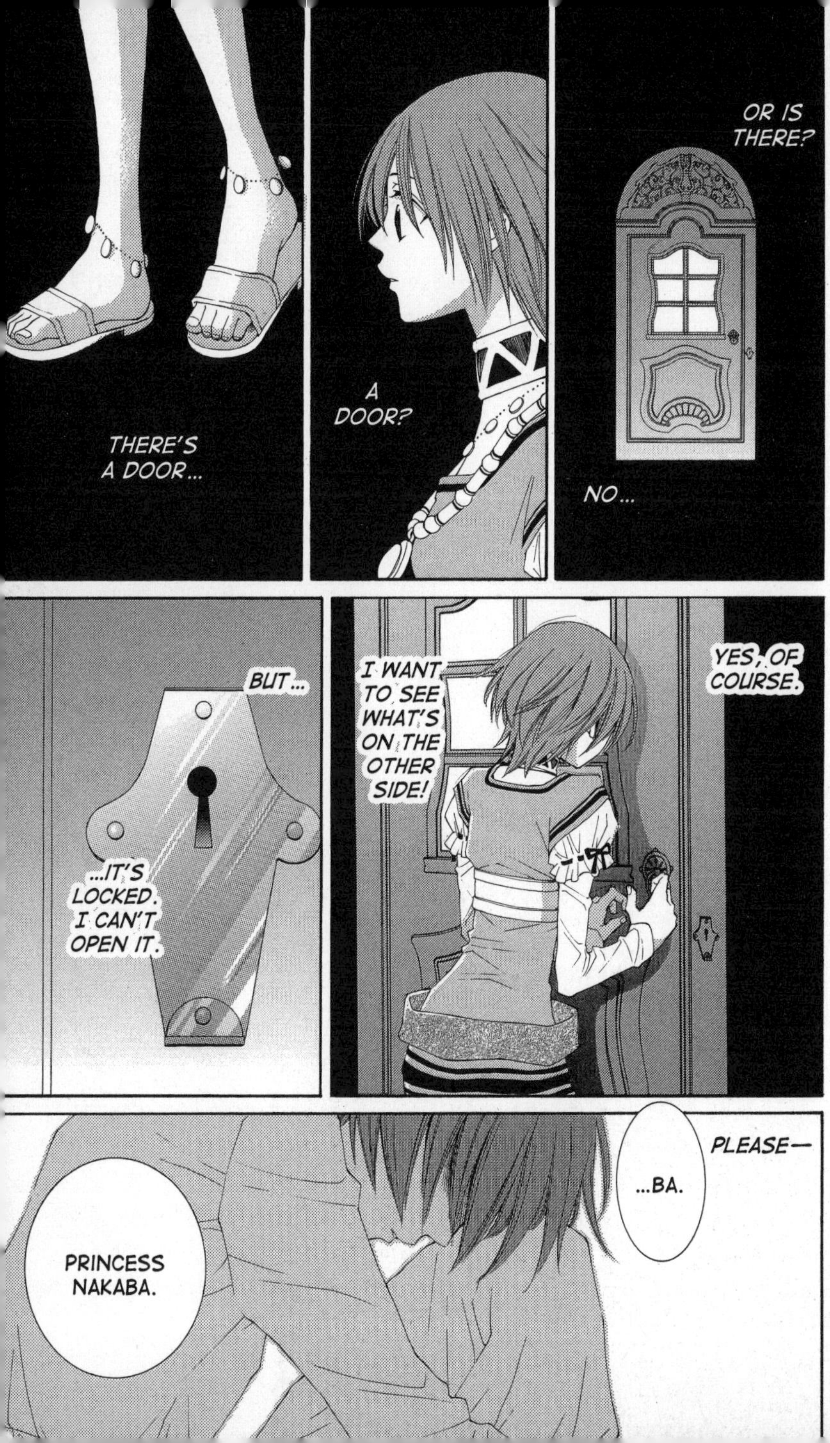
OR IS THERE?
NO...
A DOOR?
THERE'S A DOOR...
YES, OF COURSE.
I WANT TO SEE WHAT'S ON THE OTHER SIDE!
BUT...
...IT'S LOCKED. I CAN'T OPEN IT.
PLEASE—
...BA.
PRINCESS NAKABA.

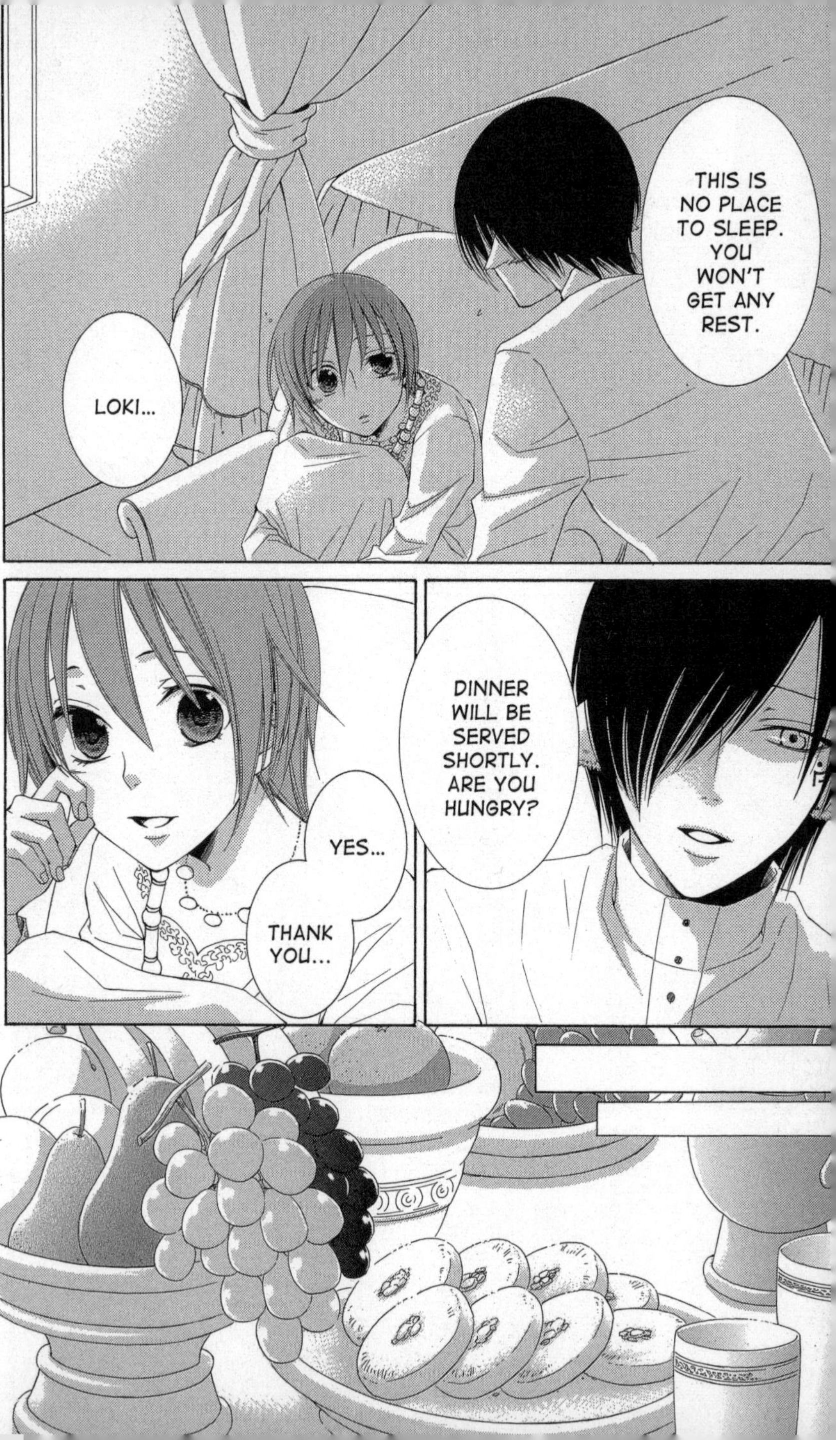
THIS IS NO PLACE TO SLEEP. YOU WON'T GET ANY REST.
LOKI...
DINNER WILL BE SERVED SHORTLY. ARE YOU HUNGRY?
YES...
THANK YOU...

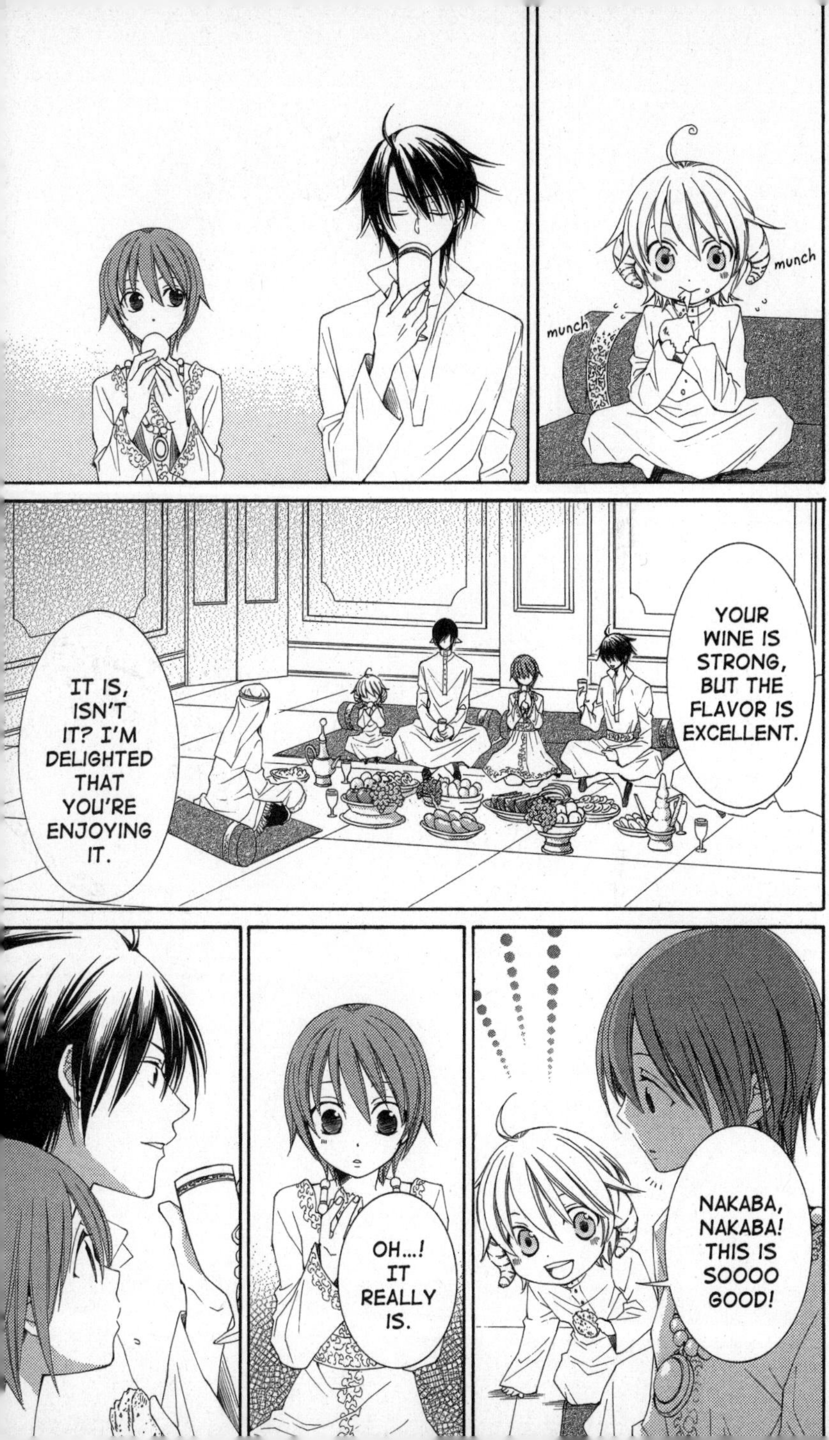
munch
munch
YOUR WINE IS STRONG, BUT THE FLAVOR IS EXCELLENT.
IT IS, ISN'T IT? I'M DELIGHTED THAT YOU'RE ENJOYING IT.
NAKABA, NAKABA! THIS IS SOOOO GOOD!
OH...! IT REALLY IS.

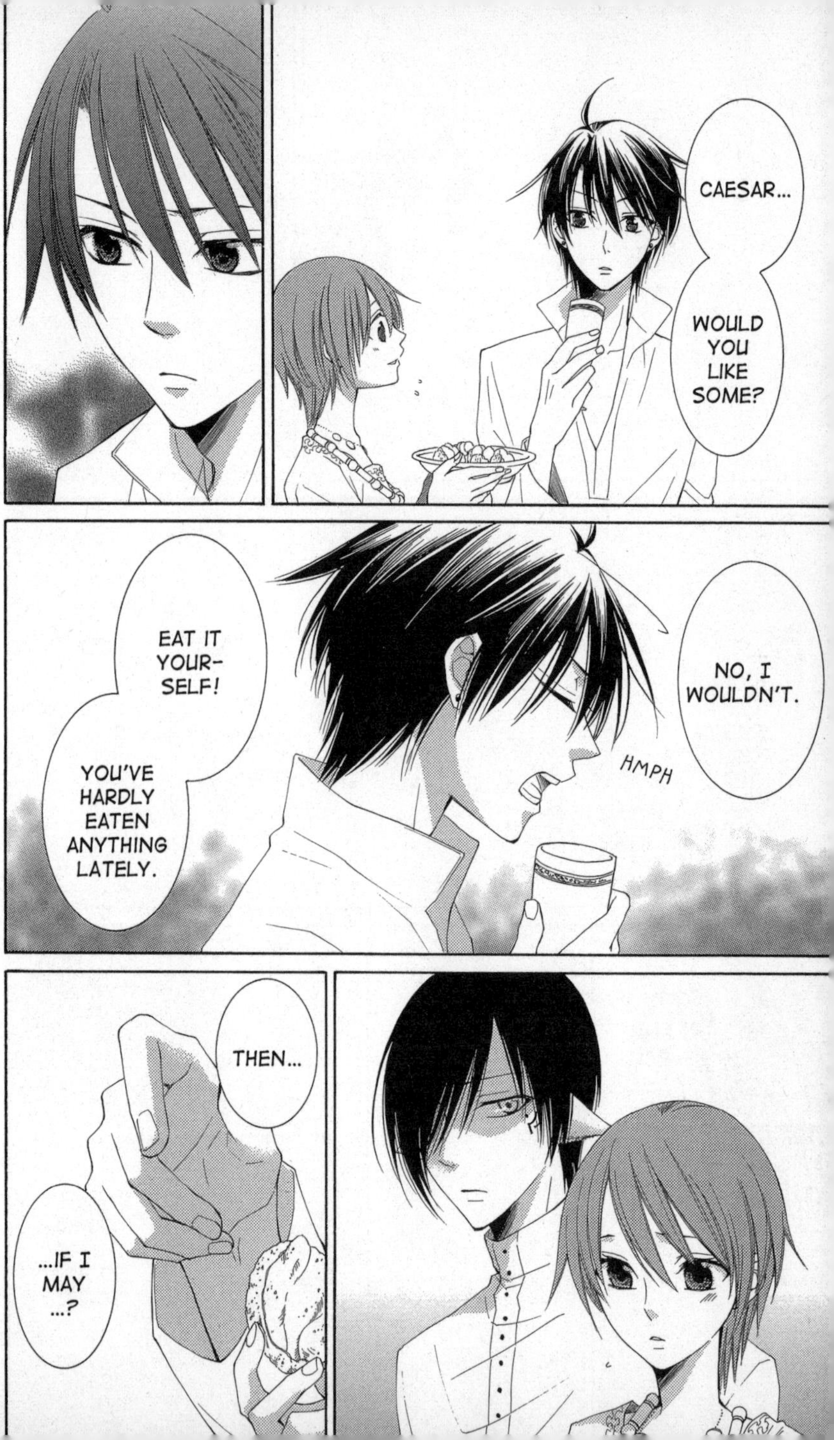
CAESAR...
WOULD YOU LIKE SOME?
NO, I WOULDN'T.
HMPH
EAT IT YOUR-SELF!
YOU'VE HARDLY EATEN ANYTHING LATELY.
THEN...
...IF I MAY ...?

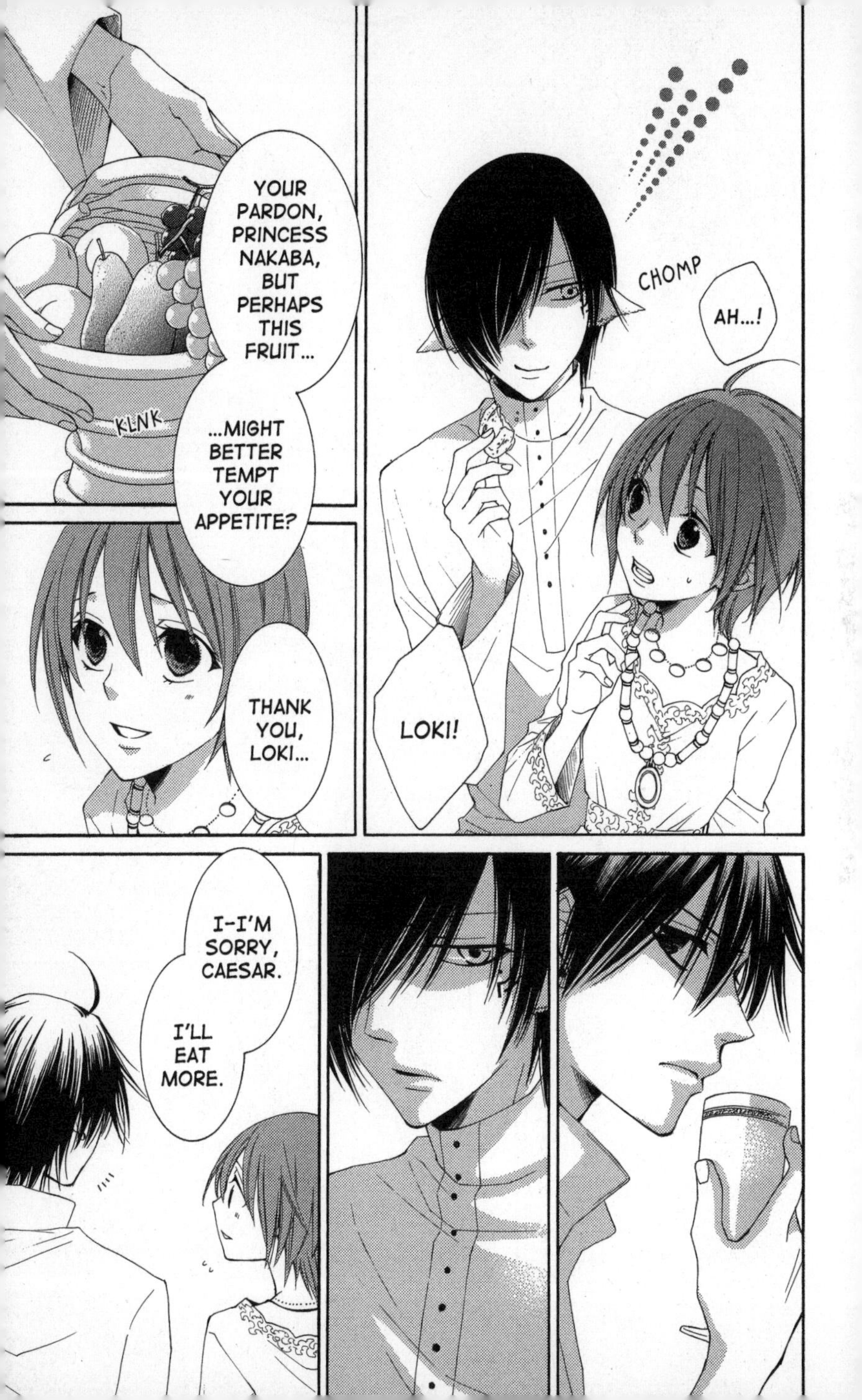
CHOMP
AH...!
LOKI!
KLNK
YOUR PARDON, PRINCESS NAKABA, BUT PERHAPS THIS FRUIT...
...MIGHT BETTER TEMPT YOUR APPETITE?
THANK YOU, LOKI...
I-I'M SORRY, CAESAR.
I'LL EAT MORE.

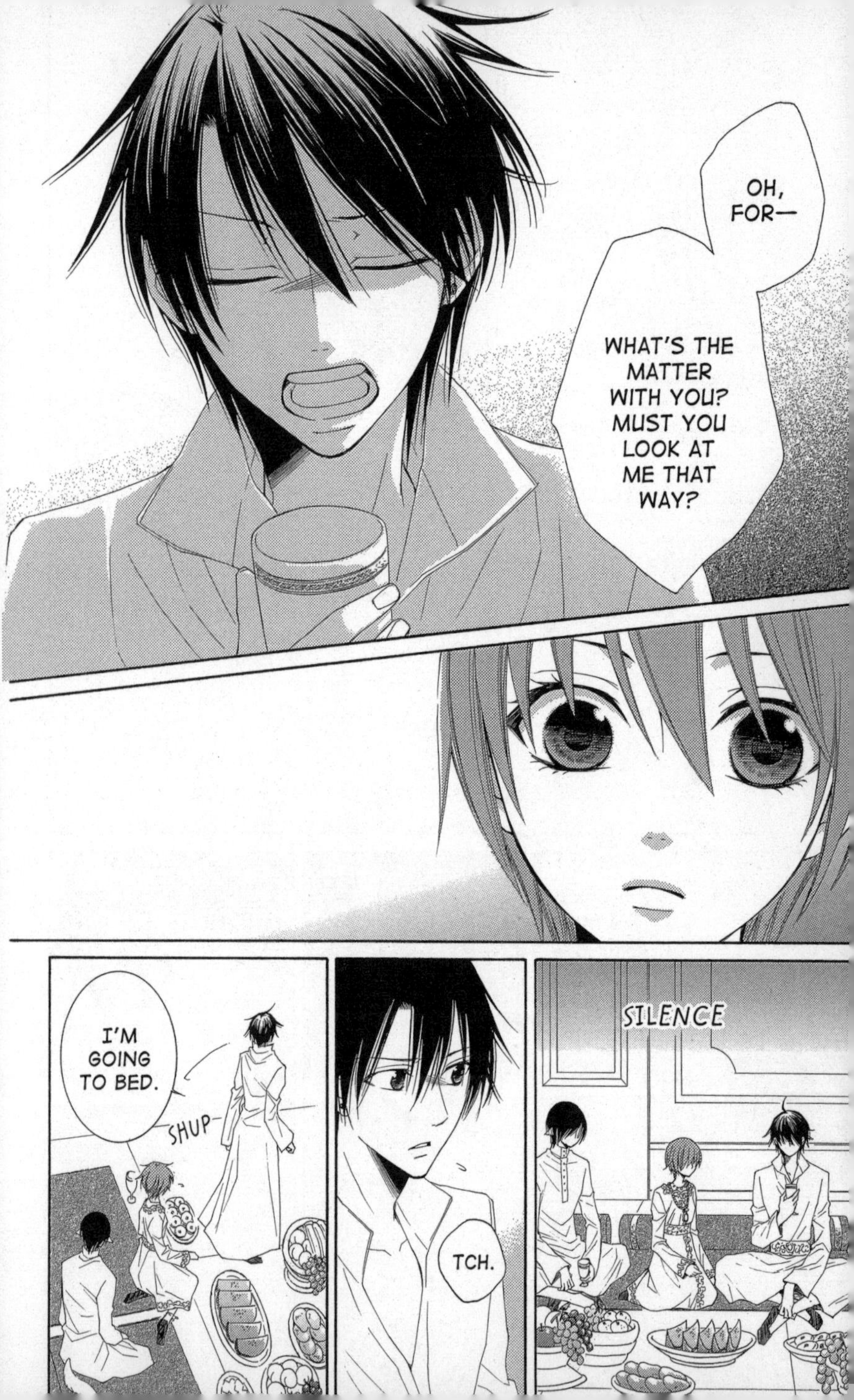
OH, FOR—
WHAT'S THE MATTER WITH YOU? MUST YOU LOOK AT ME THAT WAY?
SILENCE
TCH.
I'M GOING TO BED.
SHUP—

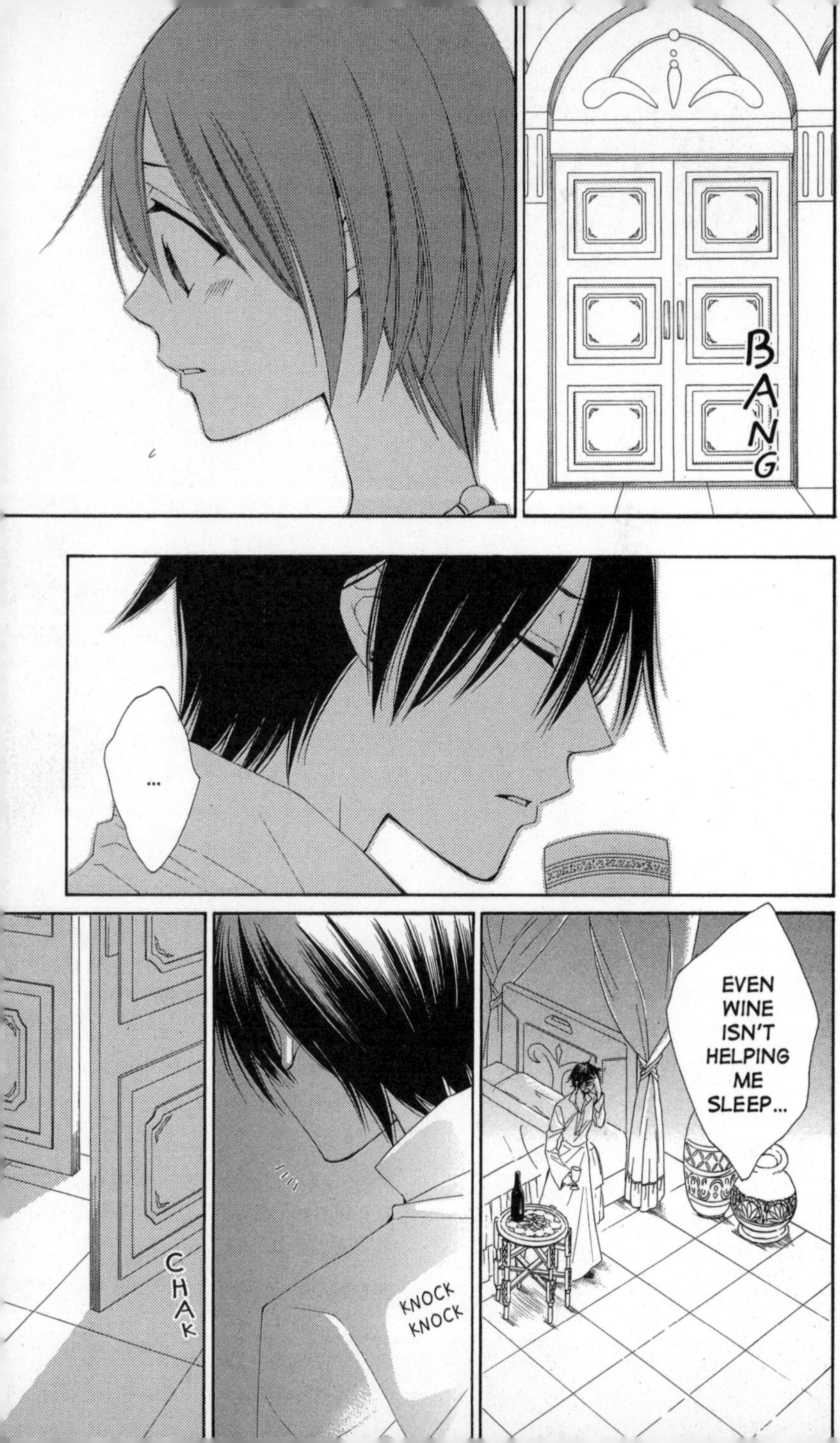
BANG
...
EVEN WINE ISN'T HELPING ME SLEEP...
KNOCK KNOCK
CHAK

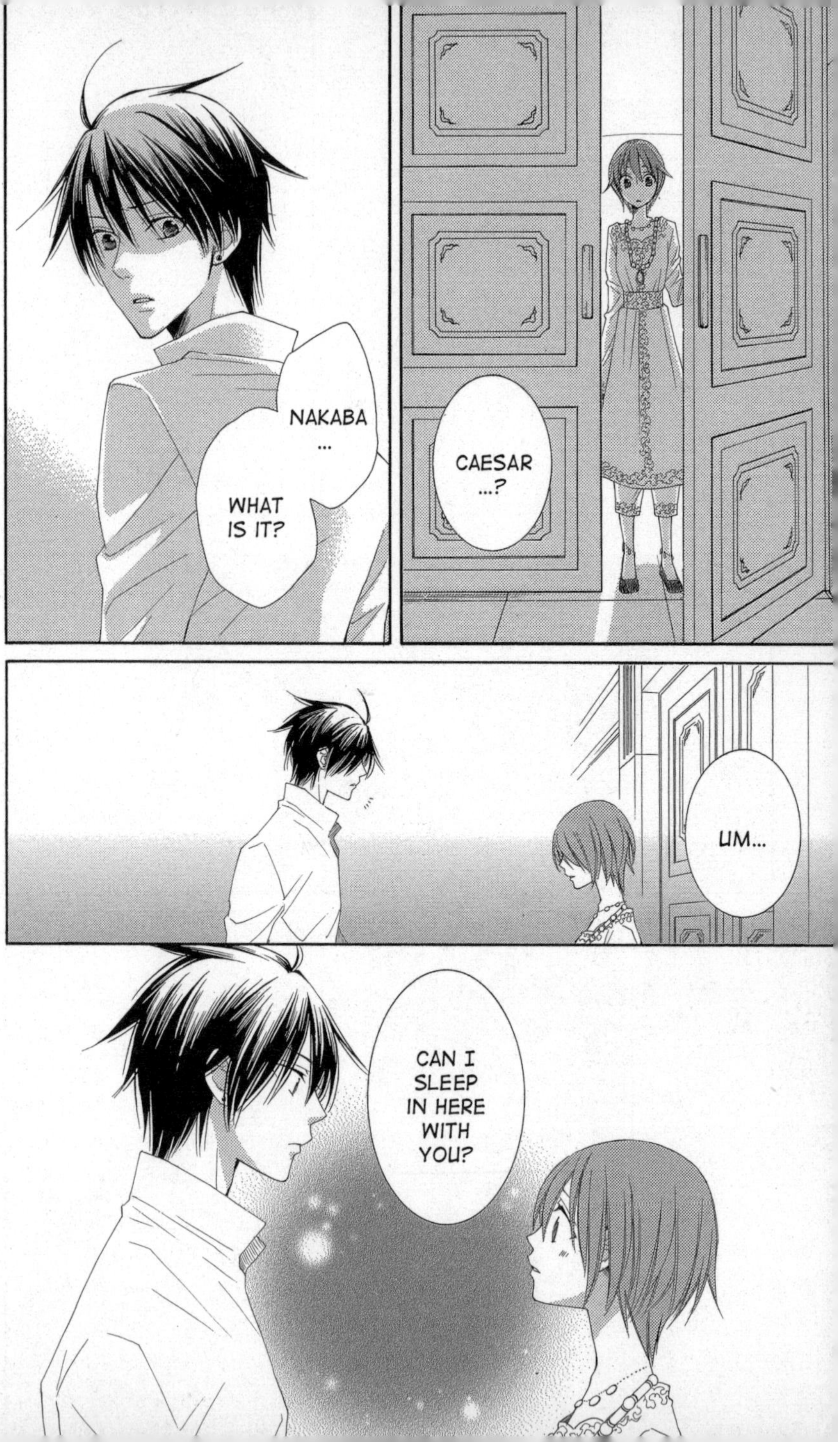
CAESAR ...?
NAKABA ... WHAT IS IT?
UM...
CAN I SLEEP IN HERE WITH YOU?

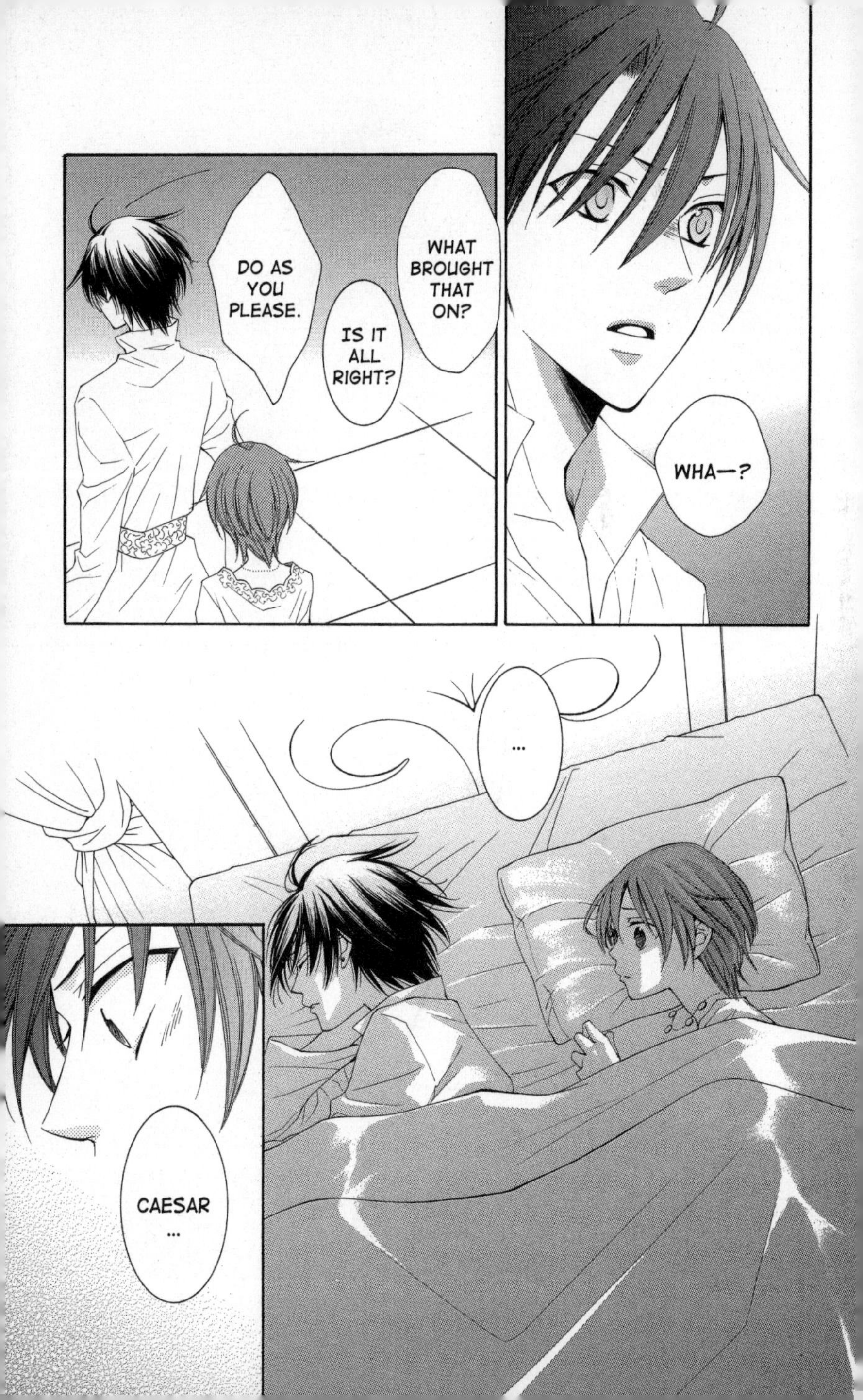
WHA—?
WHAT BROUGHT THAT ON?
IS IT ALL RIGHT?
DO AS YOU PLEASE.
...
CAESAR ...

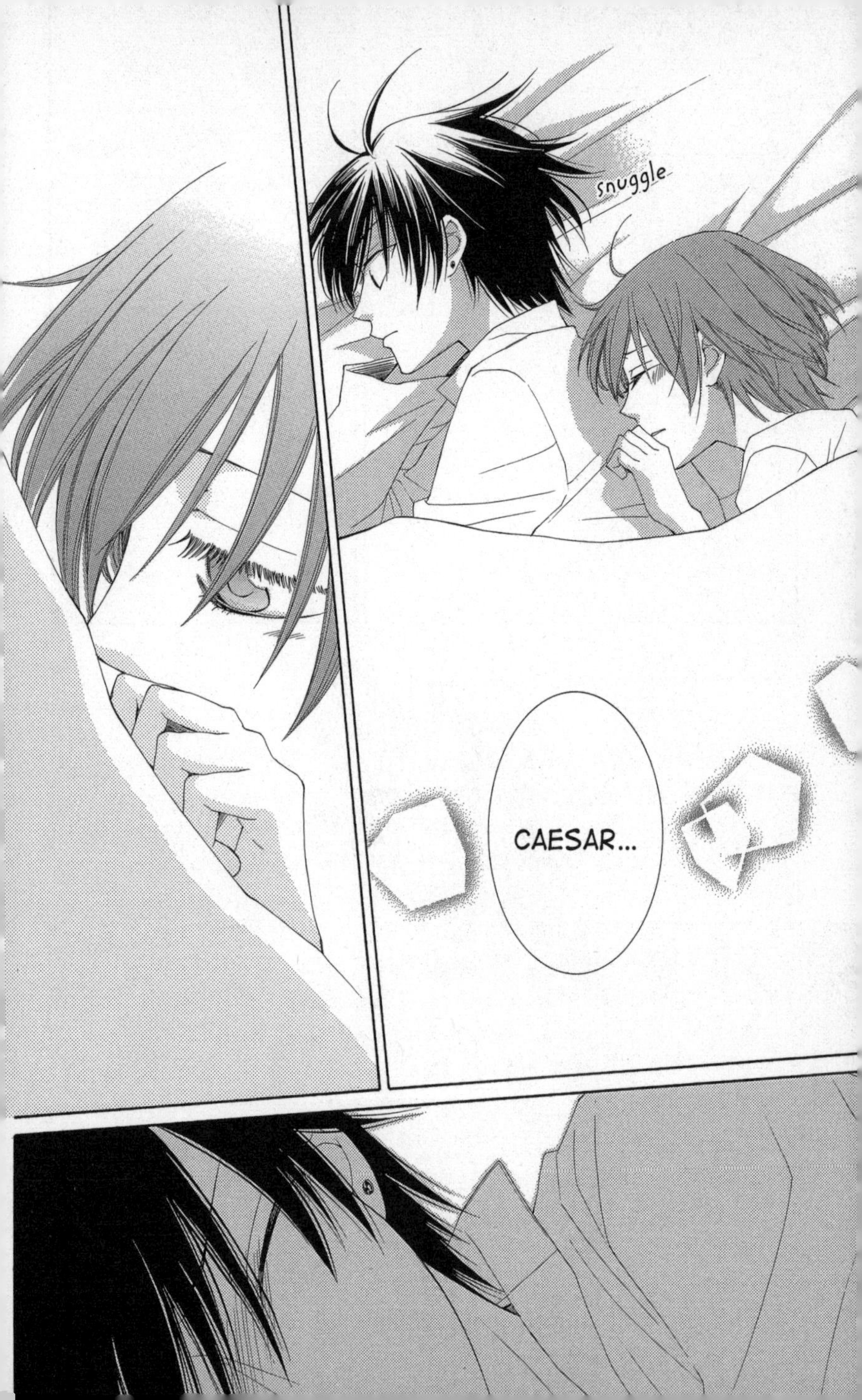
snuggle
CAESAR...

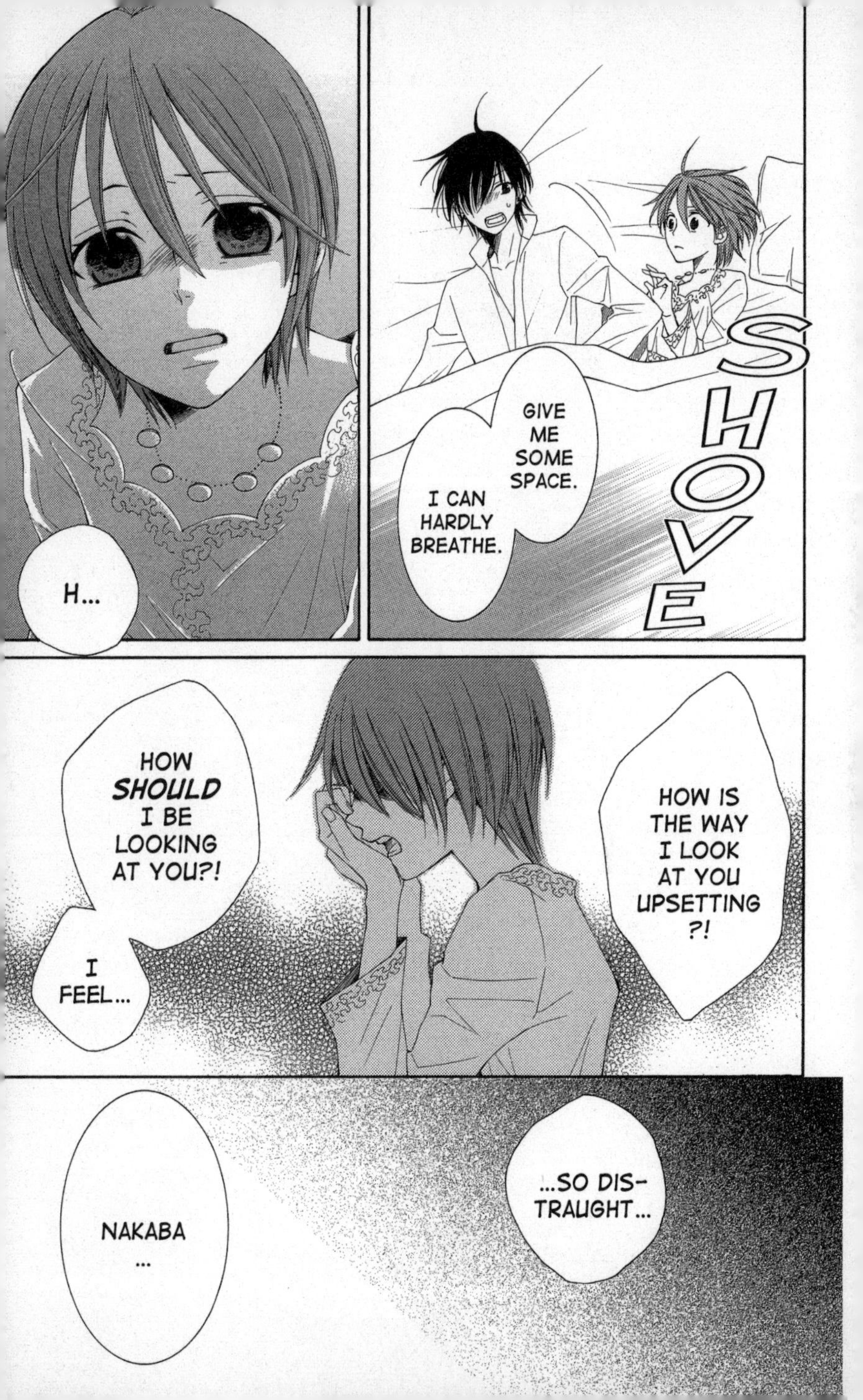
GIVE ME SOME SPACE.
I CAN HARDLY BREATHE.
SHOVE
H...
HOW IS THE WAY I LOOK AT YOU UPSETTING?!
HOW SHOULD I BE LOOKING AT YOU?!
I FEEL...
...SO DIS-TRAUGHT...
NAKABA...

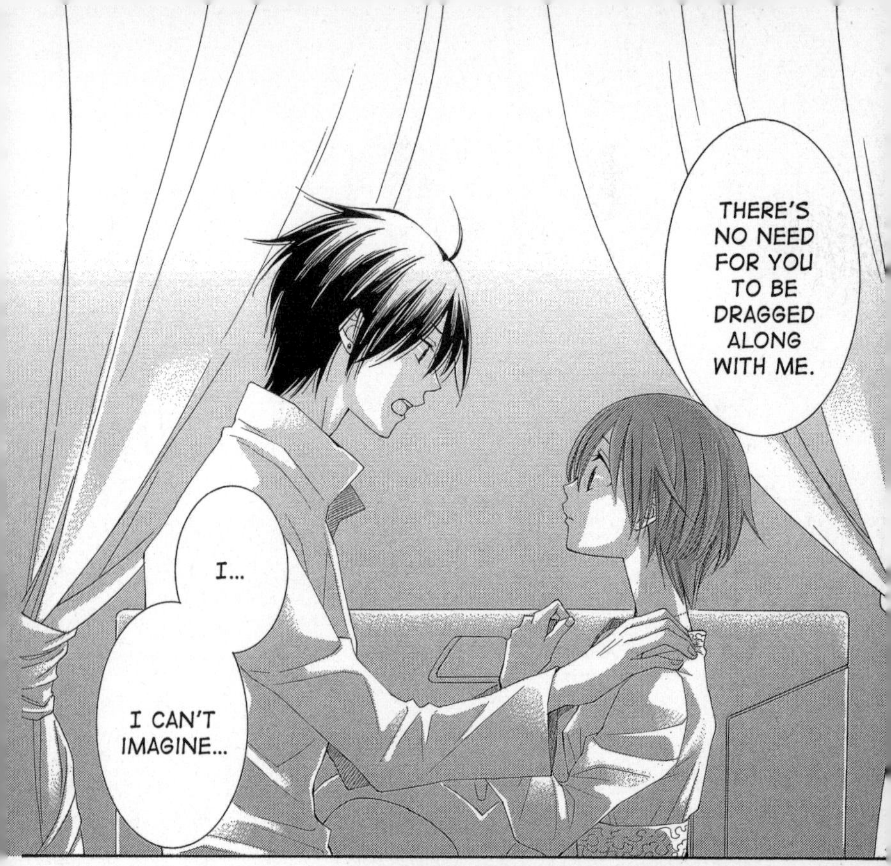
THERE'S NO NEED FOR YOU TO BE DRAGGED ALONG WITH ME.
I...
I CAN'T IMAGINE...
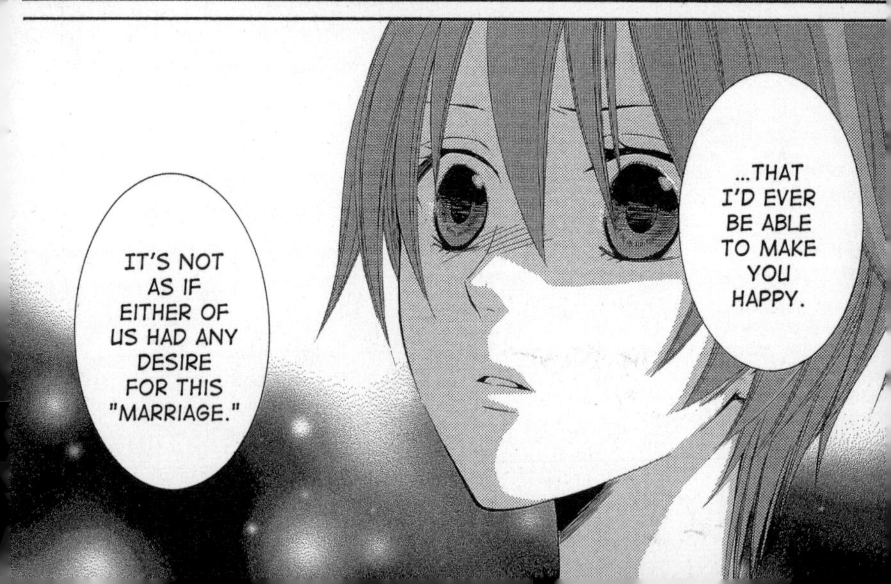
...THAT I'D EVER BE ABLE TO MAKE YOU HAPPY.
IT'S NOT AS IF EITHER OF US HAD ANY DESIRE FOR THIS "MARRIAGE."

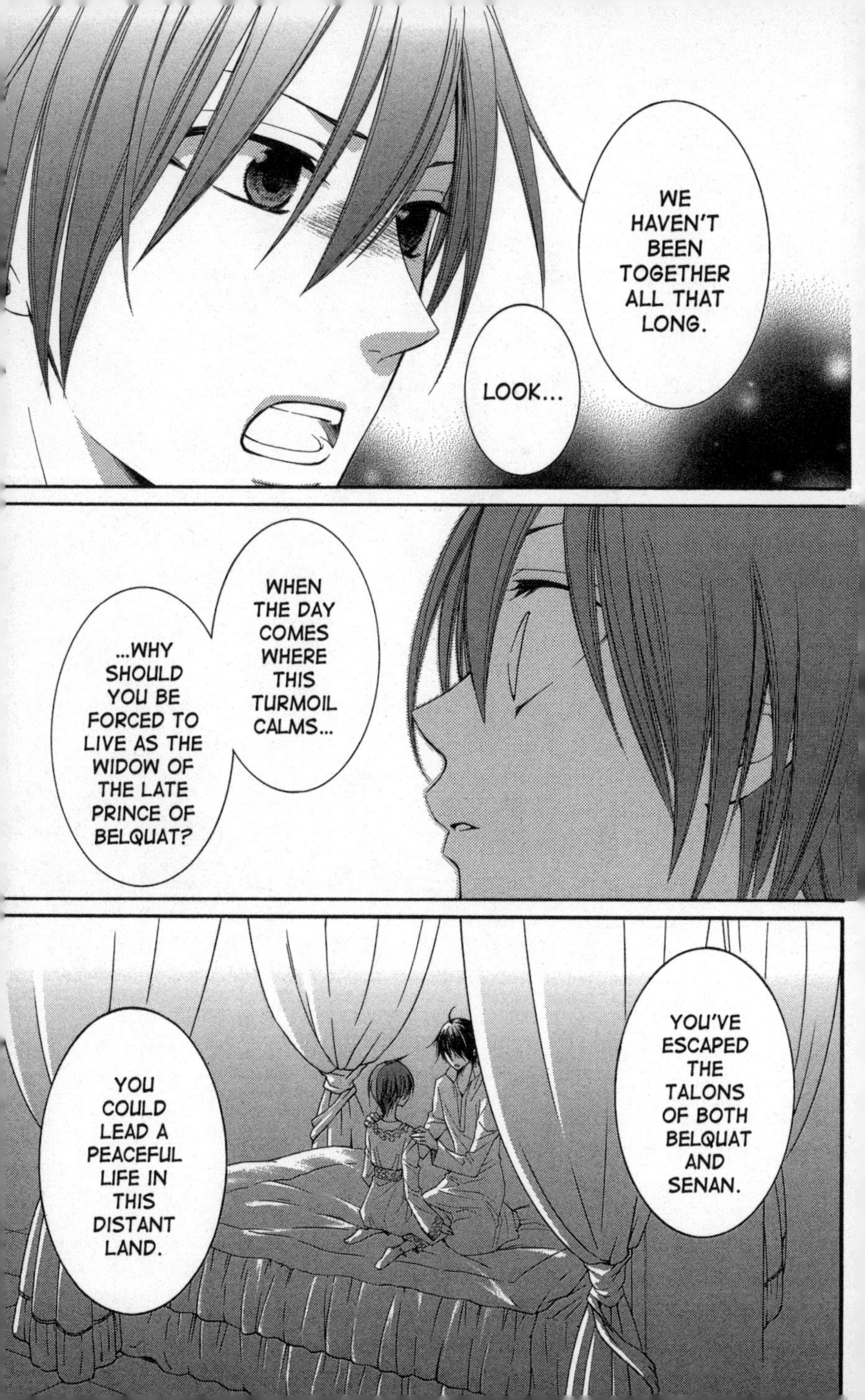
WE HAVEN'T BEEN TOGETHER ALL THAT LONG.
LOOK...
WHEN THE DAY COMES WHERE THIS TURMOIL CALMS...
...WHY SHOULD YOU BE FORCED TO LIVE AS THE WIDOW OF THE LATE PRINCE OF BELQUAT?
YOU'VE ESCAPED THE TALONS OF BOTH BELQUAT AND SENAN.
YOU COULD LEAD A PEACEFUL LIFE IN THIS DISTANT LAND.

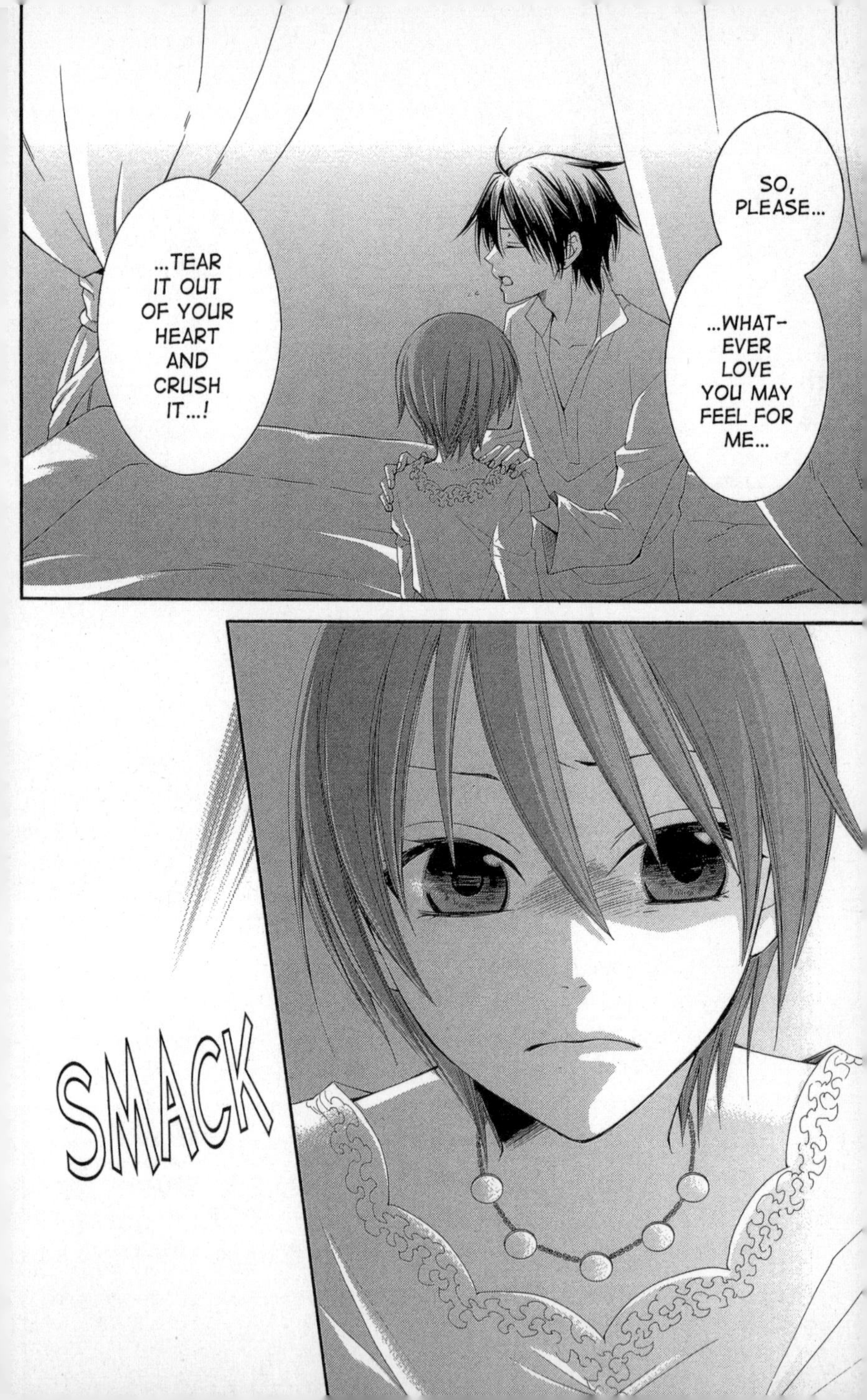
SO, PLEASE...
...WHAT-EVER LOVE YOU MAY FEEL FOR ME...
...TEAR IT OUT OF YOUR HEART AND CRUSH IT...!
SMACK

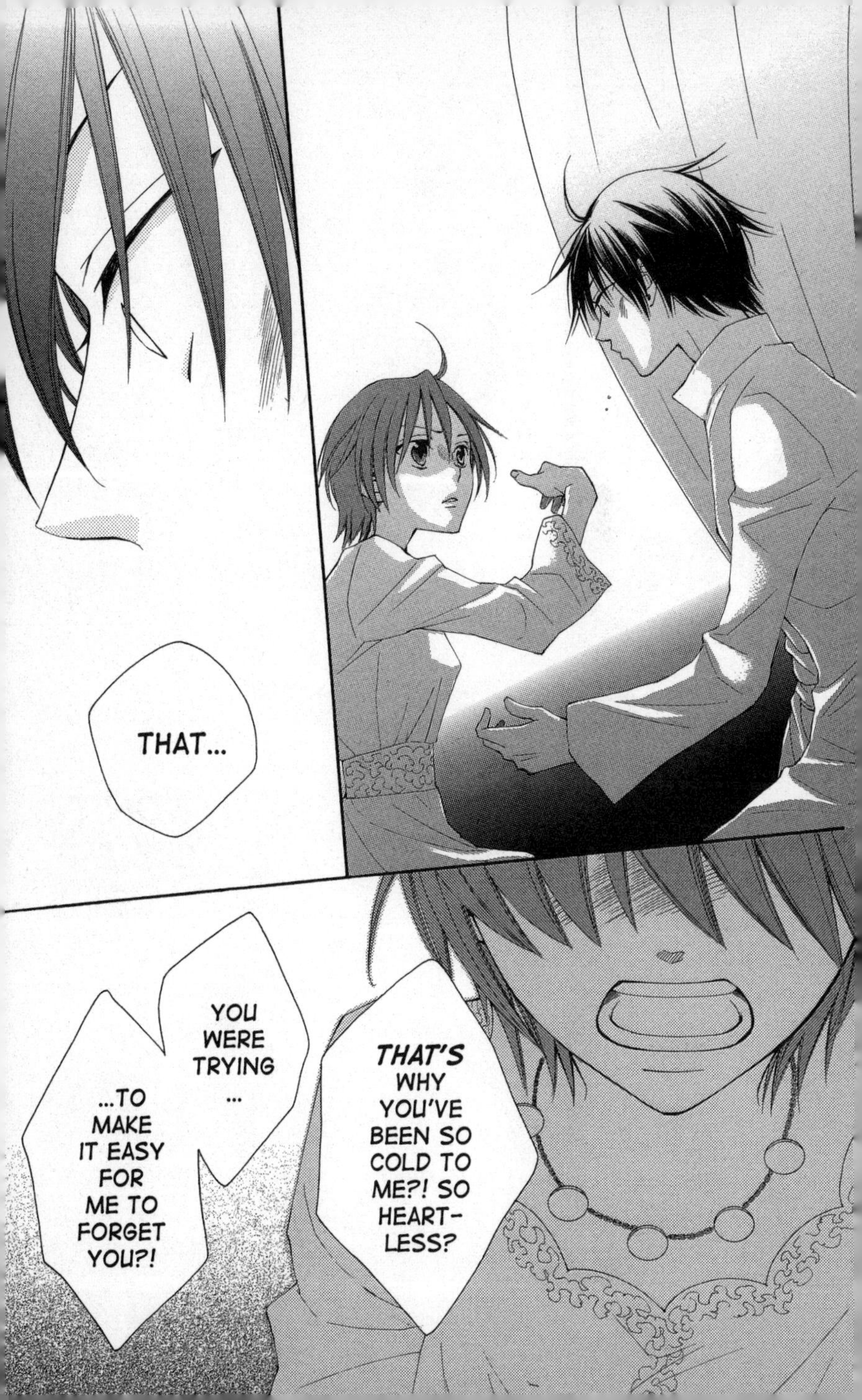
THAT...
THAT'S WHY YOU'VE BEEN SO COLD TO ME?! SO HEART-LESS?
YOU WERE TRYING ...
...TO MAKE IT EASY FOR ME TO FORGET YOU?!

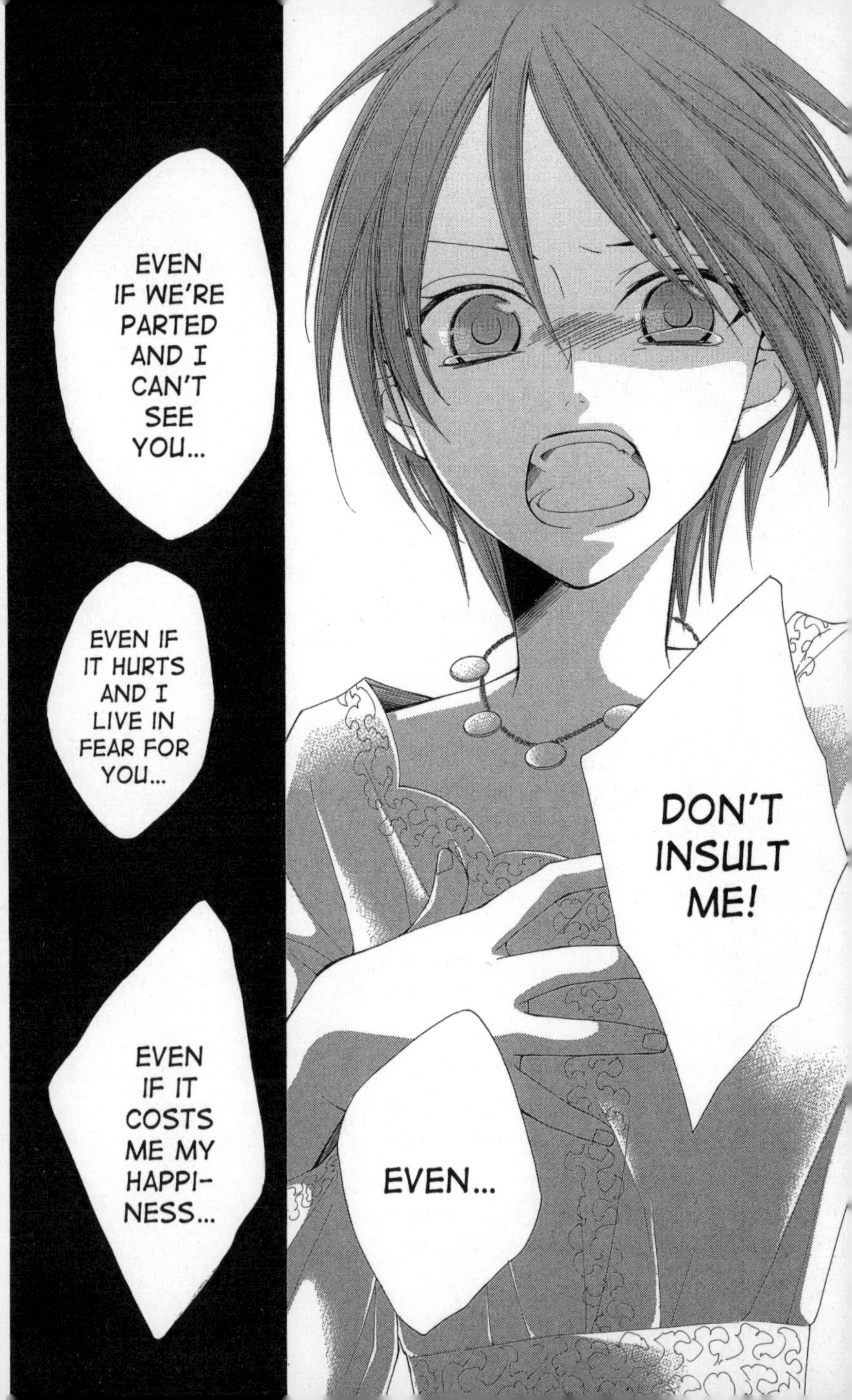
DON'T INSULT ME!
EVEN...
EVEN IF WE'RE PARTED AND I CAN'T SEE YOU...
EVEN IF IT HURTS AND I LIVE IN FEAR FOR YOU...
EVEN IF IT COSTS ME MY HAPPI-NESS...

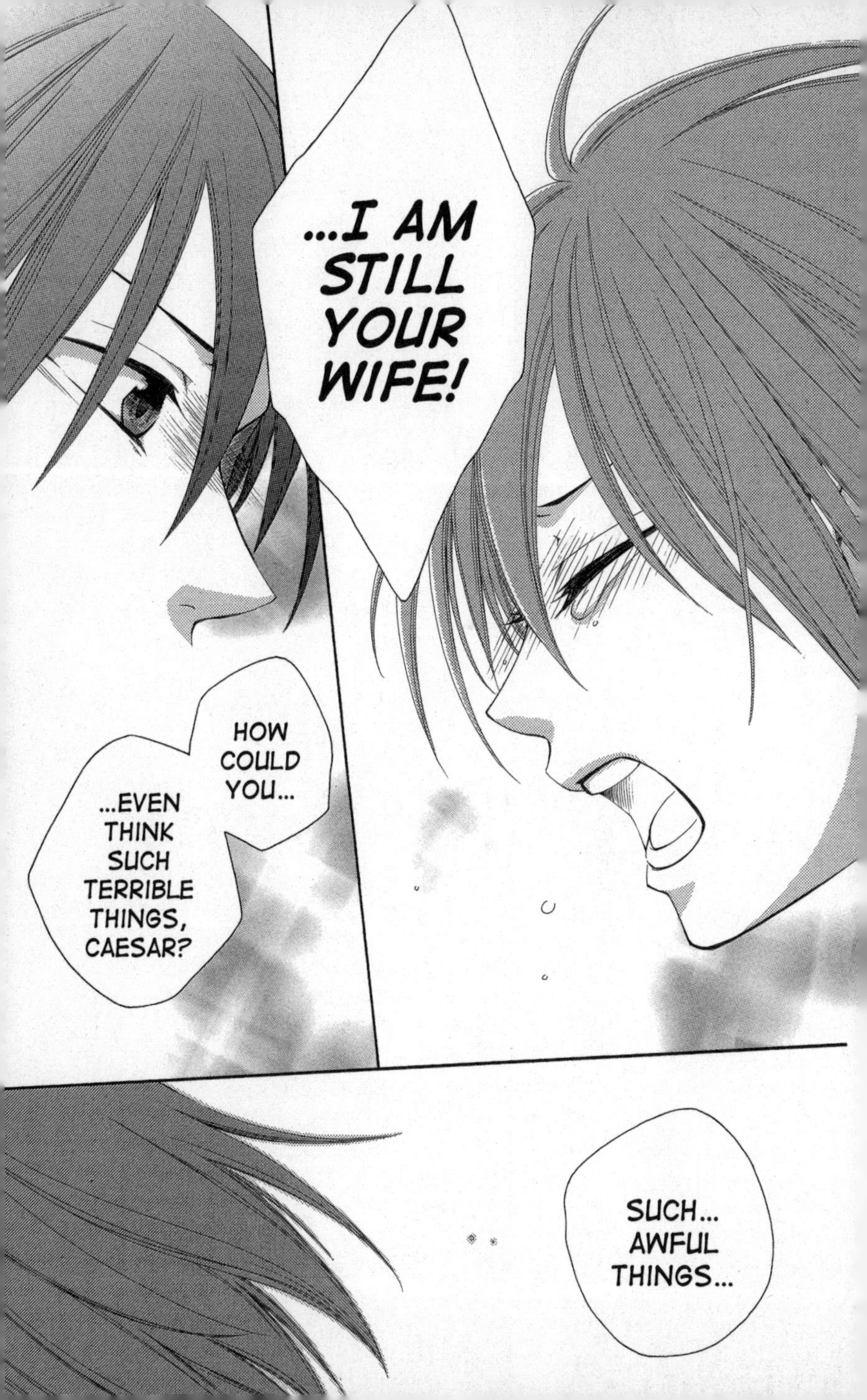
...I AM STILL YOUR WIFE!
HOW COULD YOU...
...EVEN THINK SUCH TERRIBLE THINGS, CAESAR?
SUCH... AWFUL THINGS...

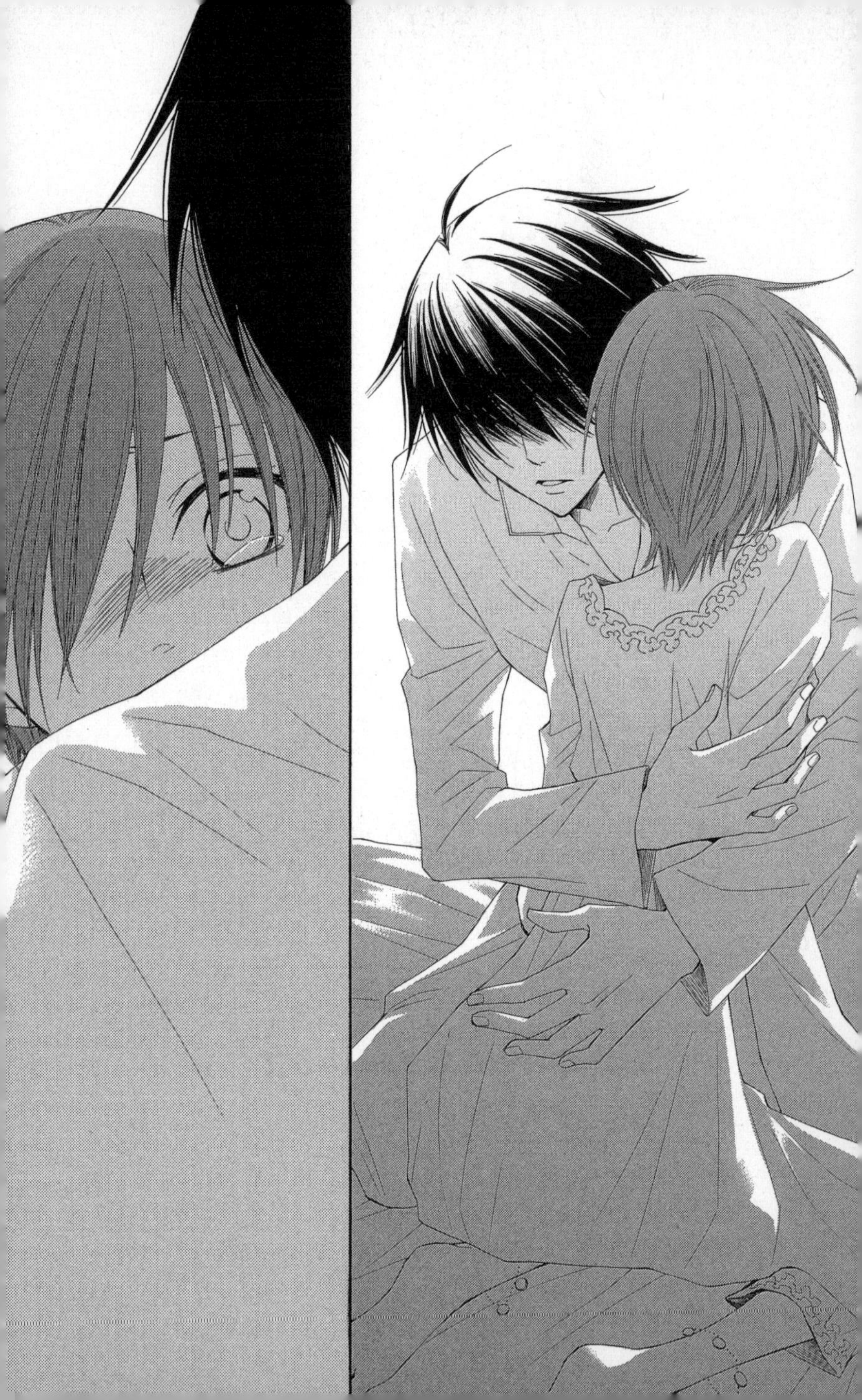

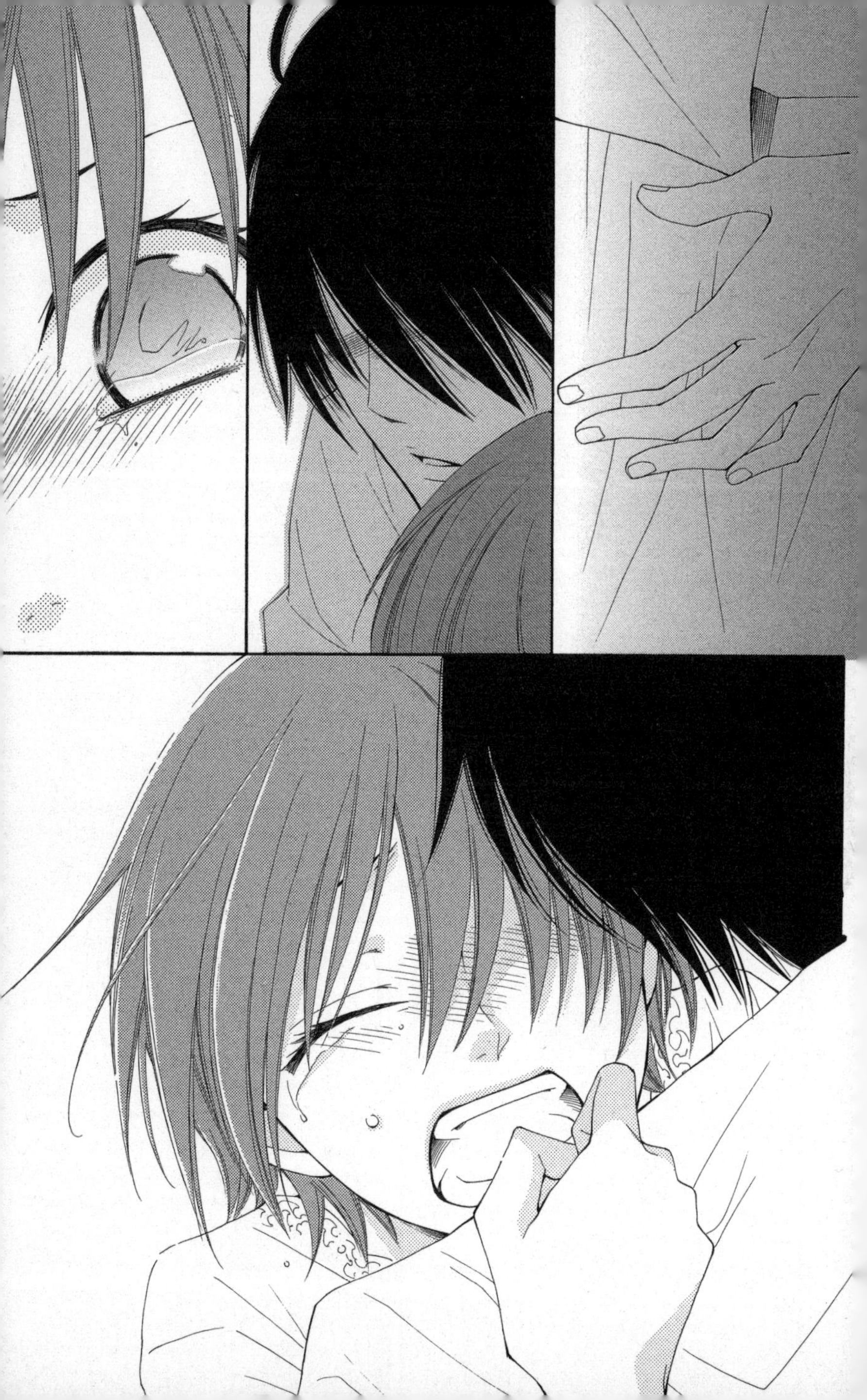

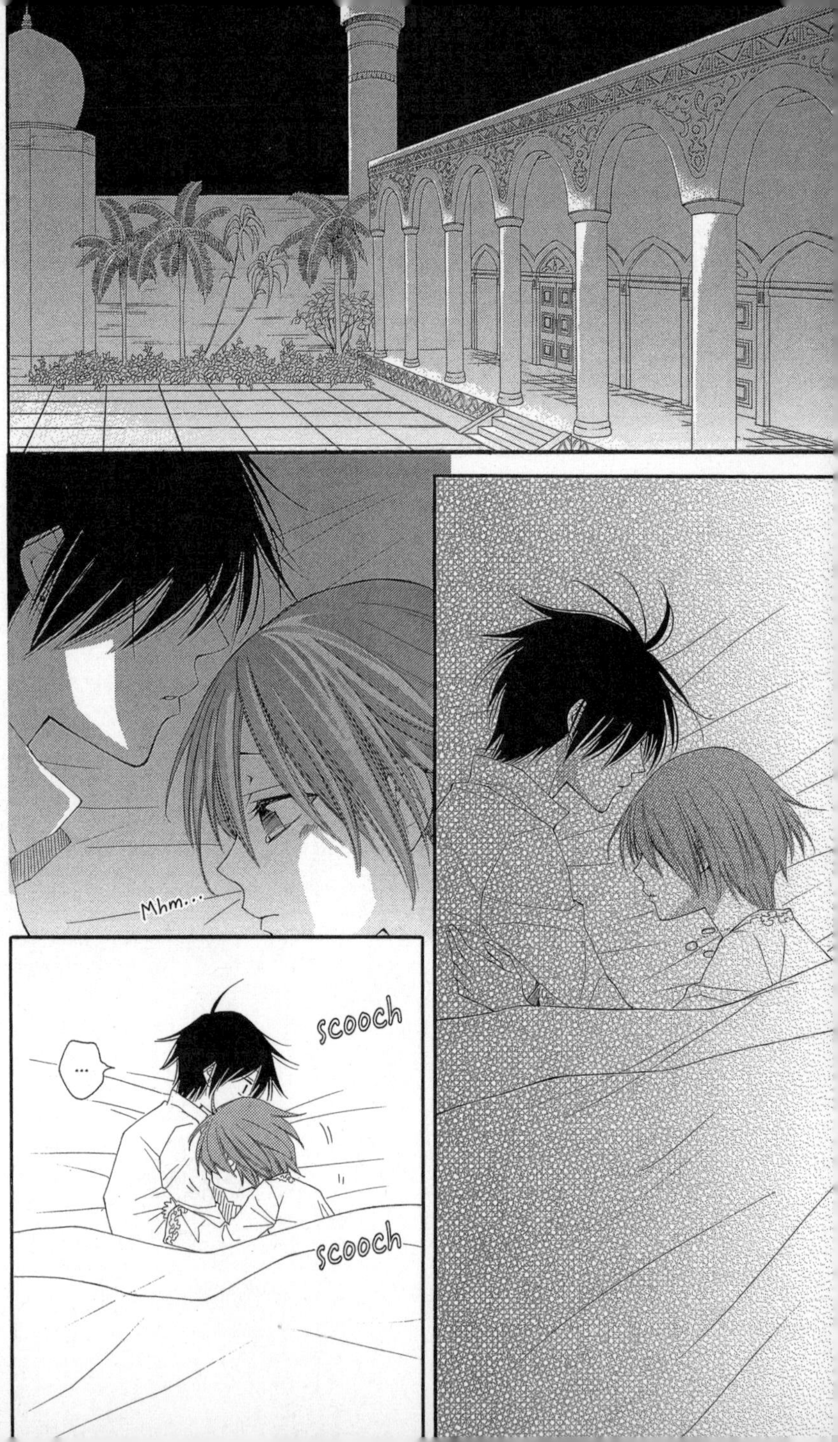
Mhm...
...
scooch
scooch

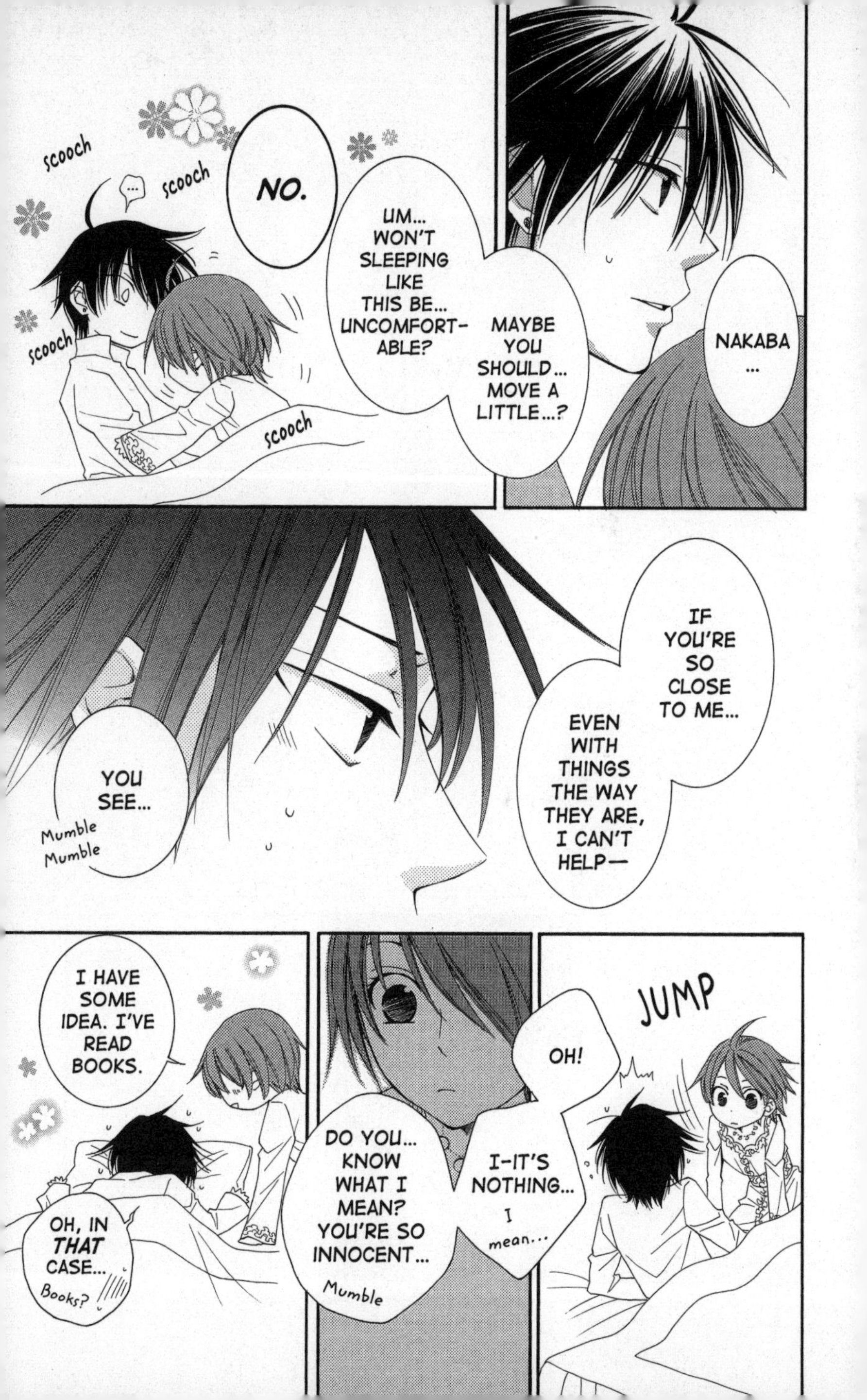
NAKABA...
MAYBE YOU SHOULD... MOVE A LITTLE...?
UM... WON'T SLEEPING LIKE THIS BE... UNCOMFORTABLE?
NO.
...
scooch
scooch
scooch
scooch
IF YOU'RE SO CLOSE TO ME...
EVEN WITH THINGS THE WAY THEY ARE, I CAN'T HELP—
YOU SEE...
Mumble Mumble
JUMP
OH!
I-IT'S NOTHING...
I mean...
DO YOU... KNOW WHAT I MEAN? YOU'RE SO INNOCENT...
Mumble
I HAVE SOME IDEA. I'VE READ BOOKS.
OH, IN *THAT* CASE...
Books?

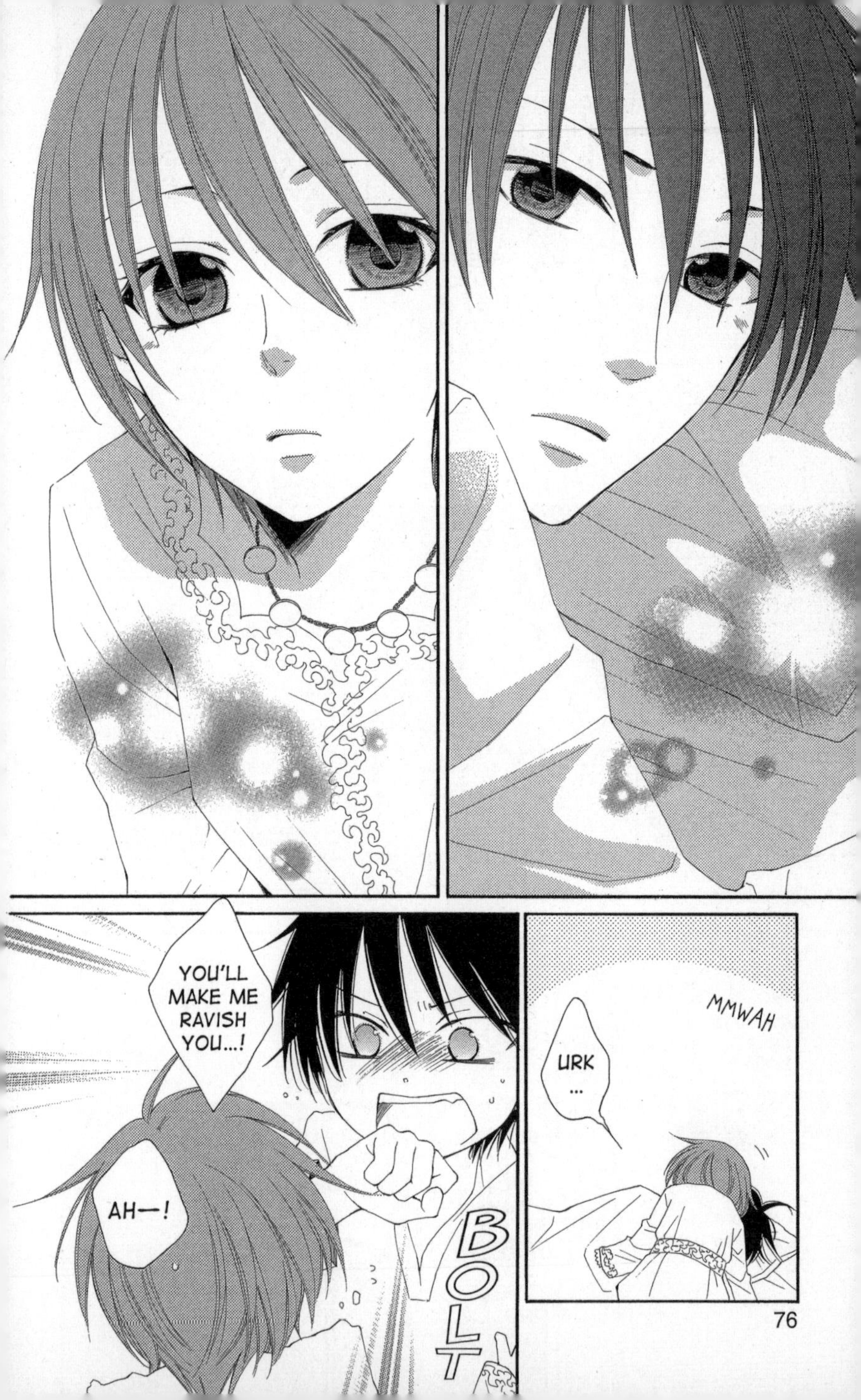
MMWAH
URK ...
YOU'LL MAKE ME RAVISH YOU...!
AH—!
BOLT

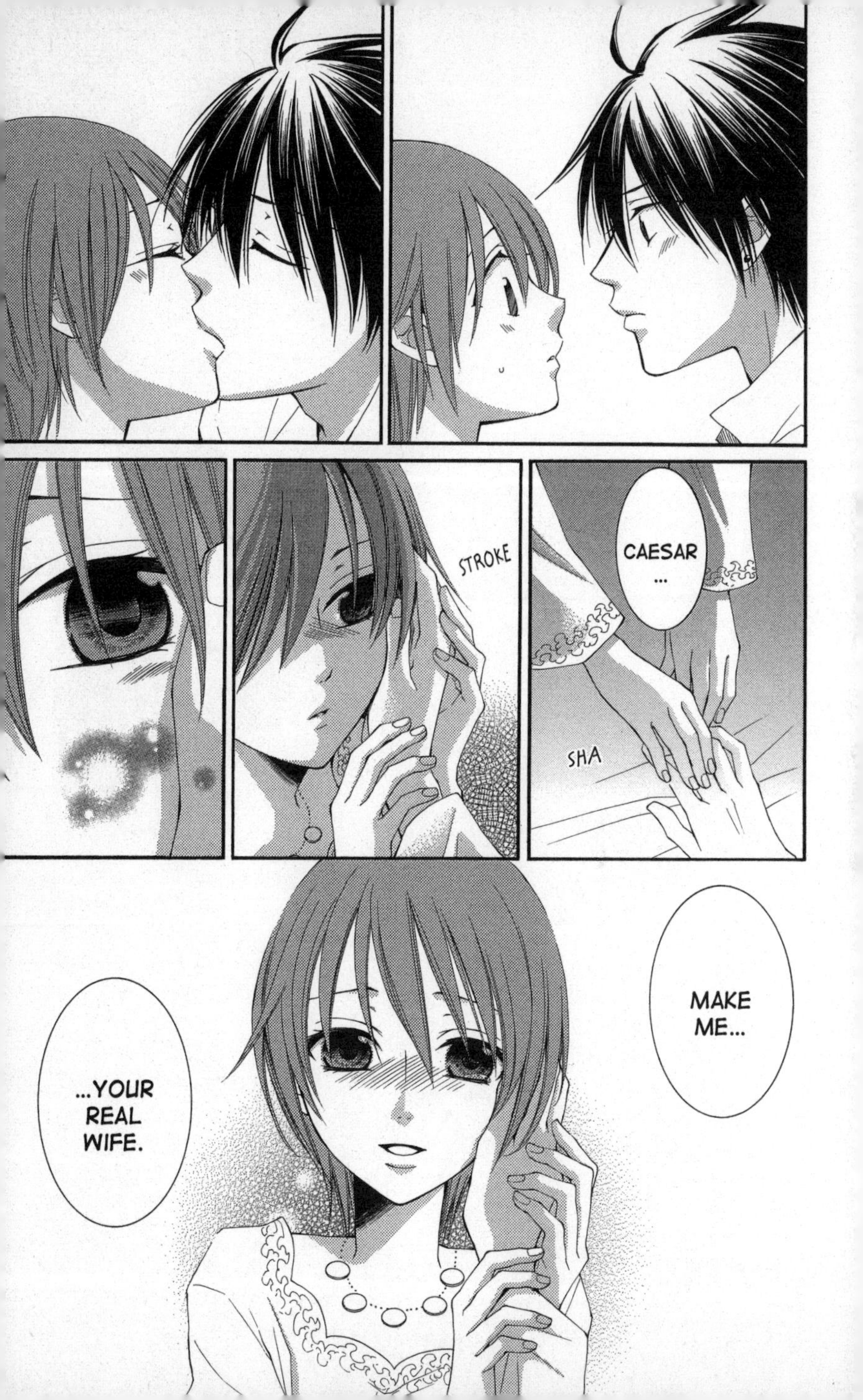
CAESAR ...
STROKE
SHA
MAKE ME...
...YOUR REAL WIFE.

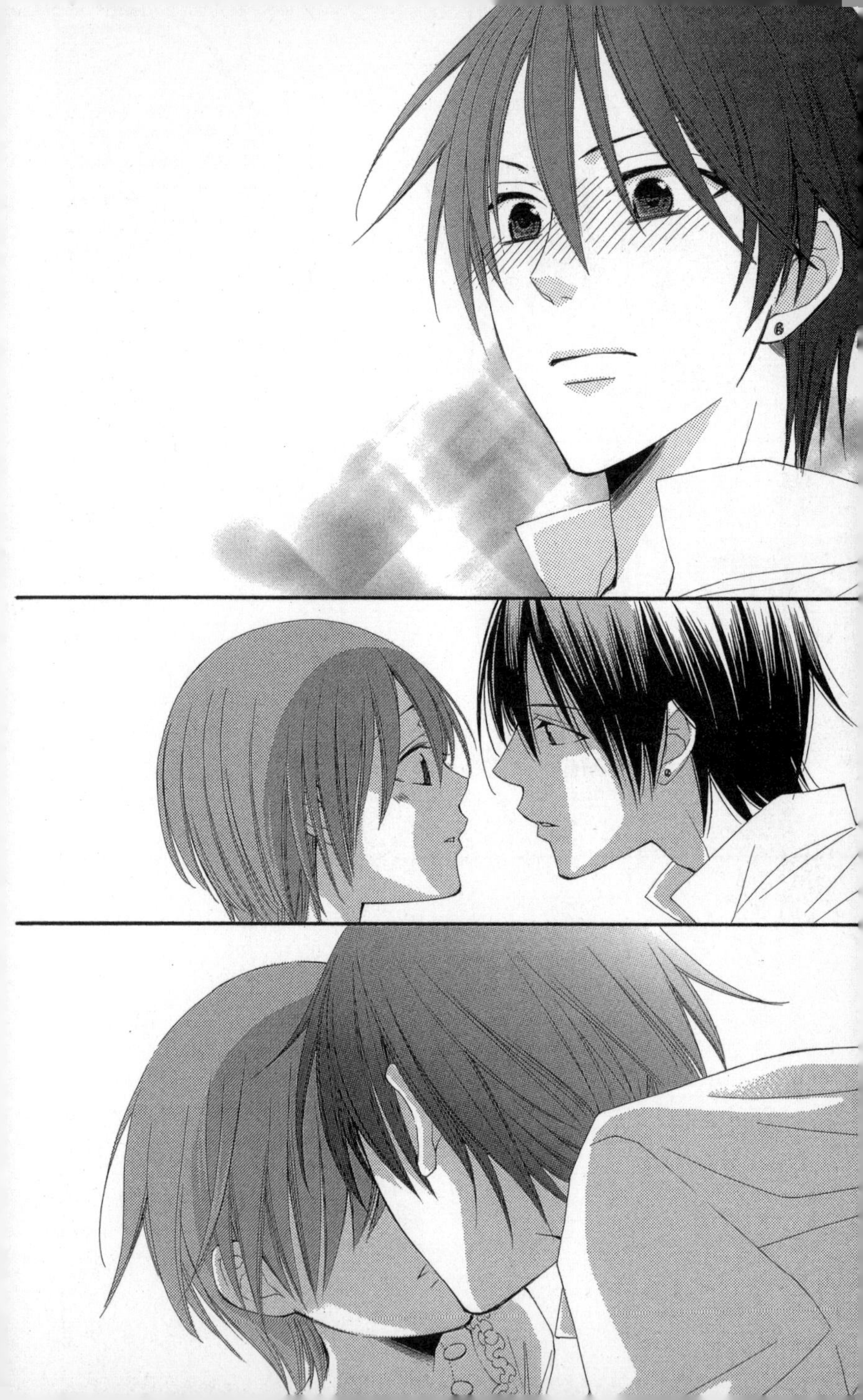

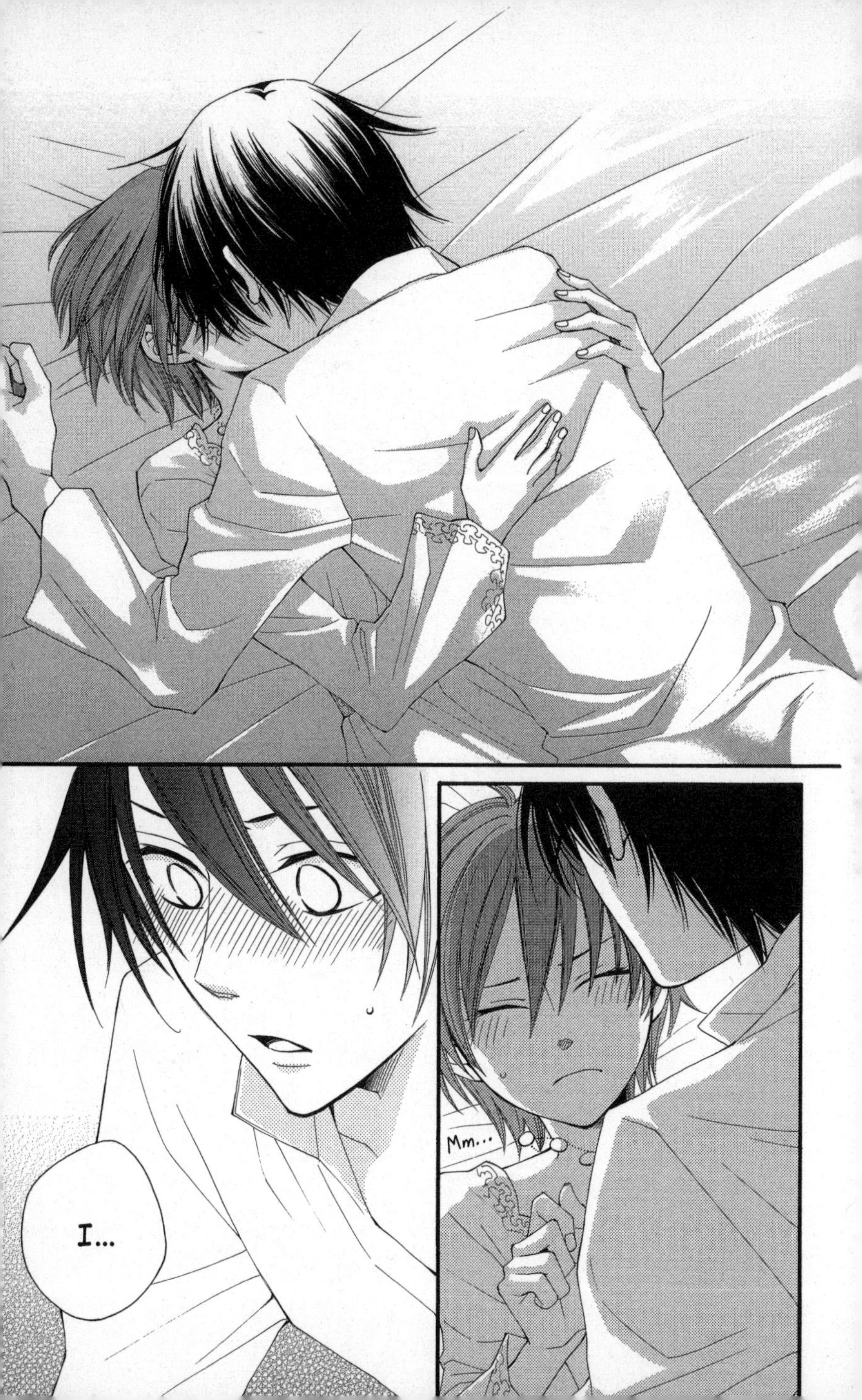
Mm...
I...

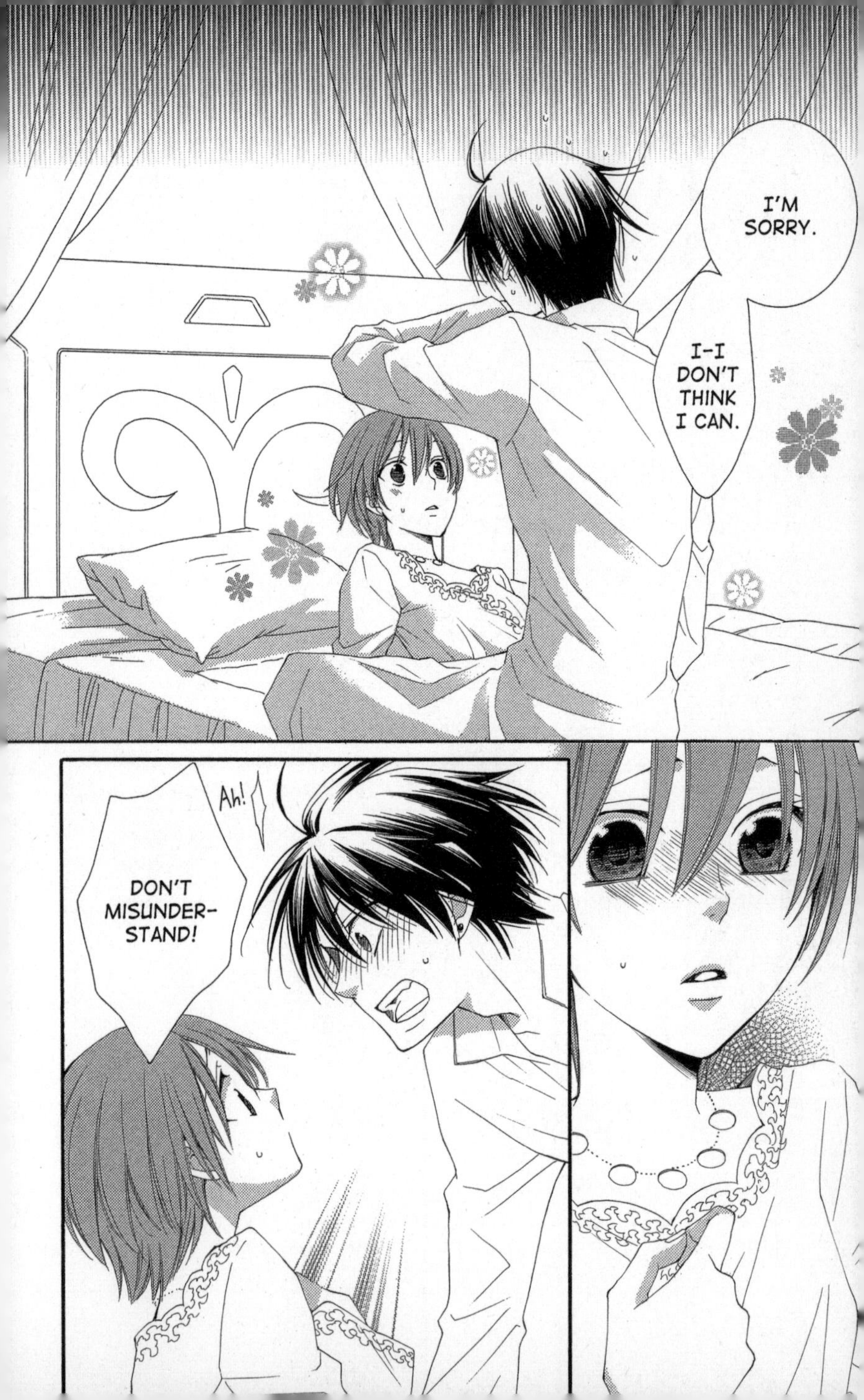
I'M SORRY.
I-I DON'T THINK I CAN.
Ah!
DON'T MISUNDERSTAND!

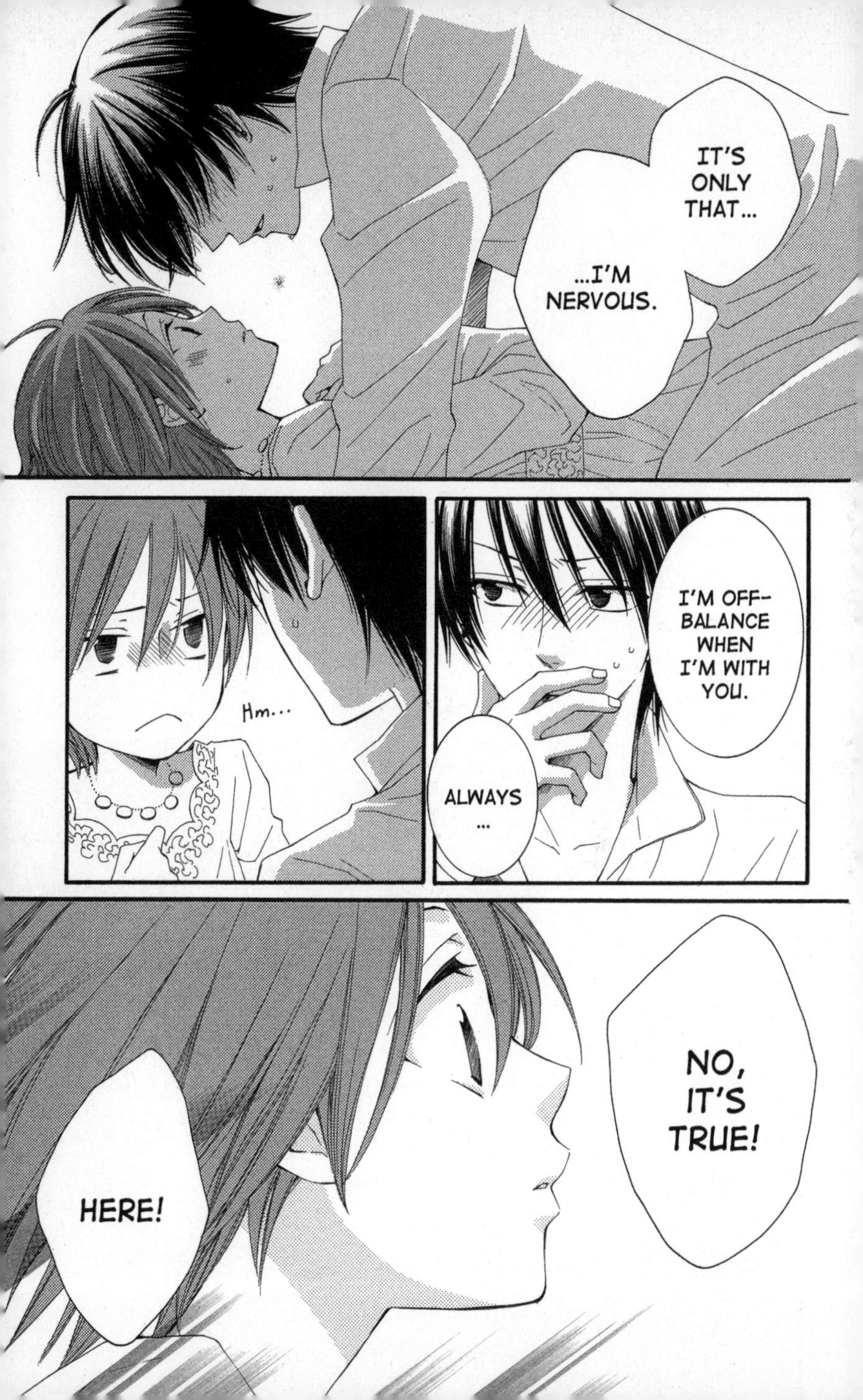
IT'S ONLY THAT...
...I'M NERVOUS.
I'M OFF-BALANCE WHEN I'M WITH YOU.
ALWAYS ...
Hm...
NO, IT'S TRUE!
HERE!

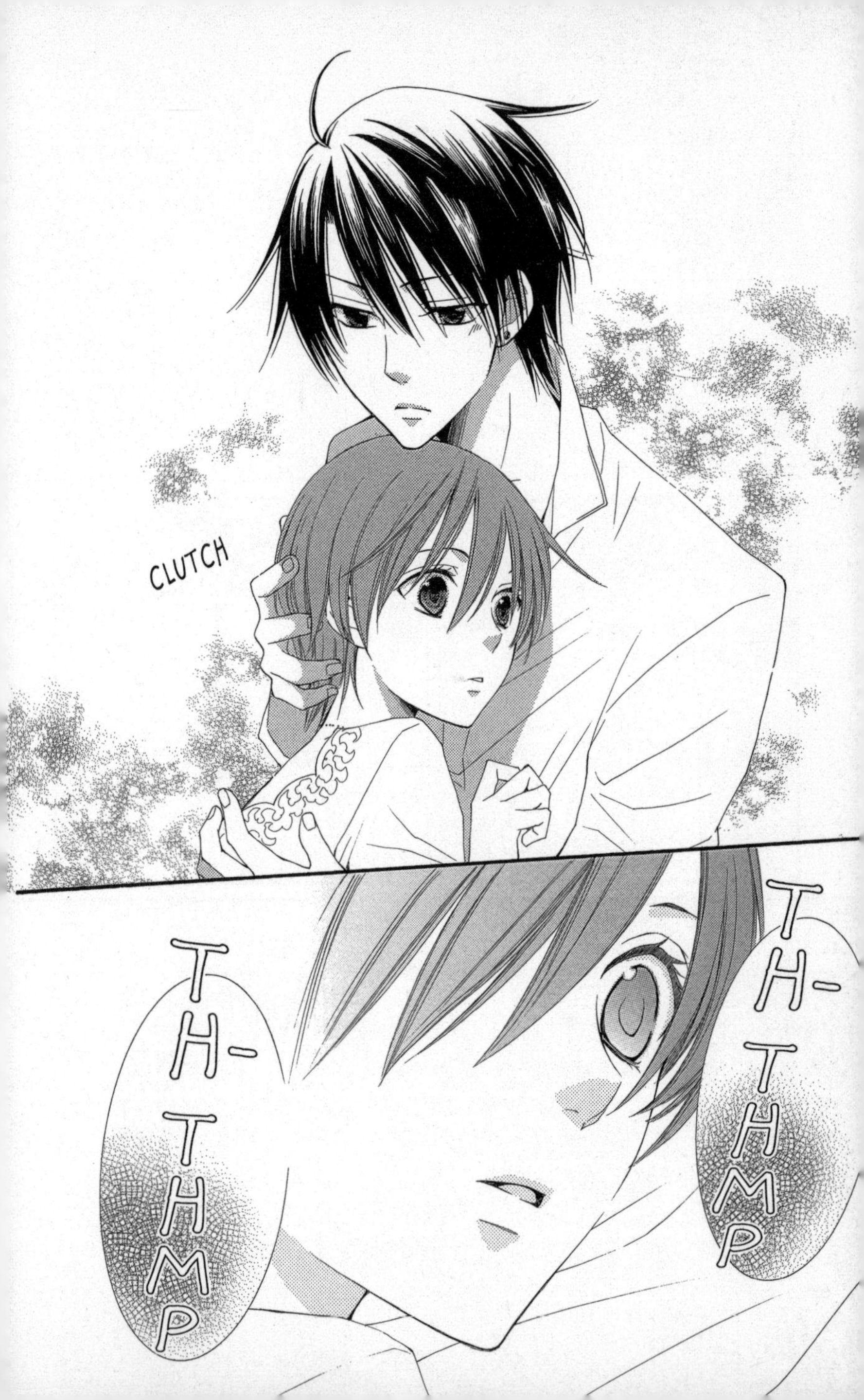
CLUTCH
TH-THMP
TH-THMP

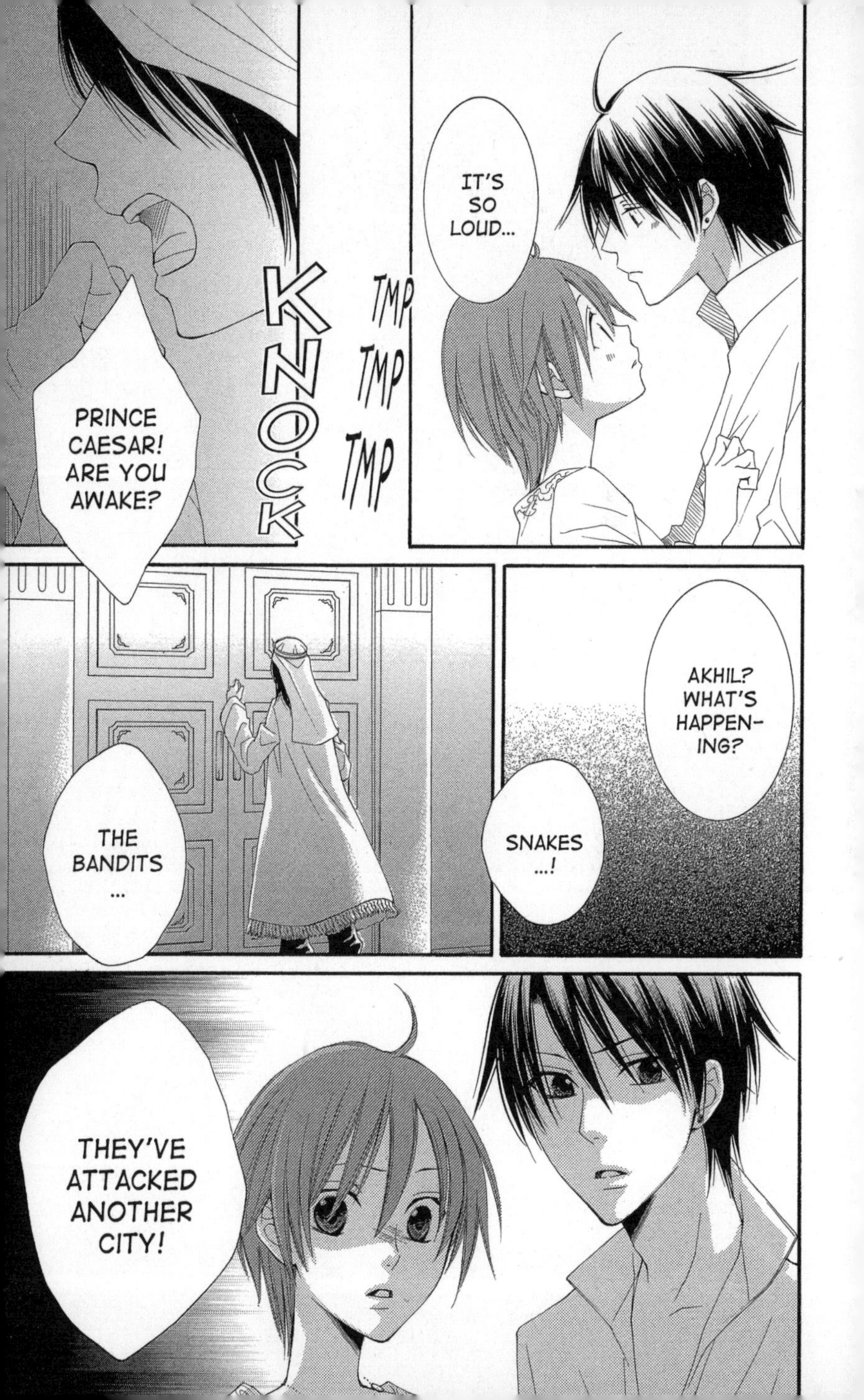
IT'S SO LOUD...
KNOCK
TMP TMP TMP
PRINCE CAESAR! ARE YOU AWAKE?
AKHIL? WHAT'S HAPPEN-ING?
SNAKES ...!
THE BANDITS ...
THEY'VE ATTACKED ANOTHER CITY!

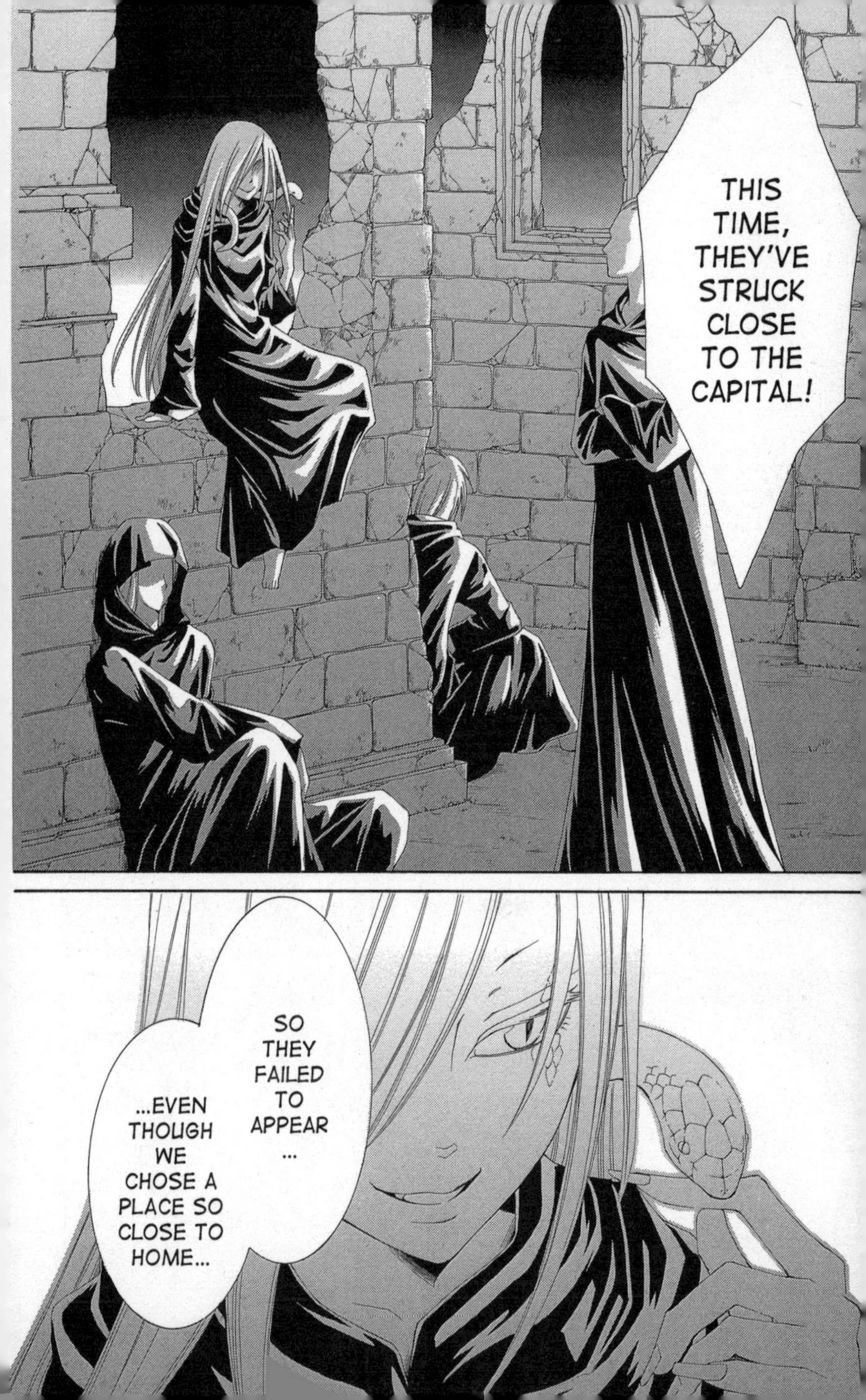
THIS TIME, THEY'VE STRUCK CLOSE TO THE CAPITAL!
SO THEY FAILED TO APPEAR ...
...EVEN THOUGH WE CHOSE A PLACE SO CLOSE TO HOME...

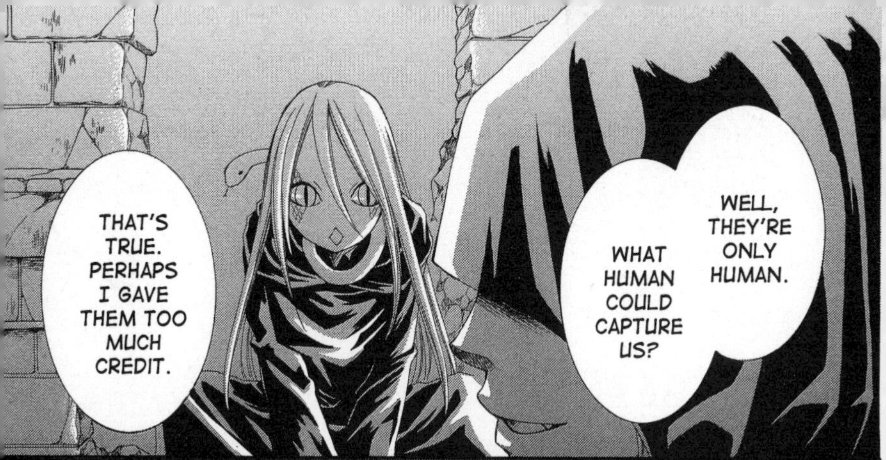
WELL, THEY'RE ONLY HUMAN.
WHAT HUMAN COULD CAPTURE US?
THAT'S TRUE. PERHAPS I GAVE THEM TOO MUCH CREDIT.
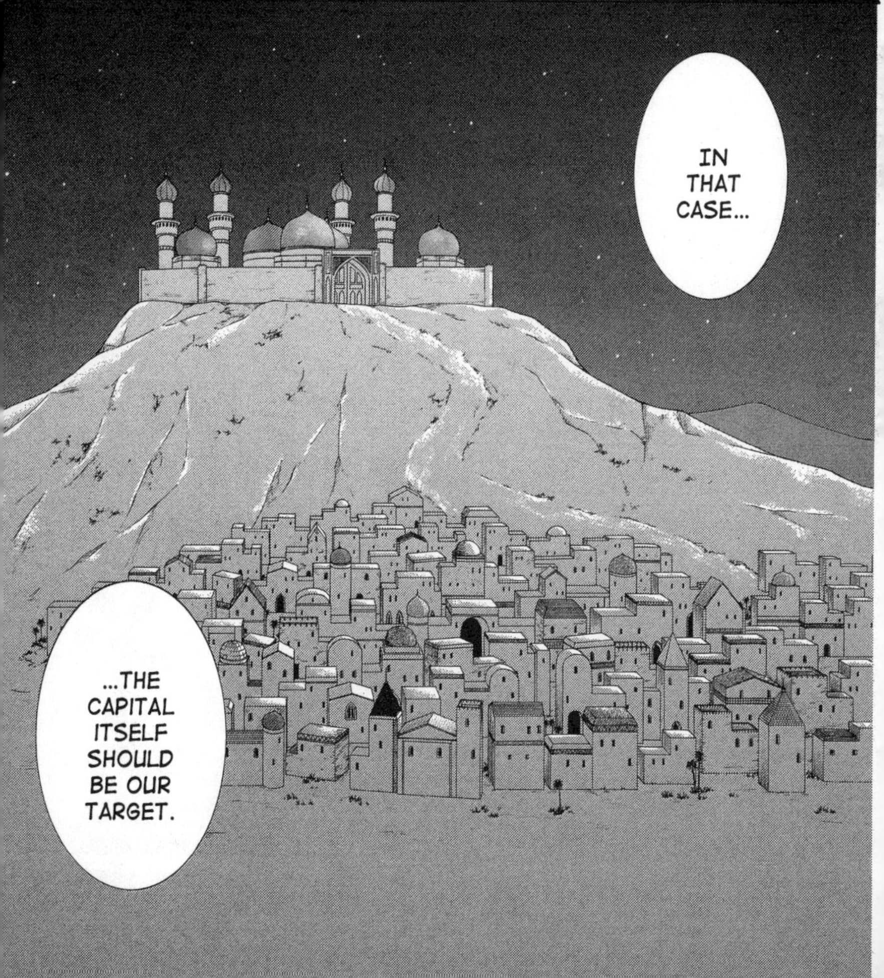
IN THAT CASE...
...THE CAPITAL ITSELF SHOULD BE OUR TARGET.

Page of Fun

Rito is around five years old now, but I felt like drawing him as an adult. He's probably about 20 here? (*Laugh*) There's no way we'll see him like this in the actual story, so it's pure conjecture.

Chapter 30

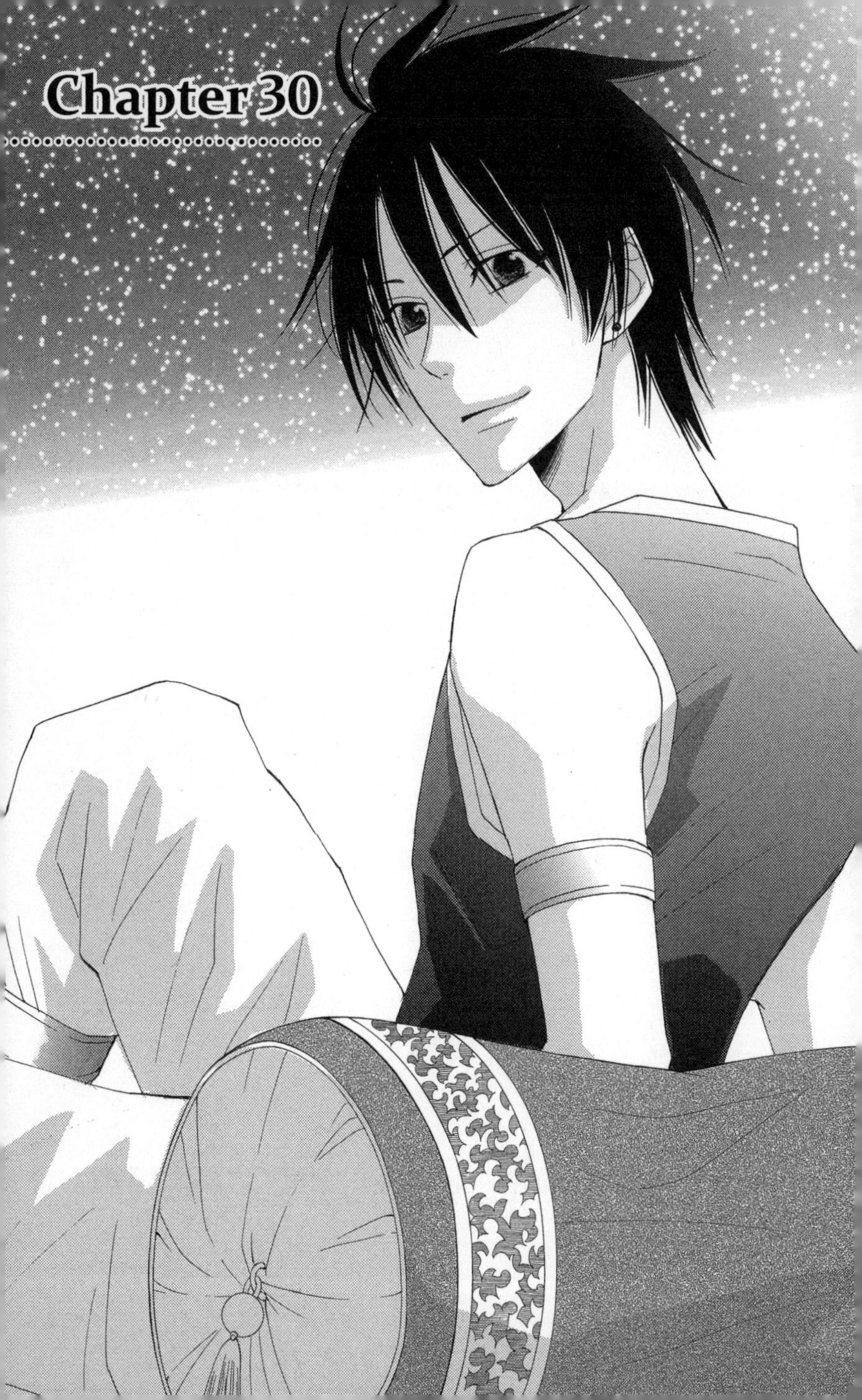

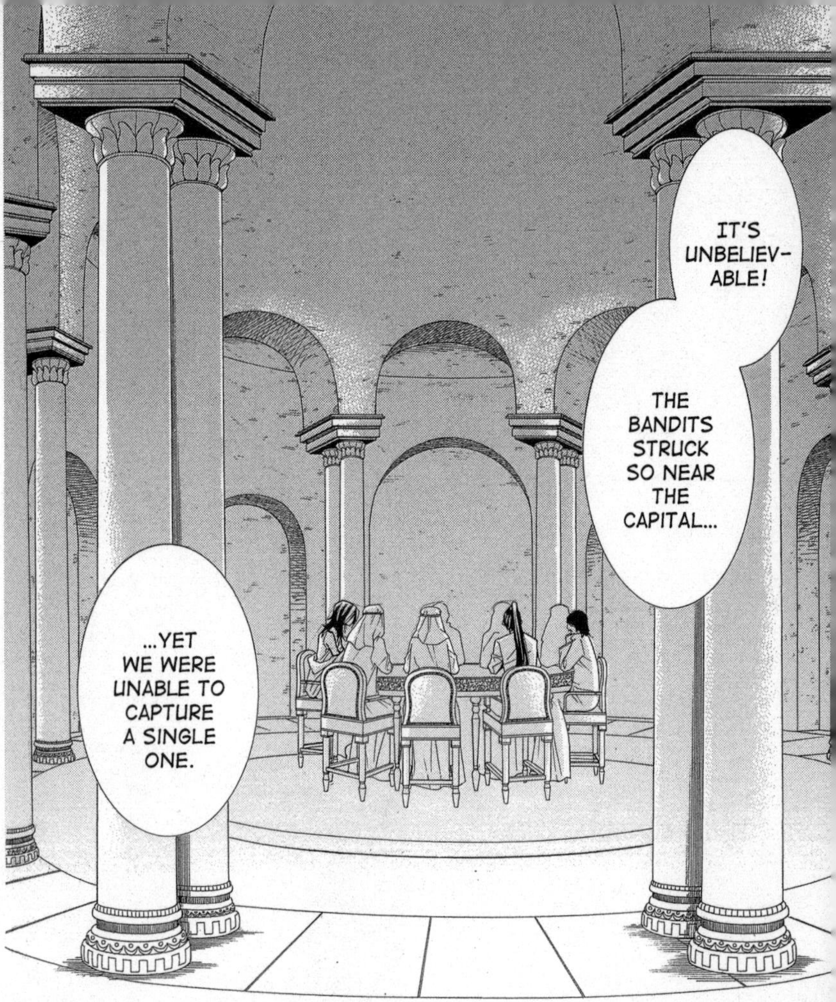
IT'S UNBELIEVABLE!
THE BANDITS STRUCK SO NEAR THE CAPITAL...
...YET WE WERE UNABLE TO CAPTURE A SINGLE ONE.

Dawn of the Arcana

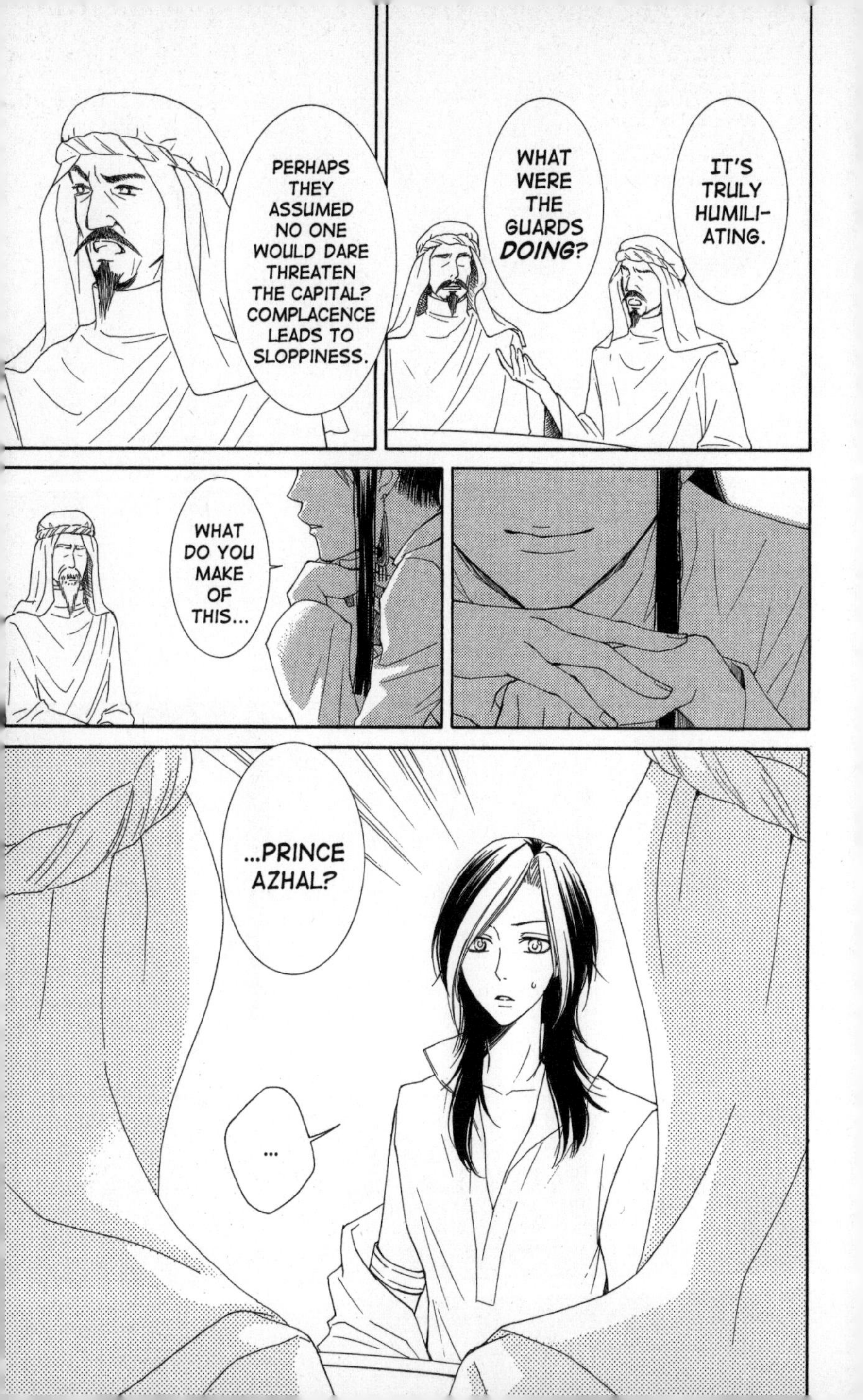
IT'S TRULY HUMILI-ATING.
WHAT WERE THE GUARDS *DOING*?
PERHAPS THEY ASSUMED NO ONE WOULD DARE THREATEN THE CAPITAL? COMPLACENCE LEADS TO SLOPPINESS.
WHAT DO YOU MAKE OF THIS...
...PRINCE AZHAL?
...

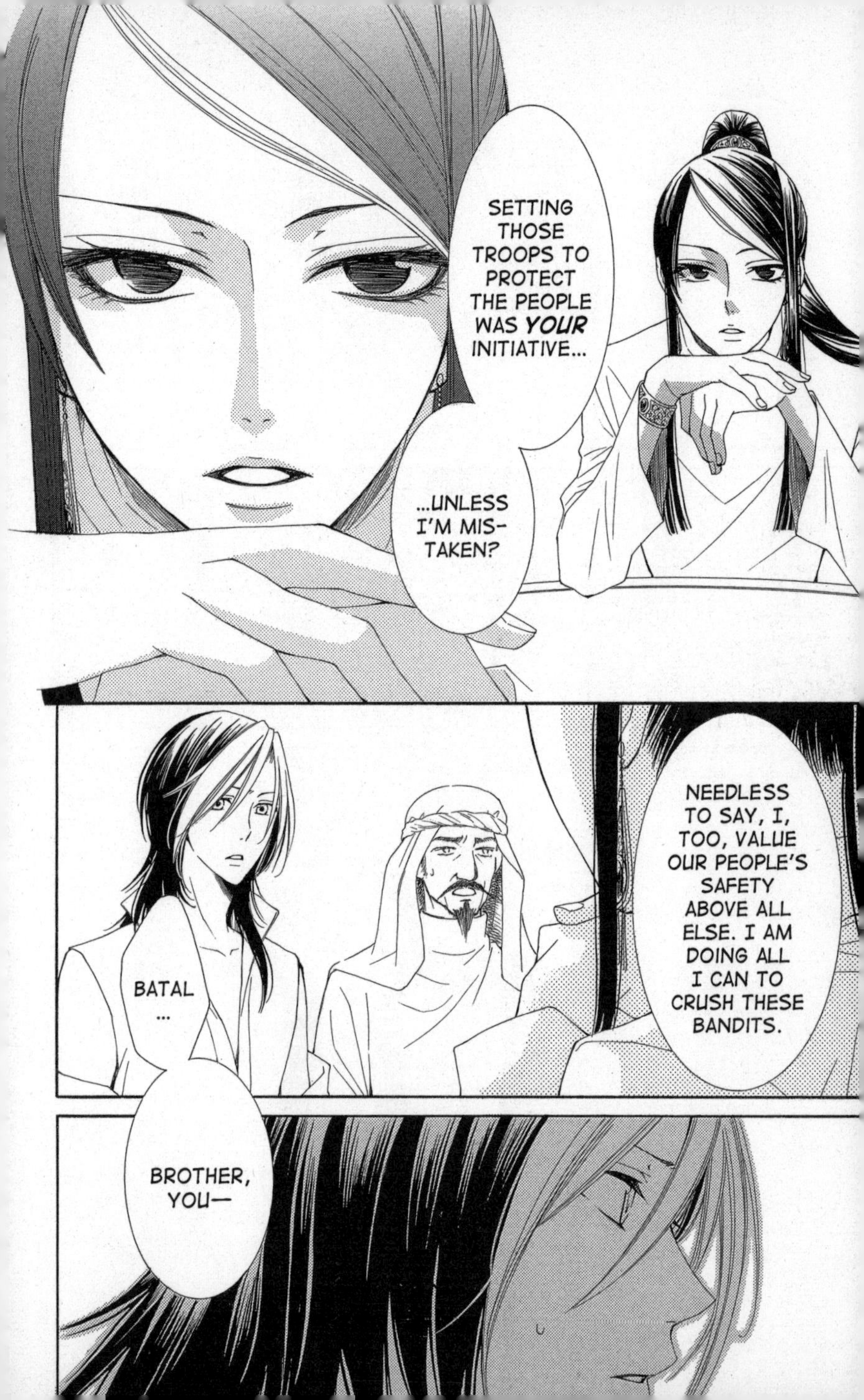
SETTING THOSE TROOPS TO PROTECT THE PEOPLE WAS *YOUR* INITIATIVE...
...UNLESS I'M MIS-TAKEN?
NEEDLESS TO SAY, I, TOO, VALUE OUR PEOPLE'S SAFETY ABOVE ALL ELSE. I AM DOING ALL I CAN TO CRUSH THESE BANDITS.
BATAL ...
BROTHER, YOU—

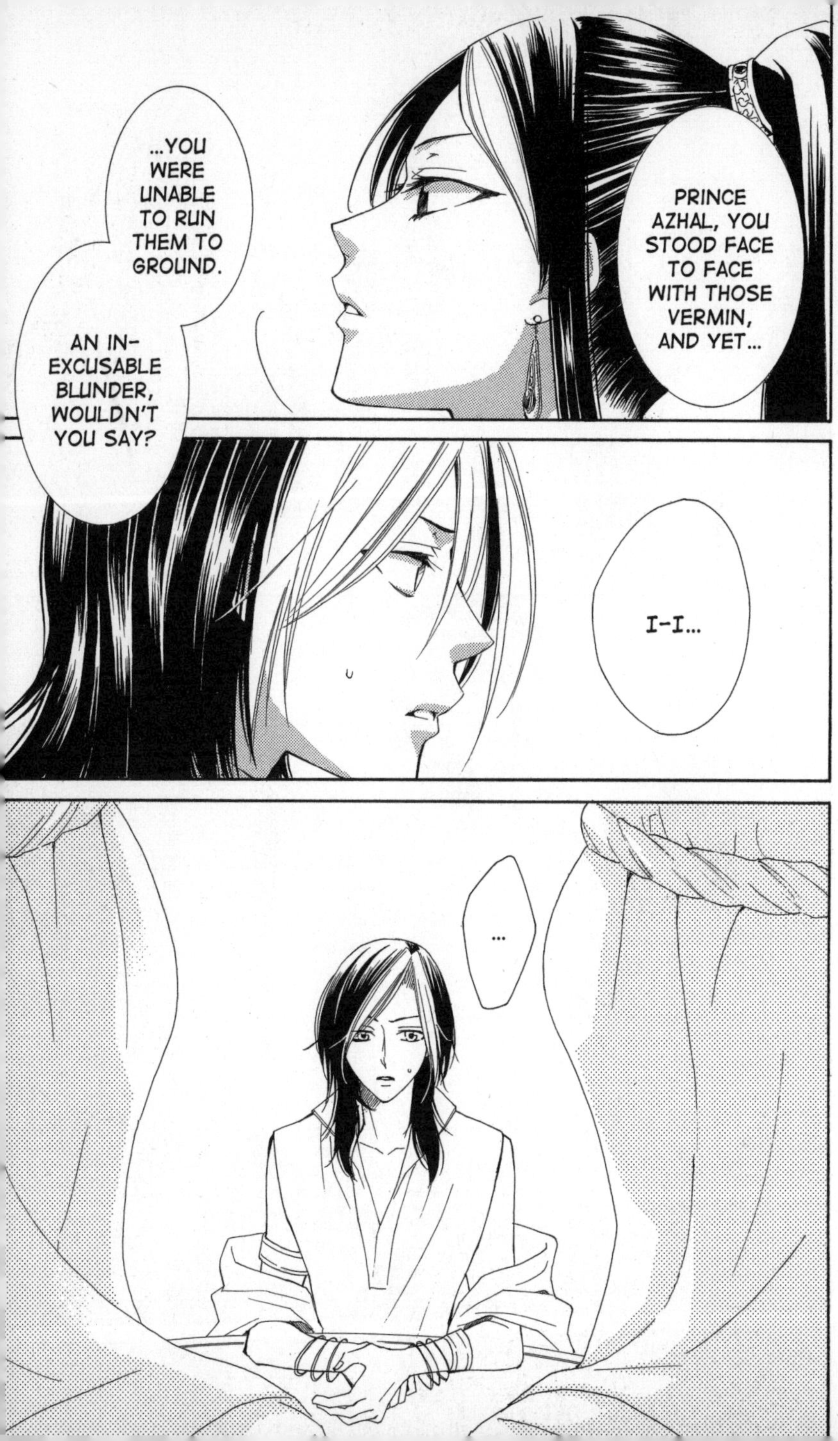
PRINCE AZHAL, YOU STOOD FACE TO FACE WITH THOSE VERMIN, AND YET...
...YOU WERE UNABLE TO RUN THEM TO GROUND.
AN IN-EXCUSABLE BLUNDER, WOULDN'T YOU SAY?
I-I...
...

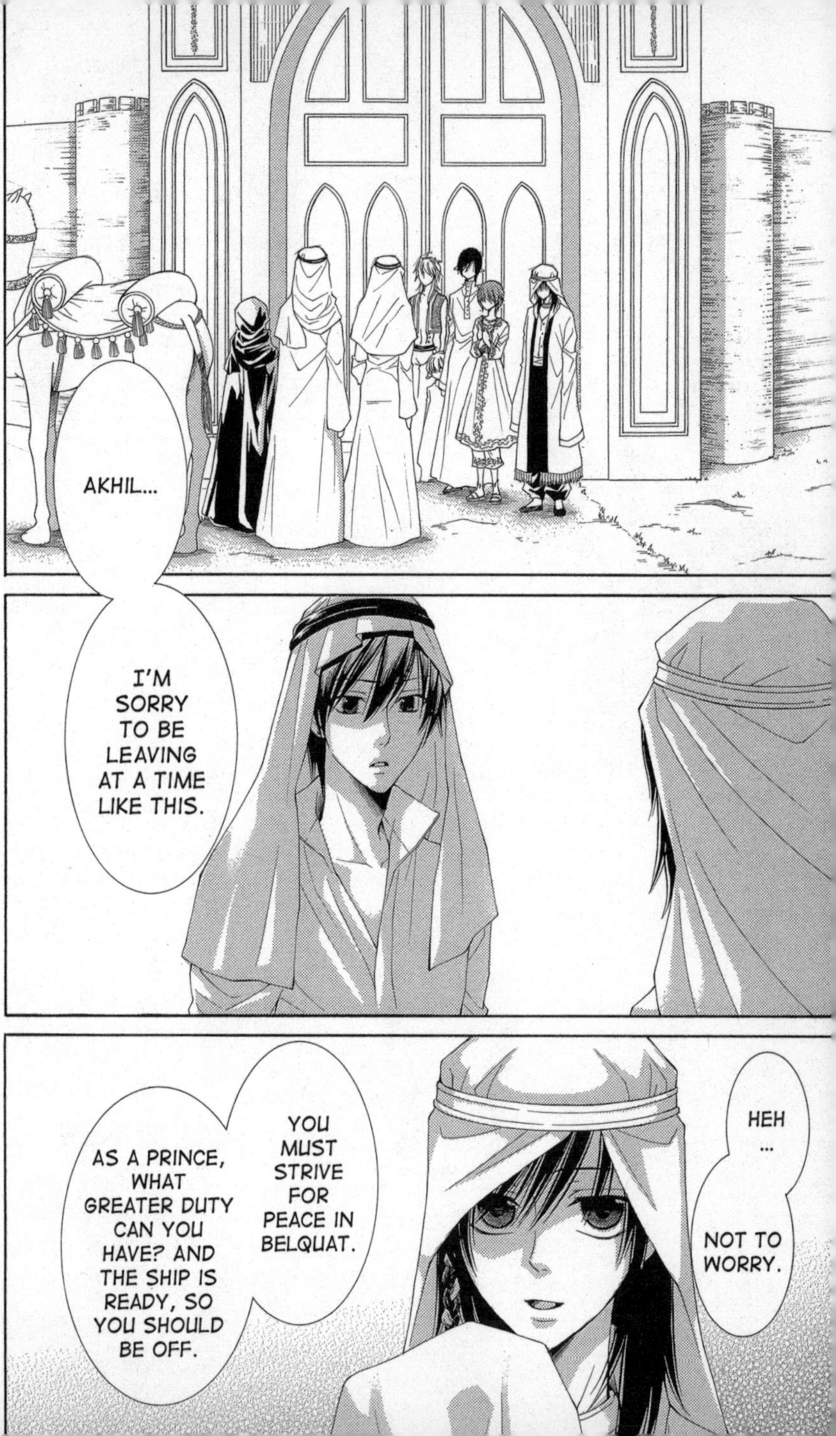
AKHIL...
I'M SORRY TO BE LEAVING AT A TIME LIKE THIS.
HEH ...
NOT TO WORRY.
YOU MUST STRIVE FOR PEACE IN BELQUAT.
AS A PRINCE, WHAT GREATER DUTY CAN YOU HAVE? AND THE SHIP IS READY, SO YOU SHOULD BE OFF.

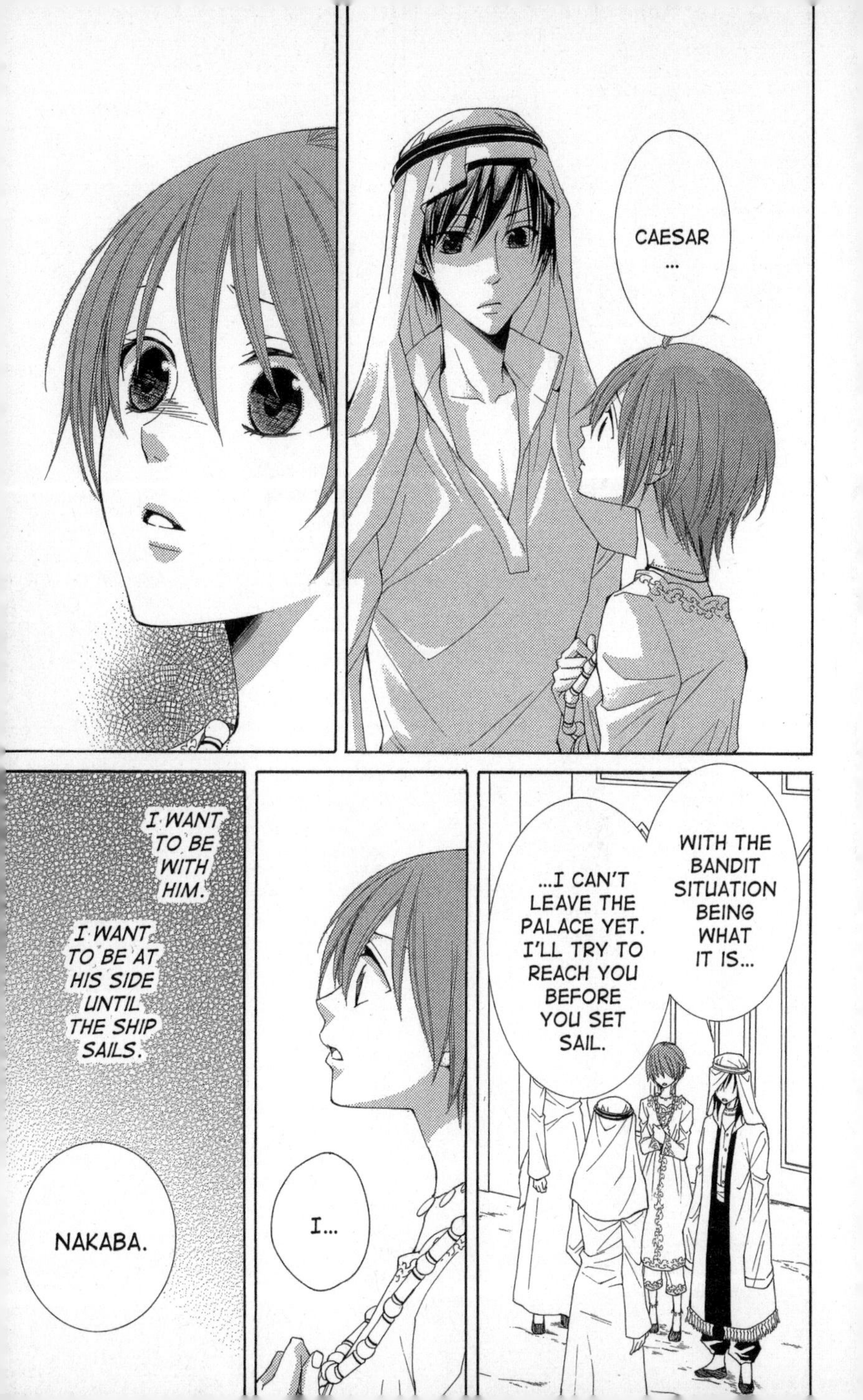
CAESAR ...
WITH THE BANDIT SITUATION BEING WHAT IT IS...
...I CAN'T LEAVE THE PALACE YET. I'LL TRY TO REACH YOU BEFORE YOU SET SAIL.
I...
I WANT TO BE WITH HIM.
I WANT TO BE AT HIS SIDE UNTIL THE SHIP SAILS.
NAKABA.

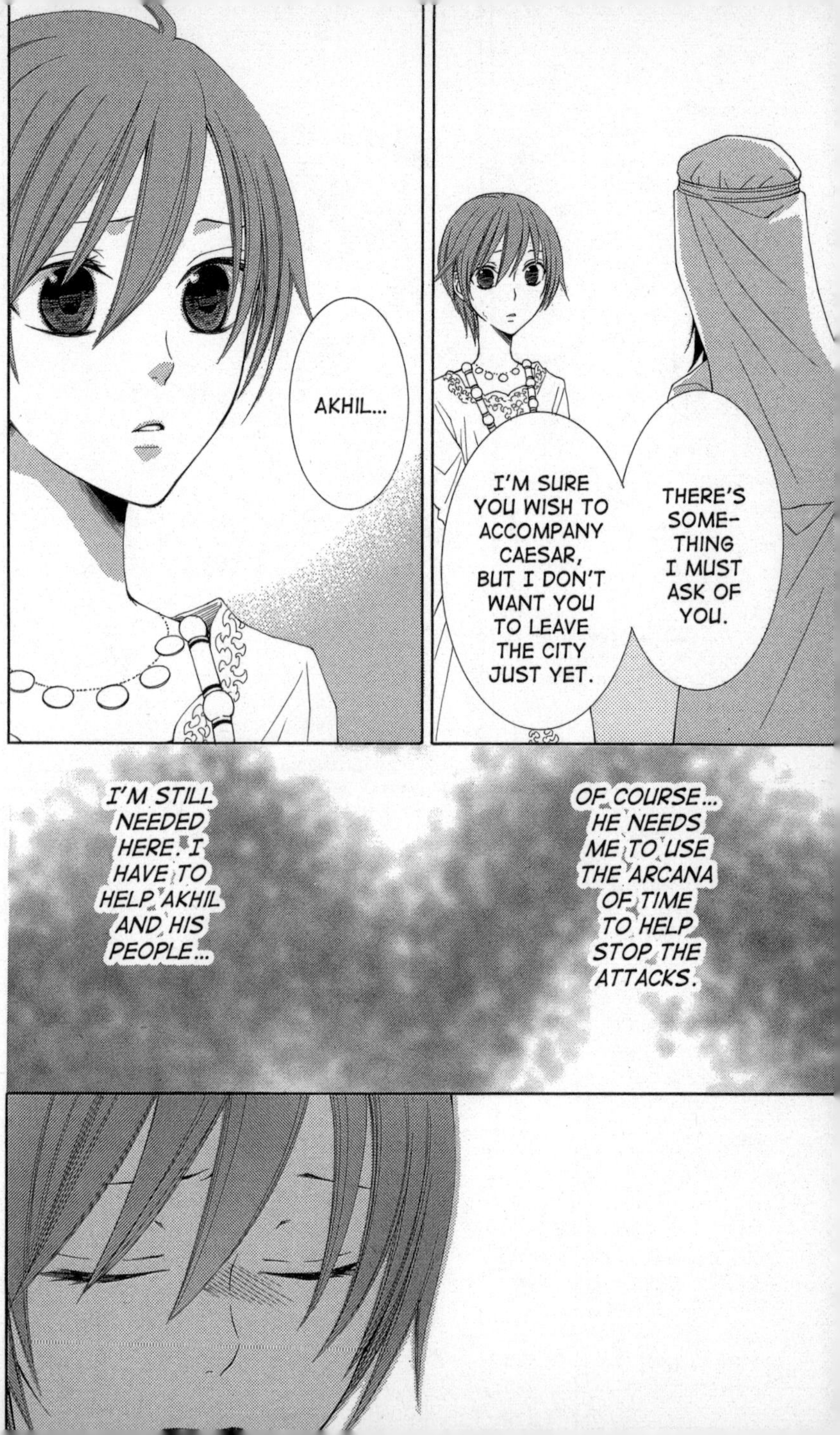
THERE'S SOMETHING I MUST ASK OF YOU.
I'M SURE YOU WISH TO ACCOMPANY CAESAR, BUT I DON'T WANT YOU TO LEAVE THE CITY JUST YET.
AKHIL...
OF COURSE... HE NEEDS ME TO USE THE ARCANA OF TIME TO HELP STOP THE ATTACKS.
I'M STILL NEEDED HERE. I HAVE TO HELP AKHIL AND HIS PEOPLE...

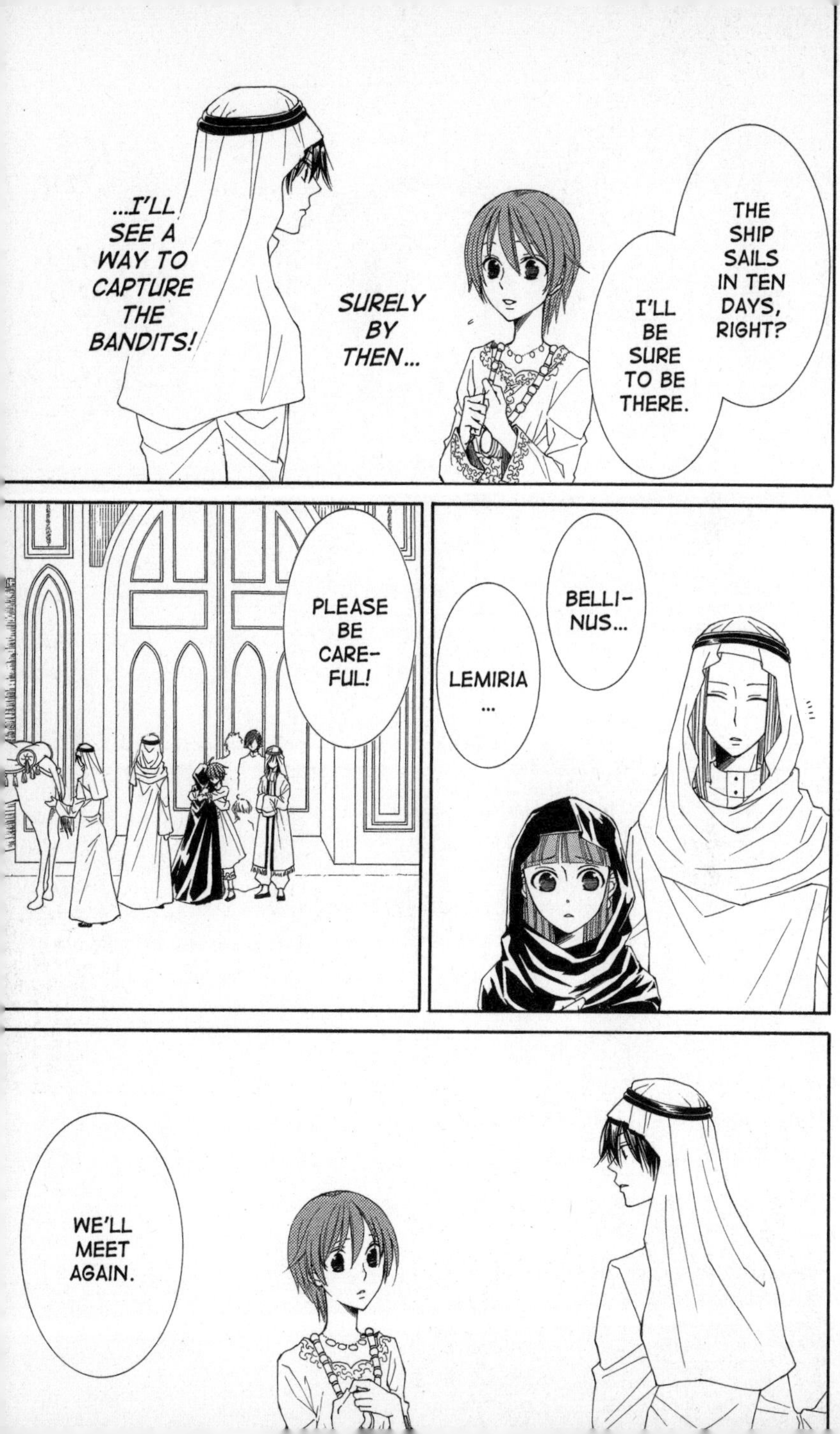
THE SHIP SAILS IN TEN DAYS, RIGHT?
I'LL BE SURE TO BE THERE.
SURELY BY THEN...
...I'LL SEE A WAY TO CAPTURE THE BANDITS!
BELLI-NUS...
LEMIRIA...
PLEASE BE CARE-FUL!
WE'LL MEET AGAIN.

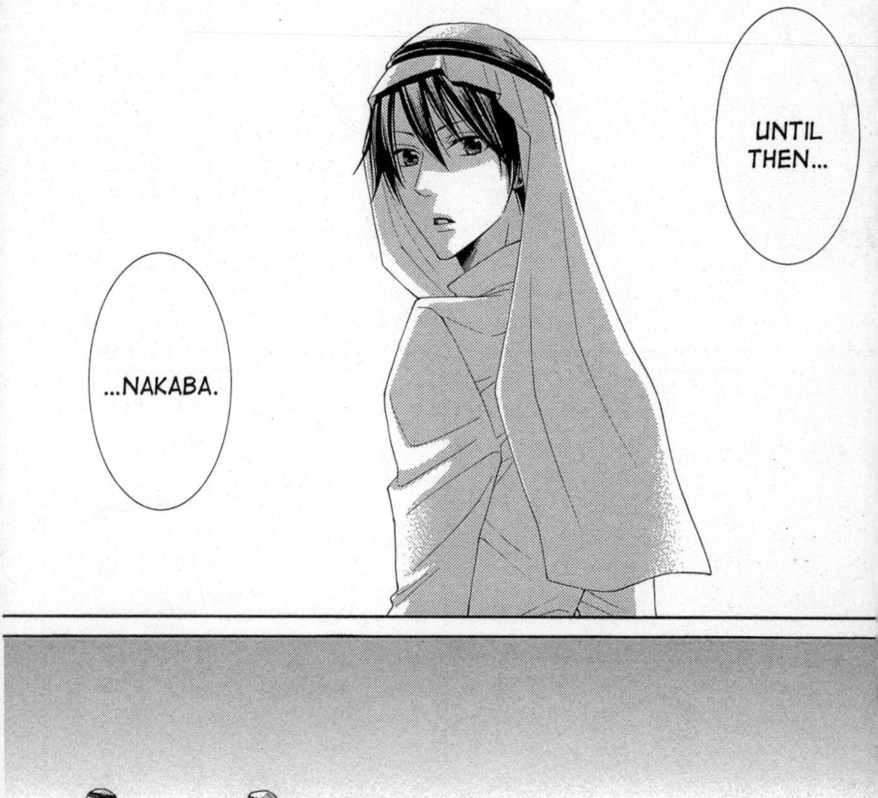
UNTIL THEN...
...NAKABA.

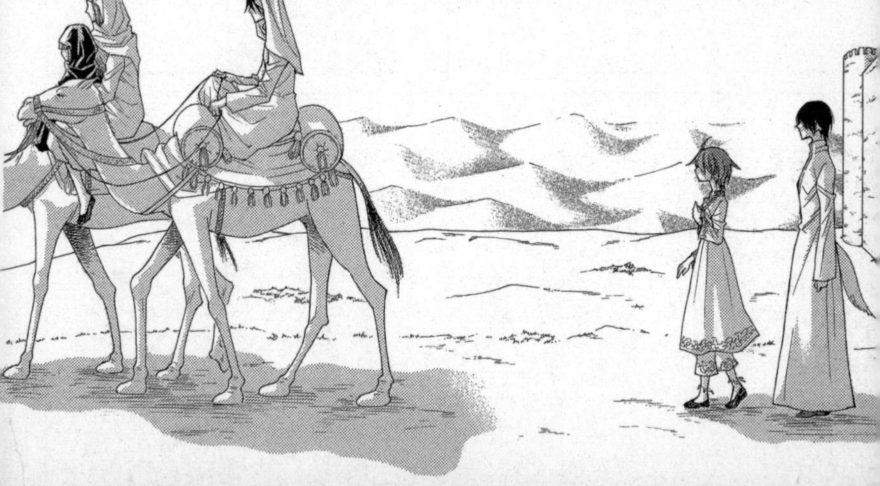

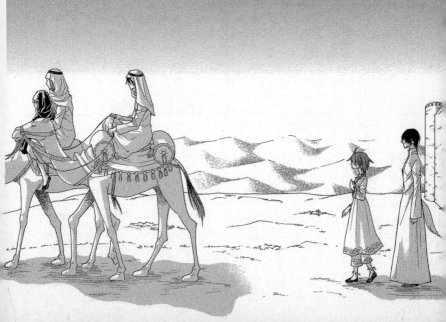

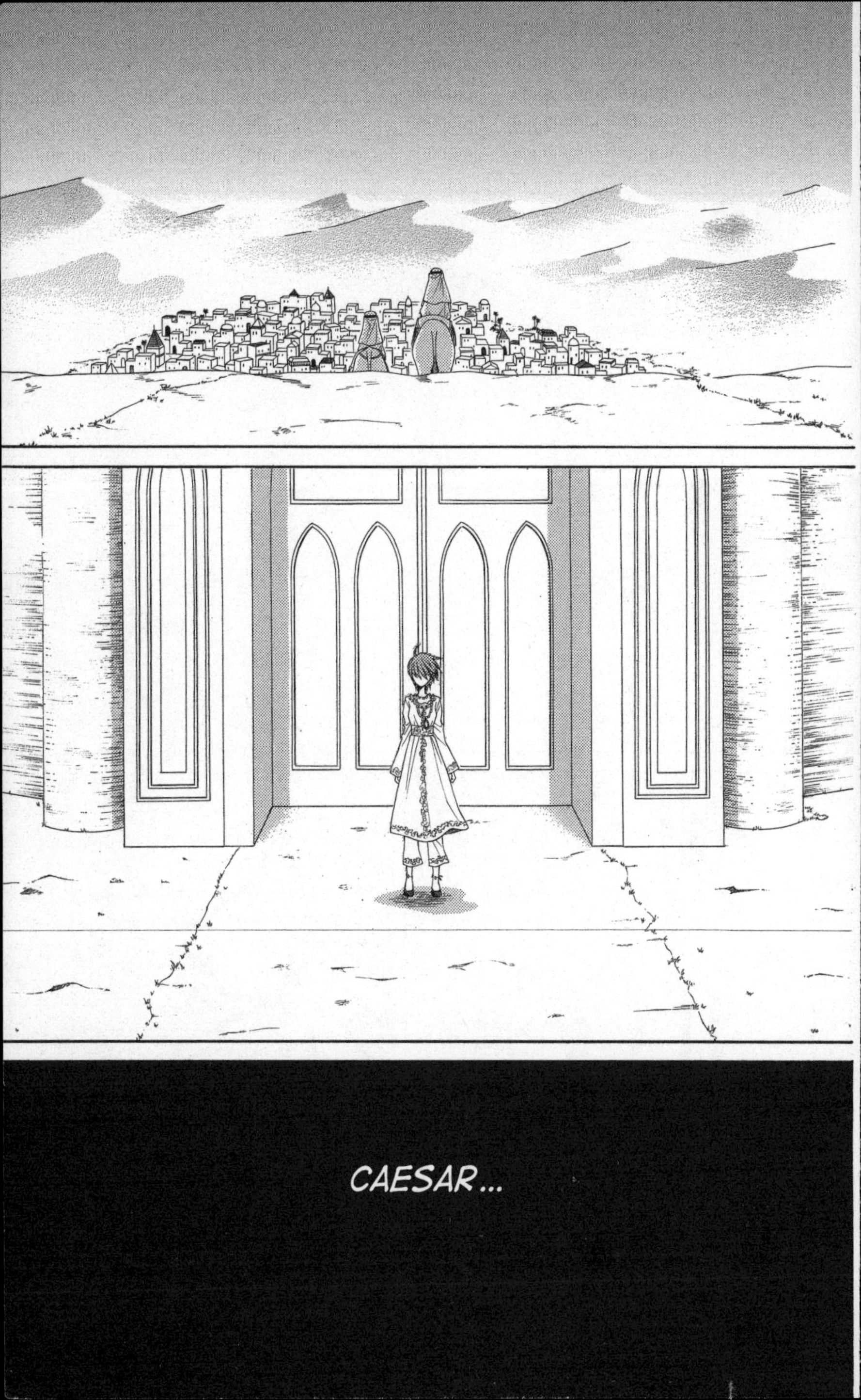
CAESAR...

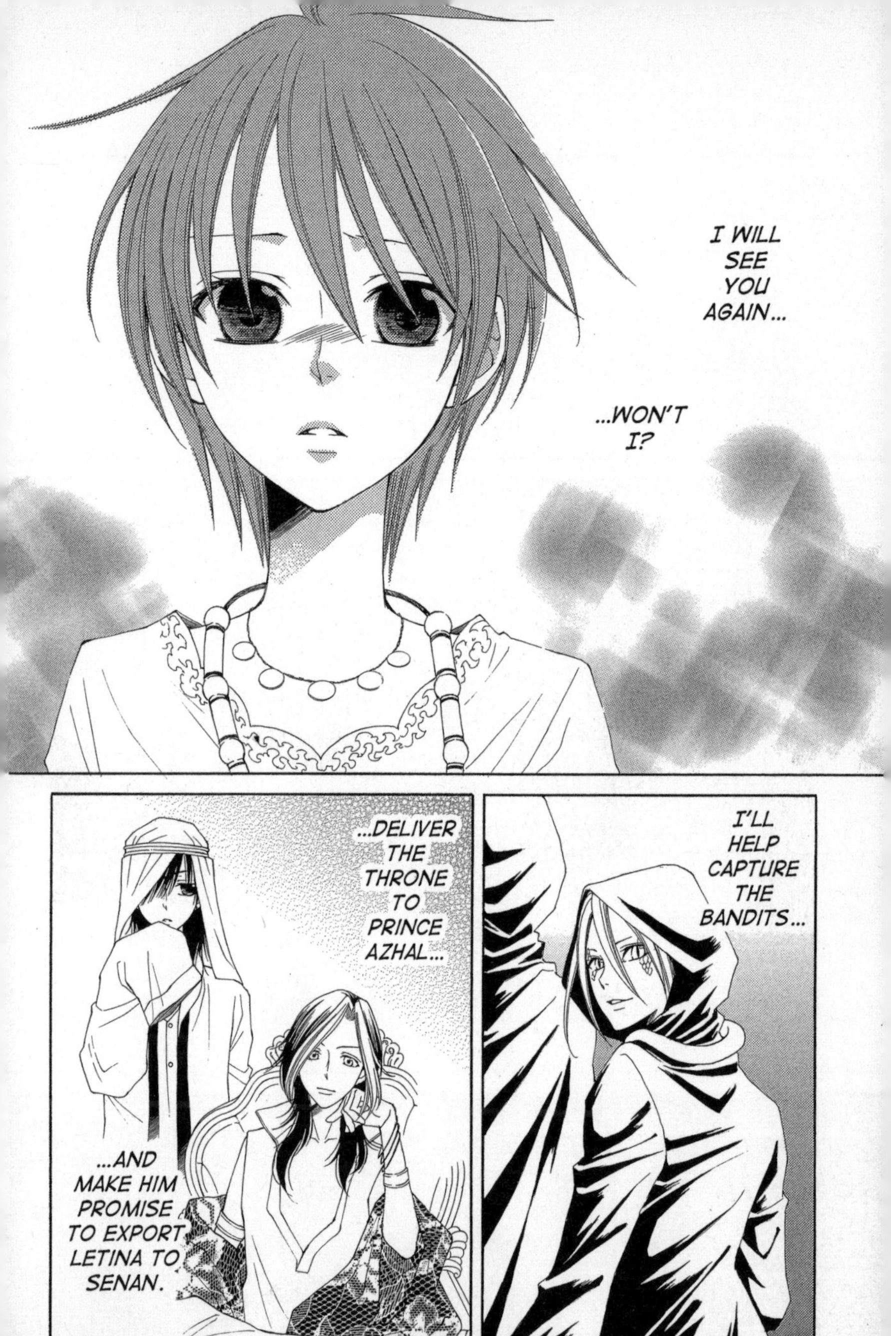
I WILL SEE YOU AGAIN...
...WON'T I?
I'LL HELP CAPTURE THE BANDITS...
...DELIVER THE THRONE TO PRINCE AZHAL...
...AND MAKE HIM PROMISE TO EXPORT LETINA TO SENAN.

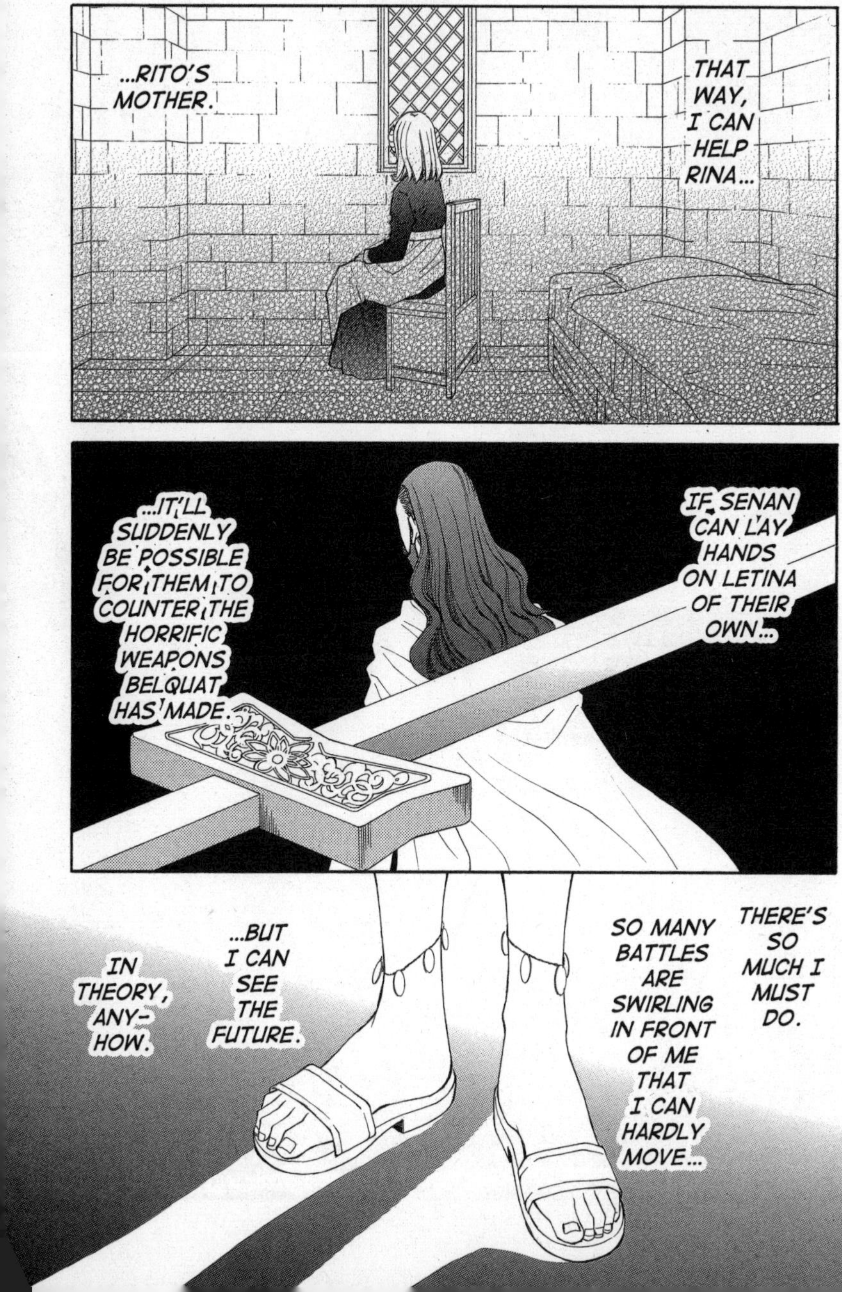
THAT WAY, I CAN HELP RINA...
...RITO'S MOTHER.
IF SENAN CAN LAY HANDS ON LETINA OF THEIR OWN...
...IT'LL SUDDENLY BE POSSIBLE FOR THEM TO COUNTER THE HORRIFIC WEAPONS BELQUAT HAS MADE.
THERE'S SO MUCH I MUST DO.
SO MANY BATTLES ARE SWIRLING IN FRONT OF ME THAT I CAN HARDLY MOVE...
...BUT I CAN SEE THE FUTURE.
IN THEORY, ANY-HOW.

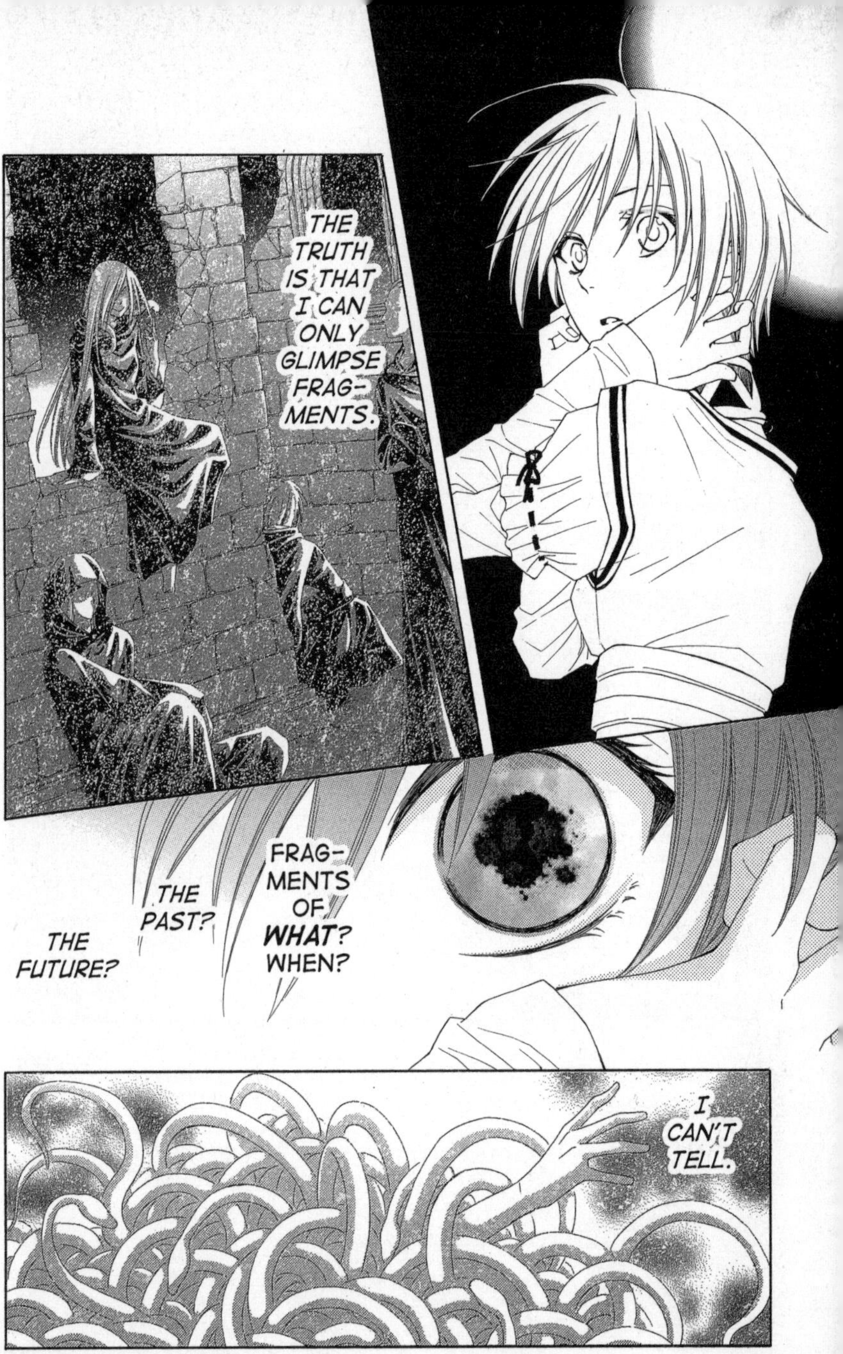
THE TRUTH IS THAT I CAN ONLY GLIMPSE FRAG-MENTS.
FRAG-MENTS OF **WHAT**? WHEN?
THE PAST?
THE FUTURE?
I CAN'T TELL.

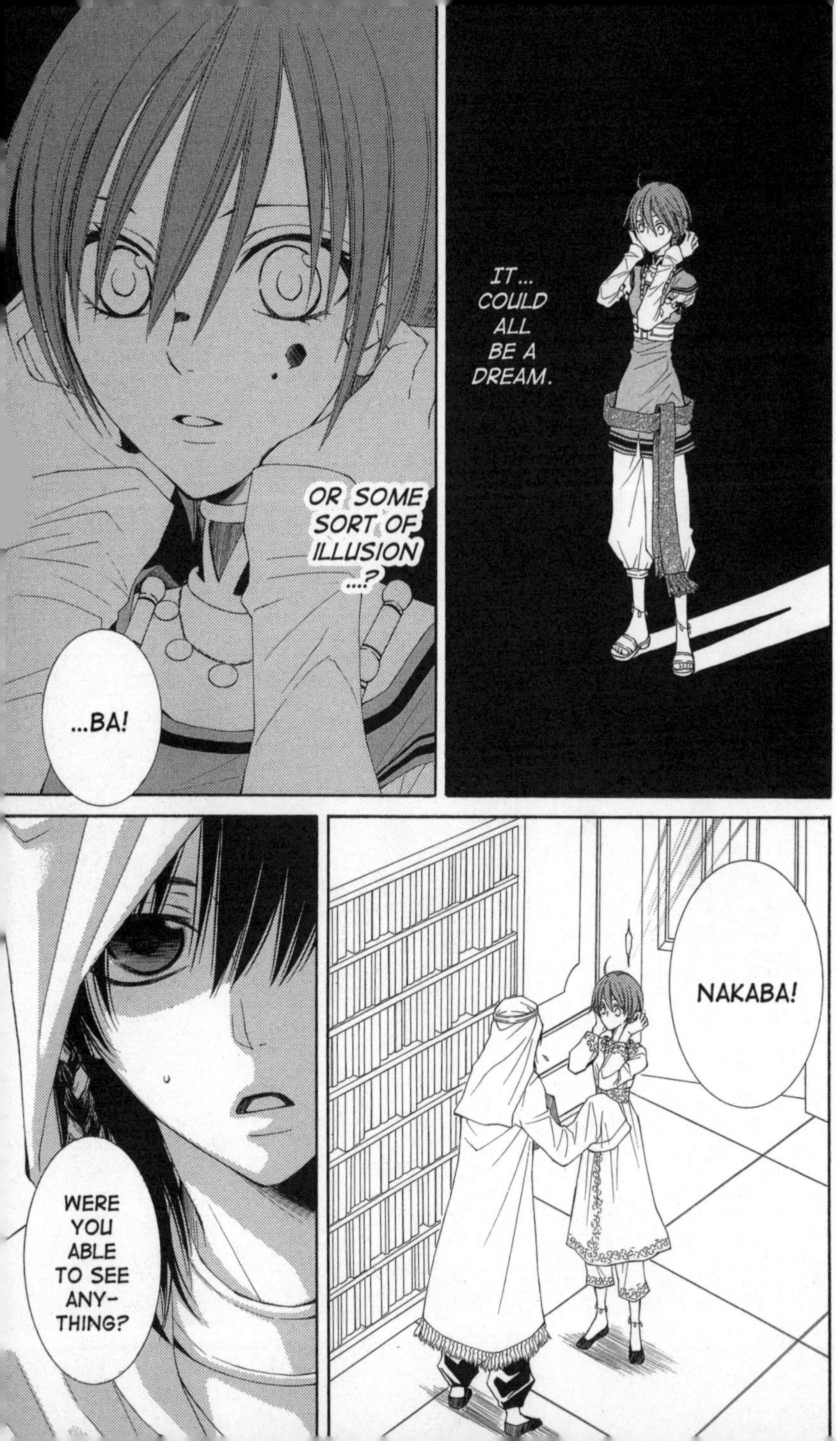
IT... COULD ALL BE A DREAM.
OR SOME SORT OF ILLUSION ...?
...BA!
NAKABA!
WERE YOU ABLE TO SEE ANYTHING?

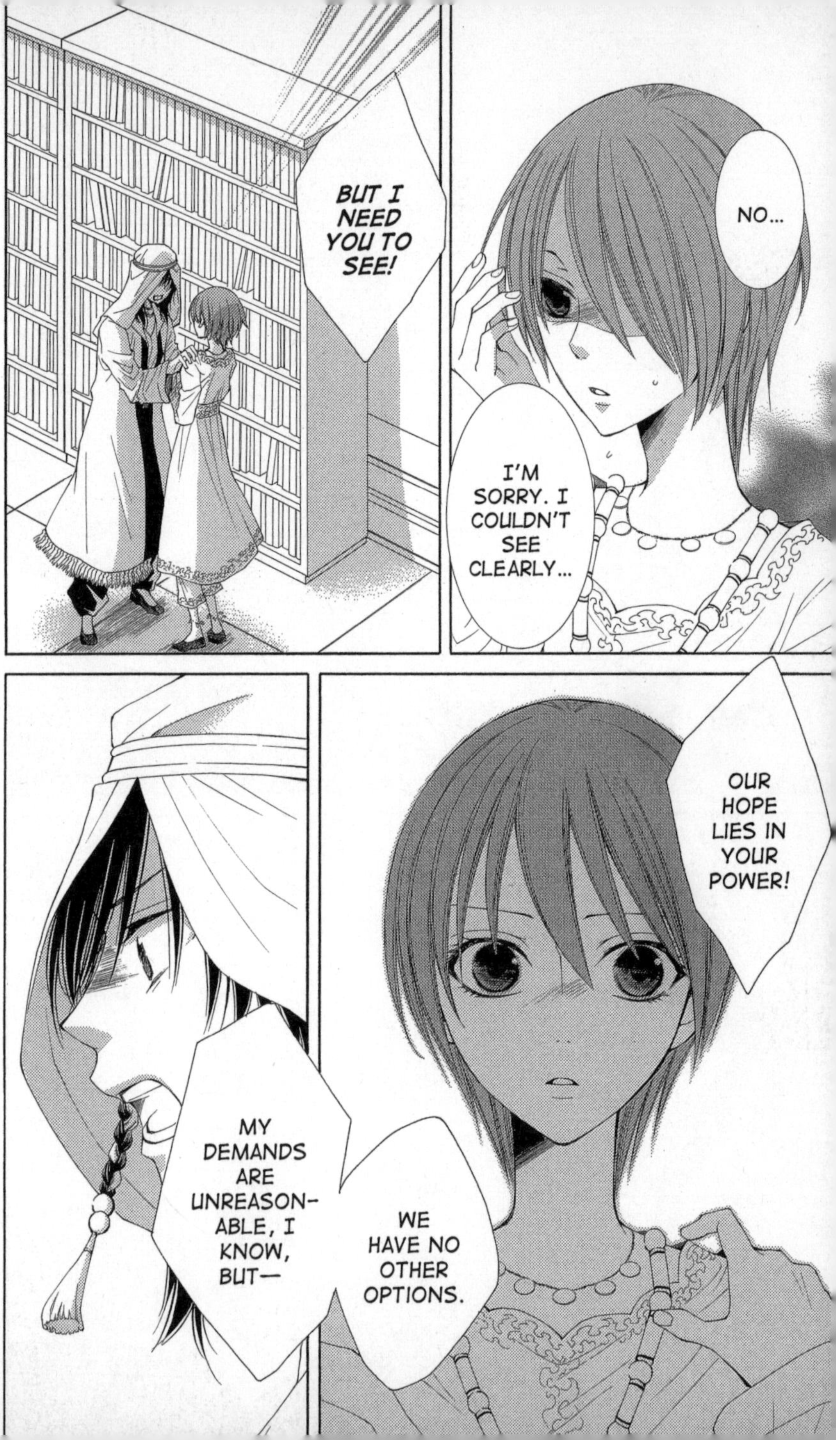
NO...
I'M SORRY. I COULDN'T SEE CLEARLY...
BUT I NEED YOU TO SEE!
OUR HOPE LIES IN YOUR POWER!
MY DEMANDS ARE UNREASON-ABLE, I KNOW, BUT—
WE HAVE NO OTHER OPTIONS.

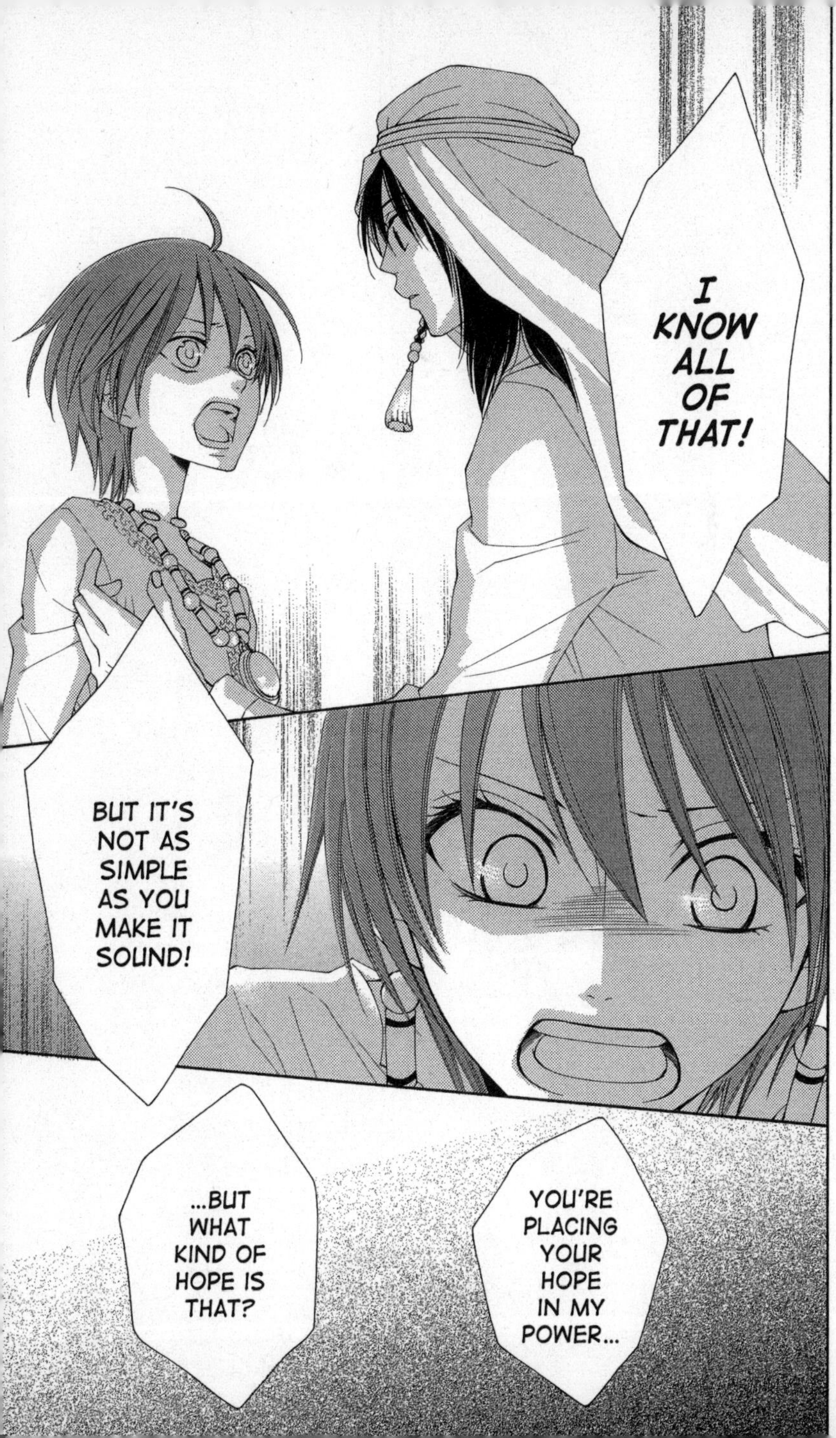
I KNOW ALL OF THAT!
BUT IT'S NOT AS SIMPLE AS YOU MAKE IT SOUND!
YOU'RE PLACING YOUR HOPE IN MY POWER...
...BUT WHAT KIND OF HOPE IS THAT?

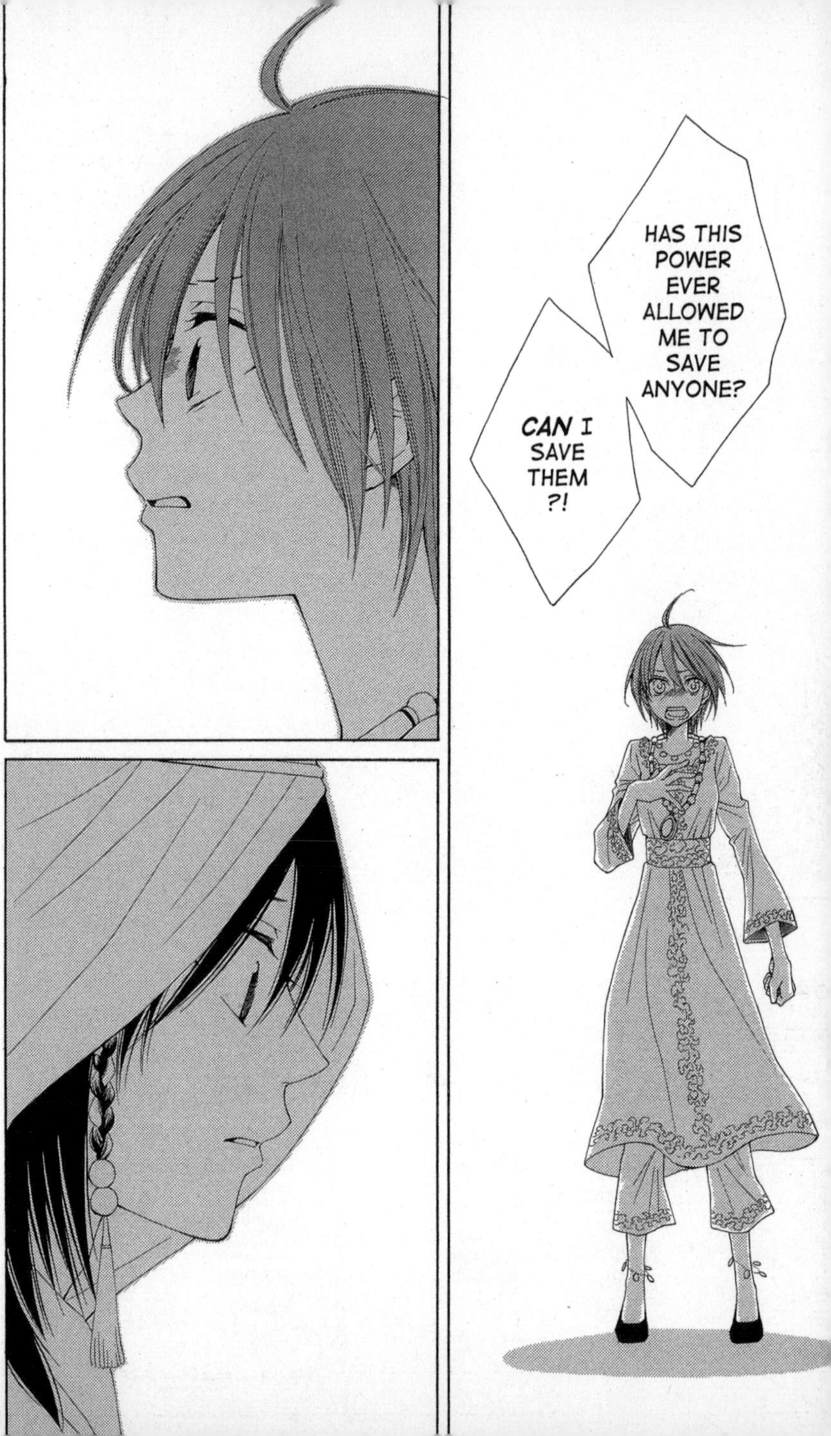
HAS THIS POWER EVER ALLOWED ME TO SAVE ANYONE?
CAN I SAVE THEM?!

I'M SORRY.

Ah...

I...
I NEED
TO GO
REST
FOR A
WHILE.

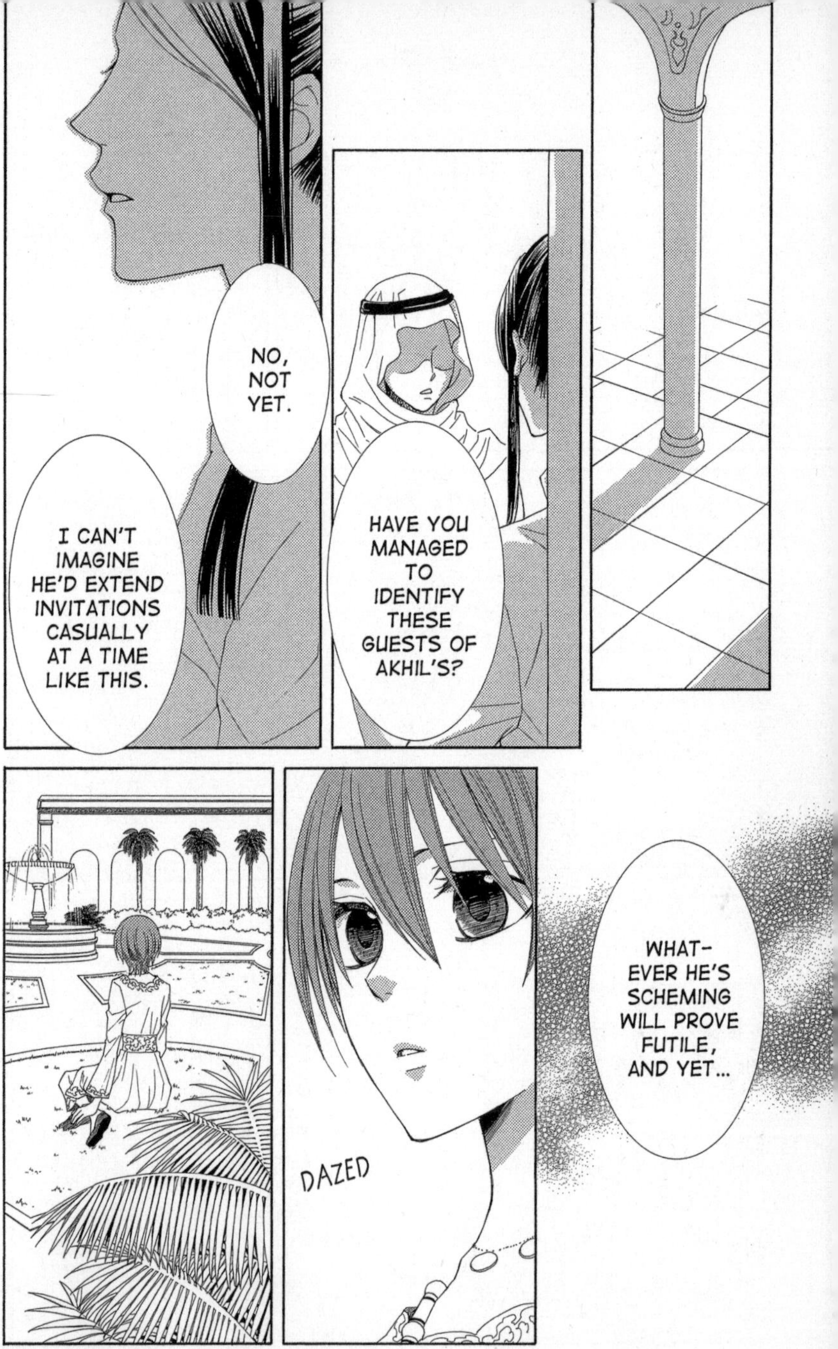
HAVE YOU MANAGED TO IDENTIFY THESE GUESTS OF AKHIL'S?
NO, NOT YET.
I CAN'T IMAGINE HE'D EXTEND INVITATIONS CASUALLY AT A TIME LIKE THIS.
WHAT-EVER HE'S SCHEMING WILL PROVE FUTILE, AND YET...
DAZED

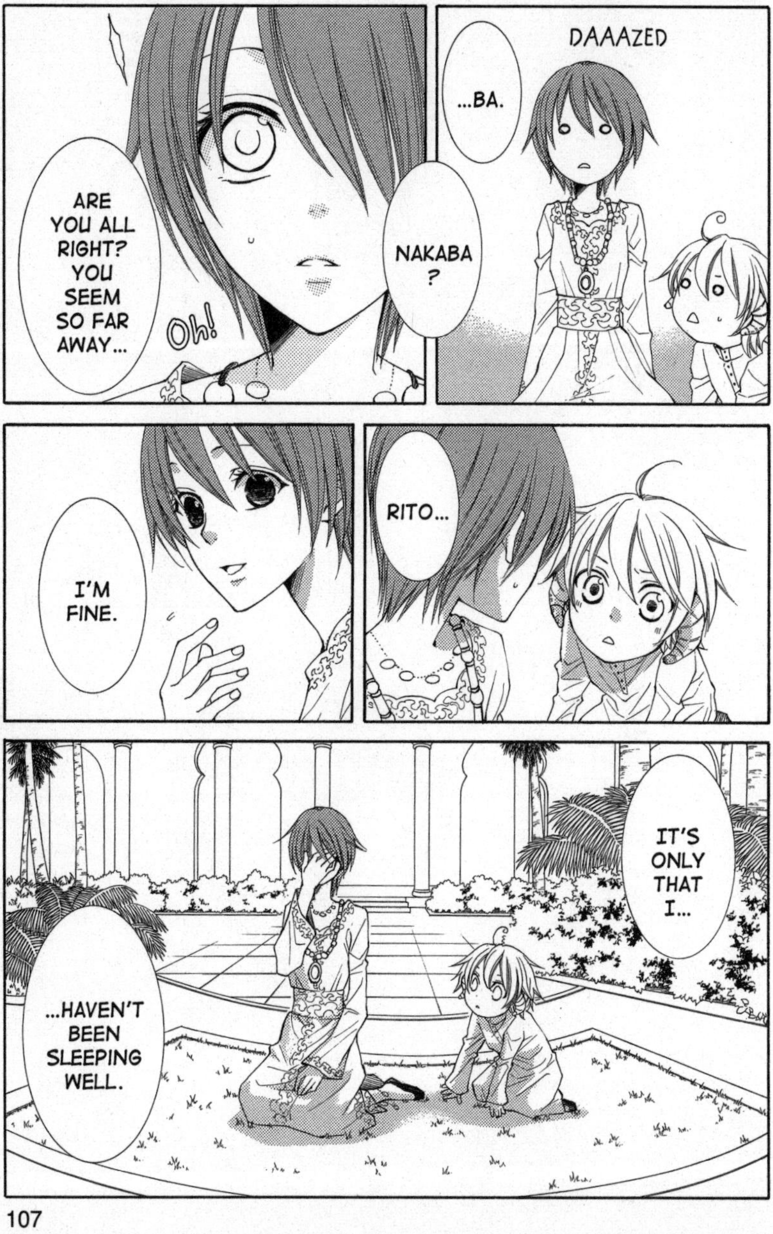
DAAAZED
...BA.
NAKABA ?
Oh!
ARE YOU ALL RIGHT? YOU SEEM SO FAR AWAY...
RITO...
I'M FINE.
IT'S ONLY THAT I...
...HAVEN'T BEEN SLEEPING WELL.

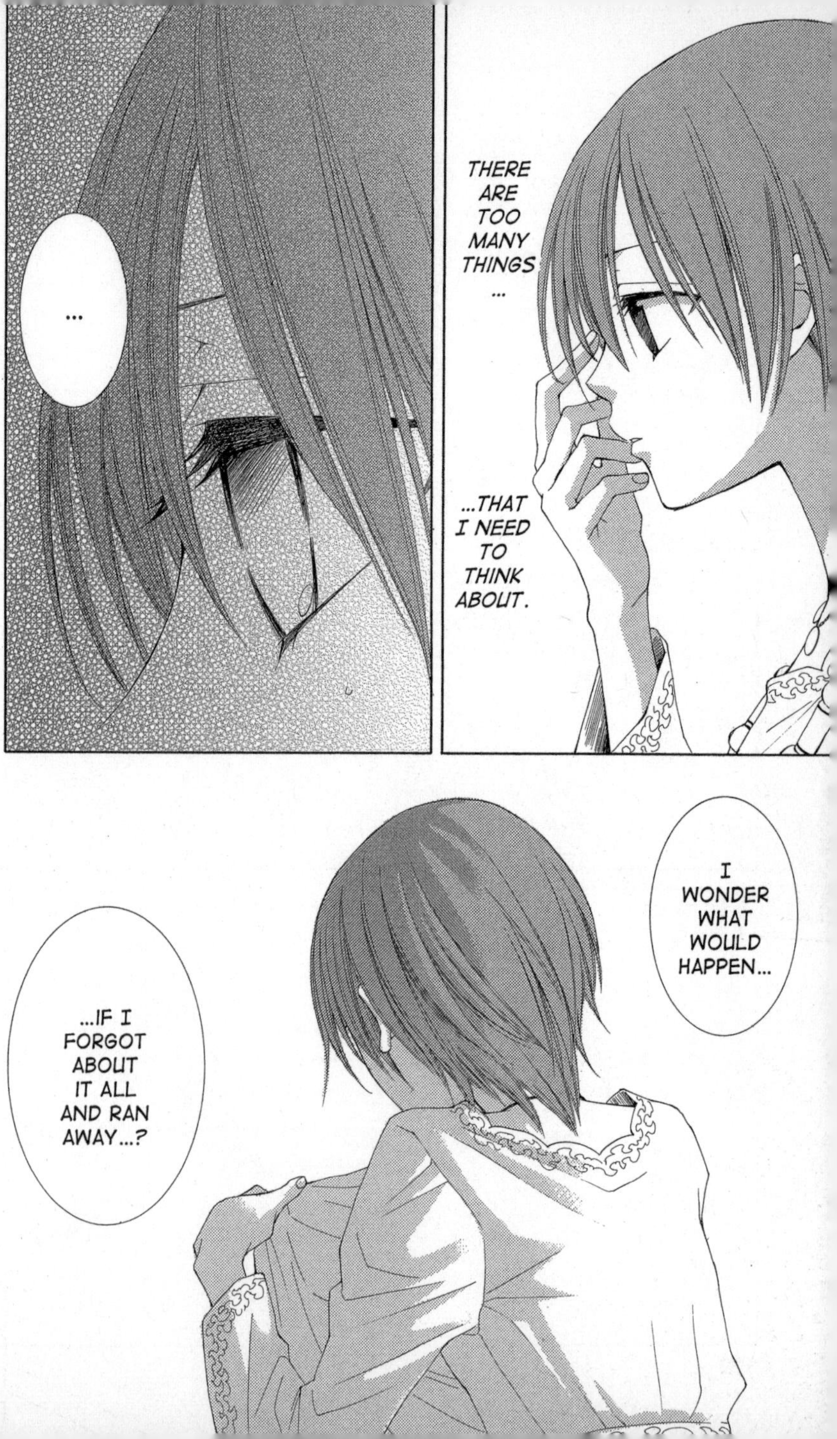
THERE ARE TOO MANY THINGS ...
...THAT I NEED TO THINK ABOUT.
...
I WONDER WHAT WOULD HAPPEN...
...IF I FORGOT ABOUT IT ALL AND RAN AWAY...?

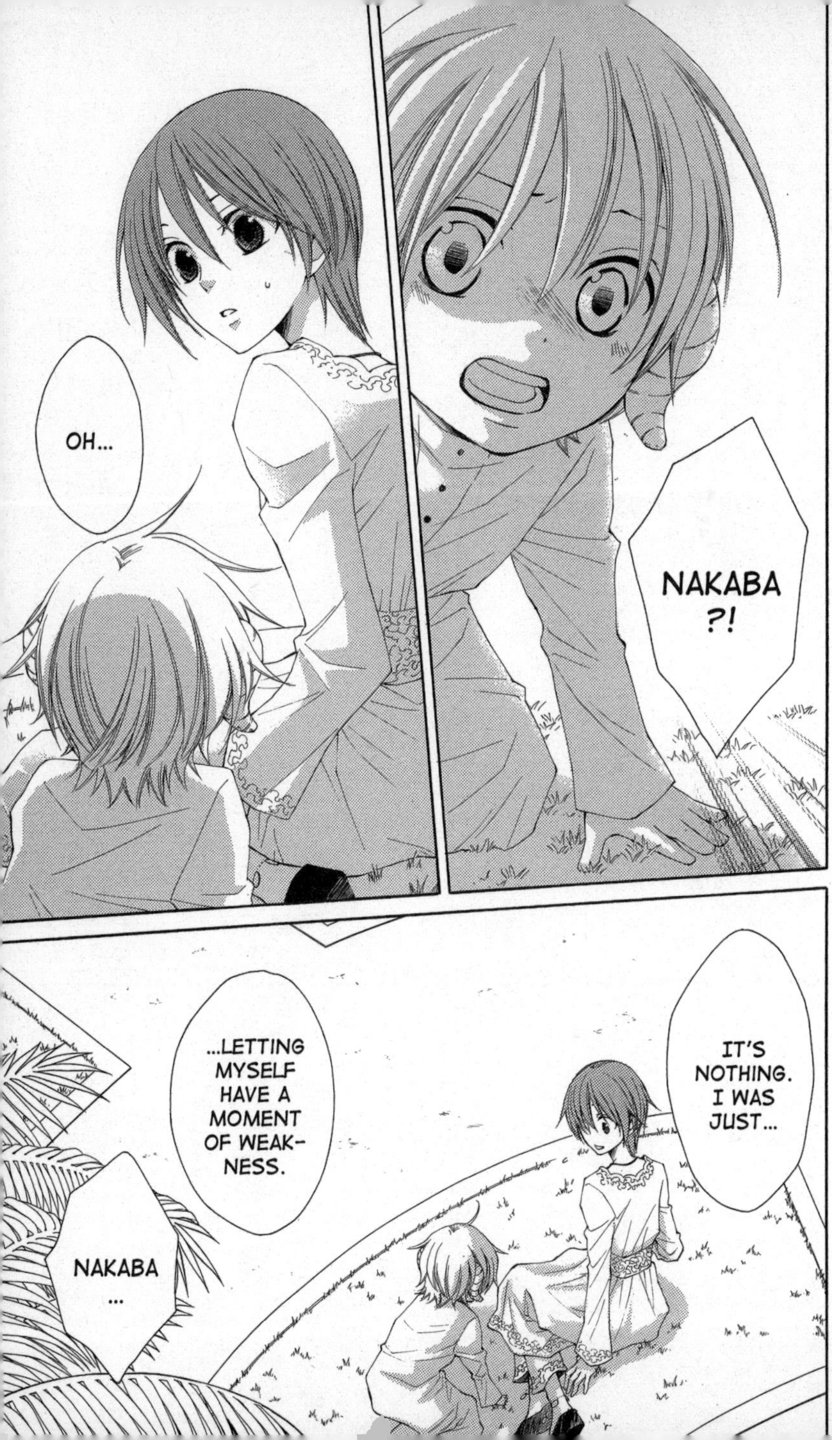
NAKABA?!
OH...
IT'S NOTHING. I WAS JUST...
...LETTING MYSELF HAVE A MOMENT OF WEAKNESS.
NAKABA...

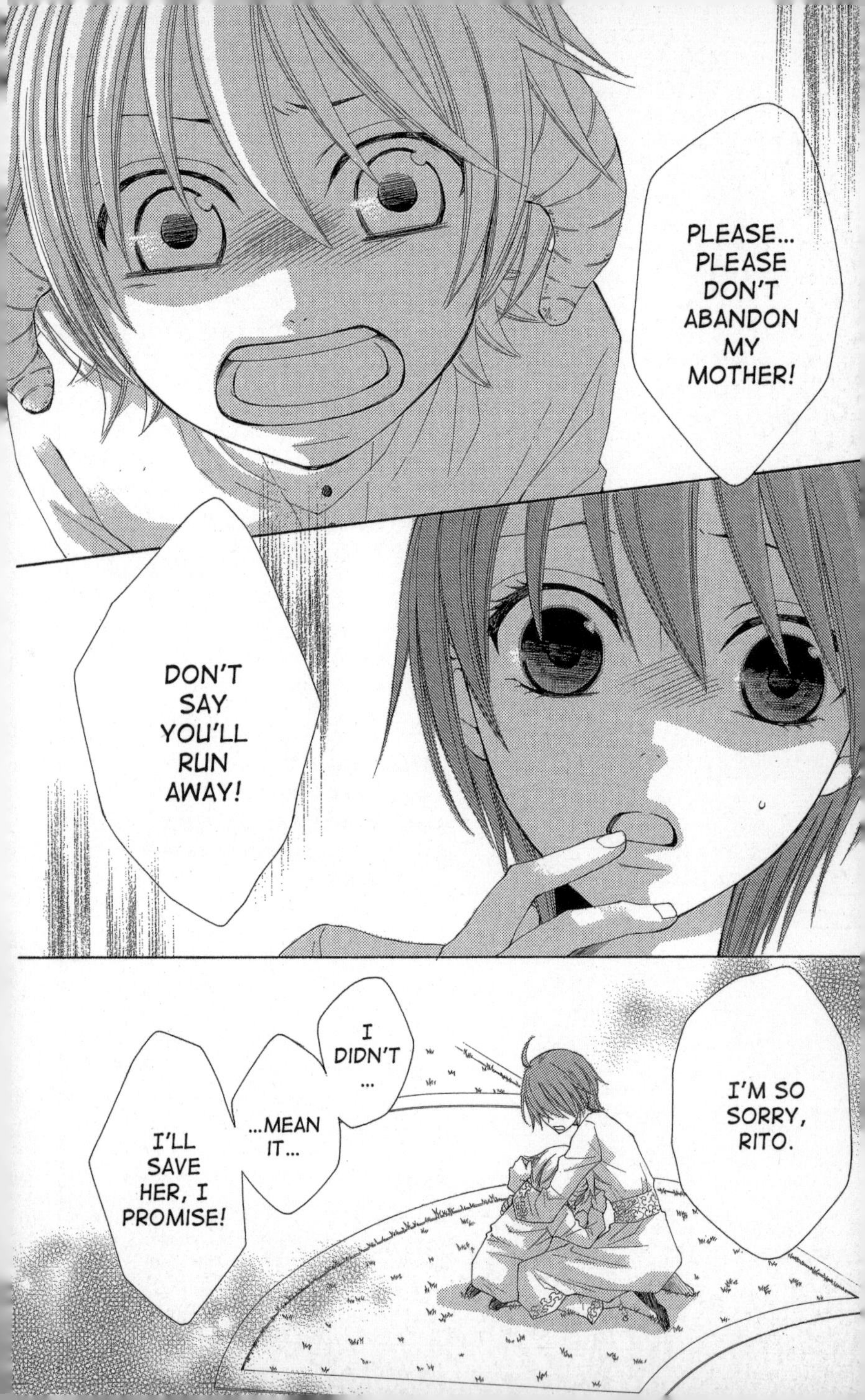
PLEASE... PLEASE DON'T ABANDON MY MOTHER!
DON'T SAY YOU'LL RUN AWAY!
I'M SO SORRY, RITO.
I DIDN'T ...
...MEAN IT...
I'LL SAVE HER, I PROMISE!

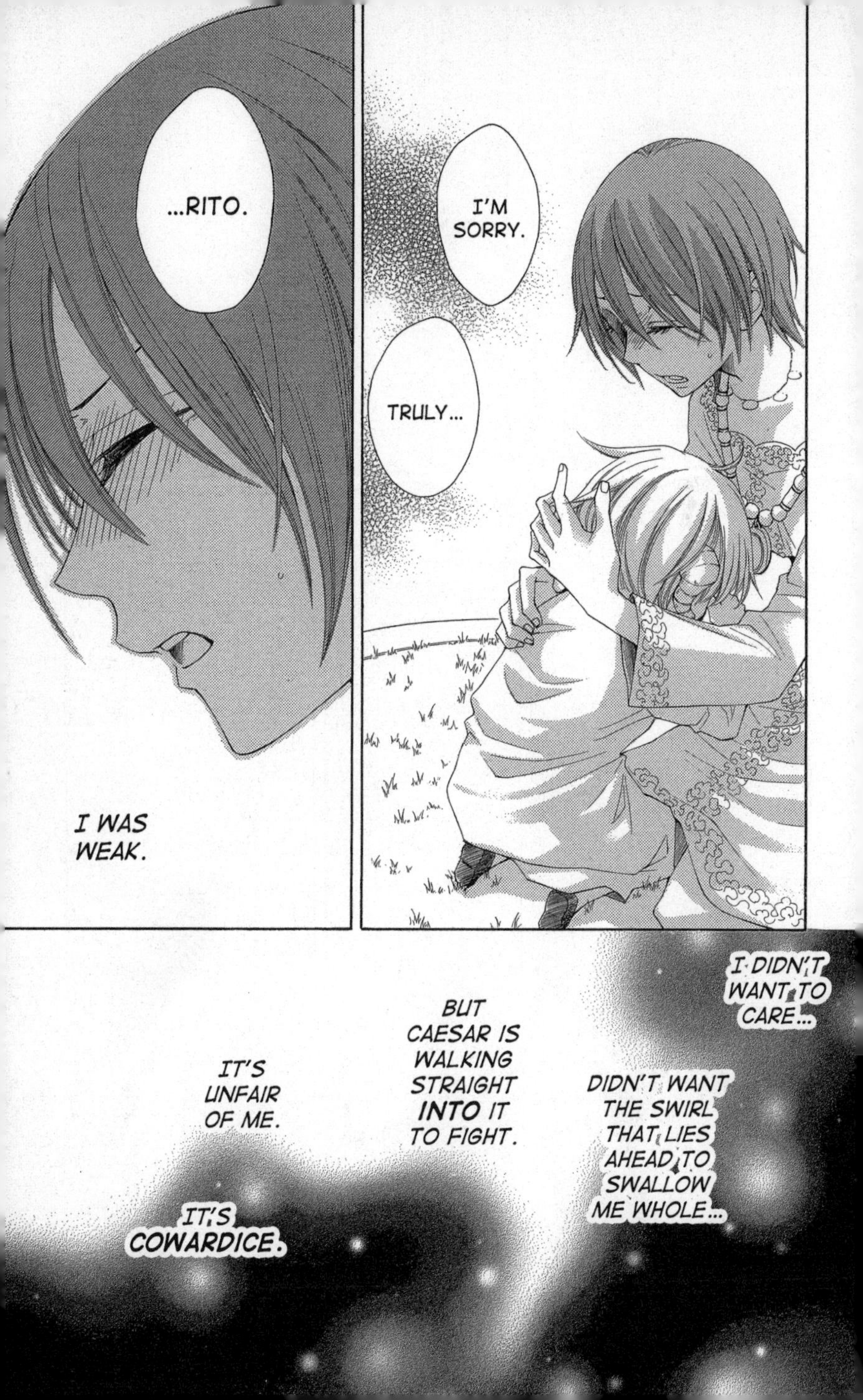
I'M SORRY.
TRULY...
...RITO.
I WAS WEAK.
I DIDN'T WANT TO CARE...
DIDN'T WANT THE SWIRL THAT LIES AHEAD TO SWALLOW ME WHOLE...
BUT CAESAR IS WALKING STRAIGHT INTO IT TO FIGHT.
IT'S UNFAIR OF ME.
IT'S COWARDICE.

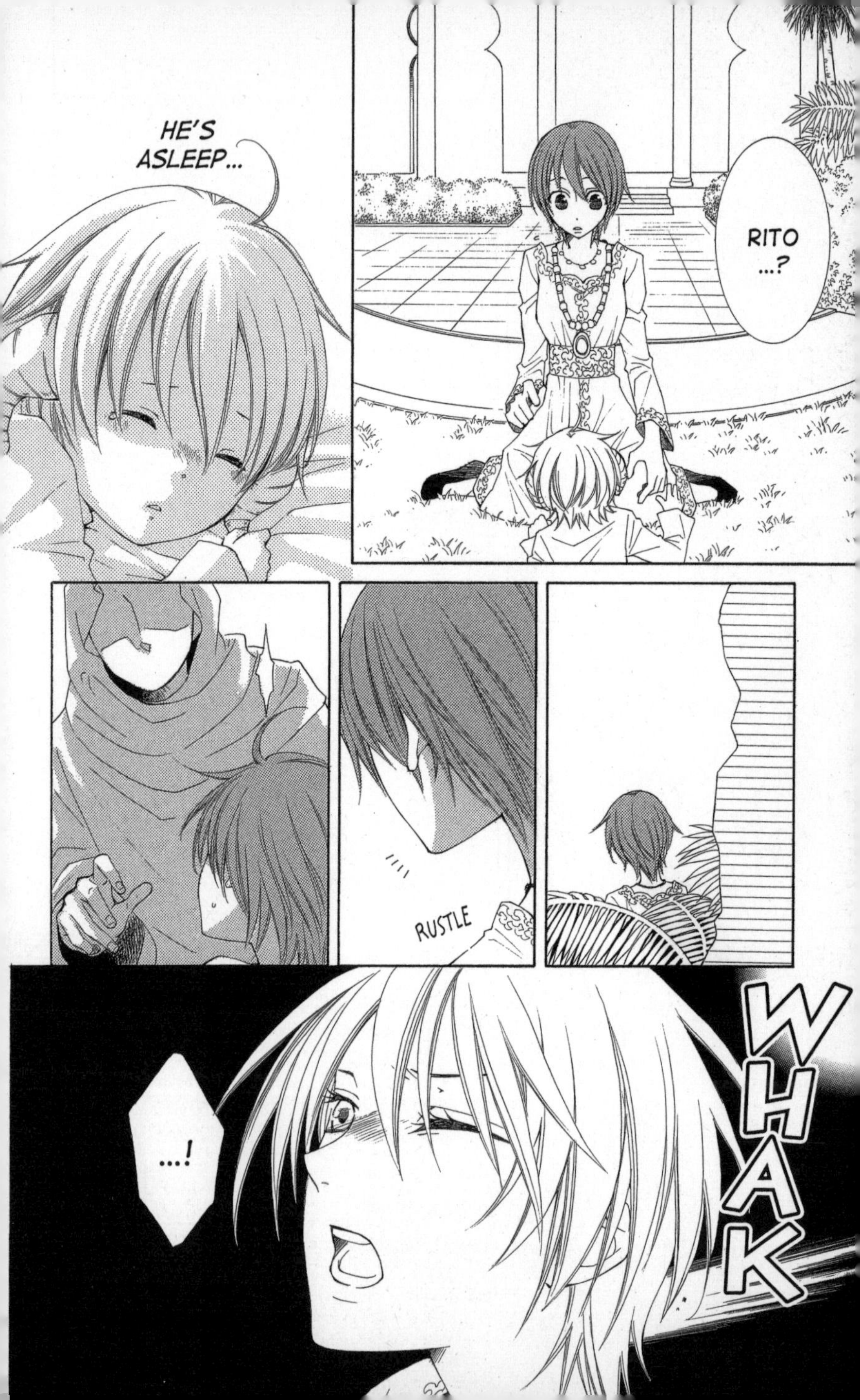
RITO ...?
HE'S ASLEEP...
RUSTLE
WHAK
...!

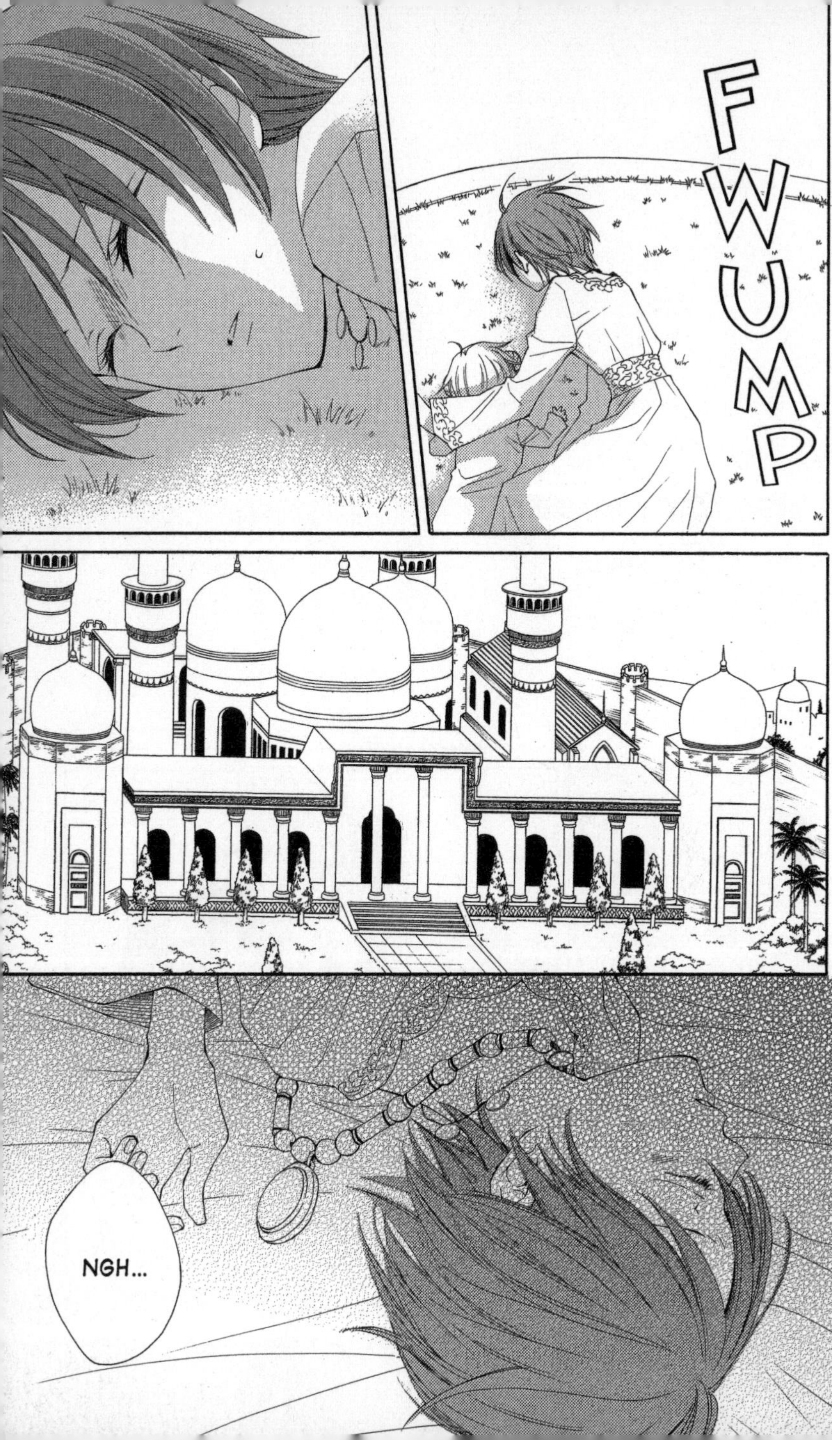
FWUMP
NGH...

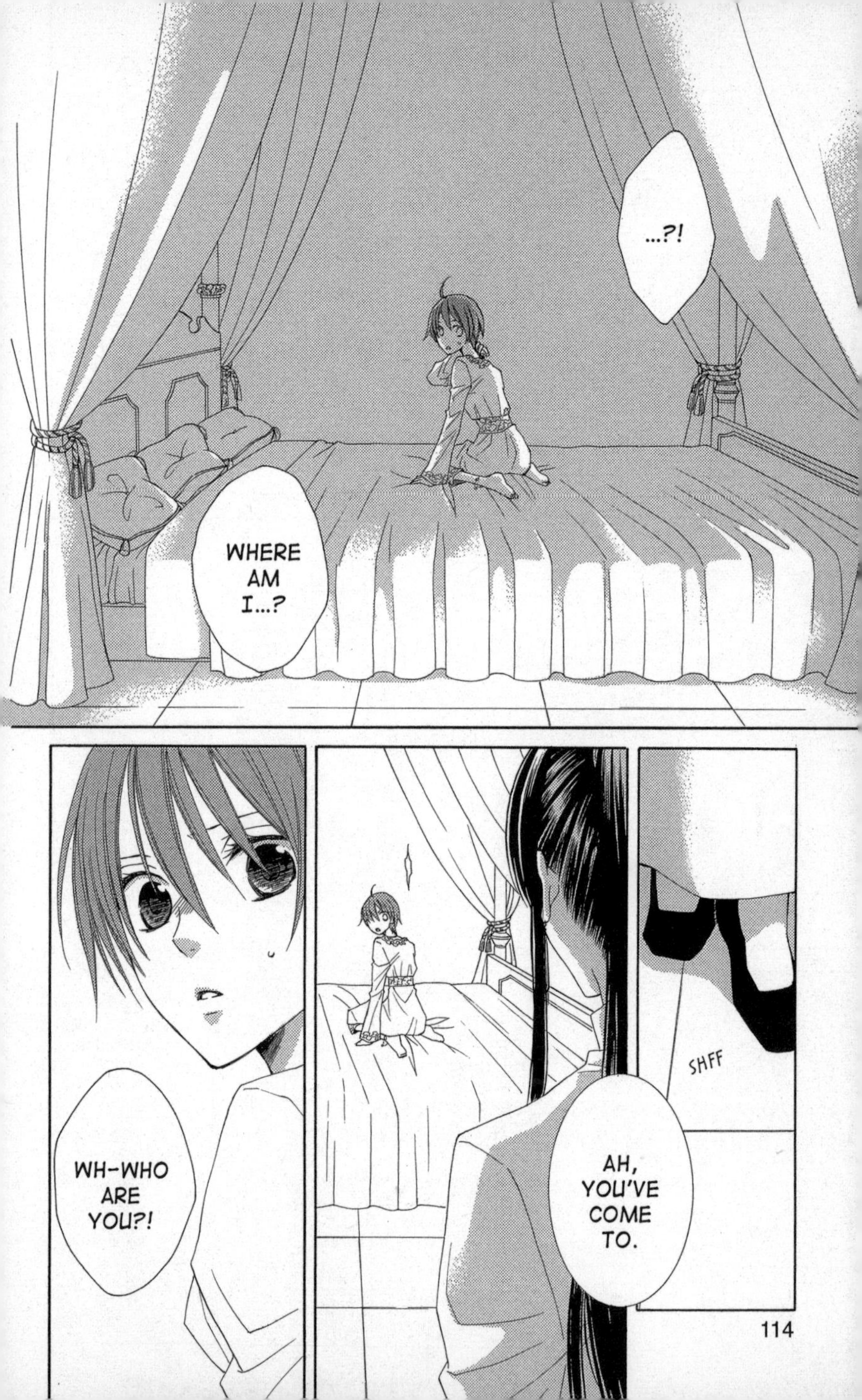
...?!
WHERE AM I...?
SHFF
AH, YOU'VE COME TO.
WH-WHO ARE YOU?!

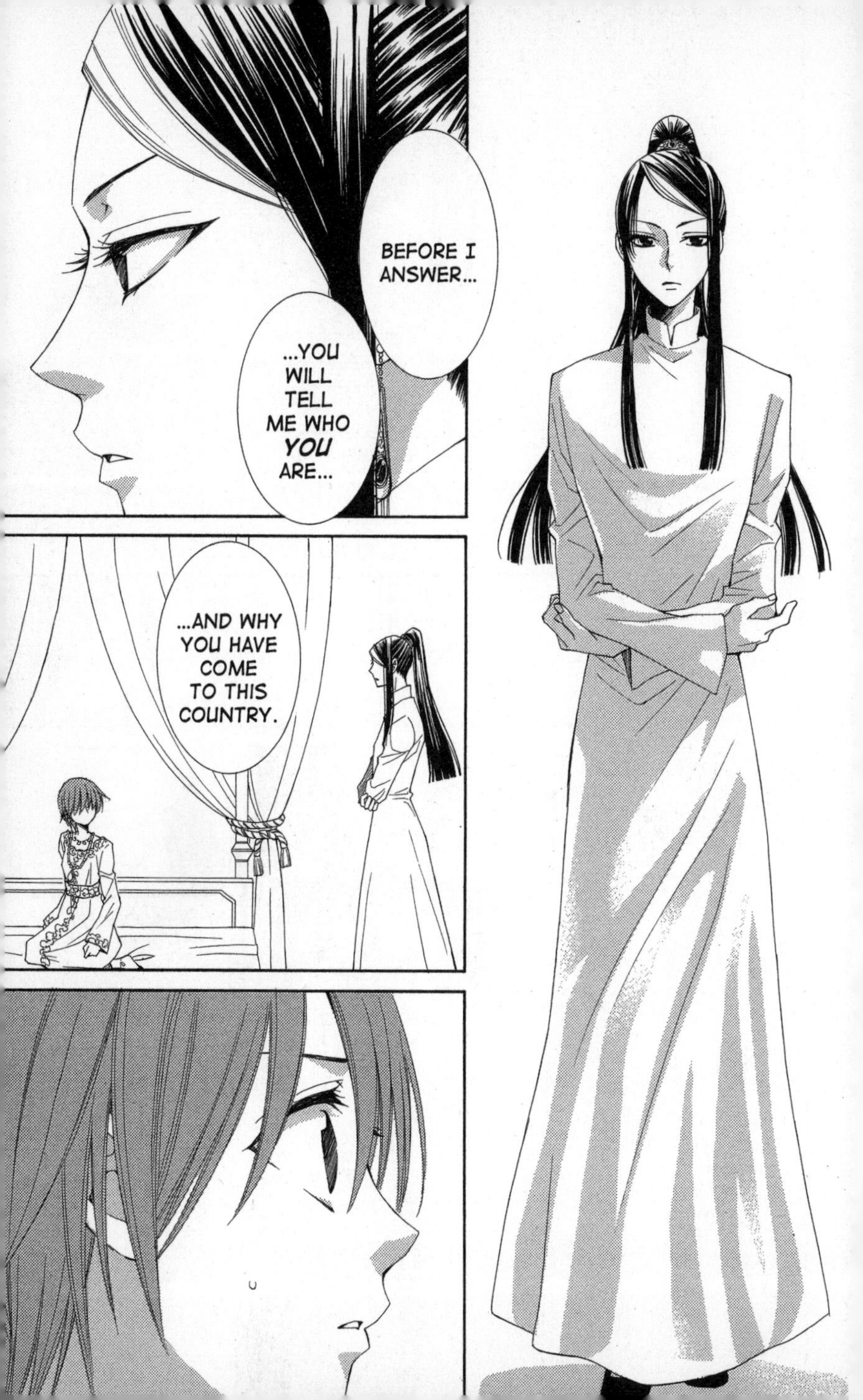
BEFORE I ANSWER...
...YOU WILL TELL ME WHO *YOU* ARE...
...AND WHY YOU HAVE COME TO THIS COUNTRY.

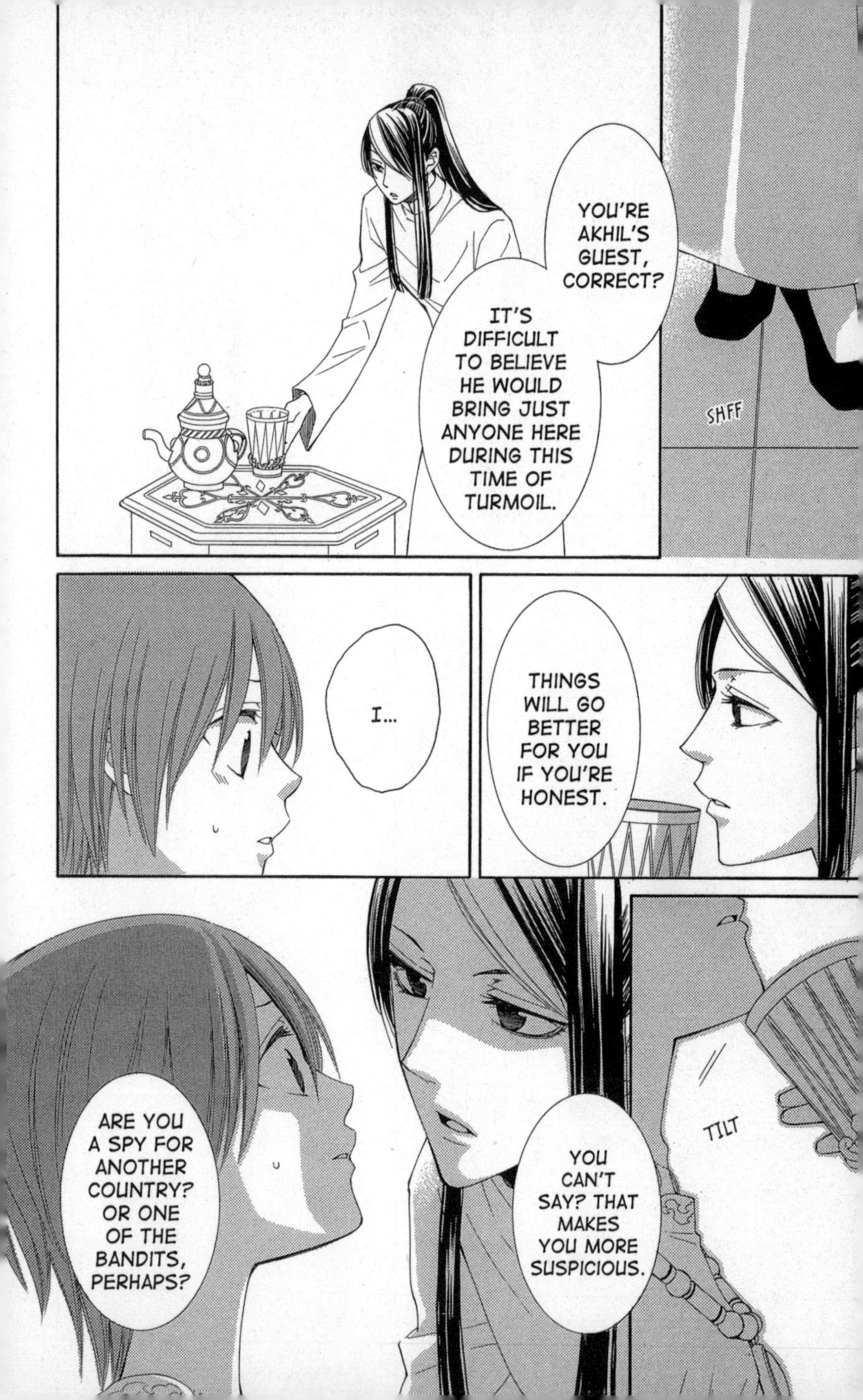
YOU'RE AKHIL'S GUEST, CORRECT?
IT'S DIFFICULT TO BELIEVE HE WOULD BRING JUST ANYONE HERE DURING THIS TIME OF TURMOIL.
SHFF
THINGS WILL GO BETTER FOR YOU IF YOU'RE HONEST.
I...
TILT
ARE YOU A SPY FOR ANOTHER COUNTRY? OR ONE OF THE BANDITS, PERHAPS?
YOU CAN'T SAY? THAT MAKES YOU MORE SUSPICIOUS.

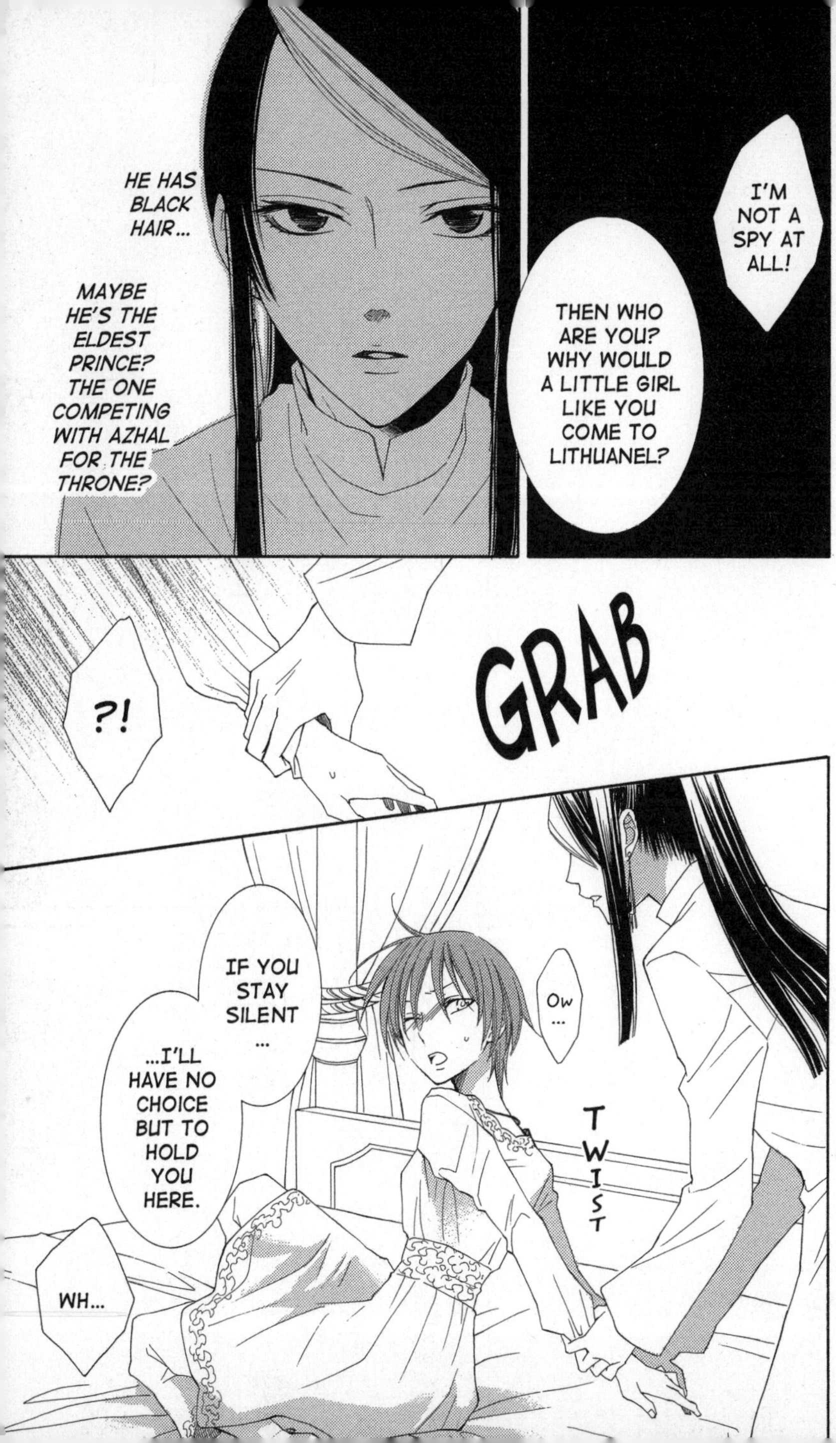
I'M NOT A SPY AT ALL!
THEN WHO ARE YOU? WHY WOULD A LITTLE GIRL LIKE YOU COME TO LITHUANEL?
HE HAS BLACK HAIR...
MAYBE HE'S THE ELDEST PRINCE? THE ONE COMPETING WITH AZHAL FOR THE THRONE?
GRAB
?!
Ow...
TWIST
IF YOU STAY SILENT...
...I'LL HAVE NO CHOICE BUT TO HOLD YOU HERE.
WH...

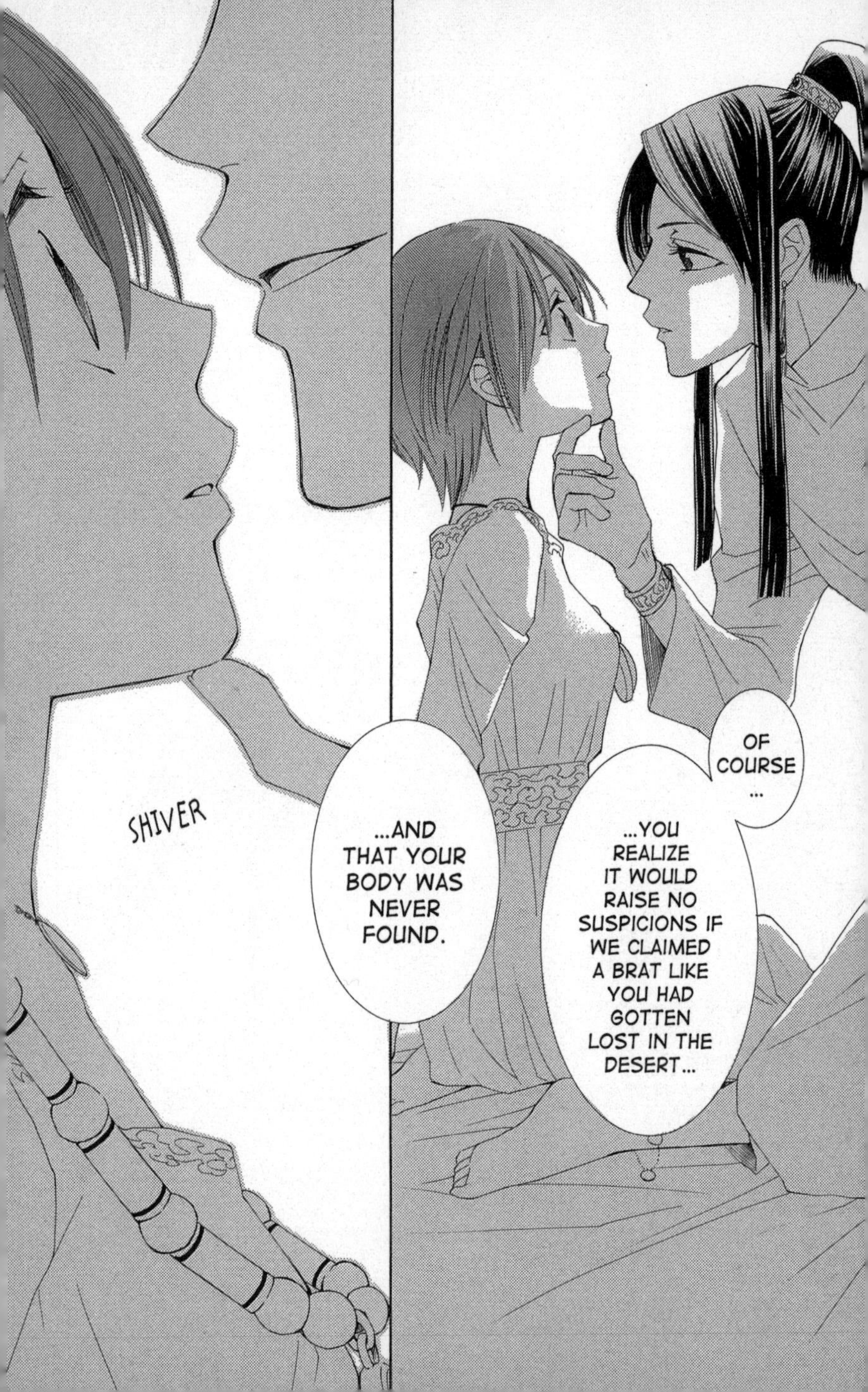
OF COURSE ...
...YOU REALIZE IT WOULD RAISE NO SUSPICIONS IF WE CLAIMED A BRAT LIKE YOU HAD GOTTEN LOST IN THE DESERT...
...AND THAT YOUR BODY WAS NEVER FOUND.
SHIVER

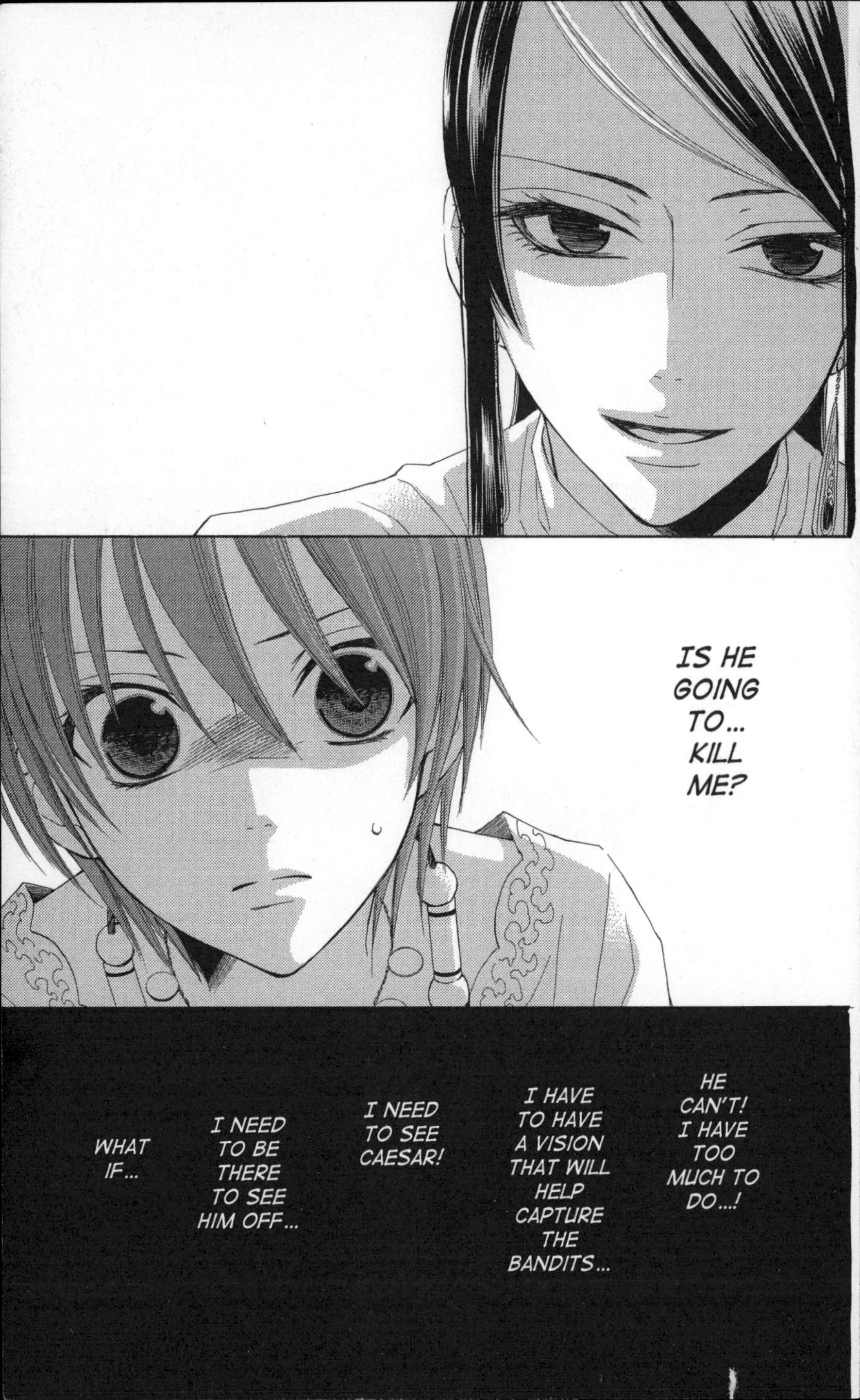
IS HE GOING TO... KILL ME?
HE CAN'T! I HAVE TOO MUCH TO DO...!
I HAVE TO HAVE A VISION THAT WILL HELP CAPTURE THE BANDITS...
I NEED TO SEE CAESAR!
I NEED TO BE THERE TO SEE HIM OFF...
WHAT IF...

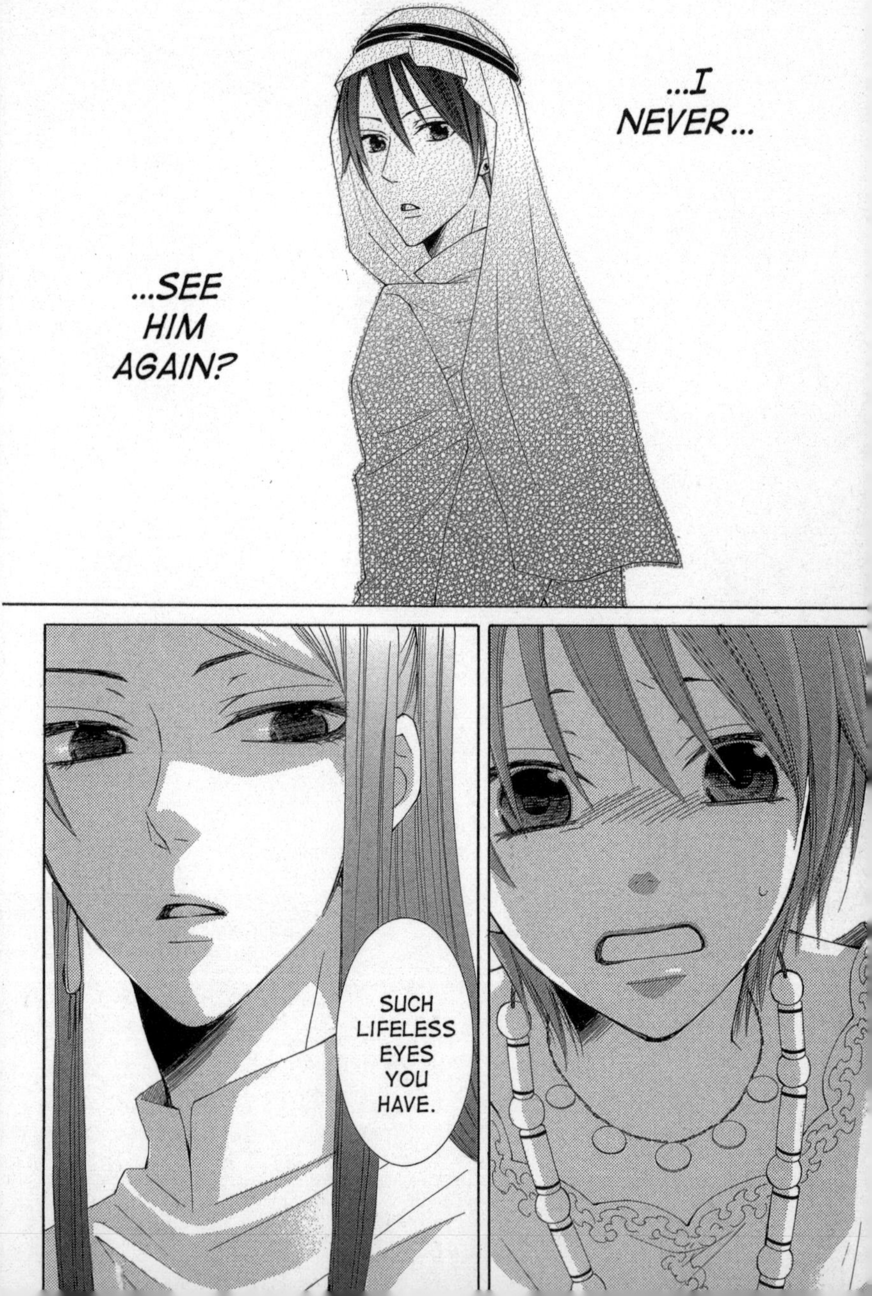
...I NEVER...
...SEE HIM AGAIN?
SUCH LIFELESS EYES YOU HAVE.

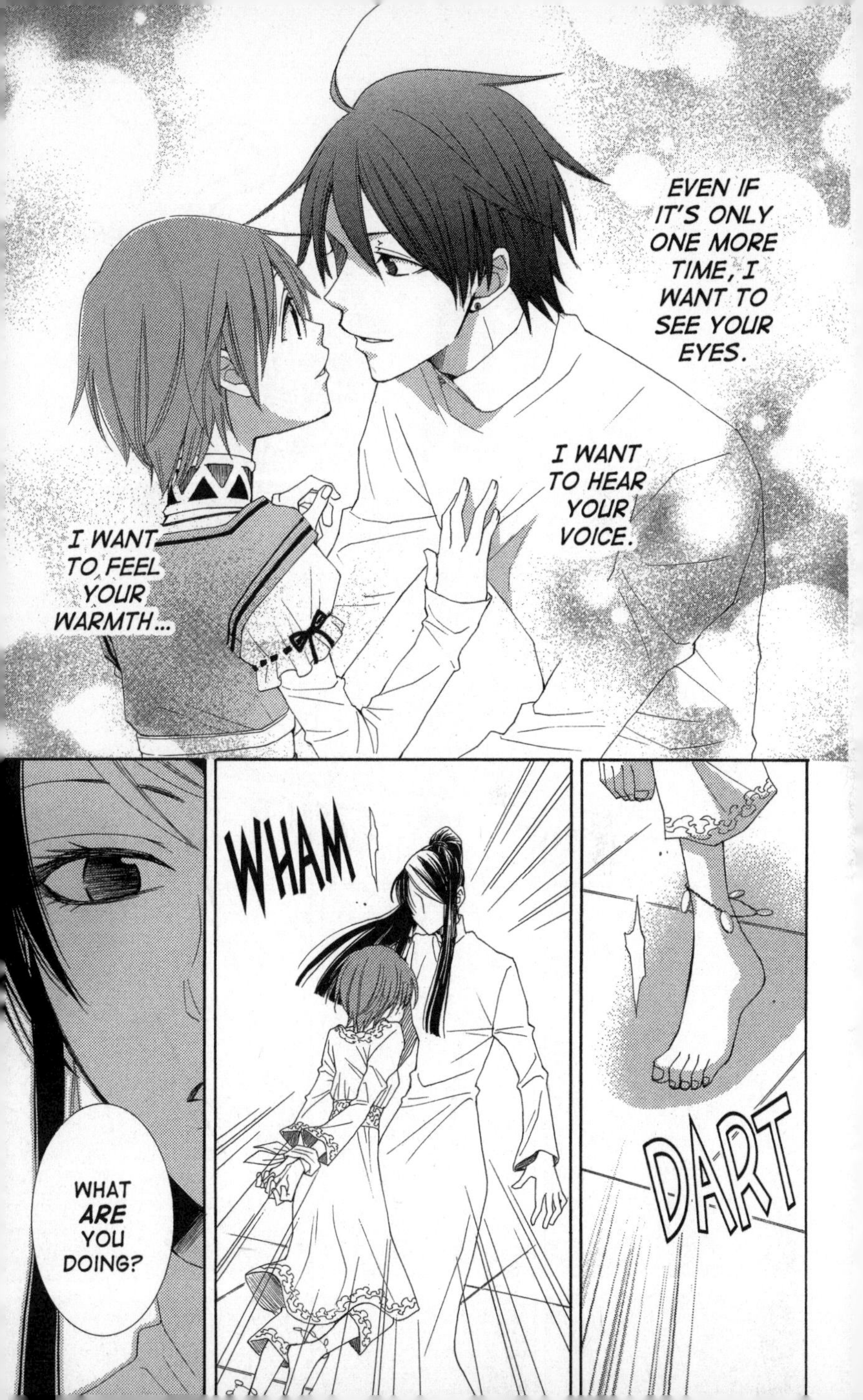
EVEN IF IT'S ONLY ONE MORE TIME, I WANT TO SEE YOUR EYES.
I WANT TO HEAR YOUR VOICE.
I WANT TO FEEL YOUR WARMTH...
DART
WHAM
WHAT ARE YOU DOING?

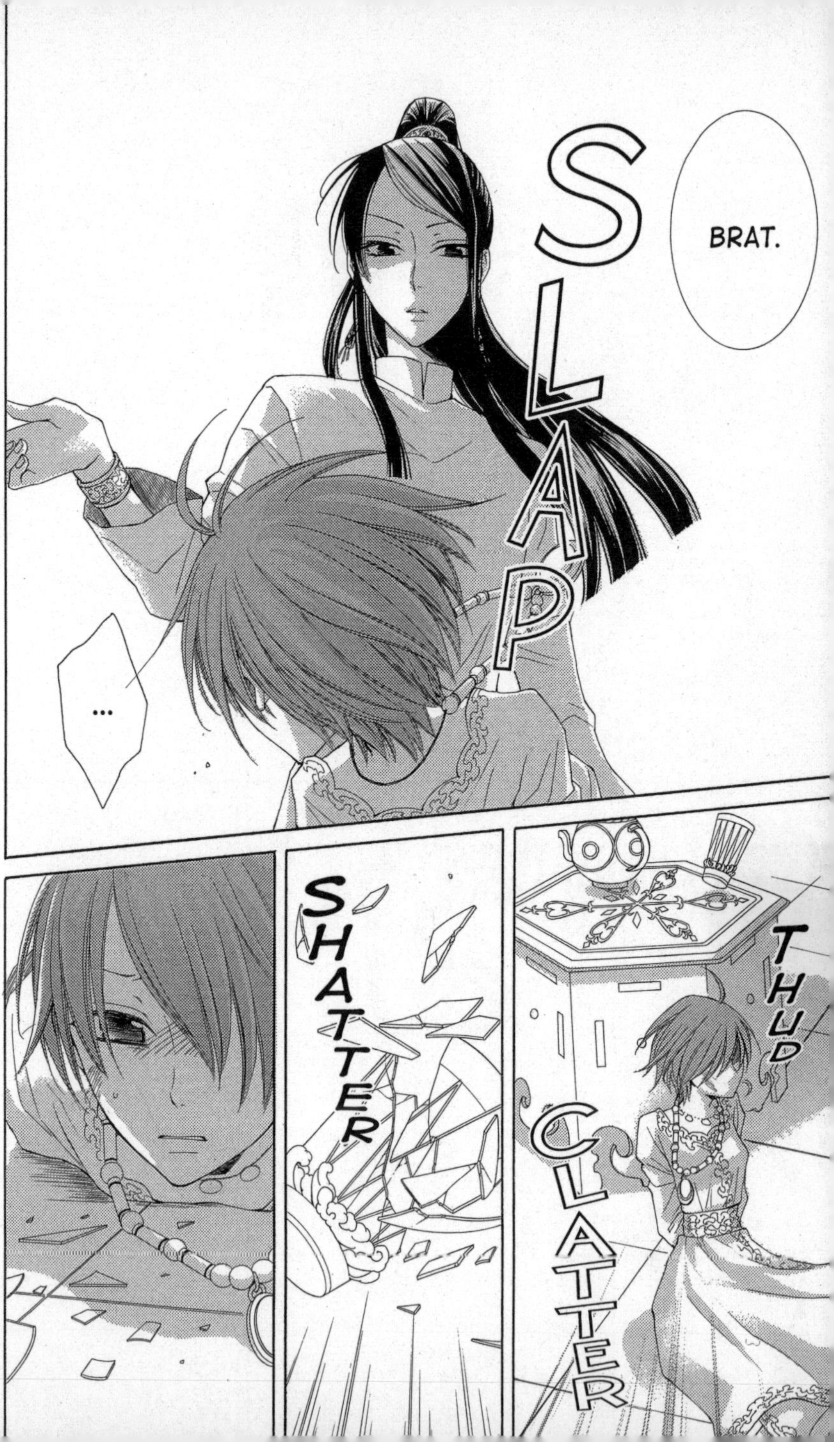
BRAT.
SLAP
...
THUD
CLATTER
SHATTER

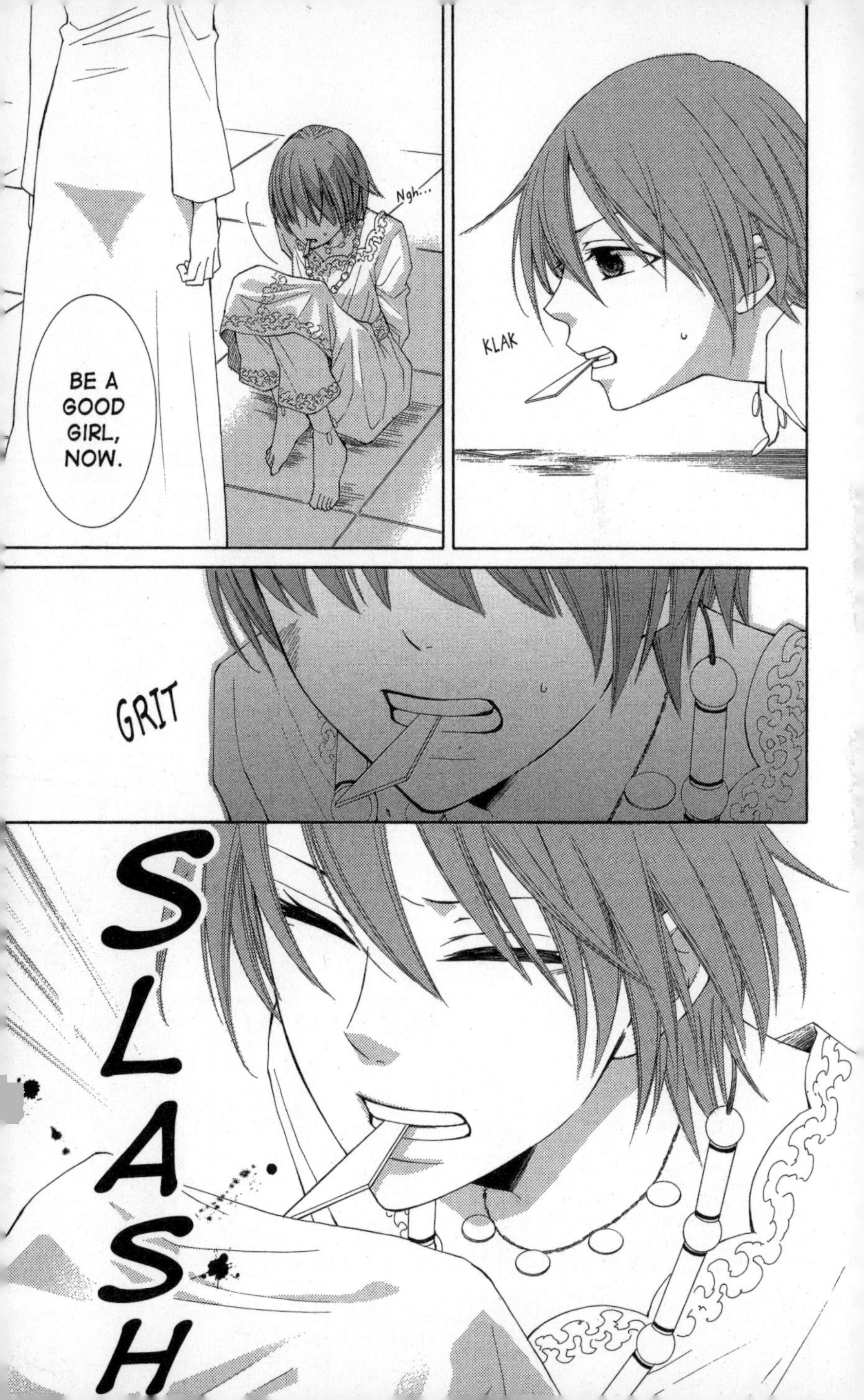
KLAK
Ngh...
BE A GOOD GIRL, NOW.
GRIT
SLASH

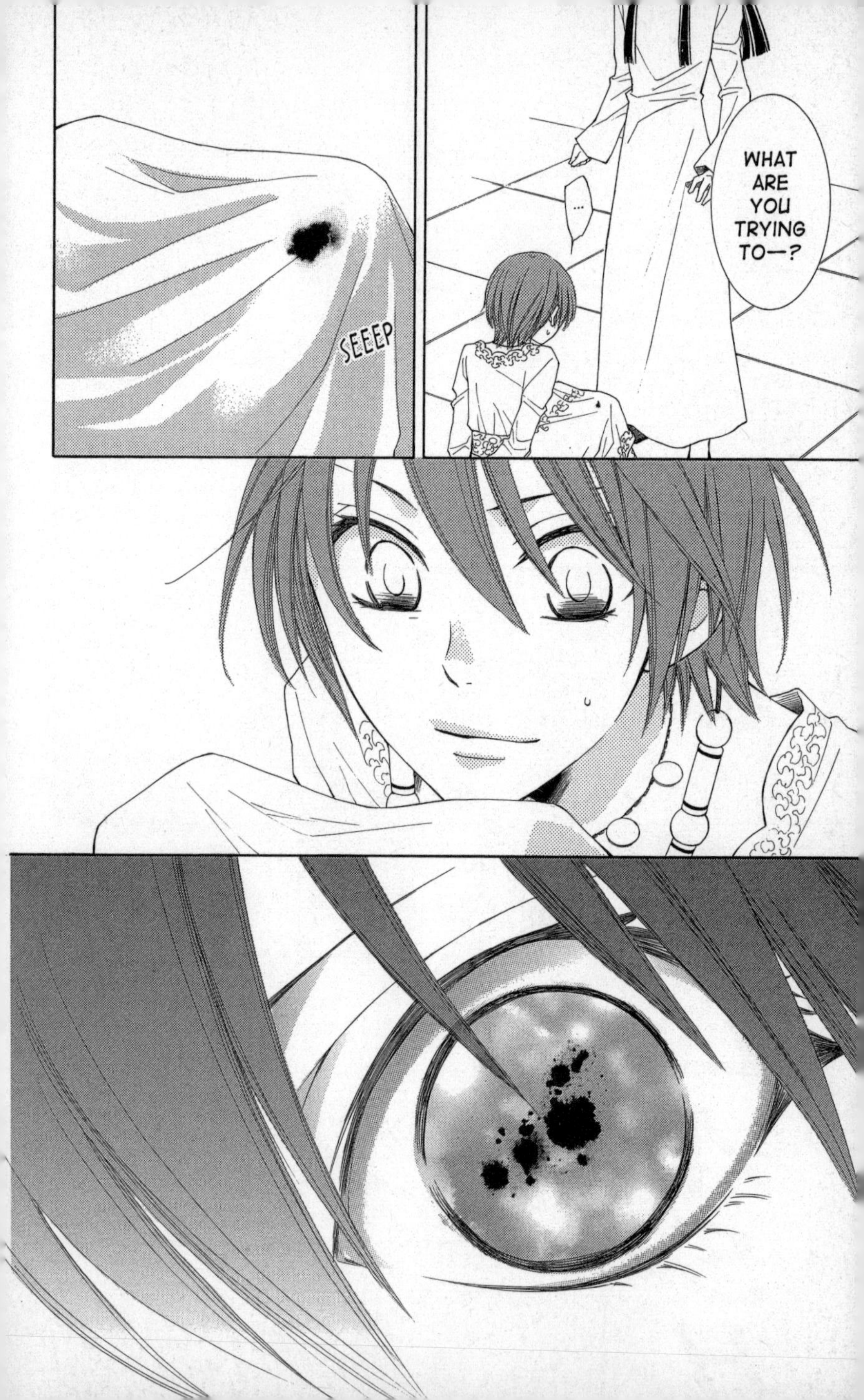
WHAT ARE YOU TRYING TO—?
...
SEEEP

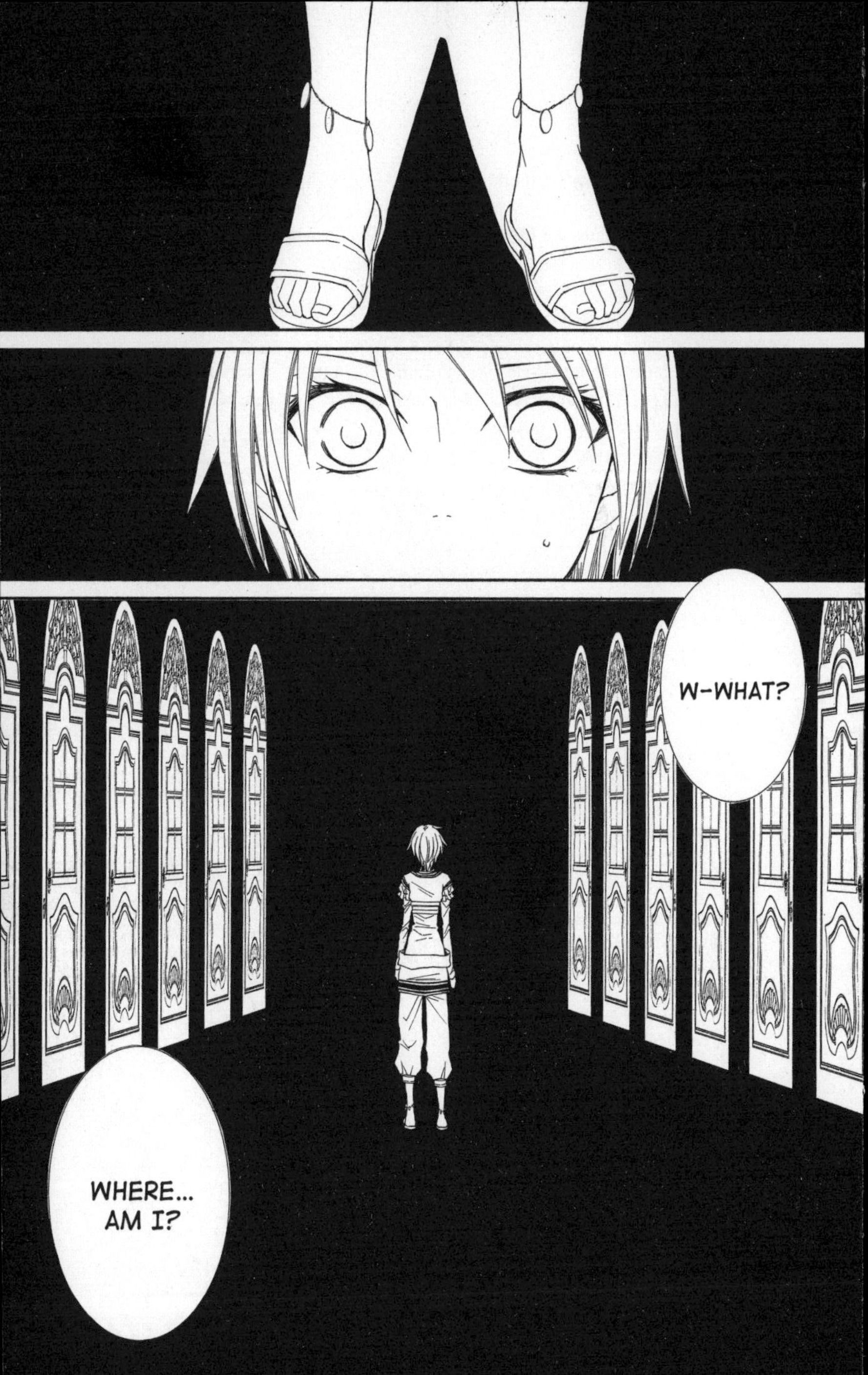
W-WHAT?
WHERE... AM I?

Mio Nanao Sensei, whose work is currently gracing the pages of
Cheese, came to help me with my manuscript. (I guess it's more
accurate to say I made her help.) Look what she drew for me!
Loki is so cool! Nanao-san draws the most gorgeous
black-haired boys. (*Pant pant*)
Rito looks just like an angel.
At first she forgot the tattoo under Loki's left eye. So even though
I'd done the same thing myself (see volume 3), I ignored that minor
detail and made a big deal of it. "Ha ha! You did it! You missed it!
You missed the tattoo!" I got her to draw it in.
Anyway, thank you so much,
Nanao-san! I'm thrilled!

リト & ロキ
Rito & Loki

I'm sorry that it doesn't
look like them. ♪

ナナオ☆
Nanao

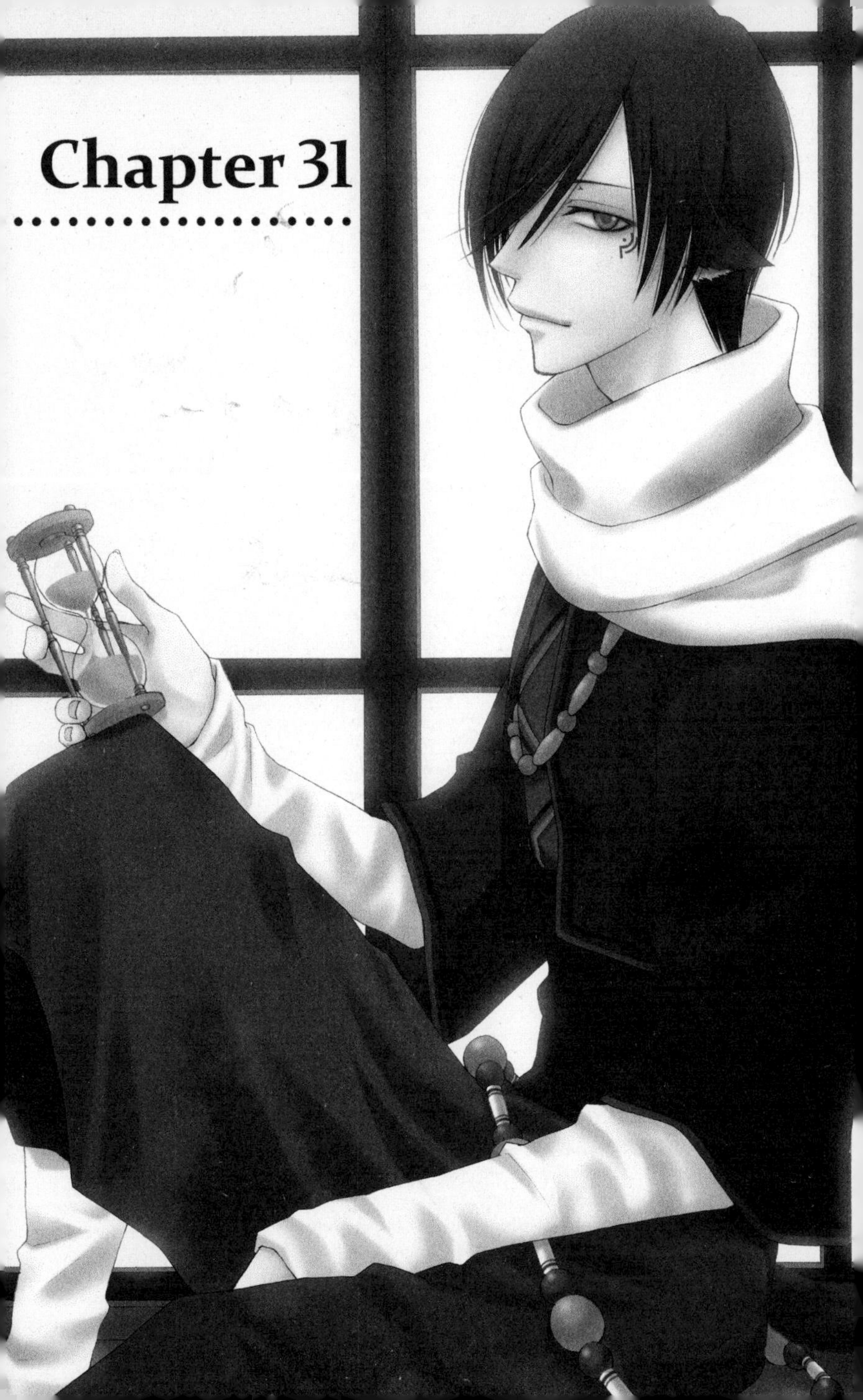
Chapter 31

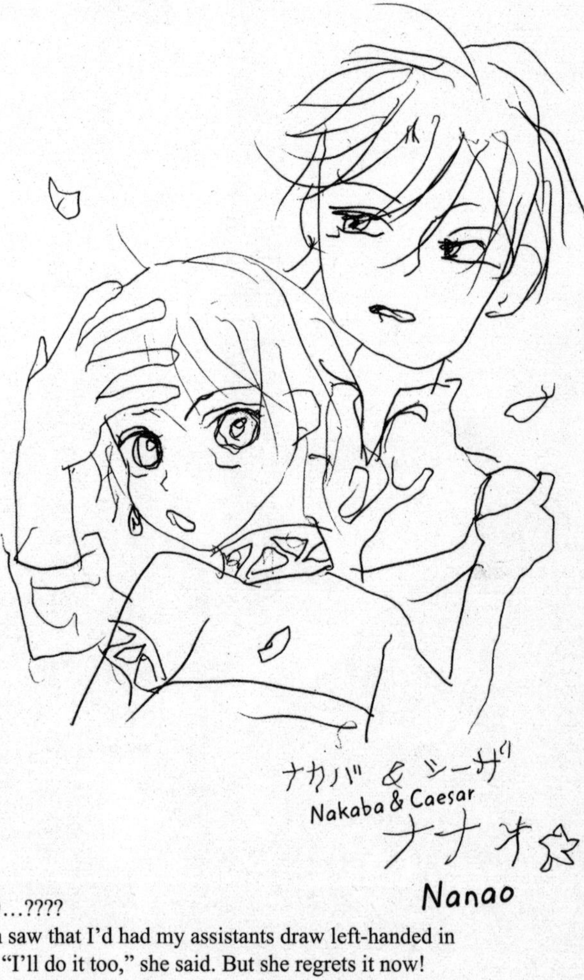
ナカバ & シーザ
Nakaba & Caesar
ナナオ
Nanao

(ˆωˆ)…????
Nanao-san saw that I'd had my assistants draw left-handed in volume 7. "I'll do it too," she said. But she regrets it now!
That's…pretty hideous, huh?
Before trying it she was looking at volume 7 and saying, "Oh, they're all awful! (*Laugh*) It's so funny!"
But all that innocent disdain led to…this.
"I get it now. Drawing left-handed sure is tough…"
I know, right?! (*Ha ha ha.*)

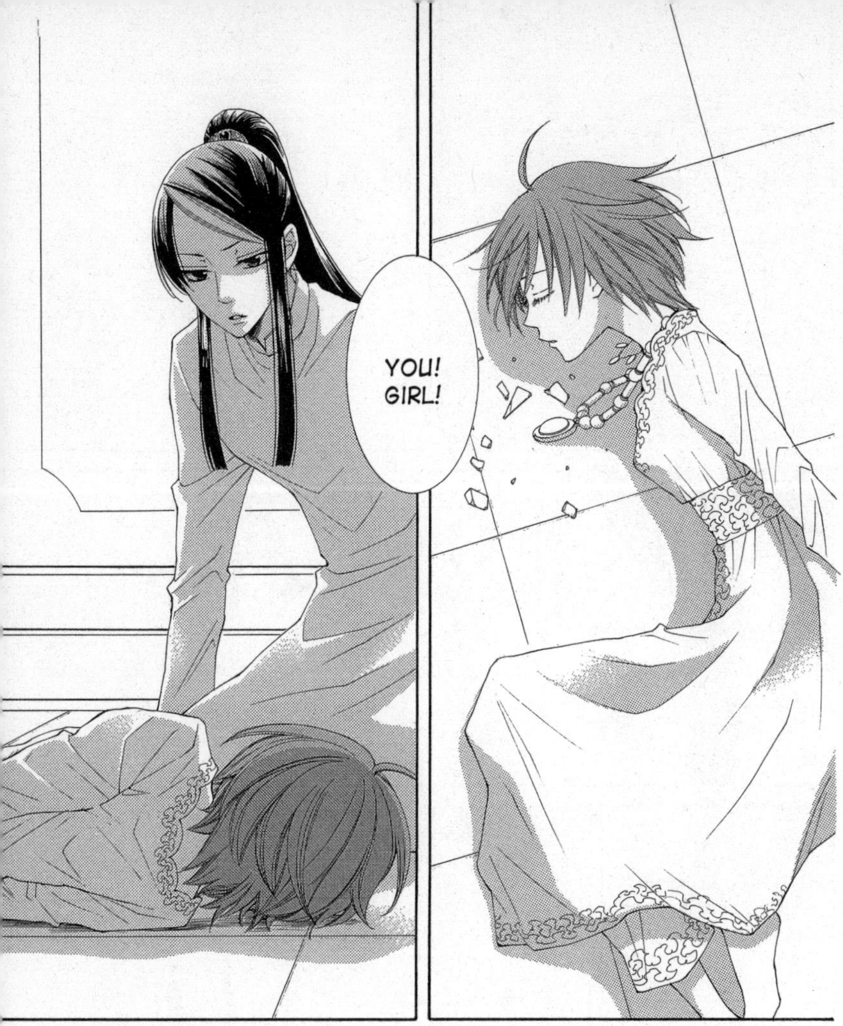
YOU! GIRL!

Dawn of the Arcana

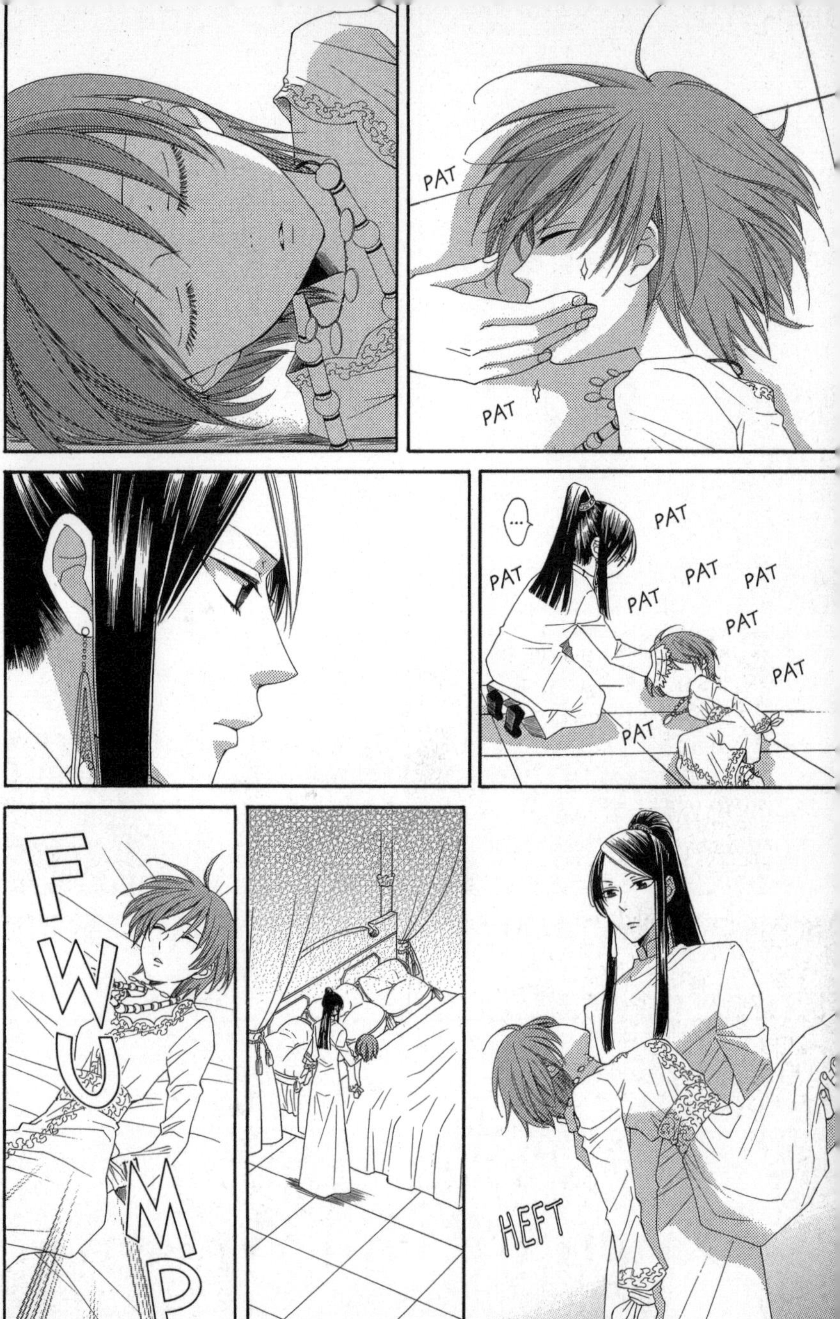
PAT
PAT
...
PAT
PAT
PAT
PAT
PAT
PAT
PAT
PAT
HEFT
FWUMP

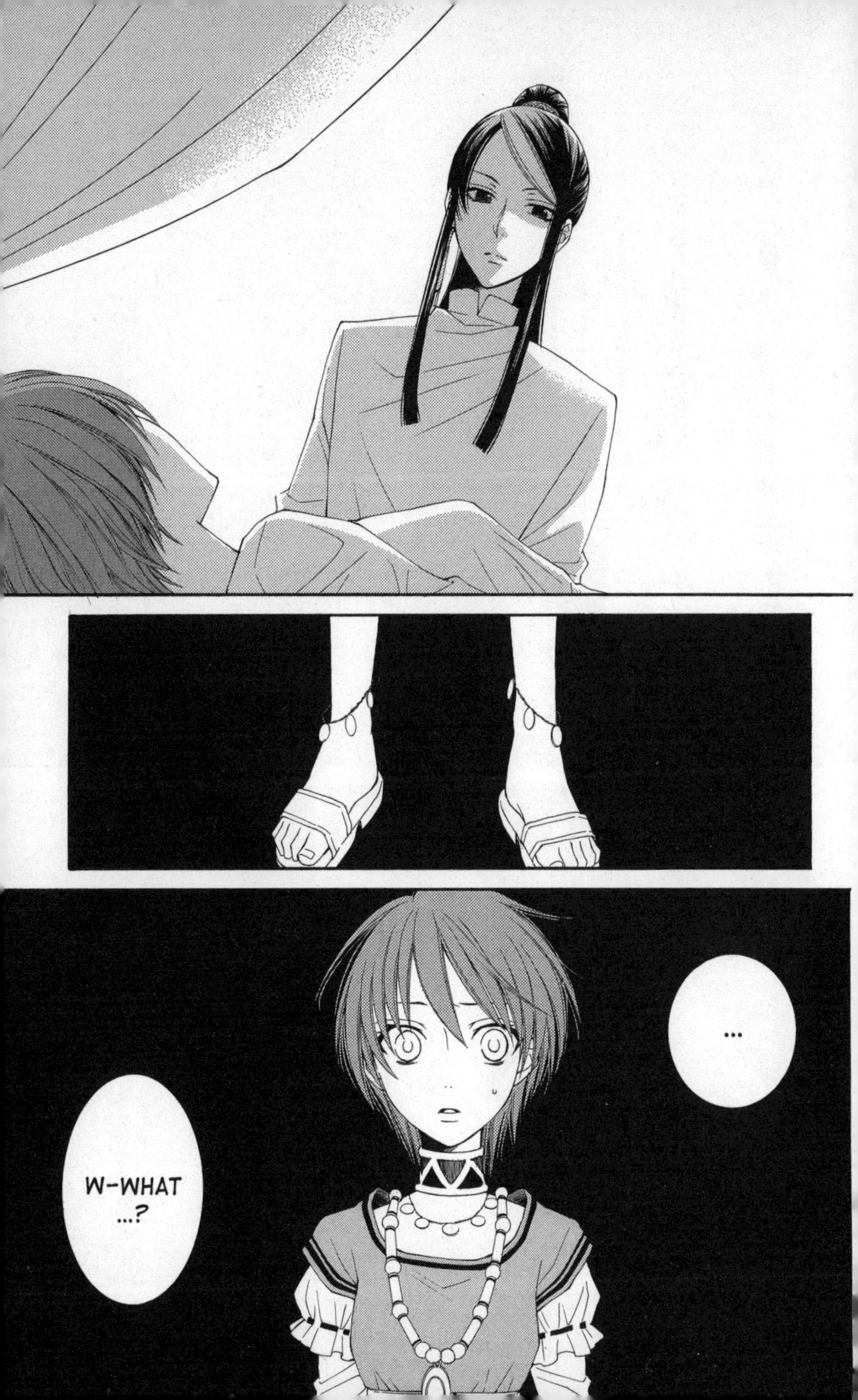
...
W-WHAT ...?

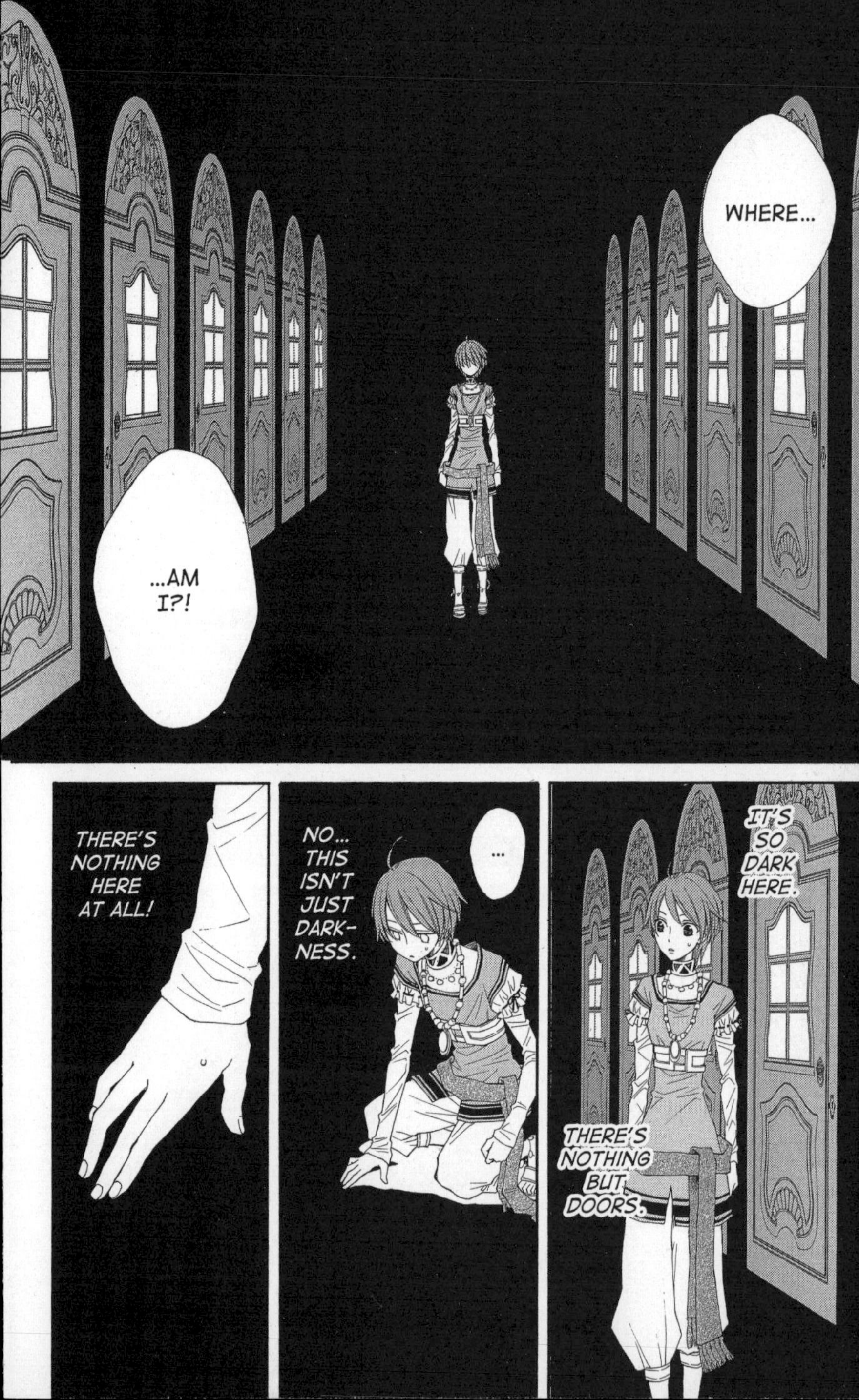
WHERE...
...AM I?!
IT'S SO DARK HERE.
THERE'S NOTHING BUT DOORS.
...
NO... THIS ISN'T JUST DARKNESS.
THERE'S NOTHING HERE AT ALL!

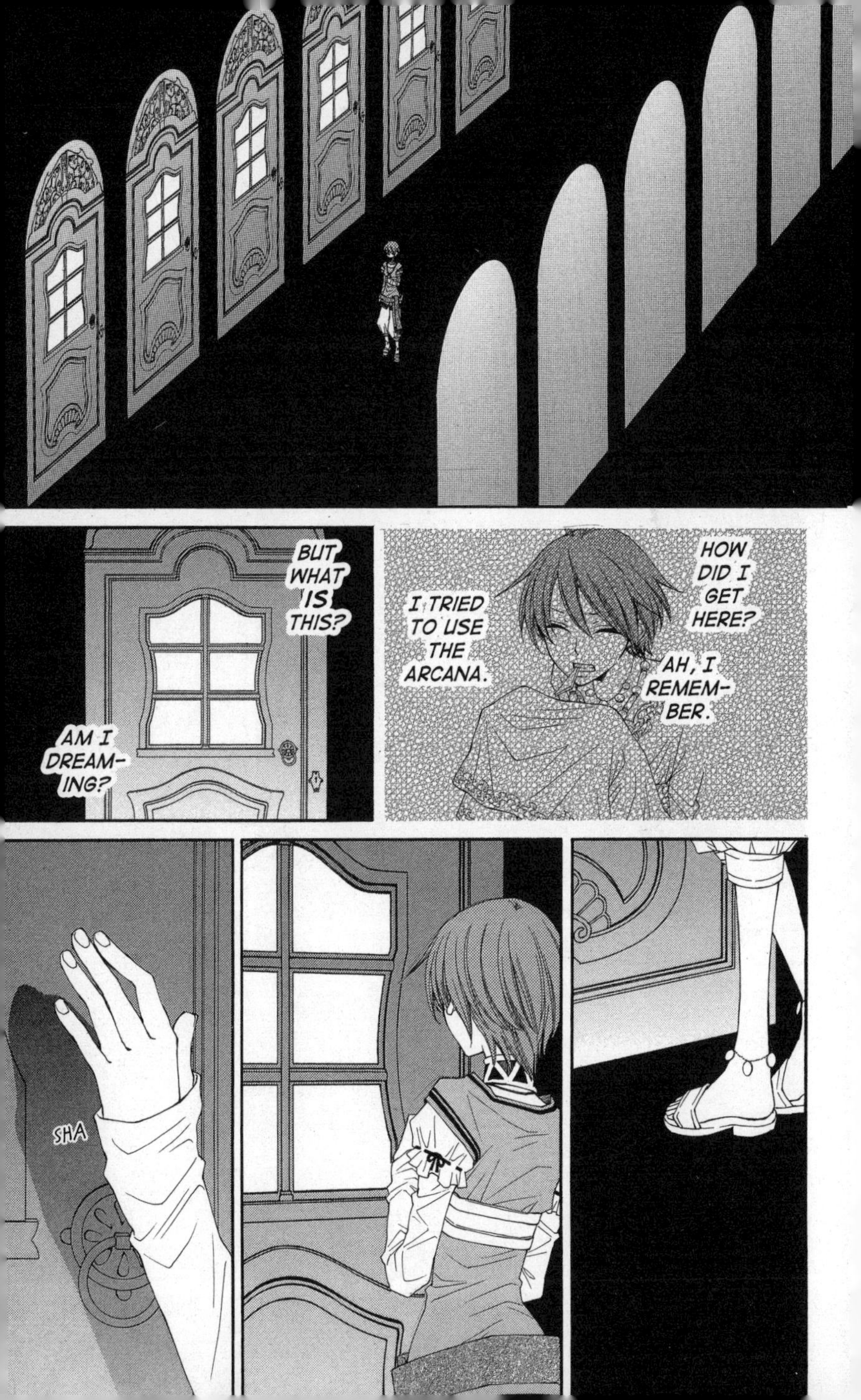
HOW DID I GET HERE?
AH, I REMEMBER.
I TRIED TO USE THE ARCANA.
BUT WHAT IS THIS?
AM I DREAMING?
SHA

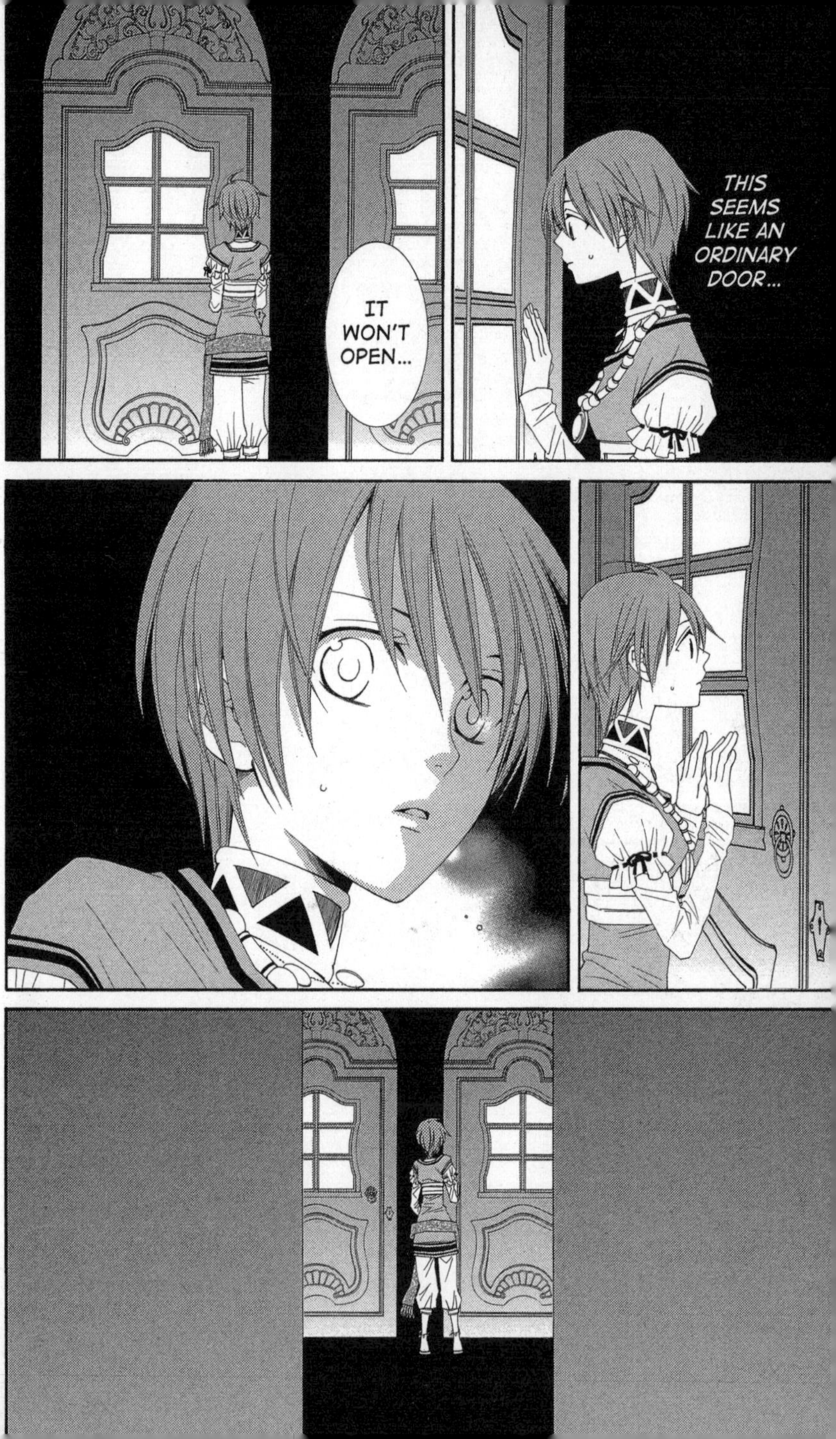
THIS SEEMS LIKE AN ORDINARY DOOR...
IT WON'T OPEN...

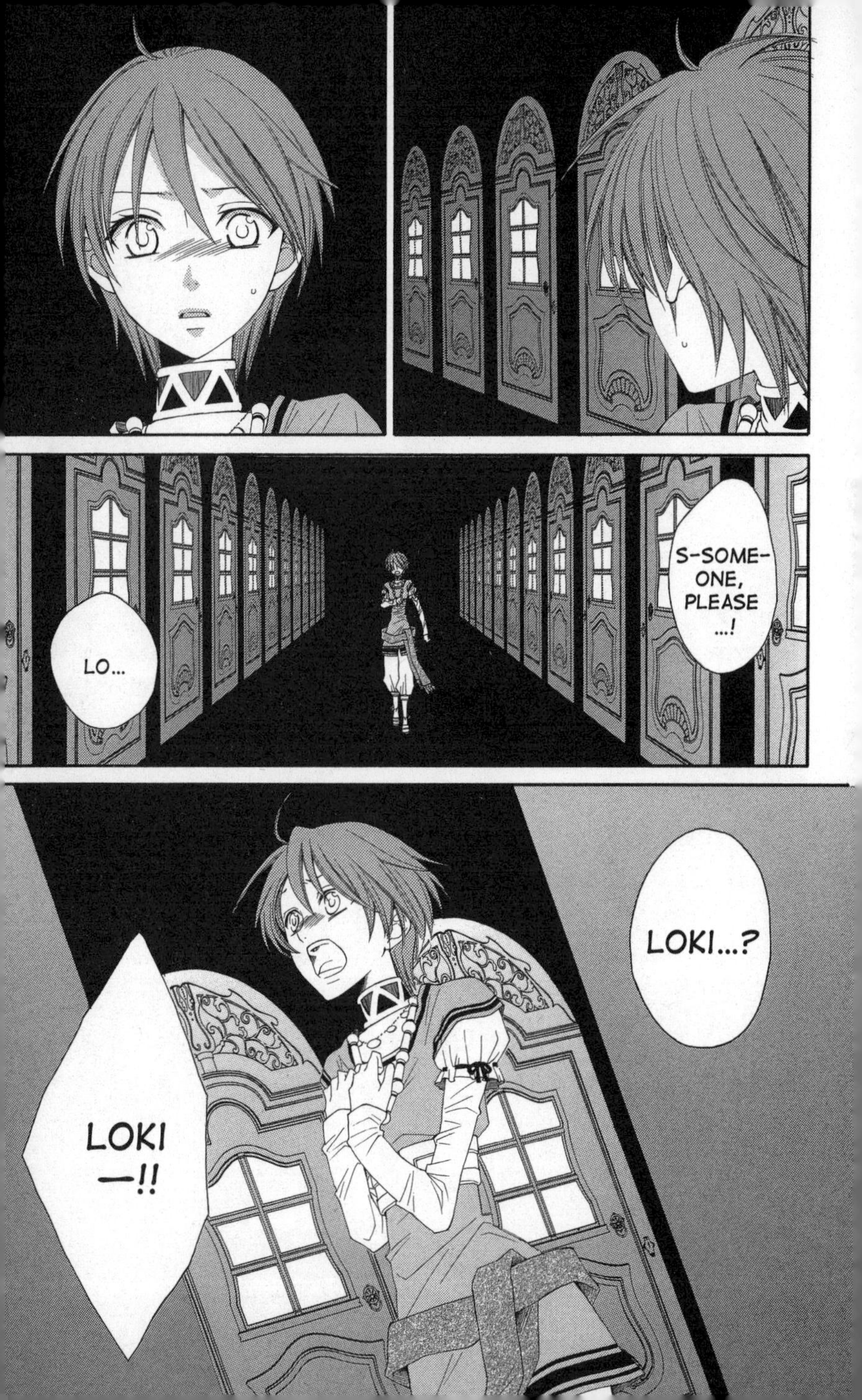
S-SOME-ONE, PLEASE ...!
LO...
LOKI...?
LOKI —!!

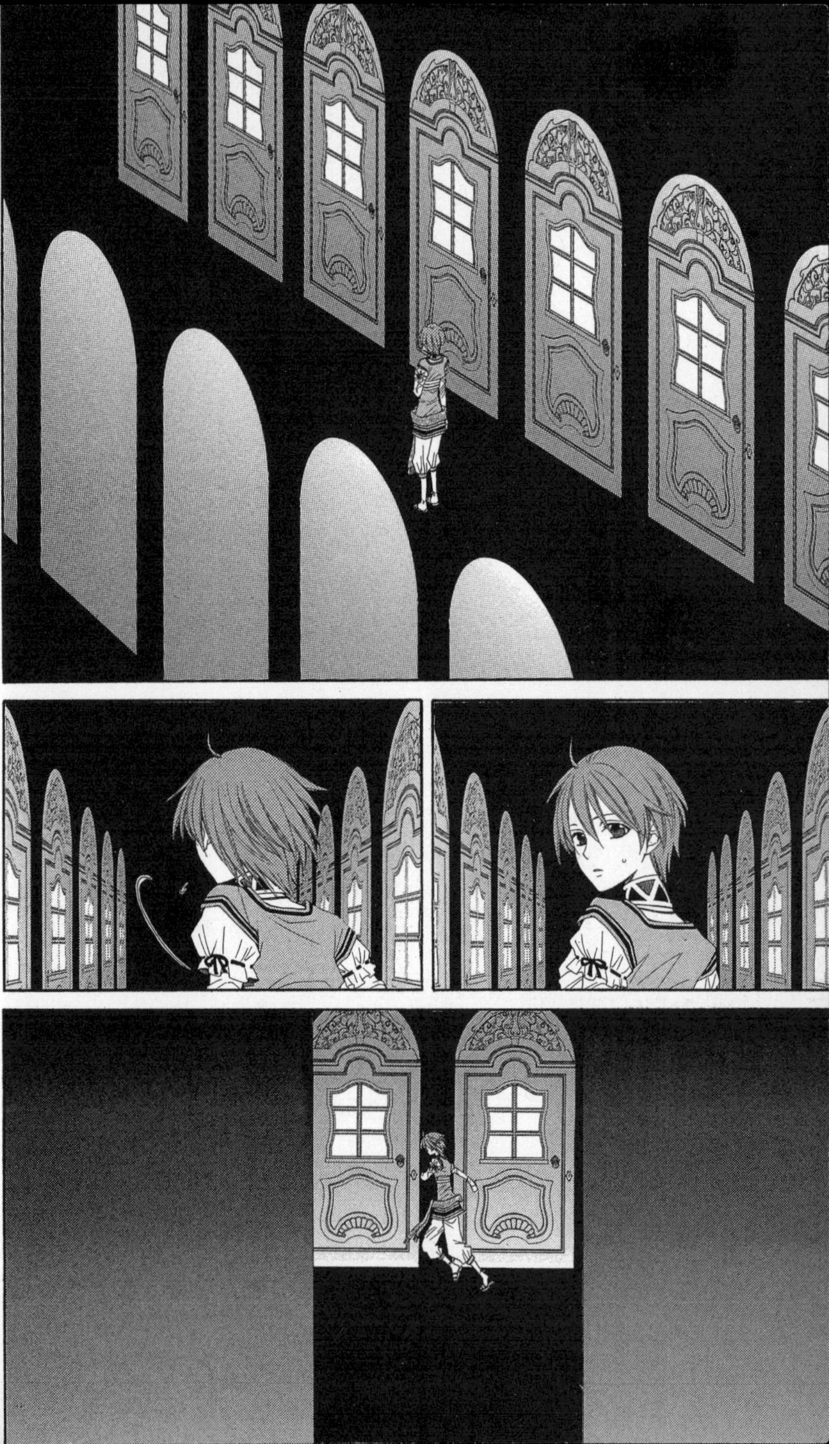

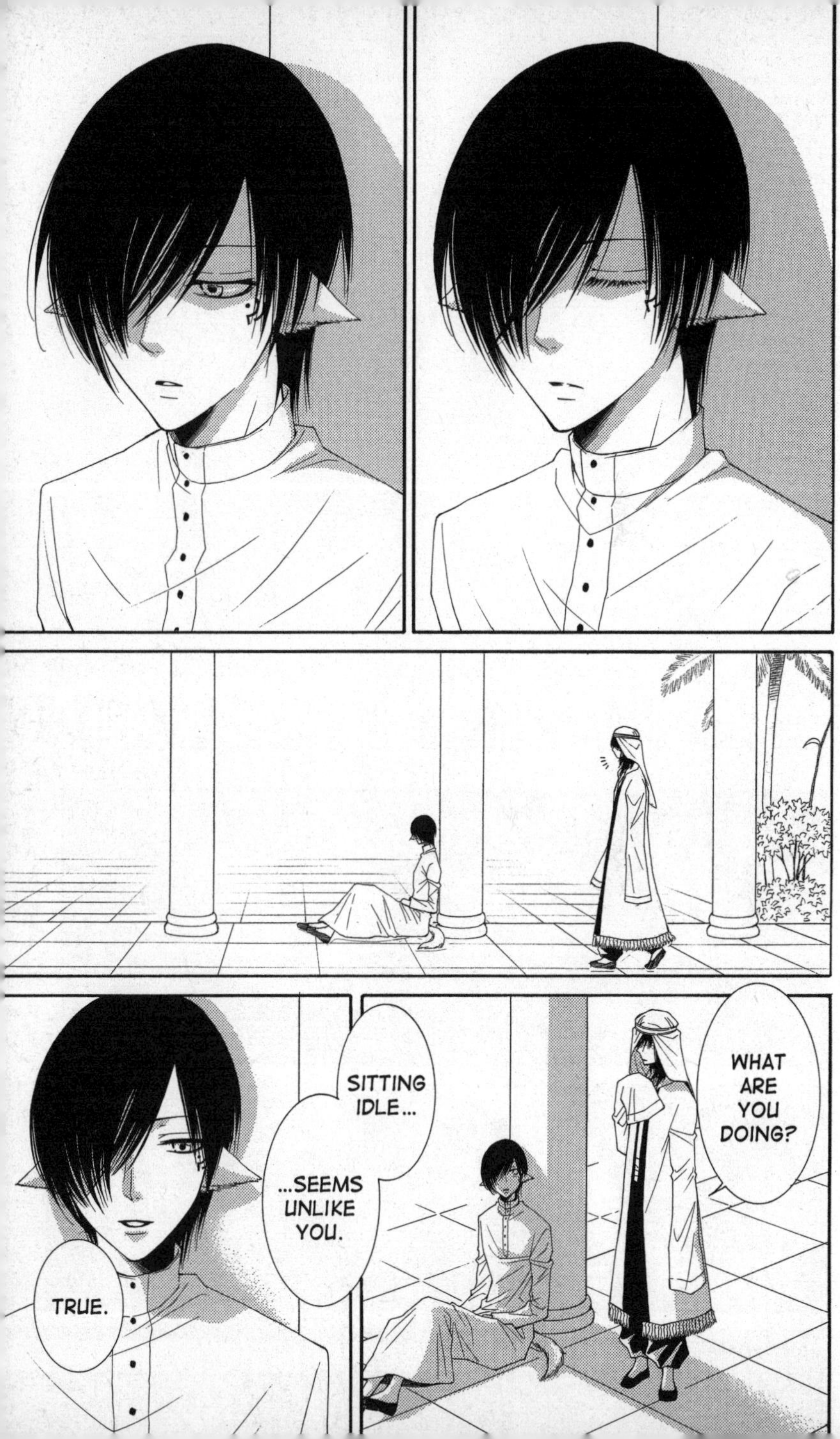
WHAT ARE YOU DOING?
SITTING IDLE...
...SEEMS UNLIKE YOU.
TRUE.

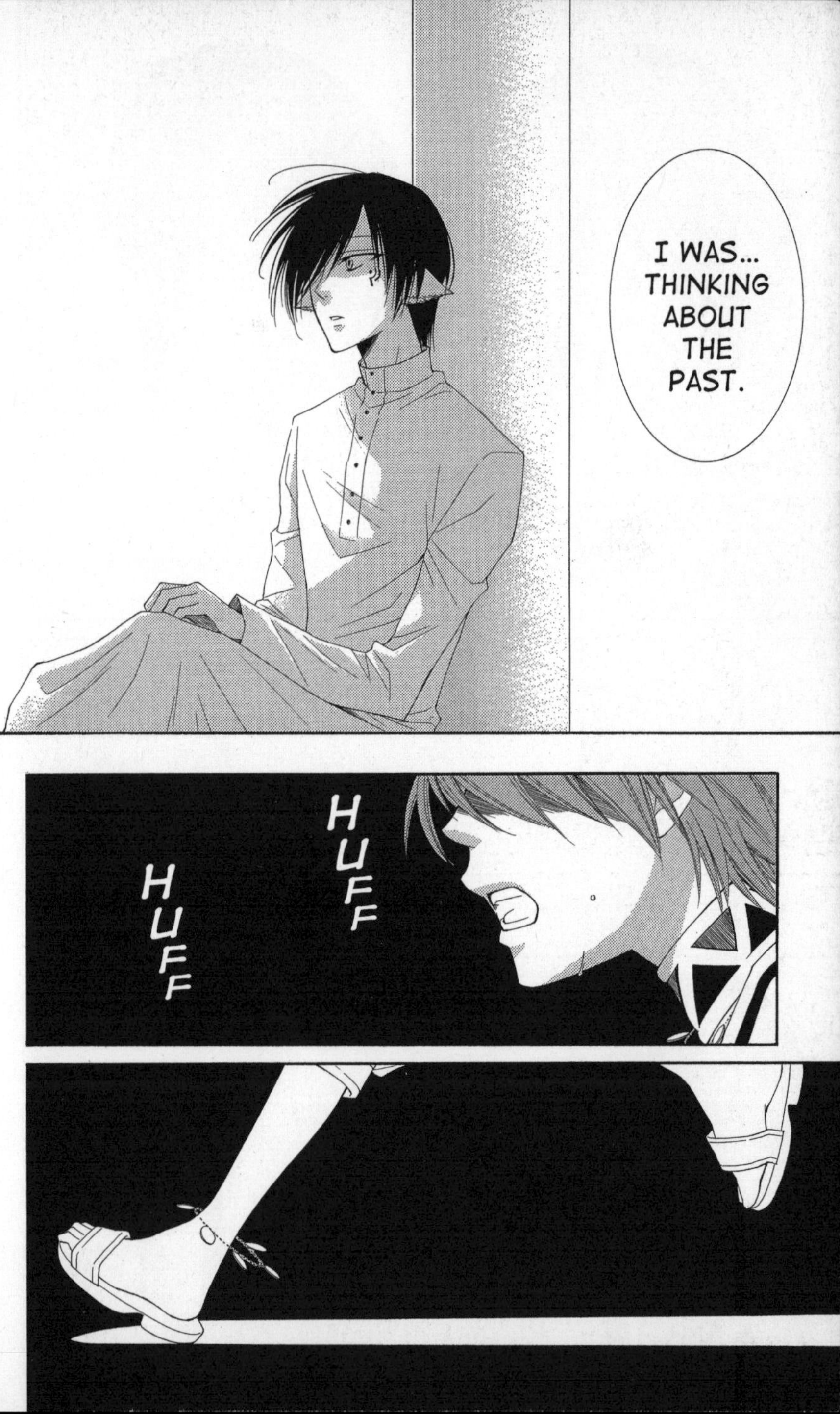
I WAS... THINKING ABOUT THE PAST.
HUFF
HUFF

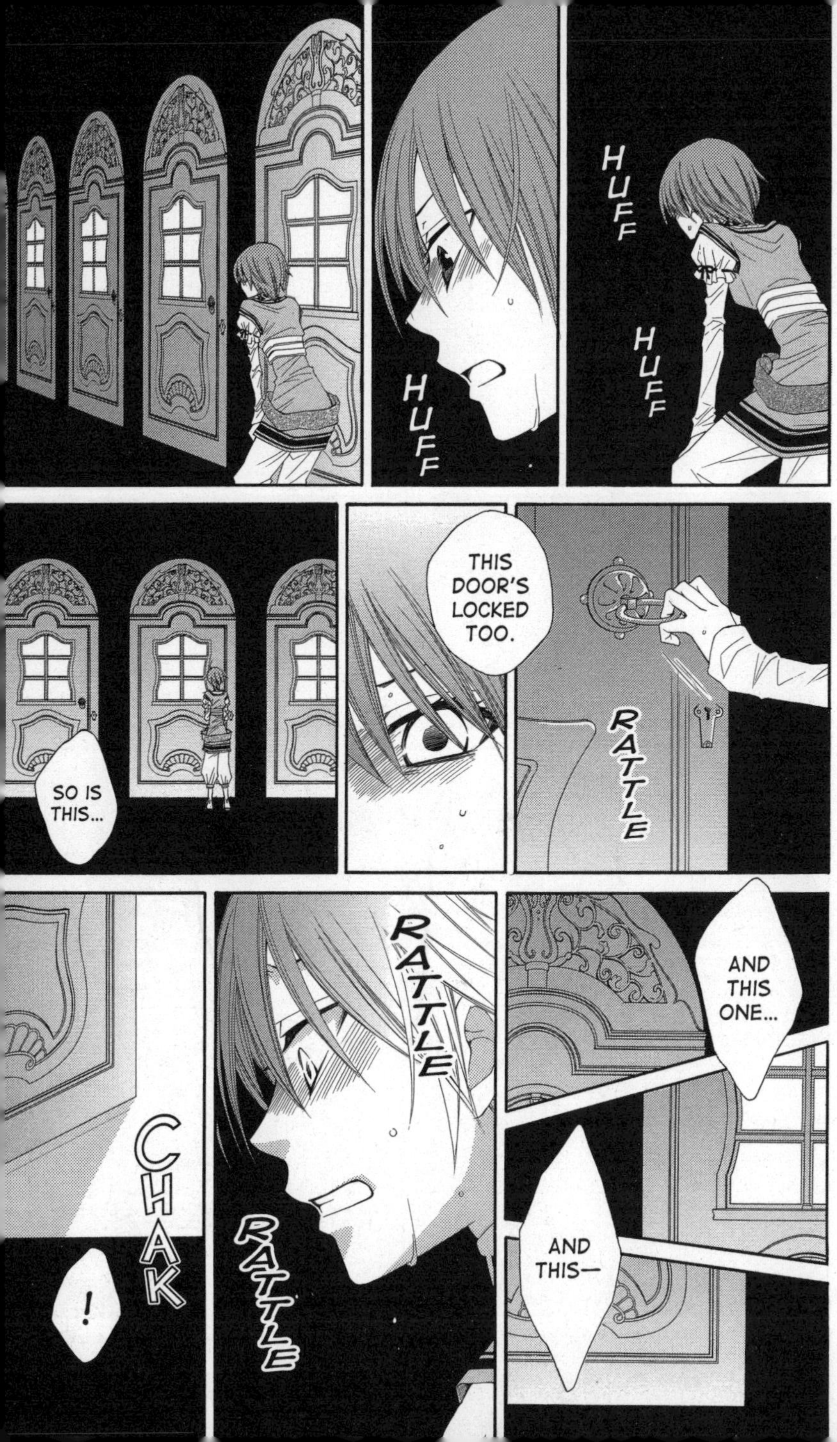
HUFF
HUFF
HUFF
RATTLE
THIS DOOR'S LOCKED TOO.
SO IS THIS...
AND THIS ONE...
AND THIS—
RATTLE
RATTLE
CHAK
!

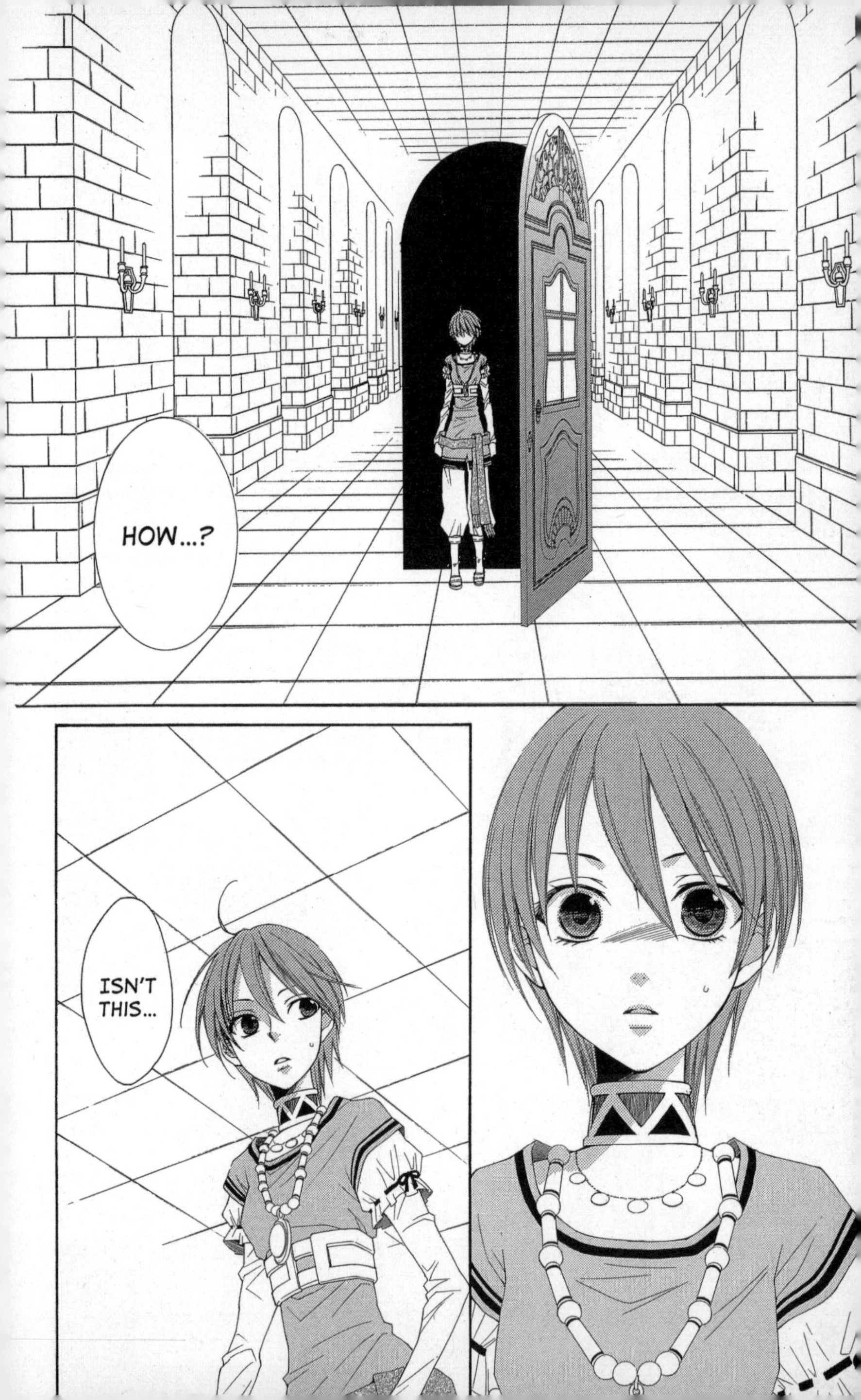
HOW...?
ISN'T THIS...

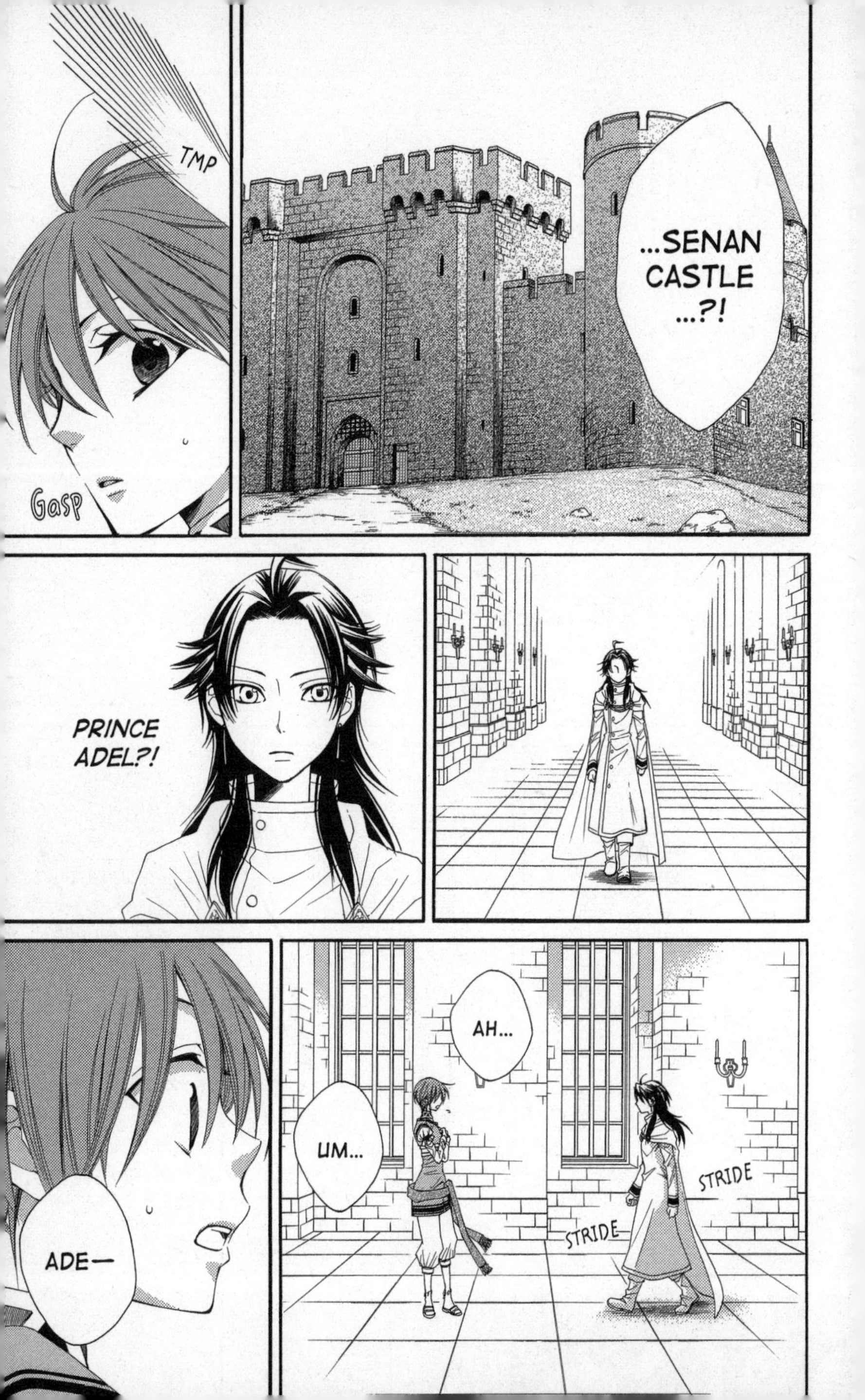
...SENAN CASTLE ...?!
TMP
Gasp
PRINCE ADEL?!
AH...
UM...
STRIDE
STRIDE
ADE—

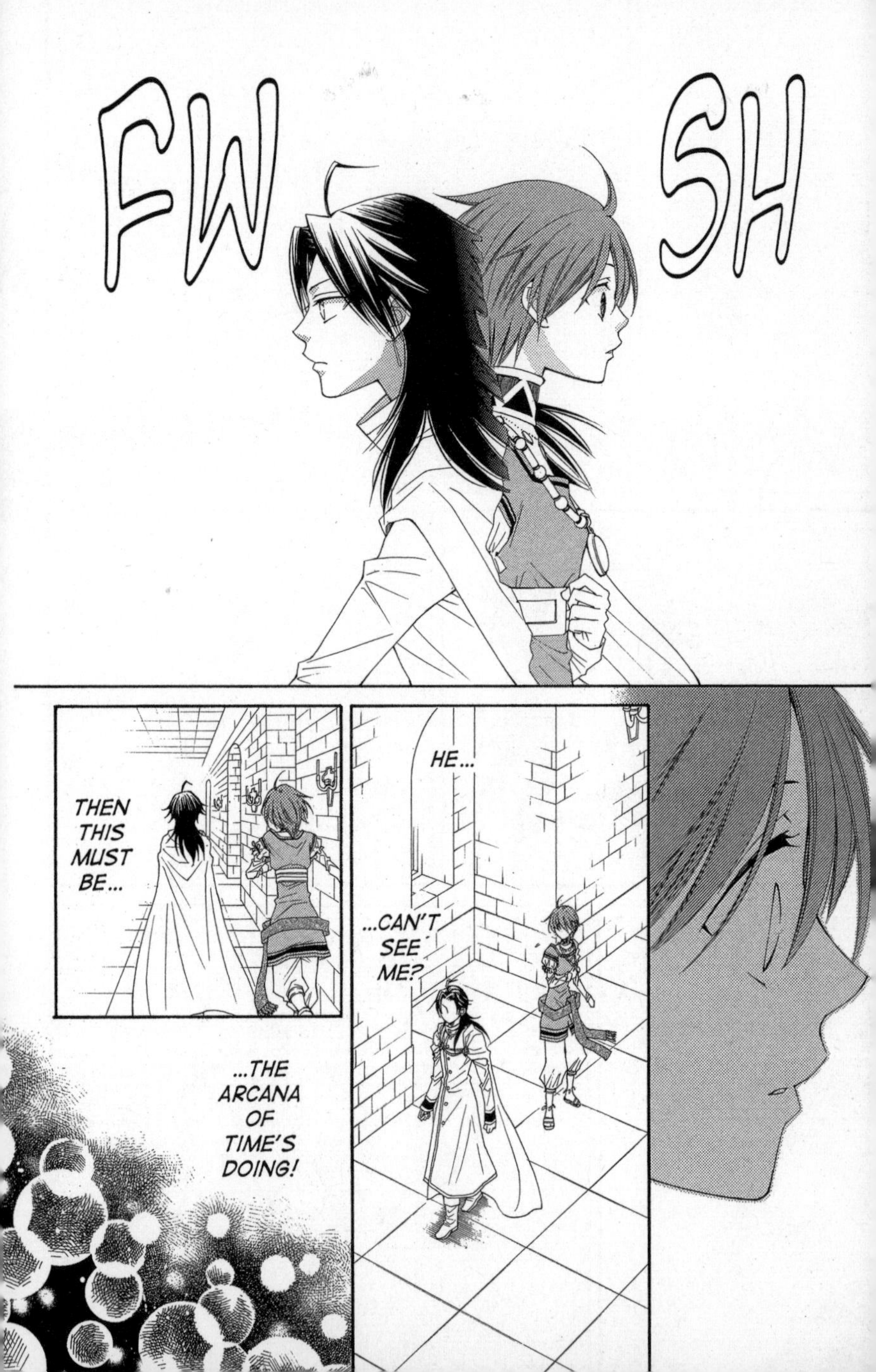
FWSH
HE...
...CAN'T SEE ME?
THEN THIS MUST BE...
...THE ARCANA OF TIME'S DOING!

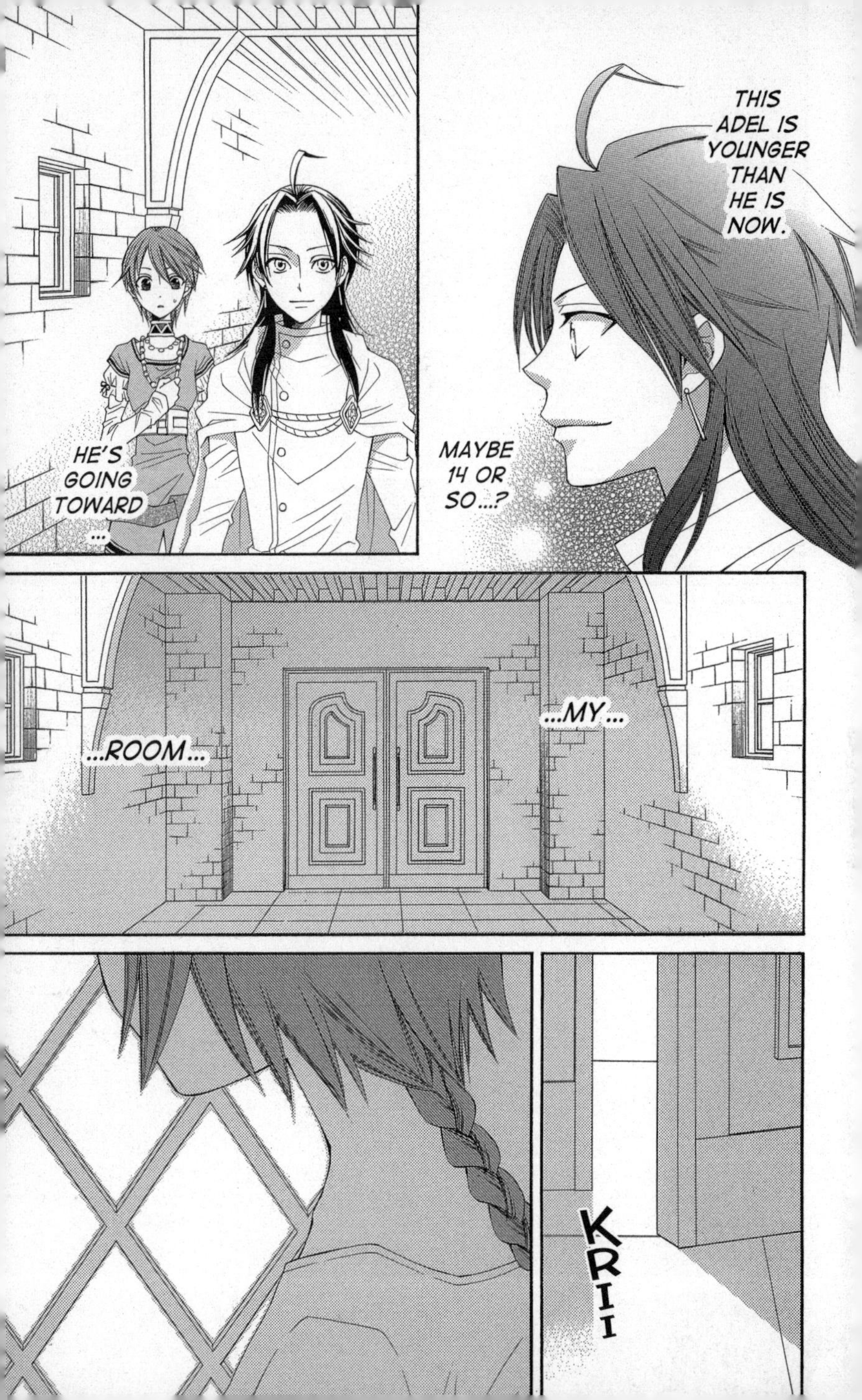
THIS ADEL IS YOUNGER THAN HE IS NOW.
MAYBE 14 OR SO...?
HE'S GOING TOWARD ...
...MY...
...ROOM...
KRII

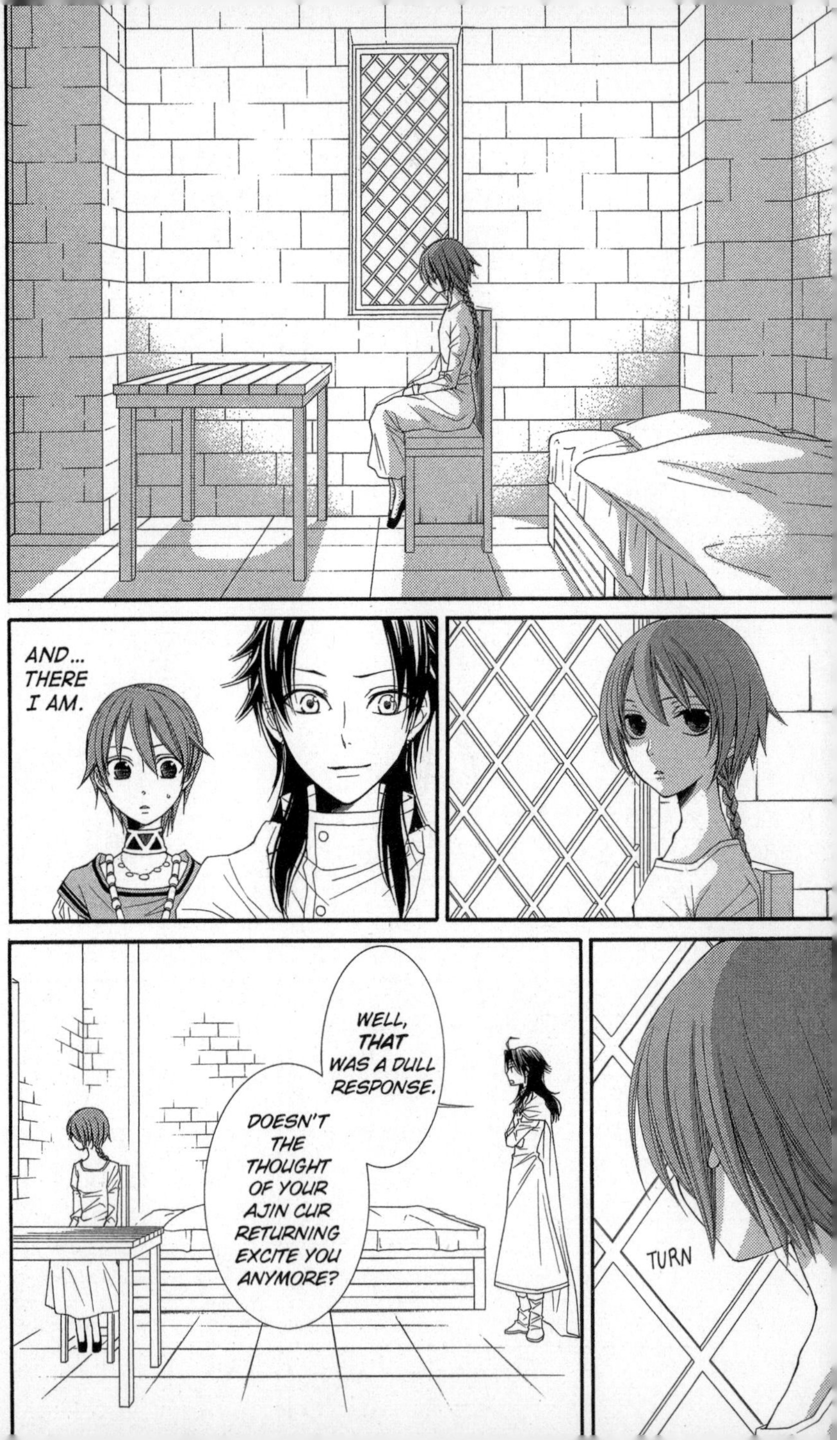
AND... THERE I AM.
WELL, THAT WAS A DULL RESPONSE.
DOESN'T THE THOUGHT OF YOUR AJIN CUR RETURNING EXCITE YOU ANYMORE?
TURN

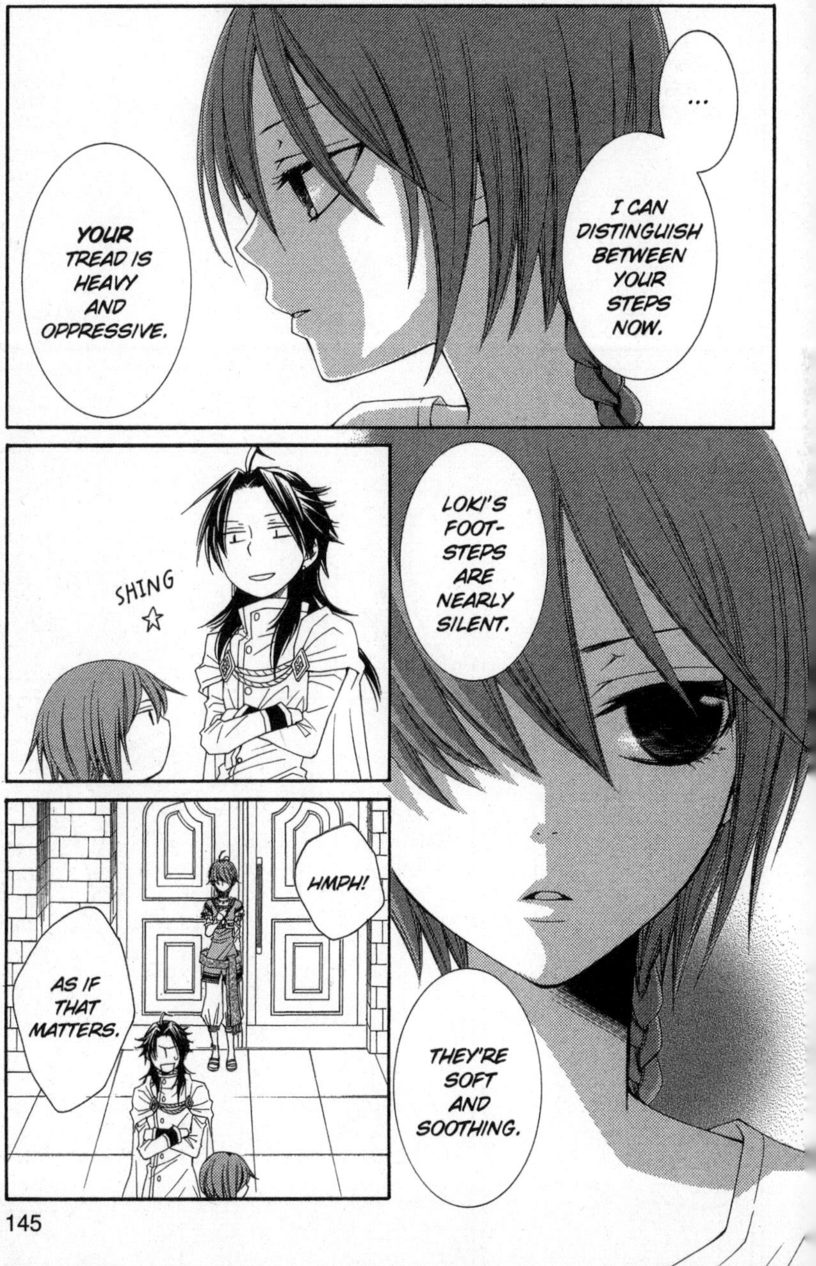
...
I CAN DISTINGUISH BETWEEN YOUR STEPS NOW.
YOUR TREAD IS HEAVY AND OPPRESSIVE.
LOKI'S FOOT-STEPS ARE NEARLY SILENT.
SHING ☆
THEY'RE SOFT AND SOOTHING.
HMPH!
AS IF THAT MATTERS.

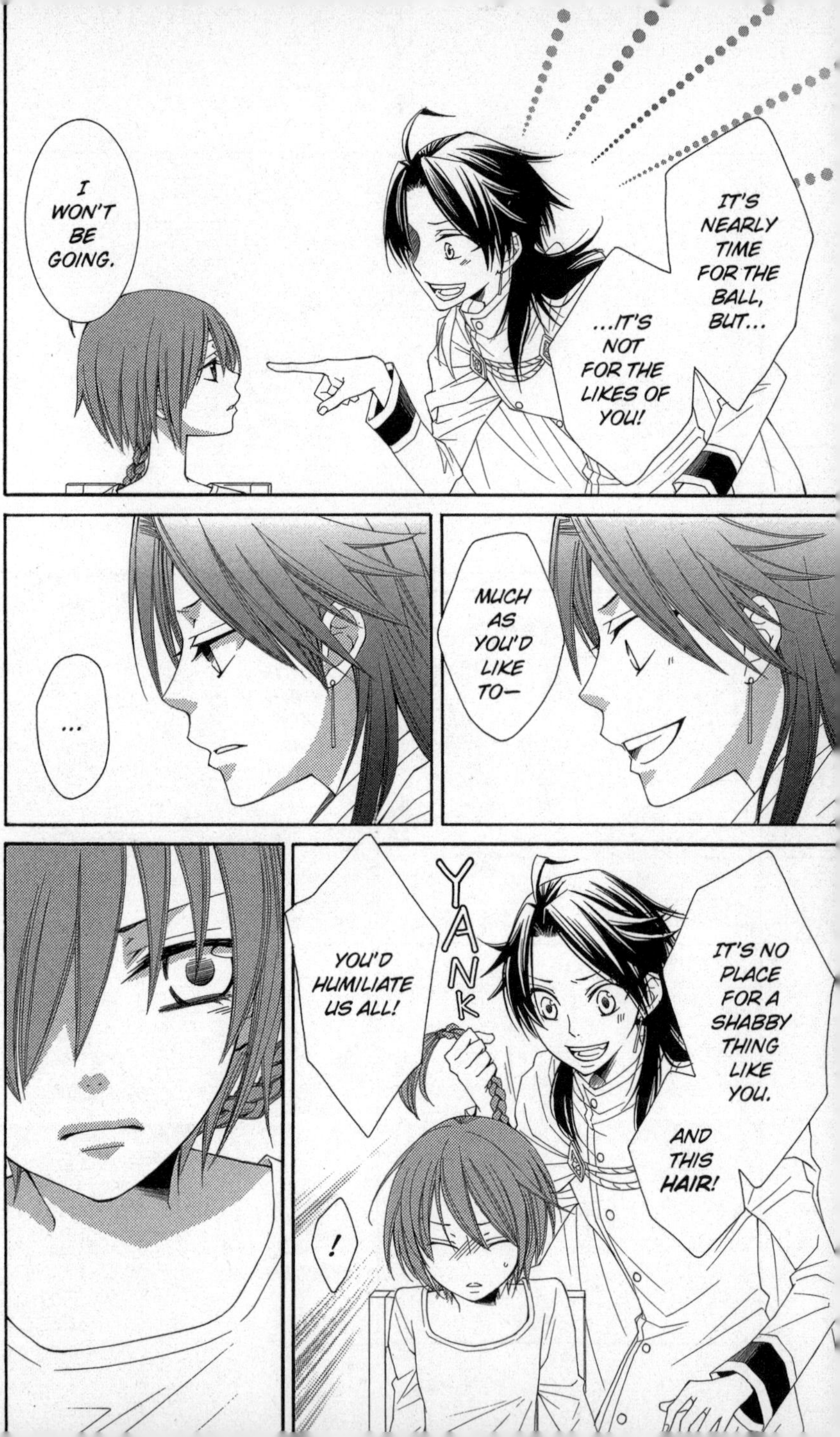
IT'S NEARLY TIME FOR THE BALL, BUT...
...IT'S NOT FOR THE LIKES OF YOU!
I WON'T BE GOING.
MUCH AS YOU'D LIKE TO—
...
IT'S NO PLACE FOR A SHABBY THING LIKE YOU.
AND THIS HAIR!
YANK
YOU'D HUMILIATE US ALL!
!

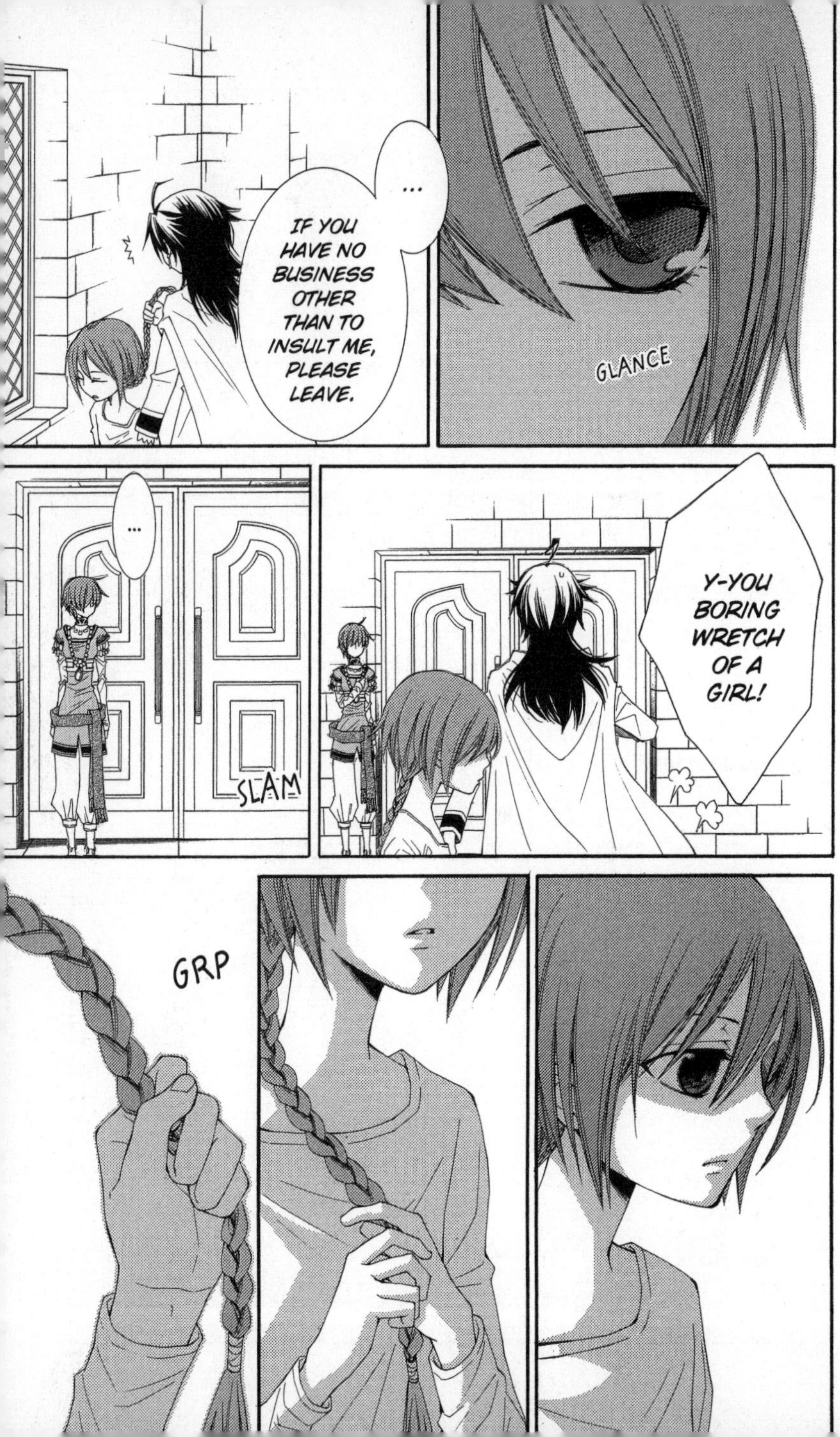
GLANCE
...
IF YOU HAVE NO BUSINESS OTHER THAN TO INSULT ME, PLEASE LEAVE.
Y-YOU BORING WRETCH OF A GIRL!
...
SLAM
GRP

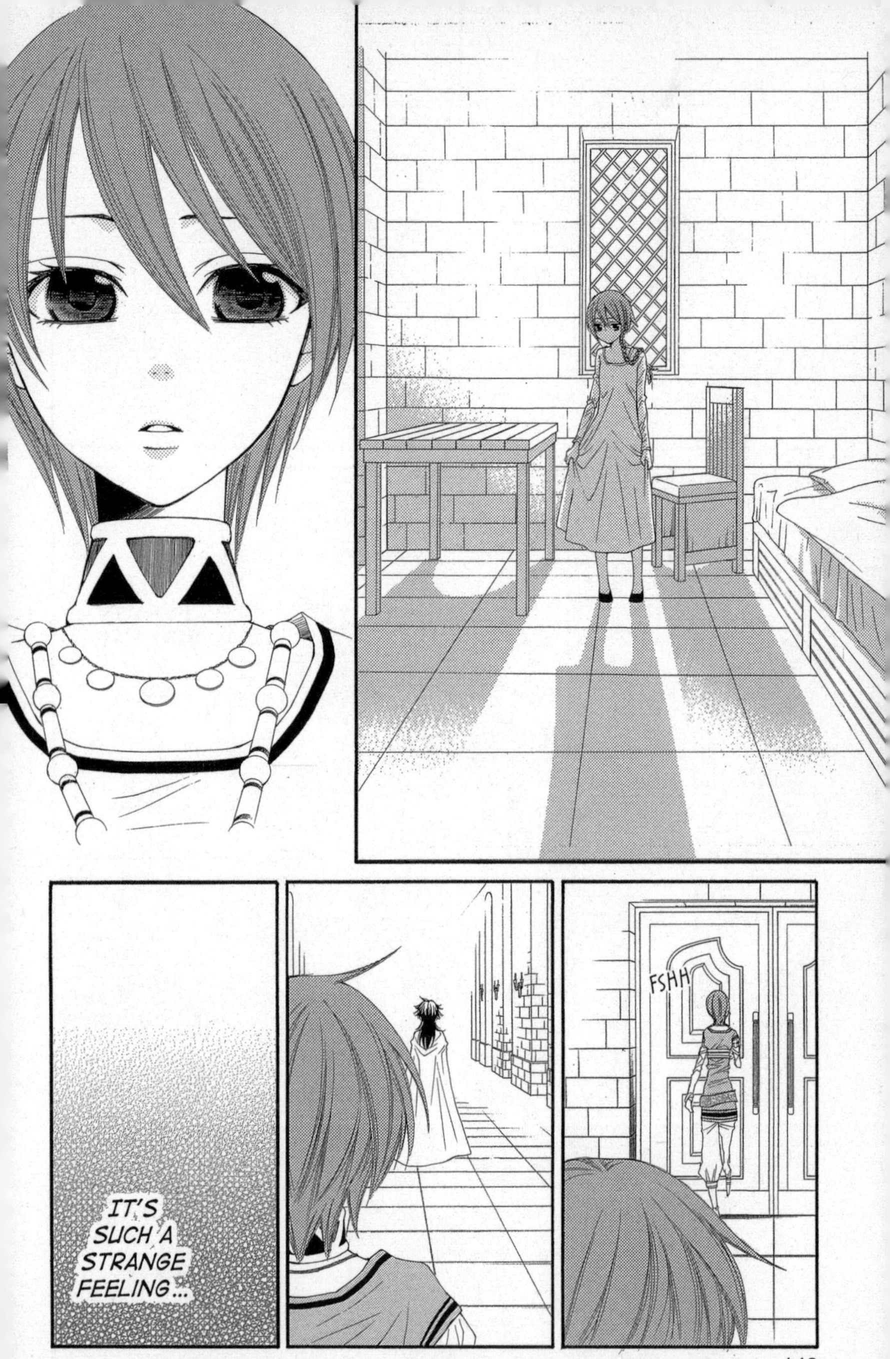
FSHH
IT'S SUCH A STRANGE FEELING...

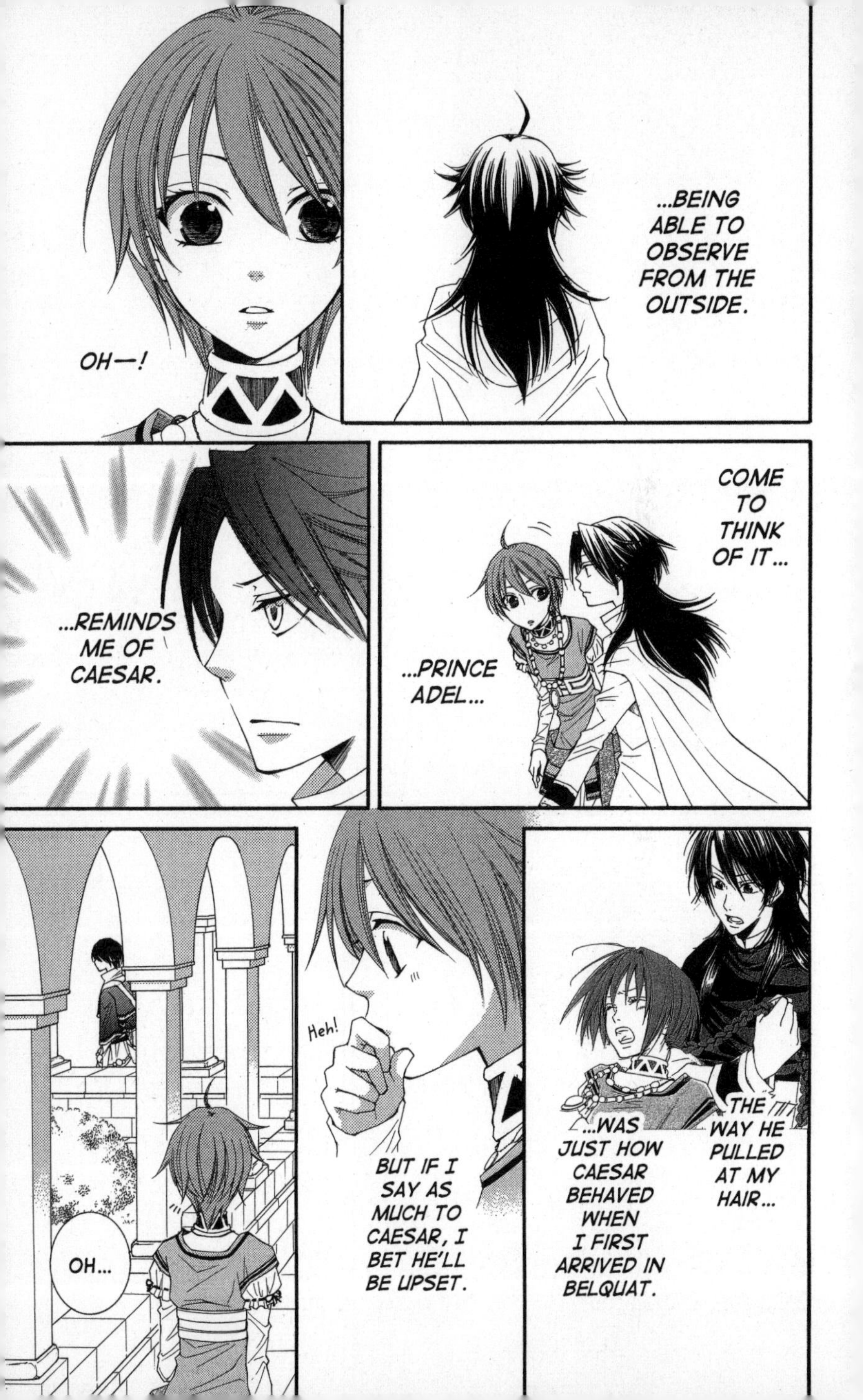
...BEING ABLE TO OBSERVE FROM THE OUTSIDE.
OH—!
COME TO THINK OF IT...
...PRINCE ADEL...
...REMINDS ME OF CAESAR.
THE WAY HE PULLED AT MY HAIR...
...WAS JUST HOW CAESAR BEHAVED WHEN I FIRST ARRIVED IN BELQUAT.
Heh!
BUT IF I SAY AS MUCH TO CAESAR, I BET HE'LL BE UPSET.
OH...

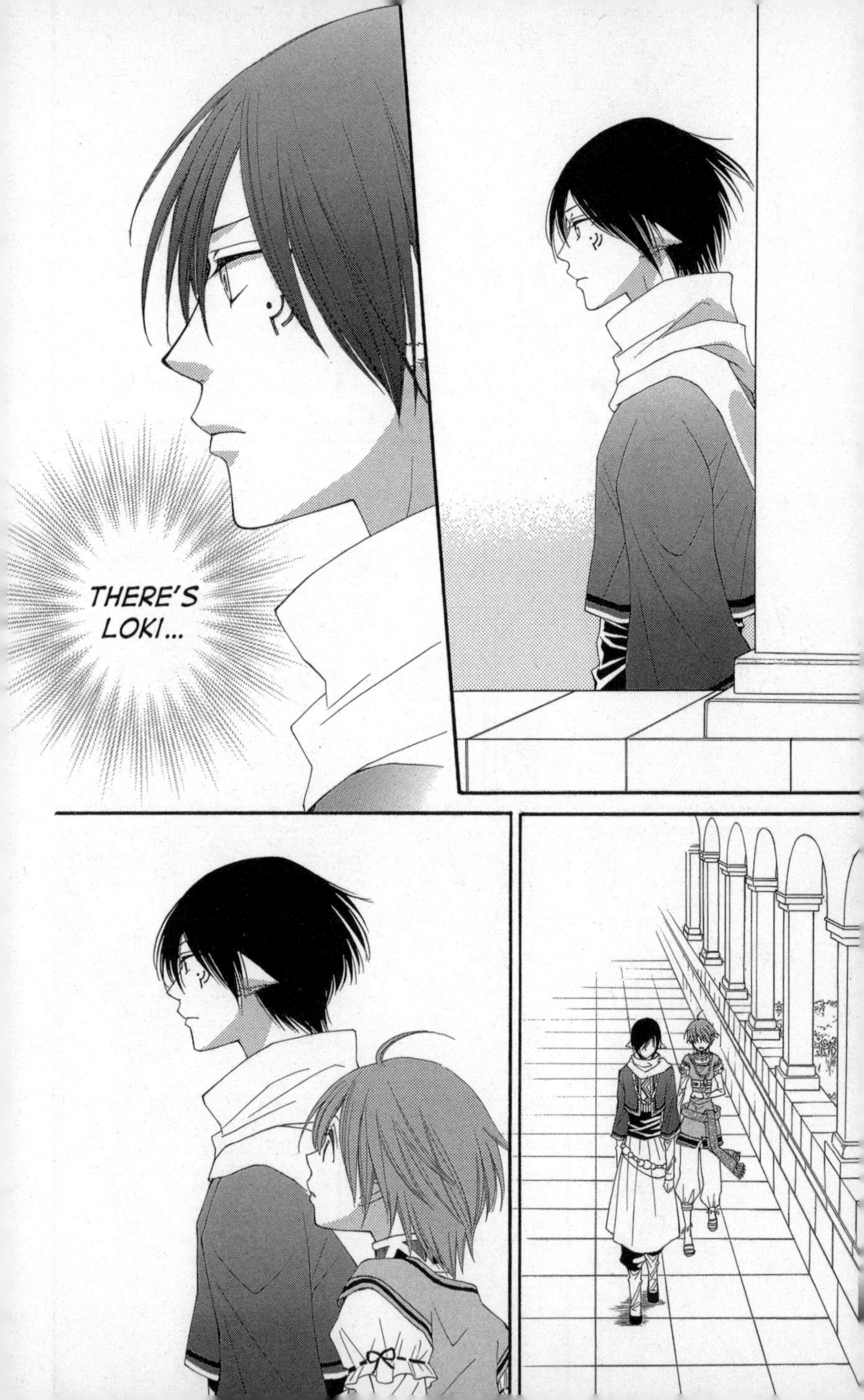
THERE'S LOKI...

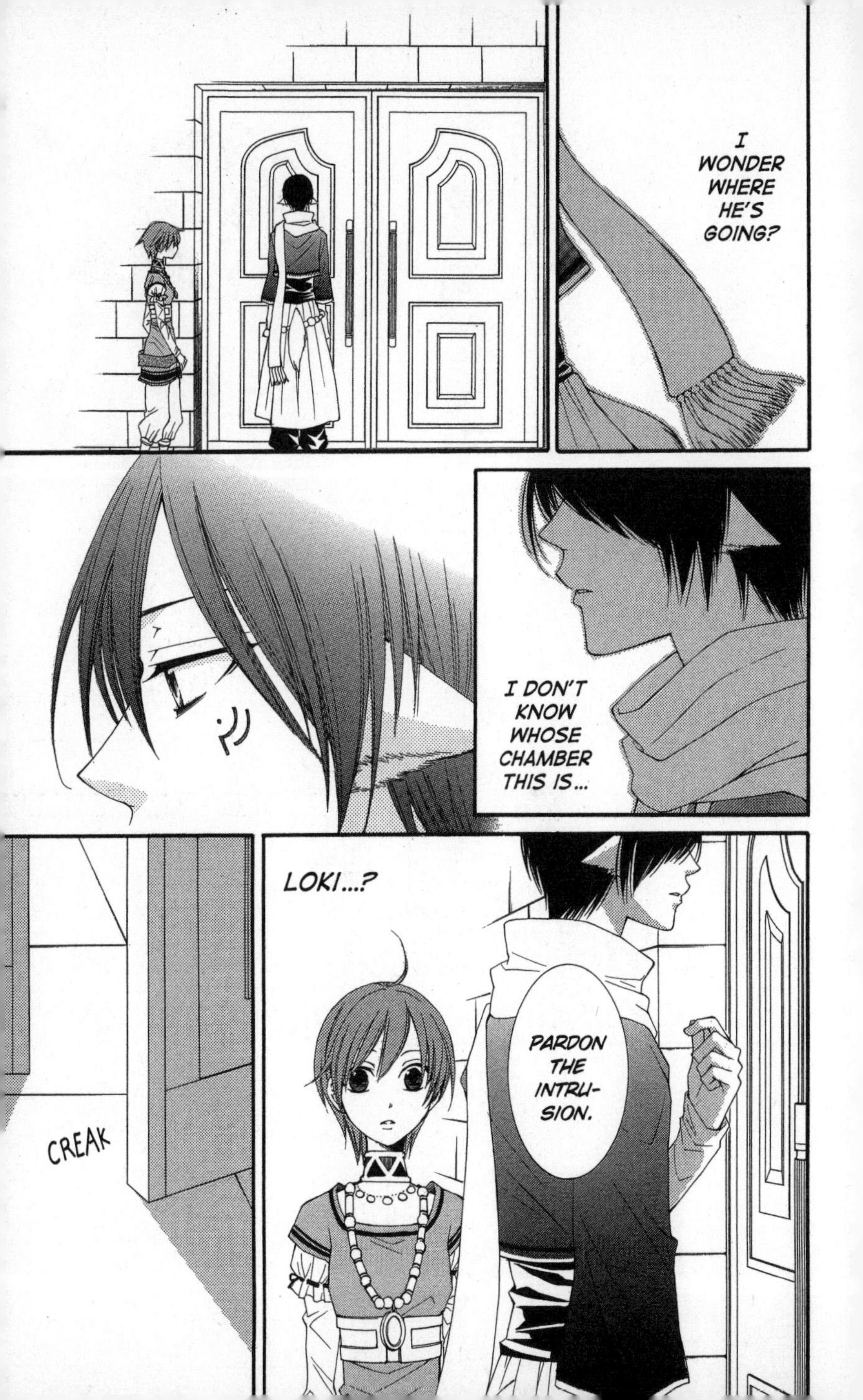
I WONDER WHERE HE'S GOING?
I DON'T KNOW WHOSE CHAMBER THIS IS...
LOKI...?
PARDON THE INTRU-SION.
CREAK

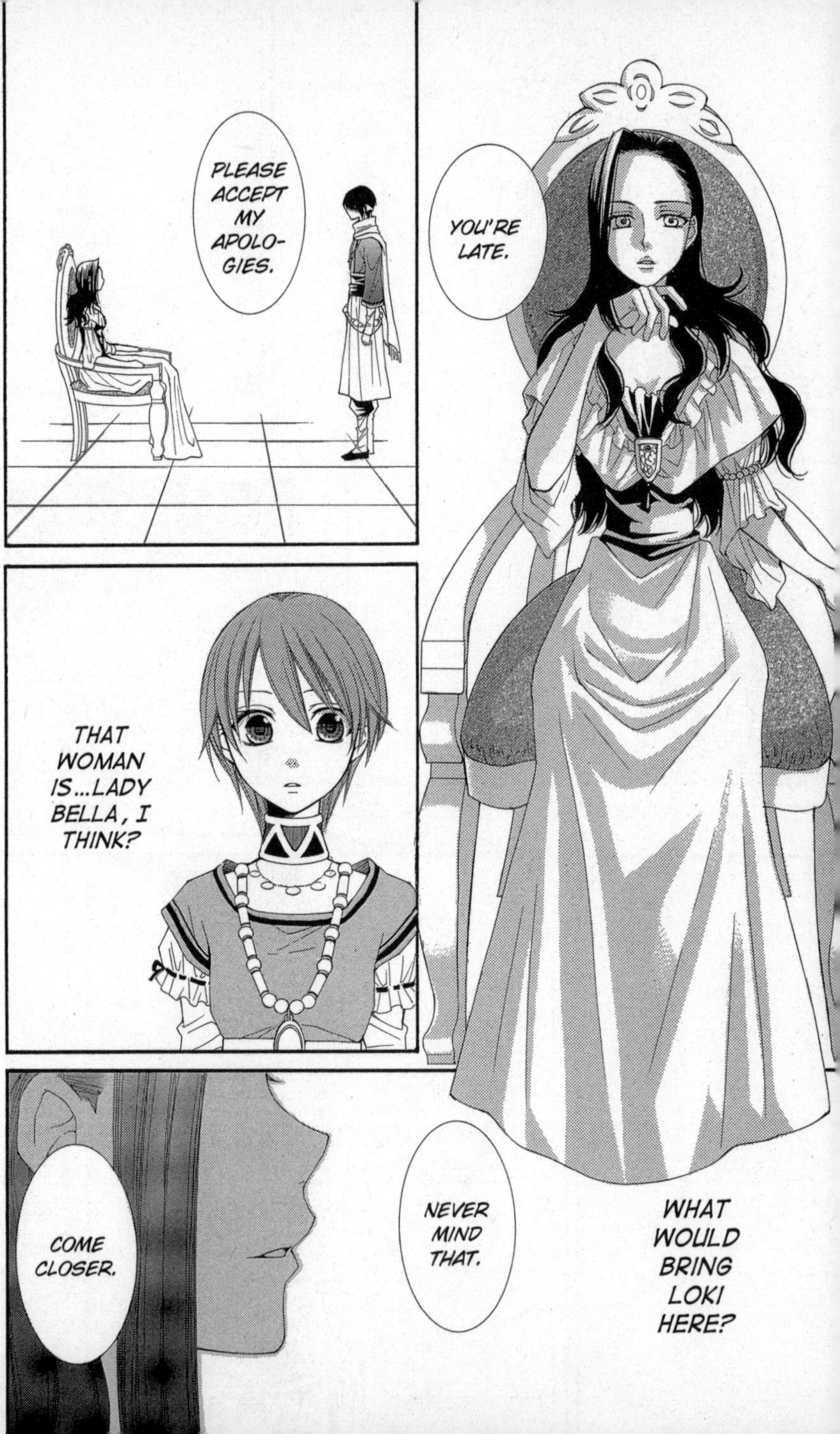
YOU'RE LATE.
PLEASE ACCEPT MY APOLO-GIES.
NEVER MIND THAT.
WHAT WOULD BRING LOKI HERE?
THAT WOMAN IS...LADY BELLA, I THINK?
COME CLOSER.

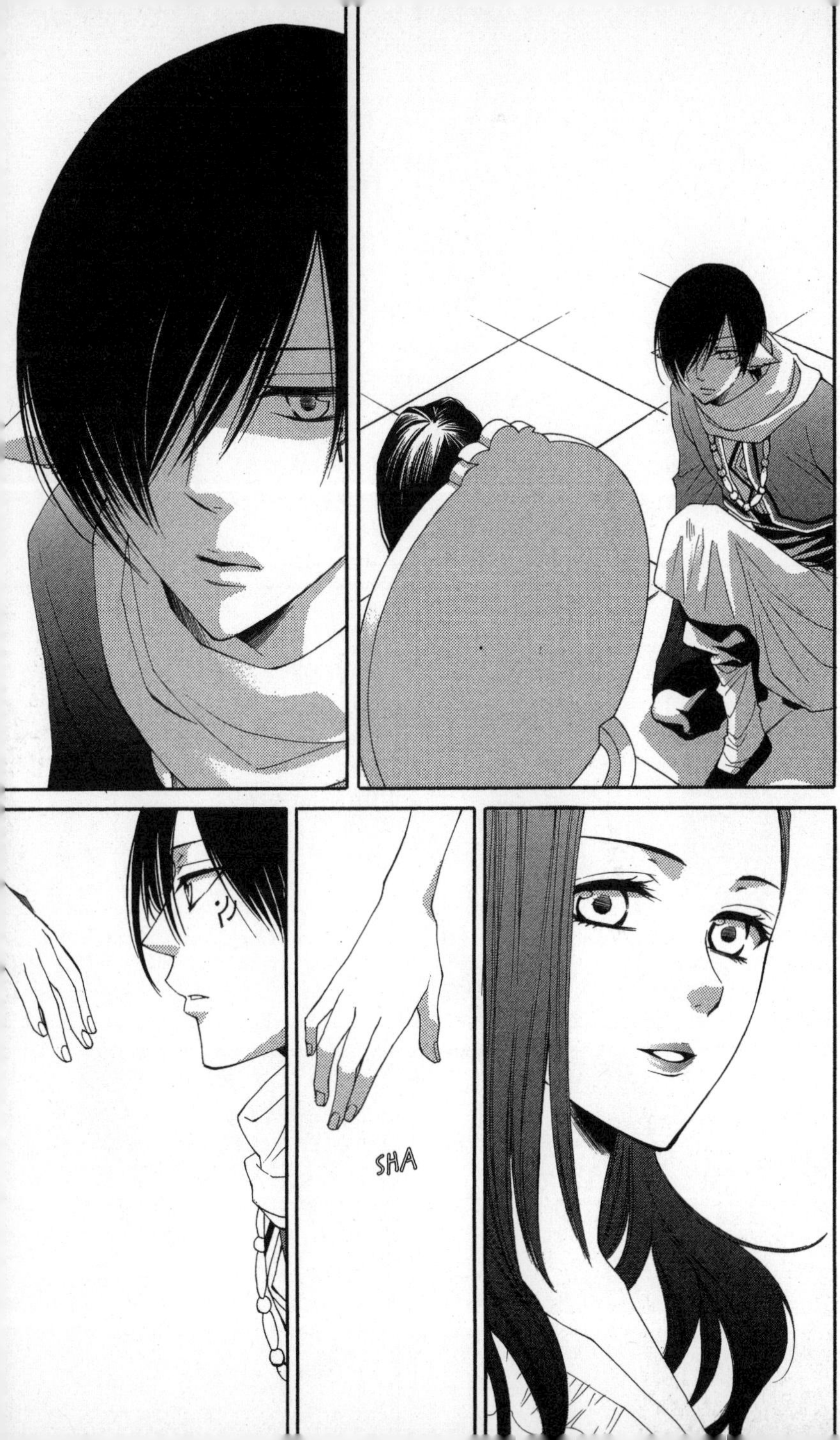
SHA

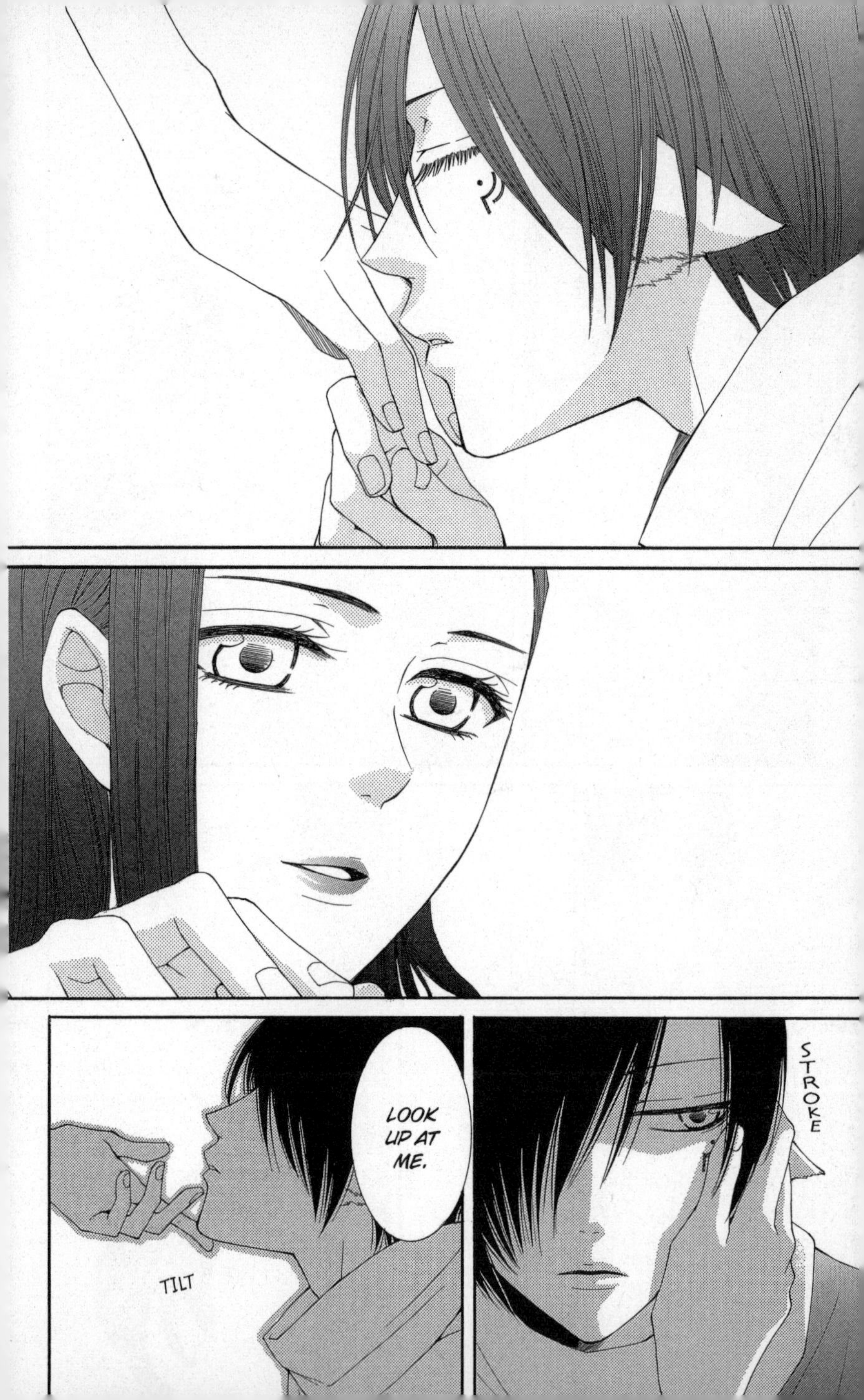
STROKE
LOOK UP AT ME.
TILT

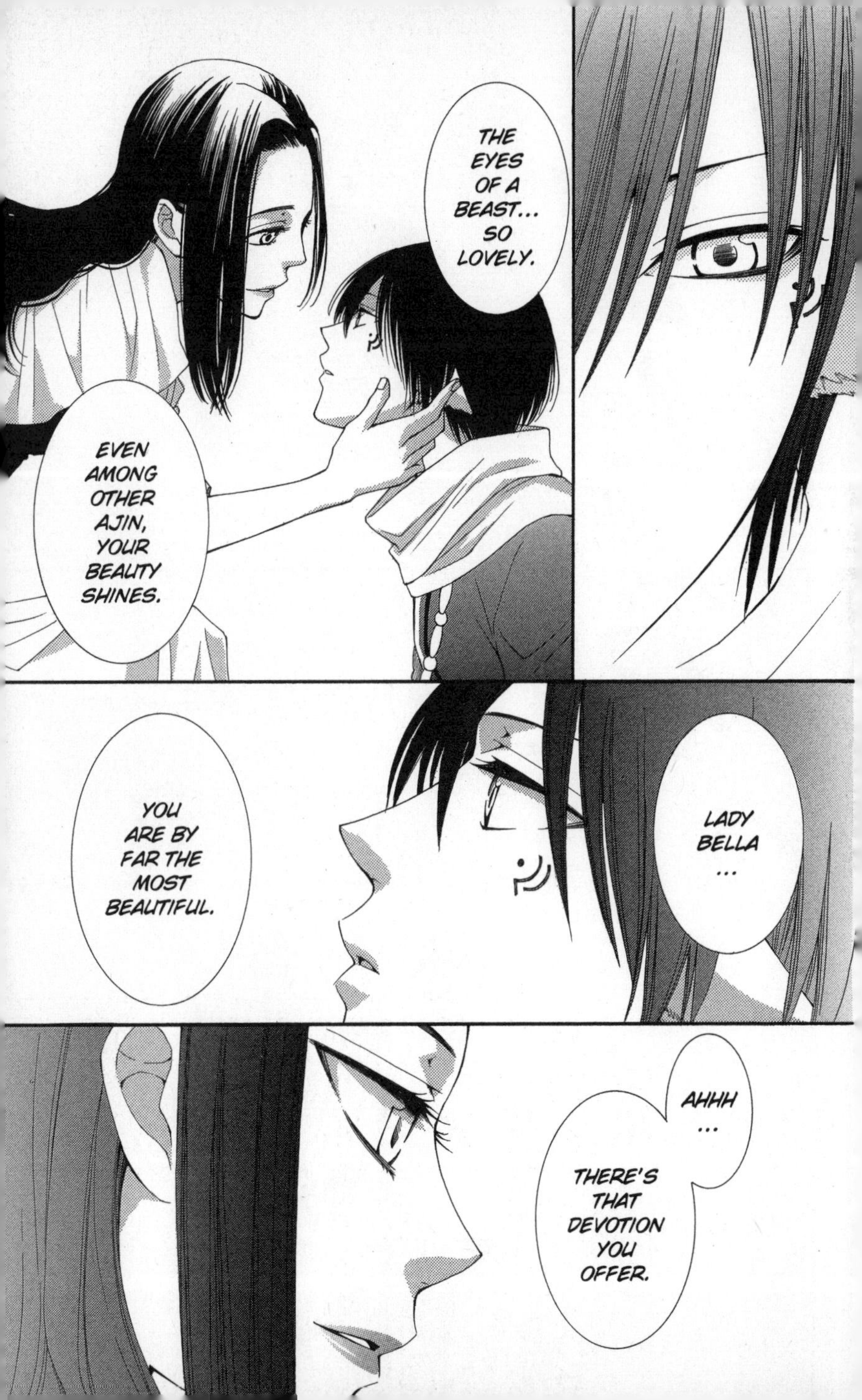
THE EYES OF A BEAST... SO LOVELY.
EVEN AMONG OTHER AJIN, YOUR BEAUTY SHINES.
LADY BELLA...
YOU ARE BY FAR THE MOST BEAUTIFUL.
AHHH...
THERE'S THAT DEVOTION YOU OFFER.

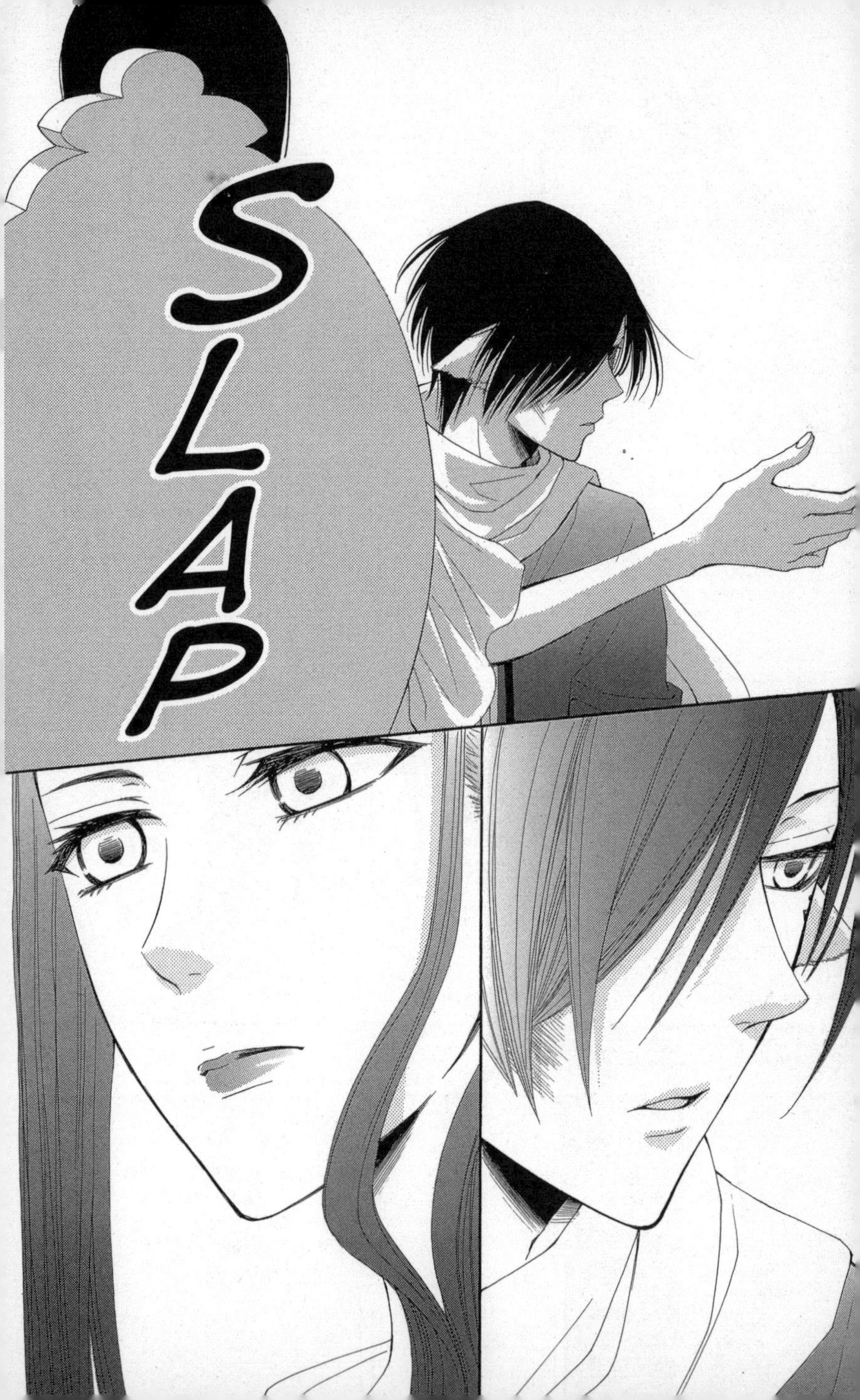
SLAP

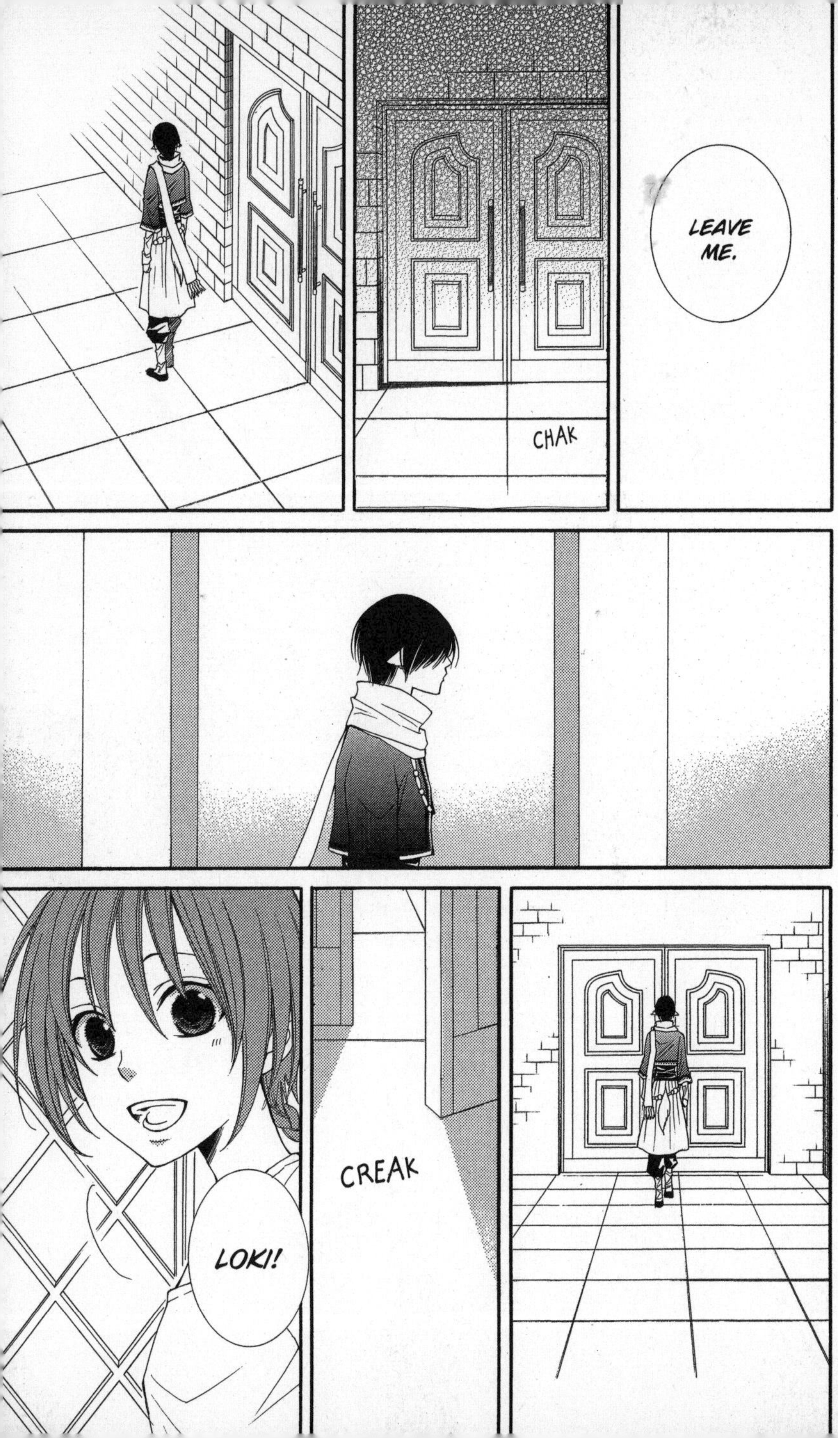
LEAVE ME.
CHAK
CREAK
LOKI!

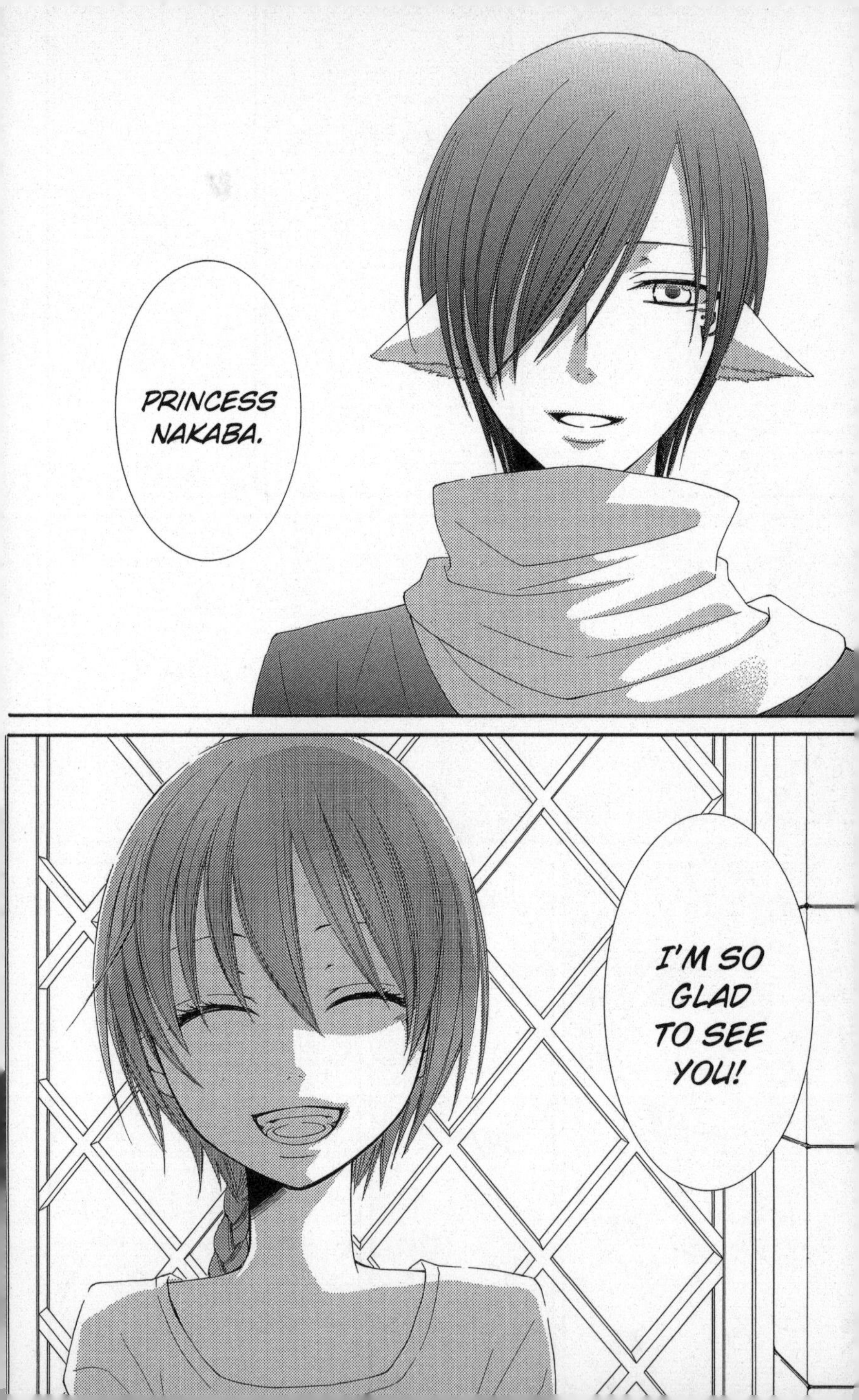
PRINCESS NAKABA.
I'M SO GLAD TO SEE YOU!

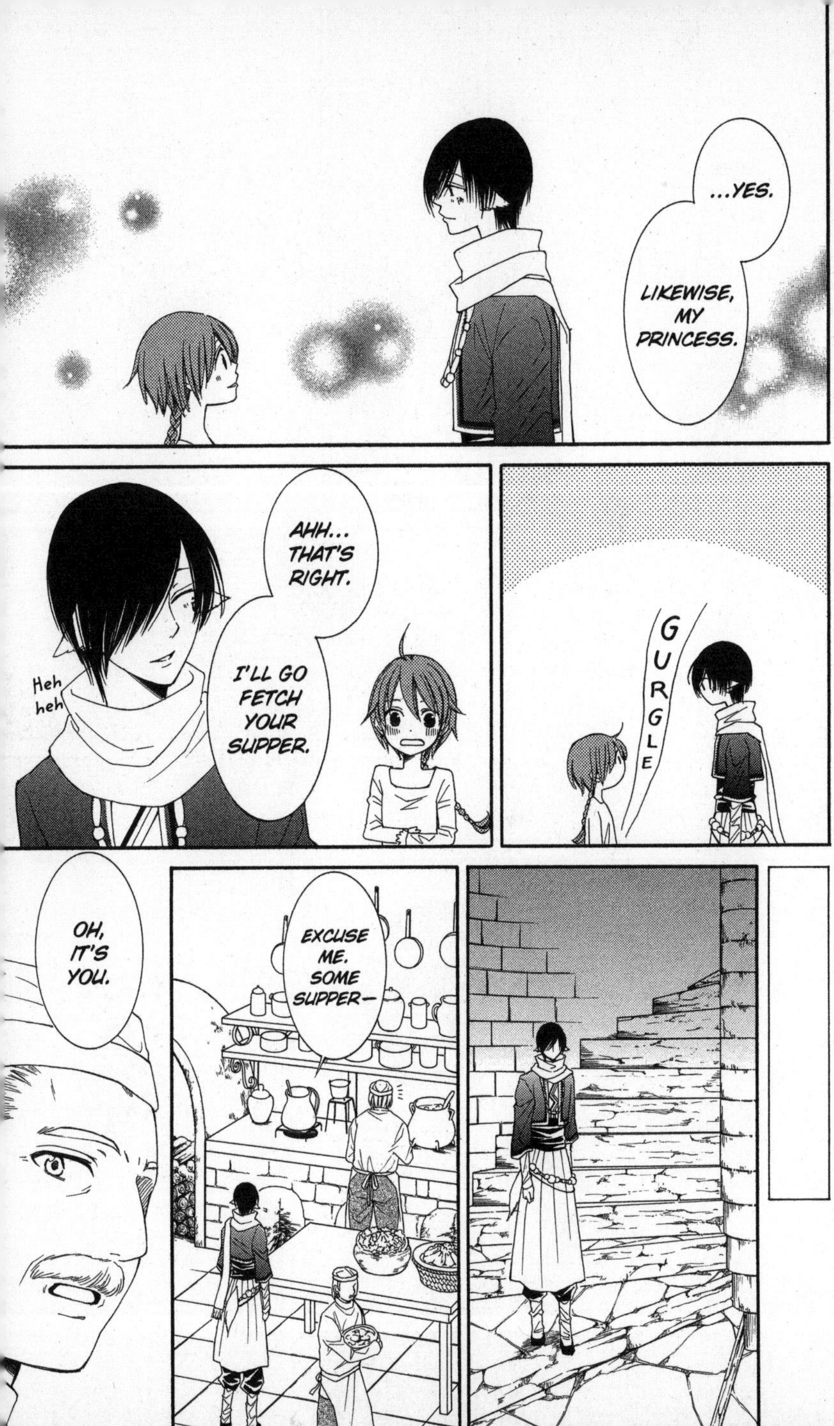
...YES.
LIKEWISE, MY PRINCESS.
GURGLE
AHH... THAT'S RIGHT.
I'LL GO FETCH YOUR SUPPER.
Heh heh
EXCUSE ME. SOME SUPPER—
OH, IT'S YOU.

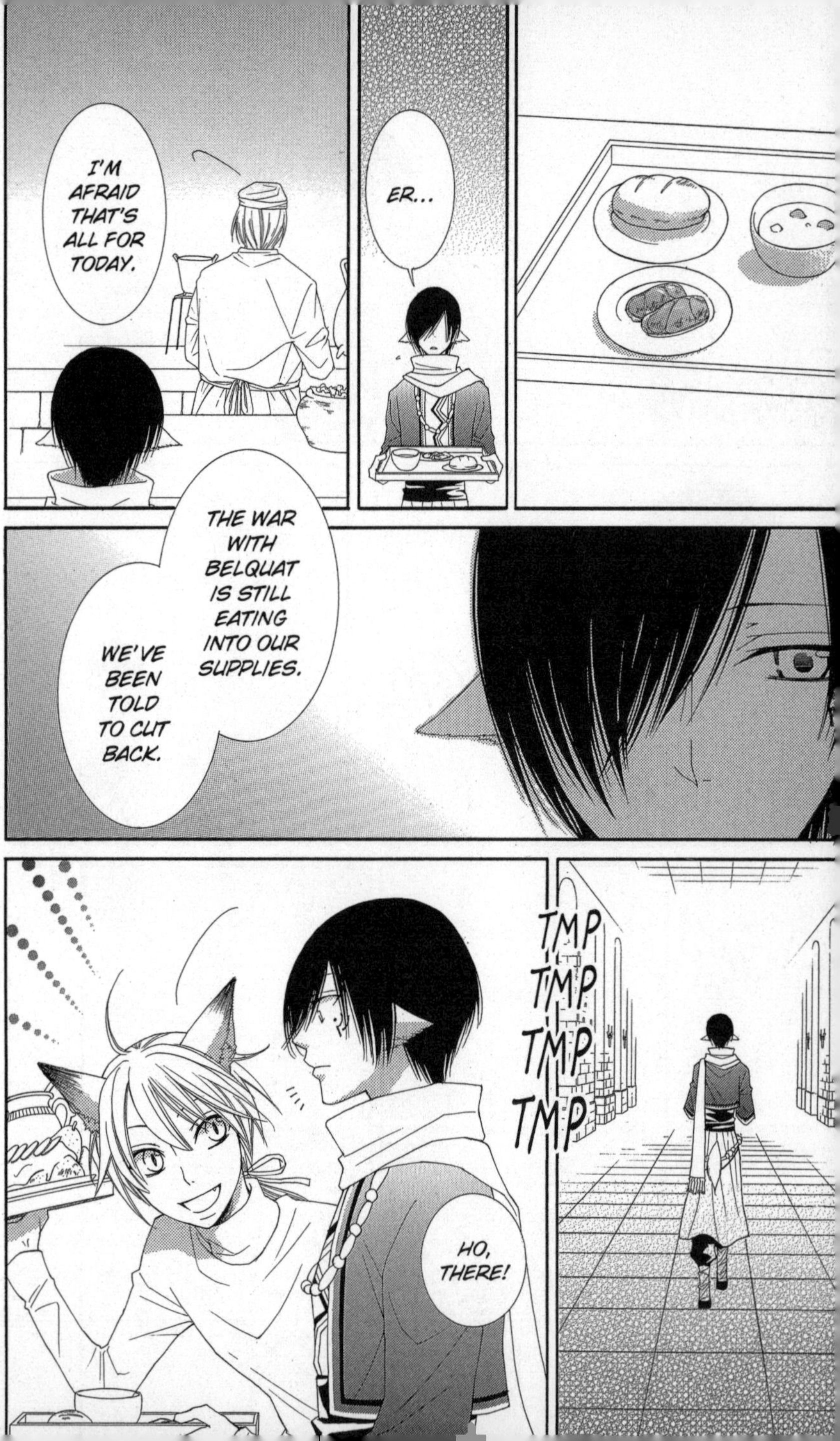
ER...
I'M AFRAID THAT'S ALL FOR TODAY.
THE WAR WITH BELQUAT IS STILL EATING INTO OUR SUPPLIES.
WE'VE BEEN TOLD TO CUT BACK.
TMP TMP TMP TMP
HO, THERE!

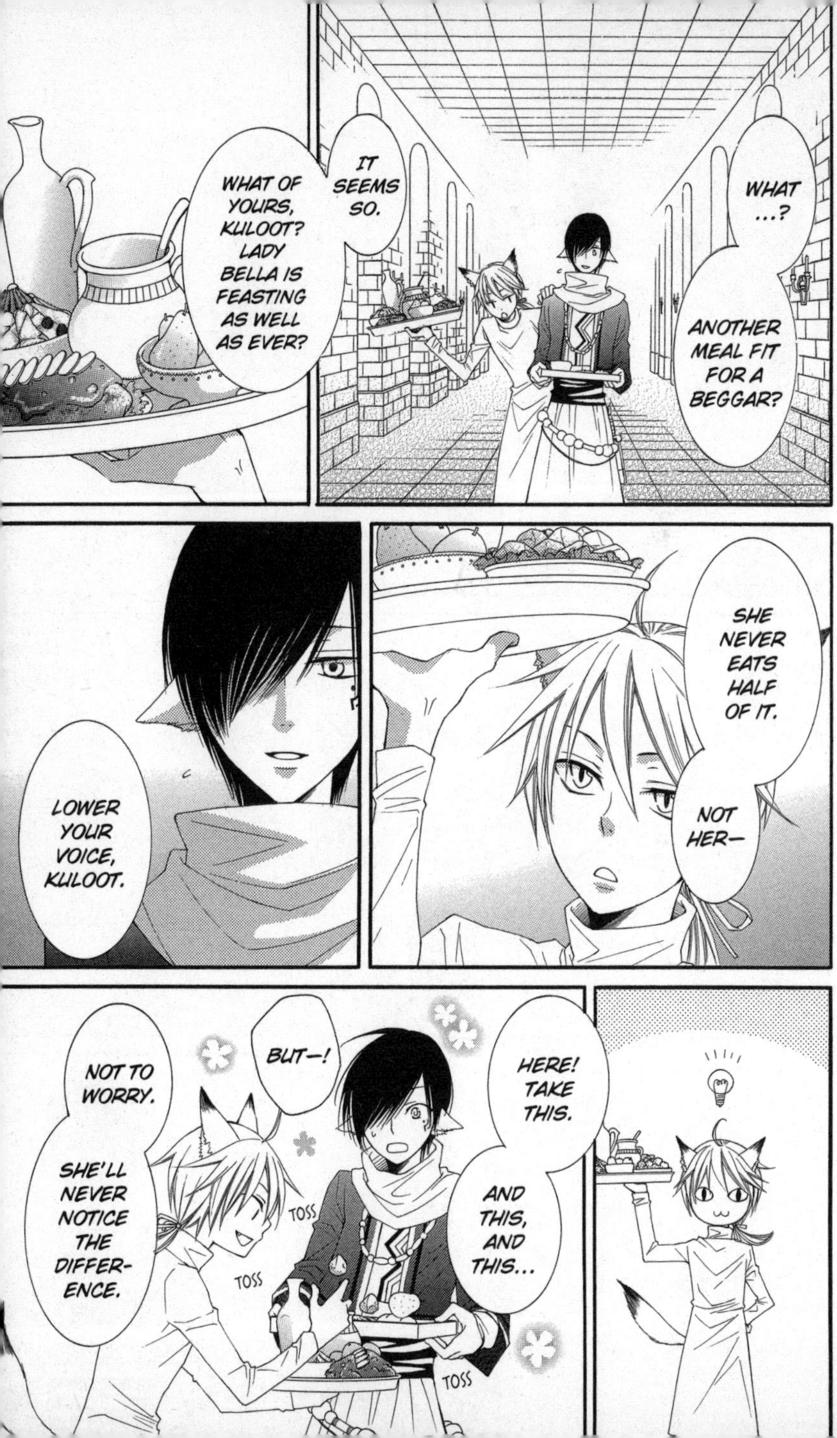
WHAT ...?
ANOTHER MEAL FIT FOR A BEGGAR?
IT SEEMS SO.
WHAT OF YOURS, KULOOT? LADY BELLA IS FEASTING AS WELL AS EVER?
SHE NEVER EATS HALF OF IT.
NOT HER—
LOWER YOUR VOICE, KULOOT.
HERE! TAKE THIS.
AND THIS, AND THIS...
BUT—!
TOSS
TOSS
TOSS
NOT TO WORRY.
SHE'LL NEVER NOTICE THE DIFFER-ENCE.

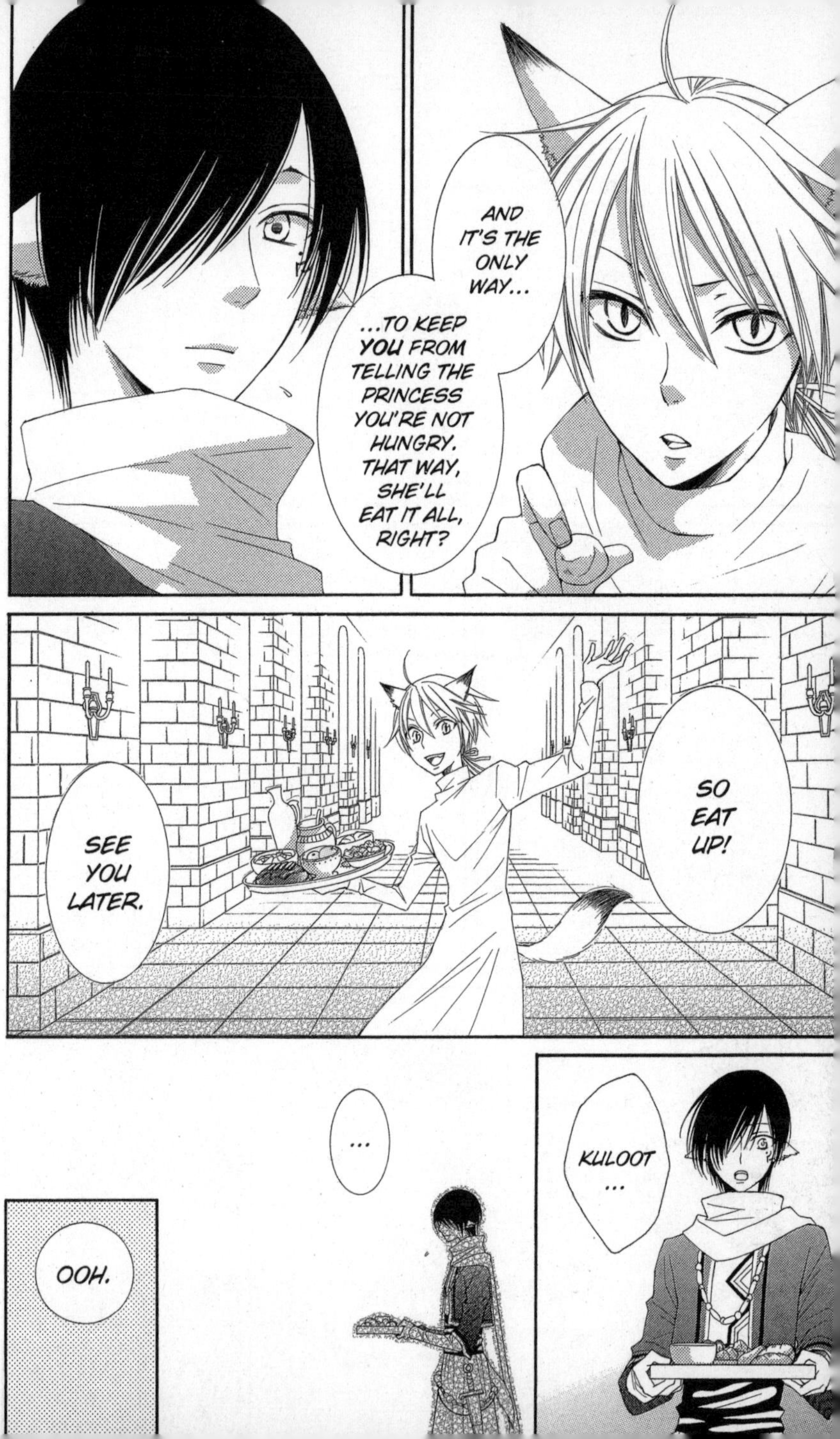
AND IT'S THE ONLY WAY...
...TO KEEP YOU FROM TELLING THE PRINCESS YOU'RE NOT HUNGRY. THAT WAY, SHE'LL EAT IT ALL, RIGHT?
SO EAT UP!
SEE YOU LATER.
KULOOT ...
...
OOH.

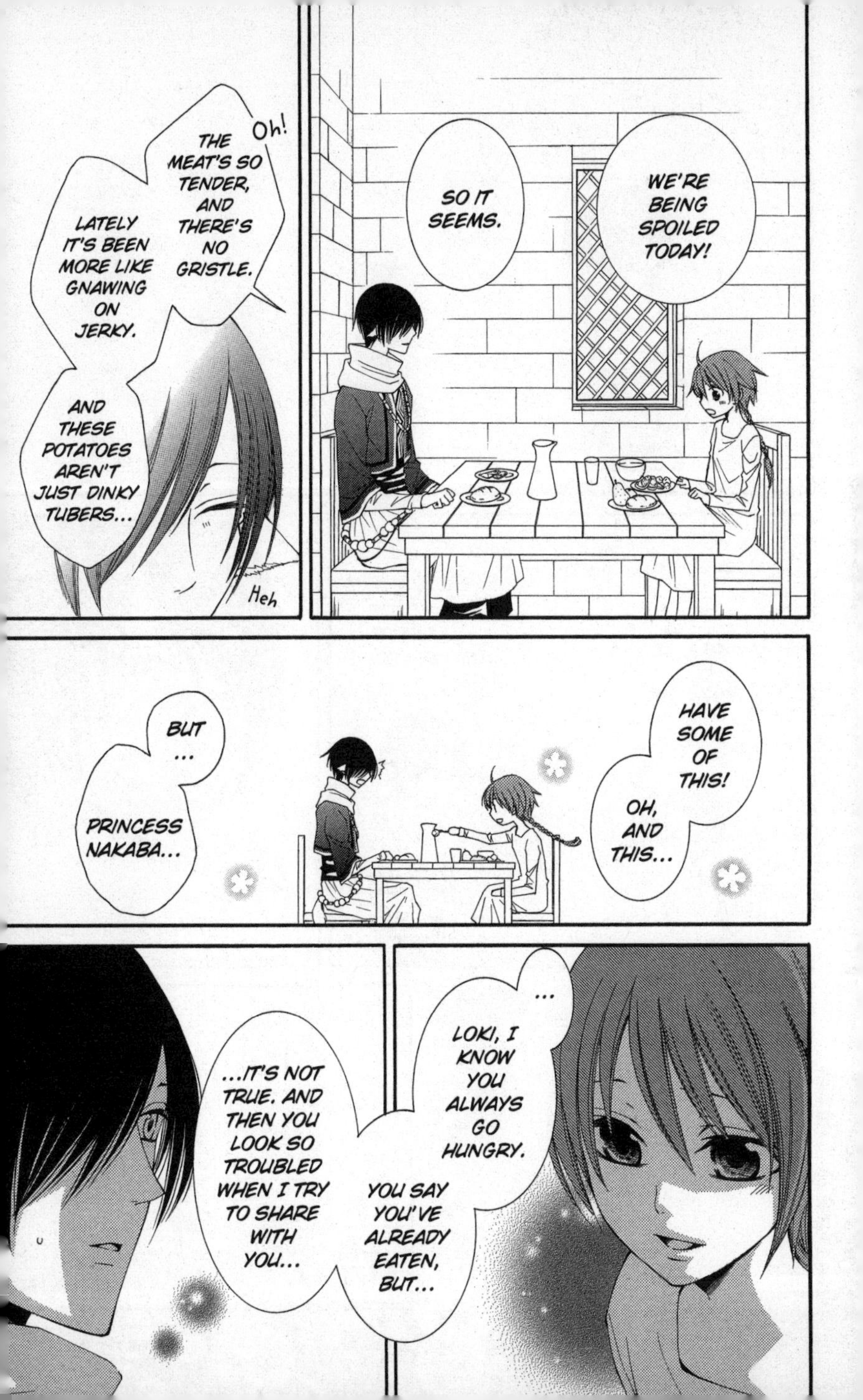
WE'RE BEING SPOILED TODAY!
SO IT SEEMS.
Oh!
THE MEAT'S SO TENDER, AND THERE'S NO GRISTLE.
LATELY IT'S BEEN MORE LIKE GNAWING ON JERKY.
AND THESE POTATOES AREN'T JUST DINKY TUBERS...
Heh
HAVE SOME OF THIS!
OH, AND THIS...
BUT ...
PRINCESS NAKABA...
...
LOKI, I KNOW YOU ALWAYS GO HUNGRY.
YOU SAY YOU'VE ALREADY EATEN, BUT...
...IT'S NOT TRUE. AND THEN YOU LOOK SO TROUBLED WHEN I TRY TO SHARE WITH YOU...

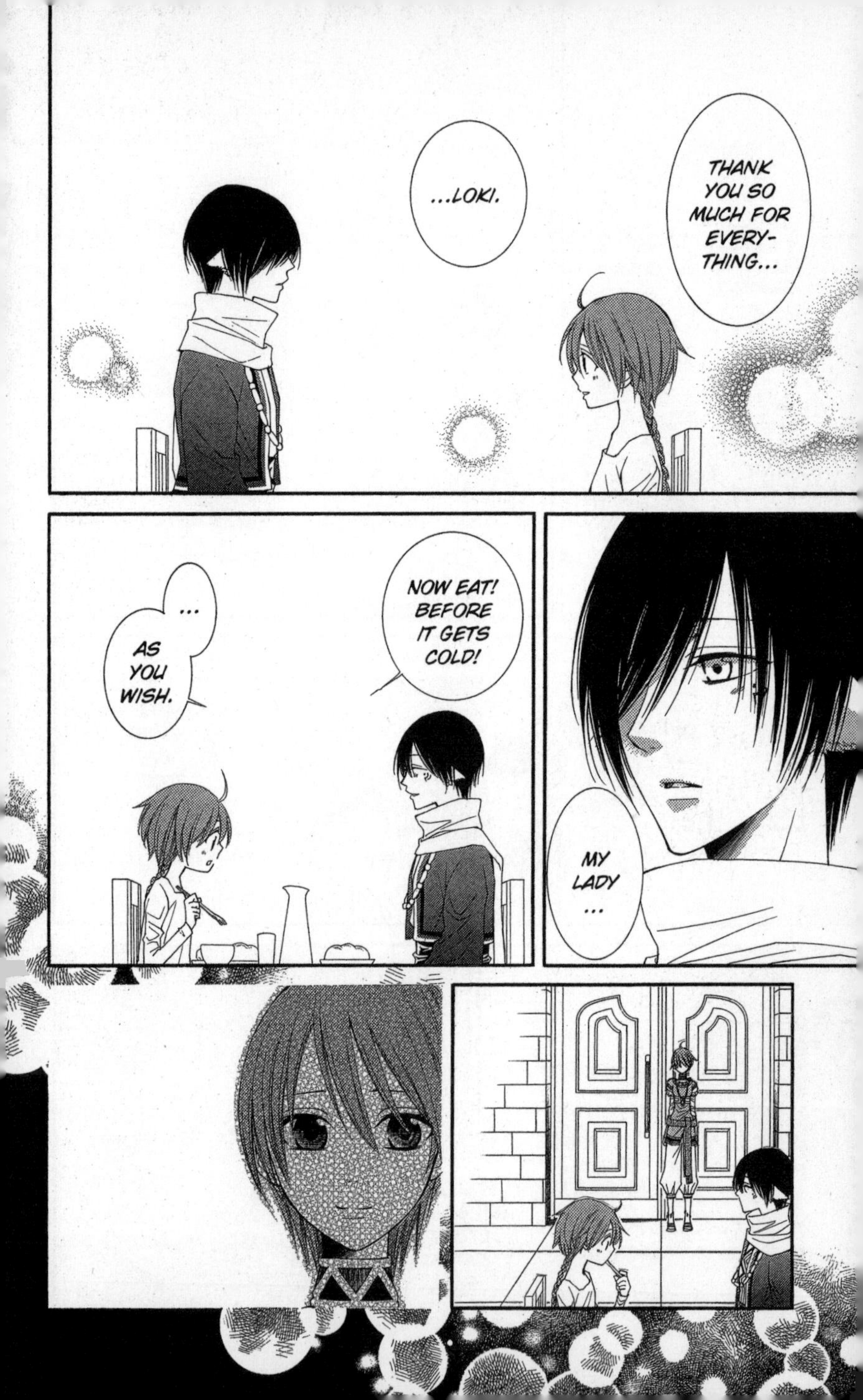
THANK YOU SO MUCH FOR EVERY-THING...
...LOKI.
MY LADY ...
NOW EAT! BEFORE IT GETS COLD!
... AS YOU WISH.

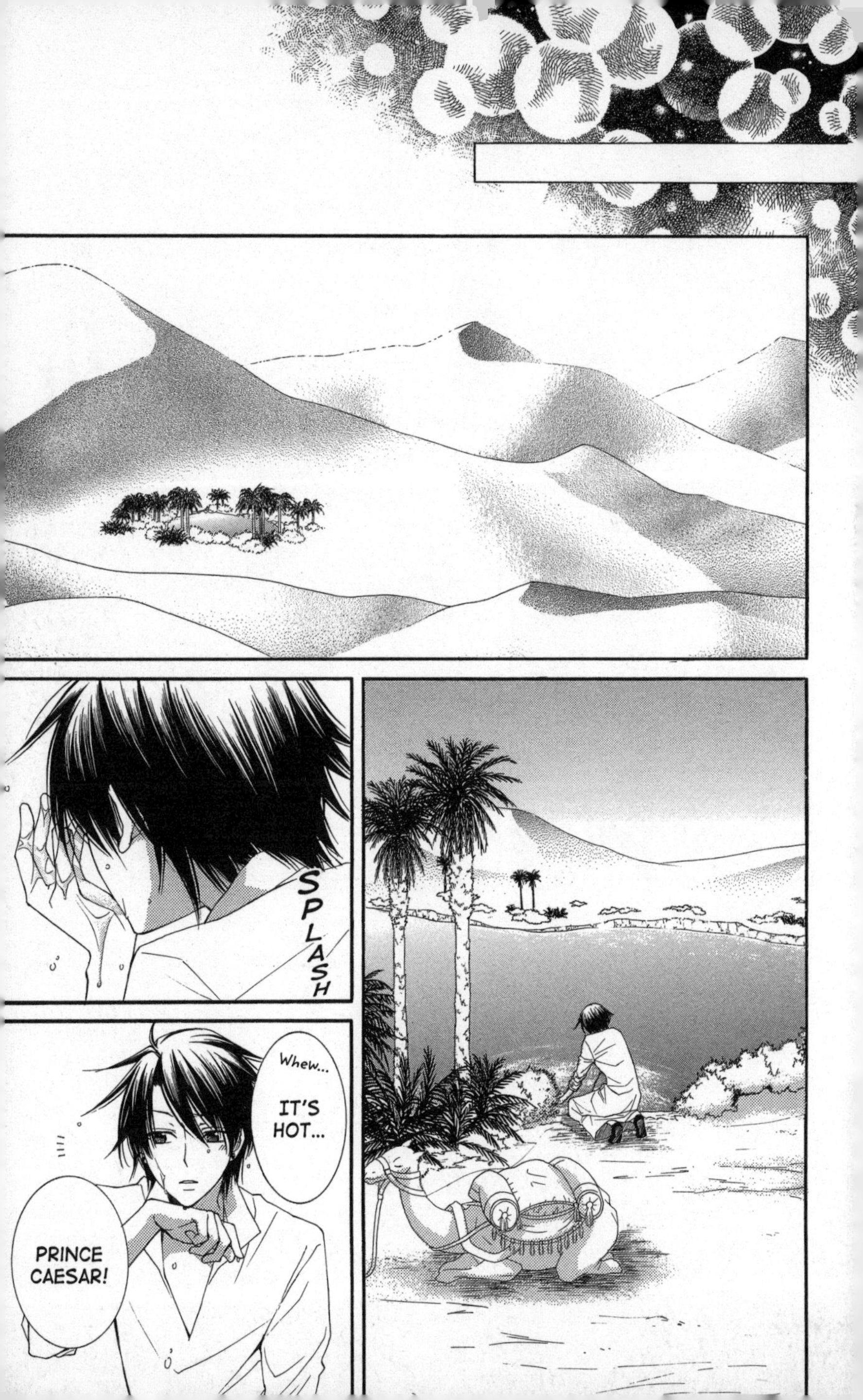
SPLASH
Whew... IT'S HOT...
PRINCE CAESAR!

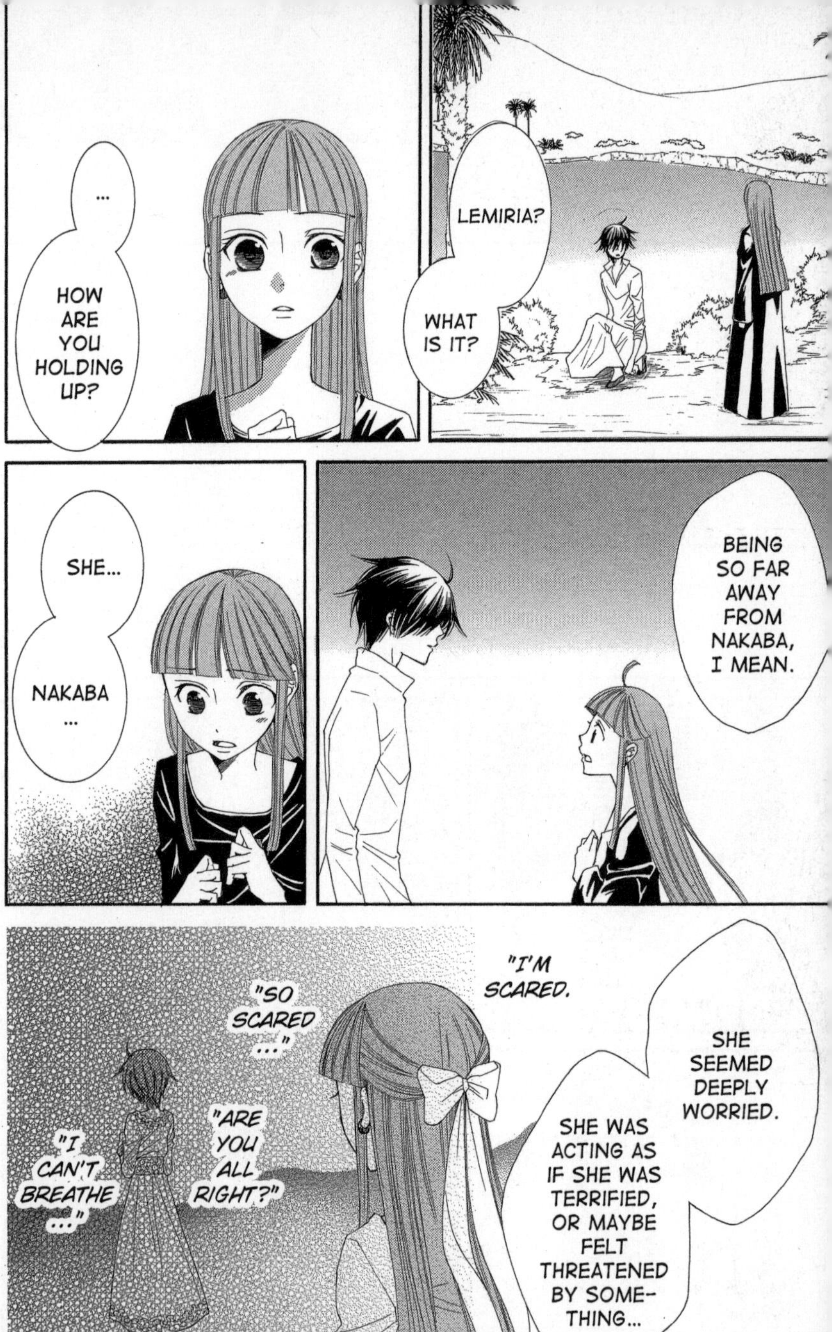
LEMIRIA?
WHAT IS IT?
...
HOW ARE YOU HOLDING UP?
BEING SO FAR AWAY FROM NAKABA, I MEAN.
SHE...
NAKABA...
SHE SEEMED DEEPLY WORRIED.
SHE WAS ACTING AS IF SHE WAS TERRIFIED, OR MAYBE FELT THREATENED BY SOME-THING...
"I'M SCARED.
"SO SCARED..."
"ARE YOU ALL RIGHT?"
"I CAN'T BREATHE..."

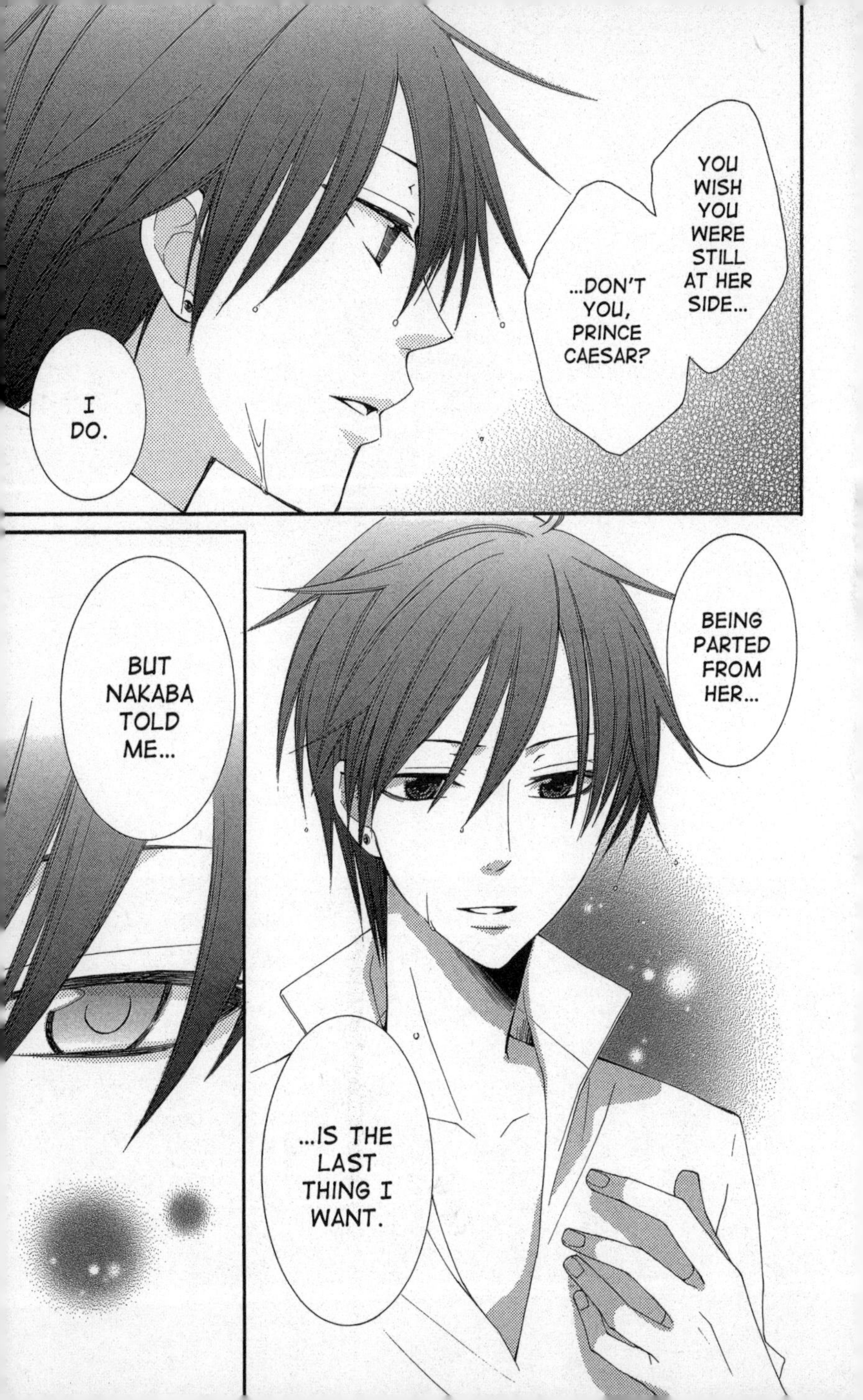
YOU WISH YOU WERE STILL AT HER SIDE...
...DON'T YOU, PRINCE CAESAR?
I DO.
BEING PARTED FROM HER...
BUT NAKABA TOLD ME...
...IS THE LAST THING I WANT.

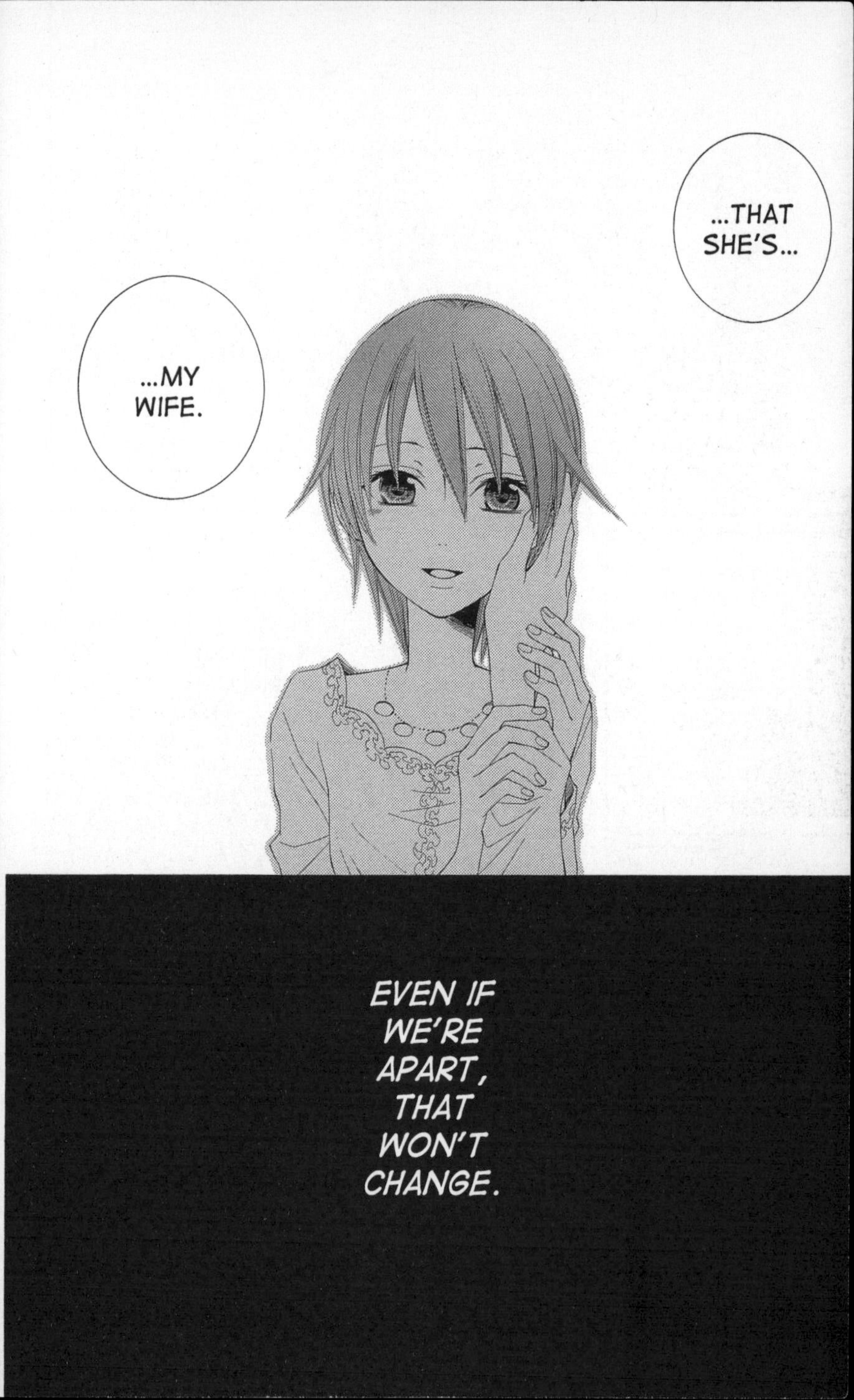
...THAT SHE'S...
...MY WIFE.
EVEN IF WE'RE APART, THAT WON'T CHANGE.

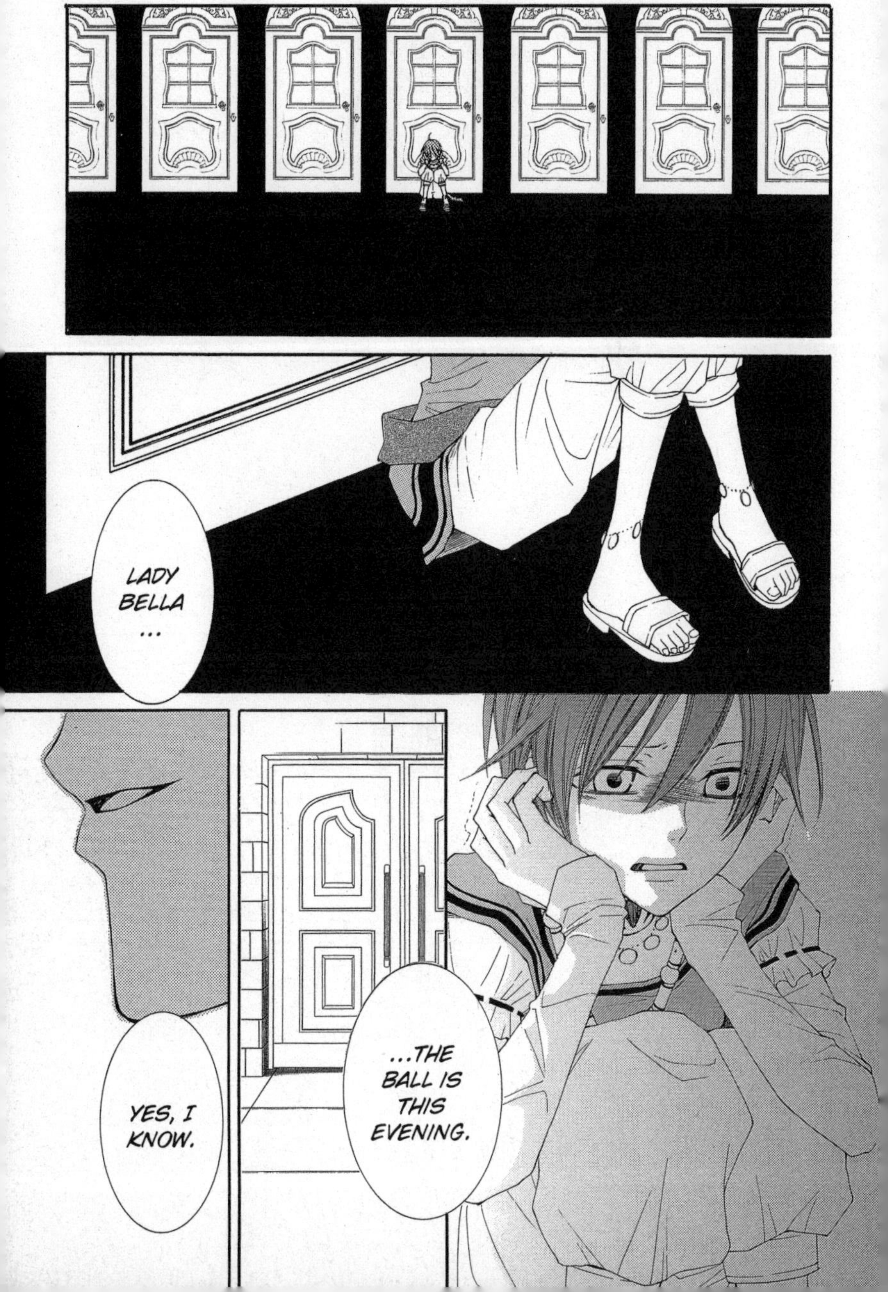
LADY BELLA ...
...THE BALL IS THIS EVENING.
YES, I KNOW.

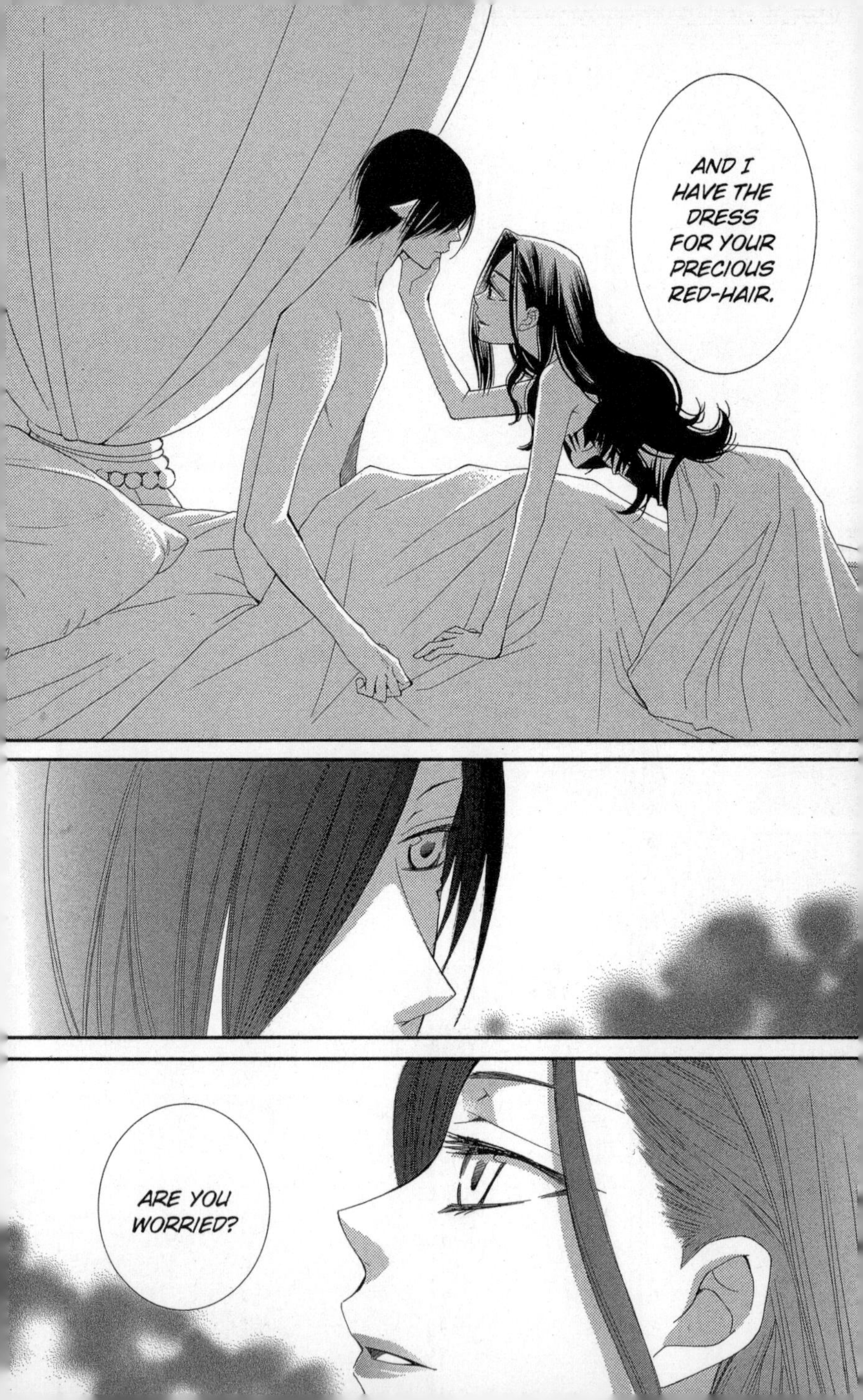
AND I HAVE THE DRESS FOR YOUR PRECIOUS RED-HAIR.
ARE YOU WORRIED?

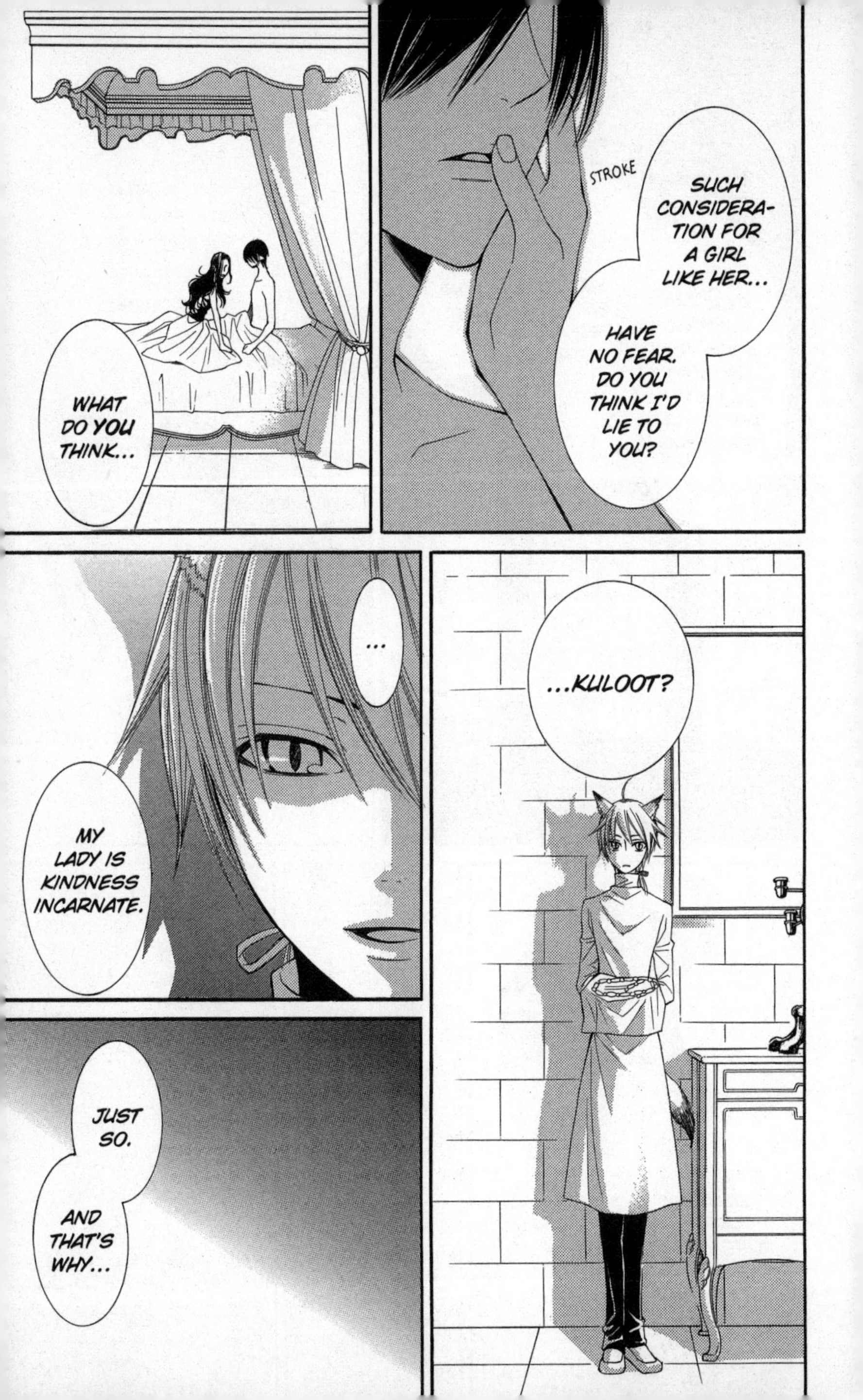
STROKE
SUCH CONSIDERATION FOR A GIRL LIKE HER...
HAVE NO FEAR. DO YOU THINK I'D LIE TO YOU?
WHAT DO YOU THINK...
...KULOOT?
...
MY LADY IS KINDNESS INCARNATE.
JUST SO.
AND THAT'S WHY...

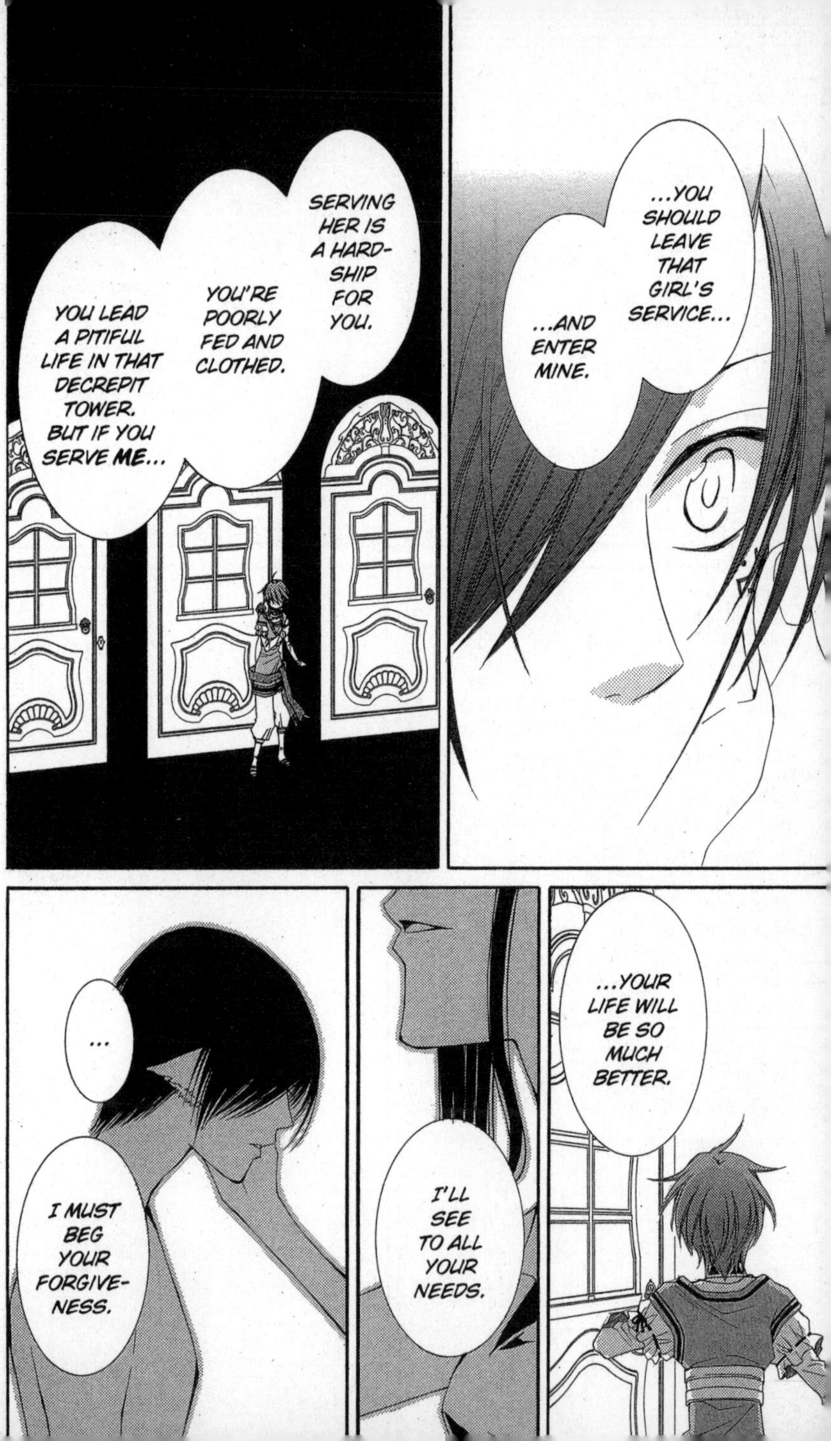
...YOU SHOULD LEAVE THAT GIRL'S SERVICE...
...AND ENTER MINE.
SERVING HER IS A HARD-SHIP FOR YOU.
YOU'RE POORLY FED AND CLOTHED.
YOU LEAD A PITIFUL LIFE IN THAT DECREPIT TOWER. BUT IF YOU SERVE **ME**...
...YOUR LIFE WILL BE SO MUCH BETTER.
I'LL SEE TO ALL YOUR NEEDS.
...
I MUST BEG YOUR FORGIVE-NESS.

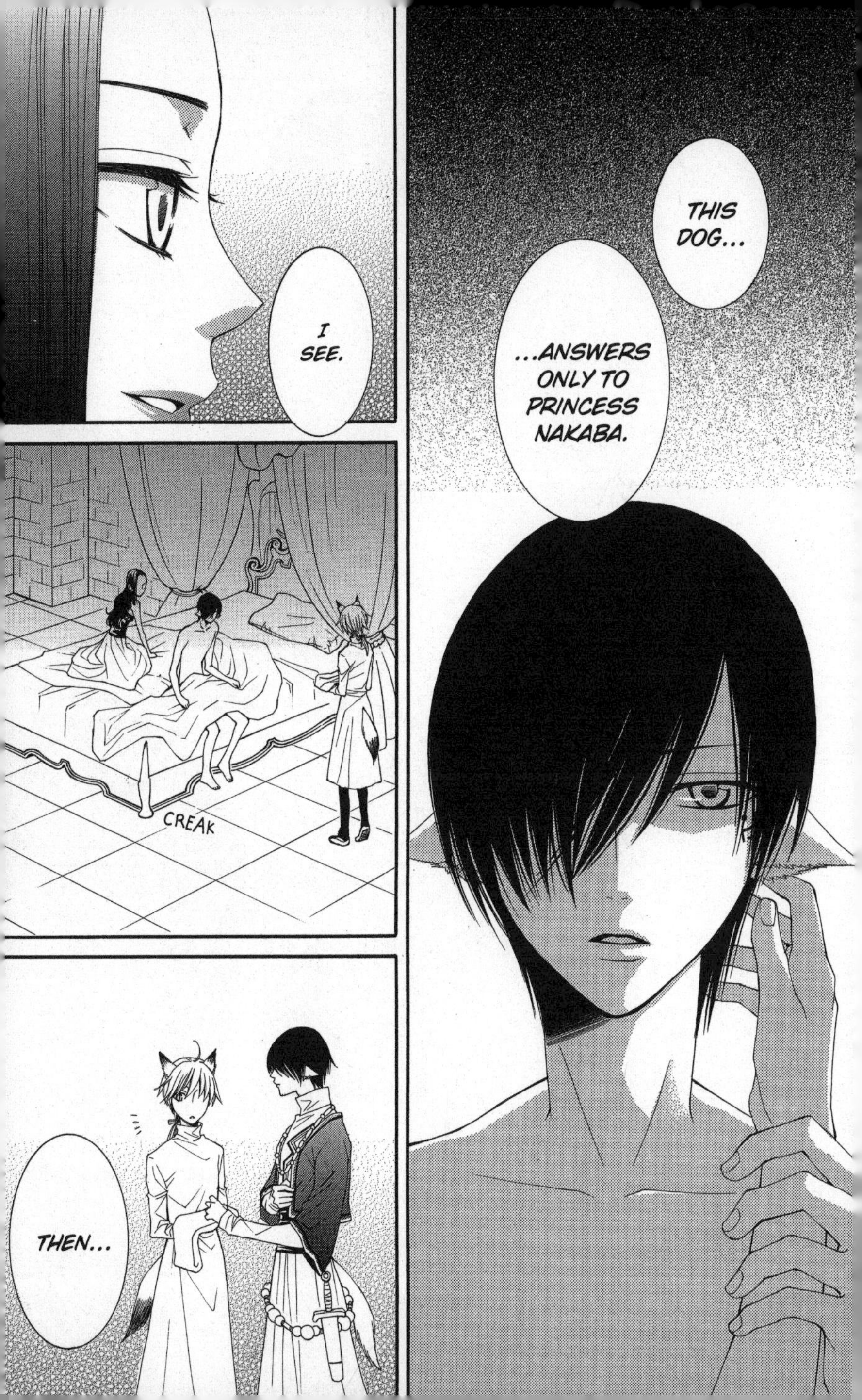
THIS DOG...
...ANSWERS ONLY TO PRINCESS NAKABA.
I SEE.
CREAK
THEN...

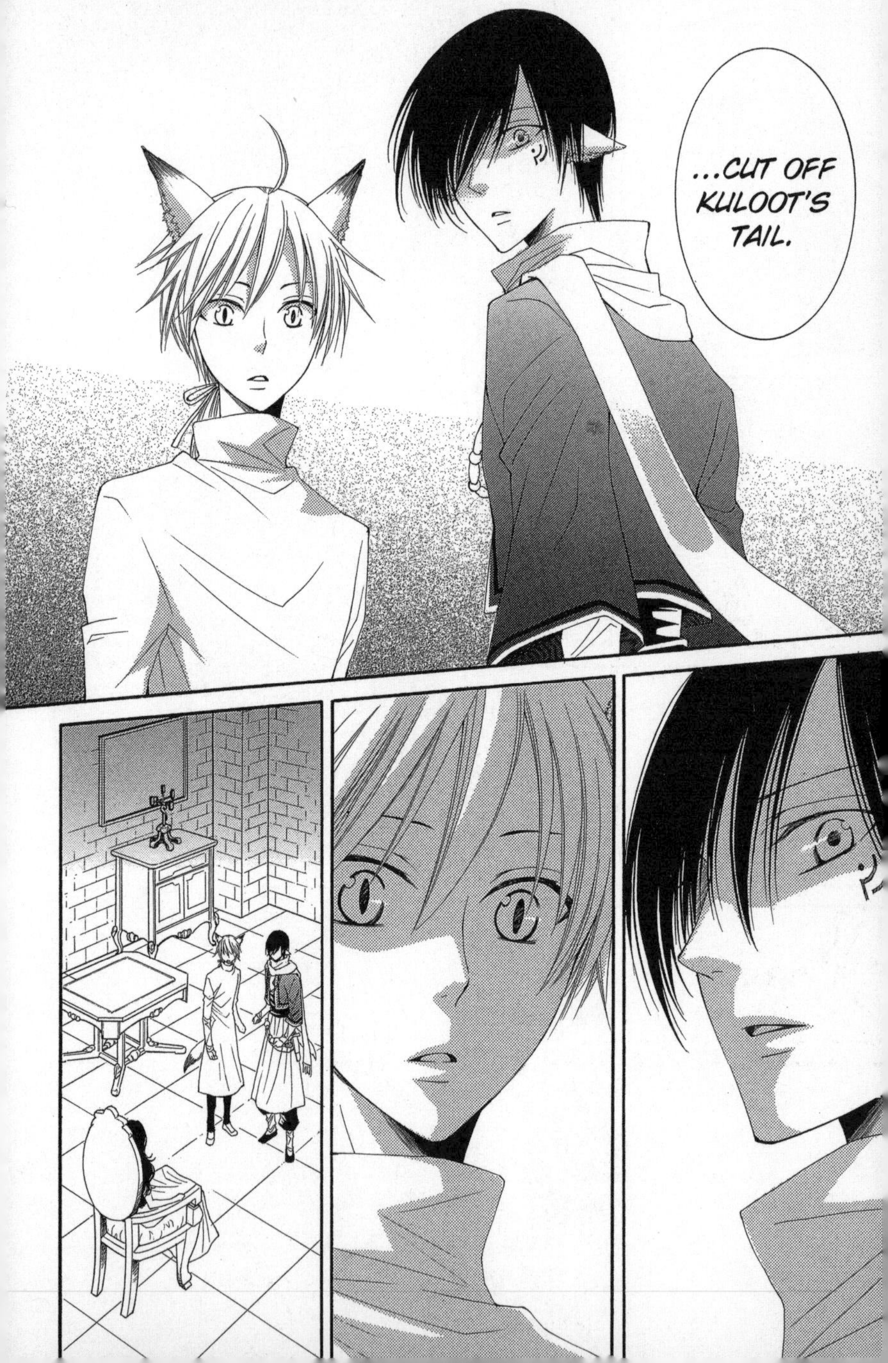
...CUT OFF KULOOT'S TAIL.

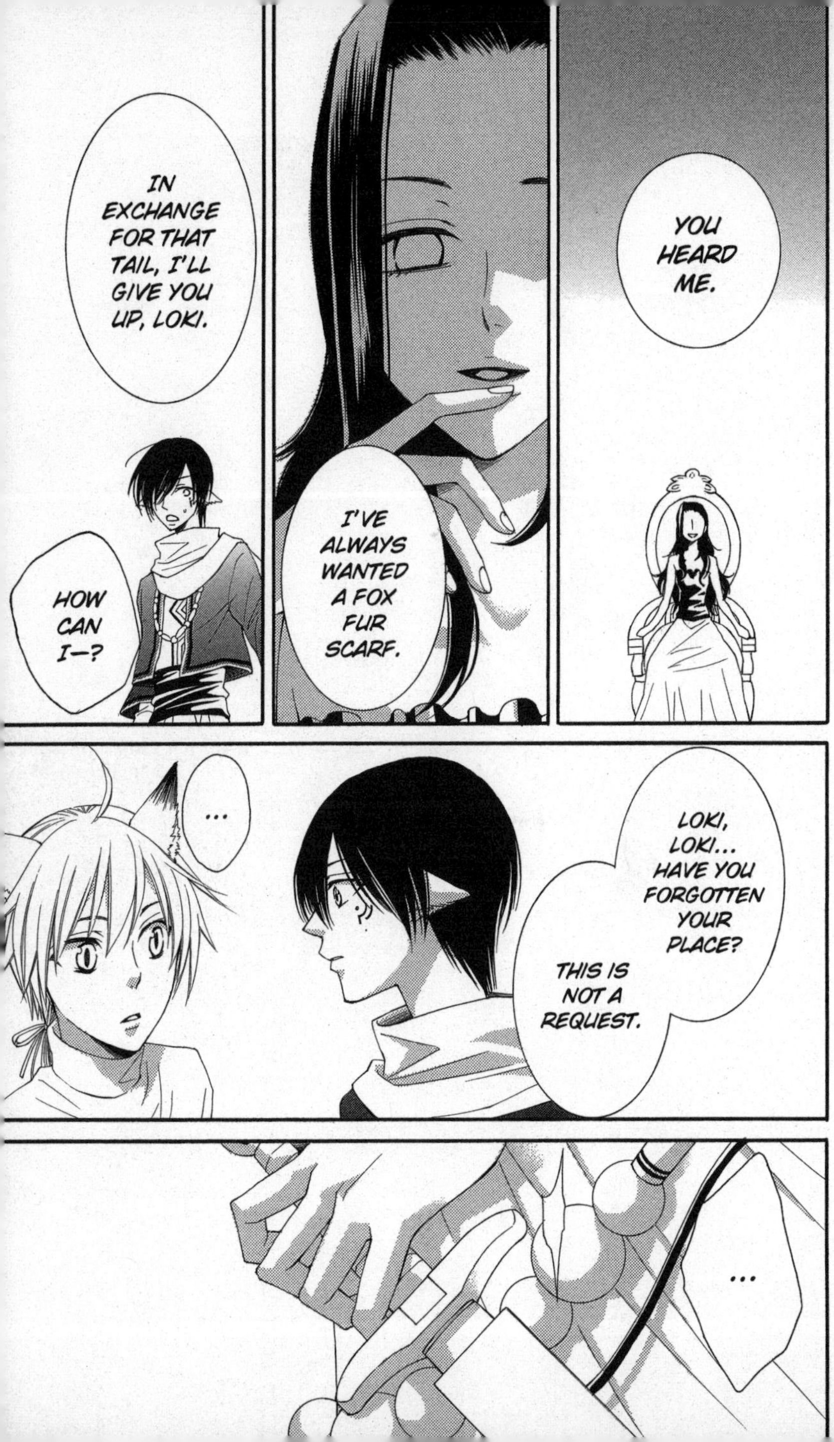
YOU HEARD ME.
I'VE ALWAYS WANTED A FOX FUR SCARF.
IN EXCHANGE FOR THAT TAIL, I'LL GIVE YOU UP, LOKI.
HOW CAN I—?
LOKI, LOKI... HAVE YOU FORGOTTEN YOUR PLACE?
THIS IS NOT A REQUEST.
...
...

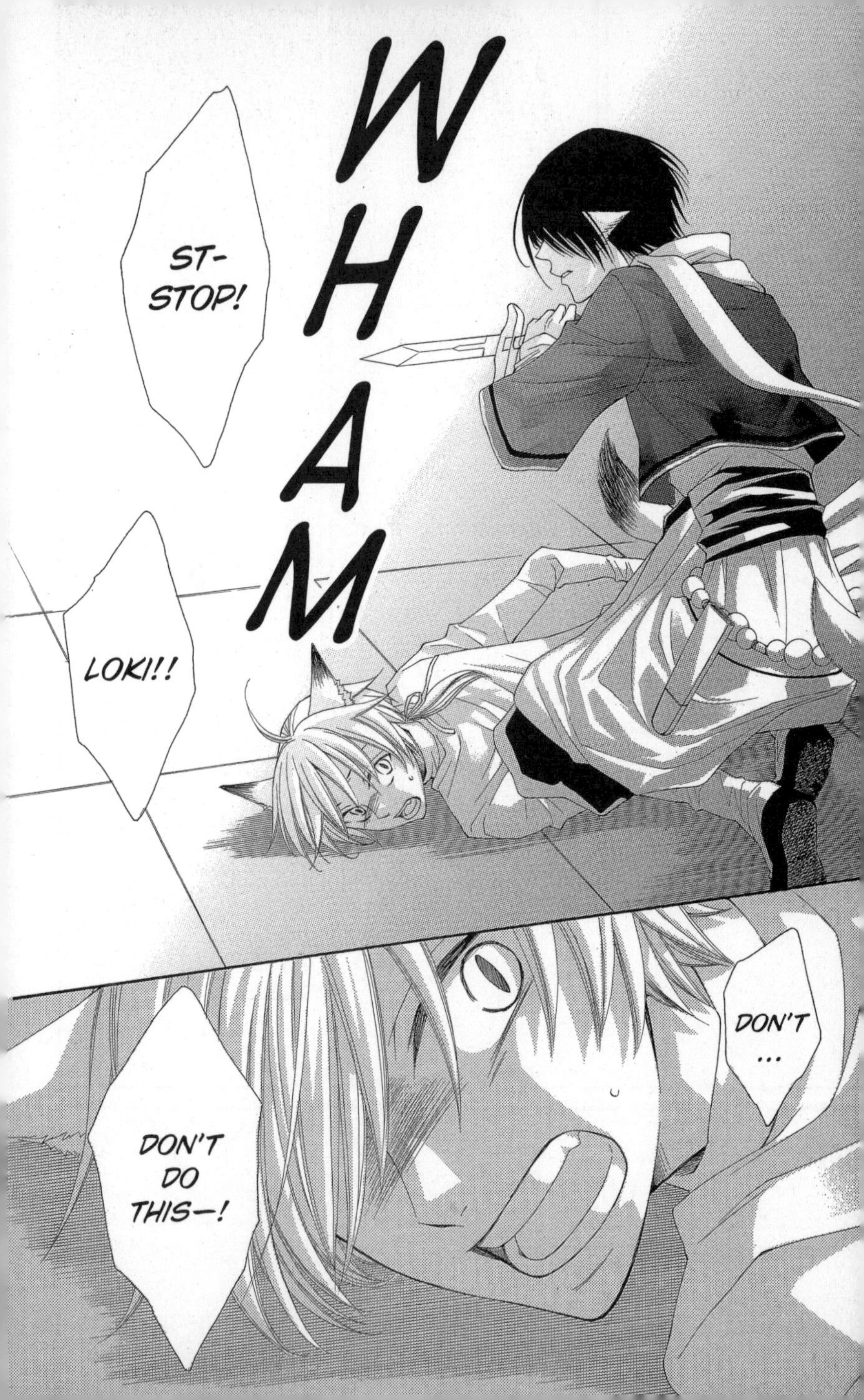
WHAM
ST- STOP!
LOKI!!
DON'T ...
DON'T DO THIS—!

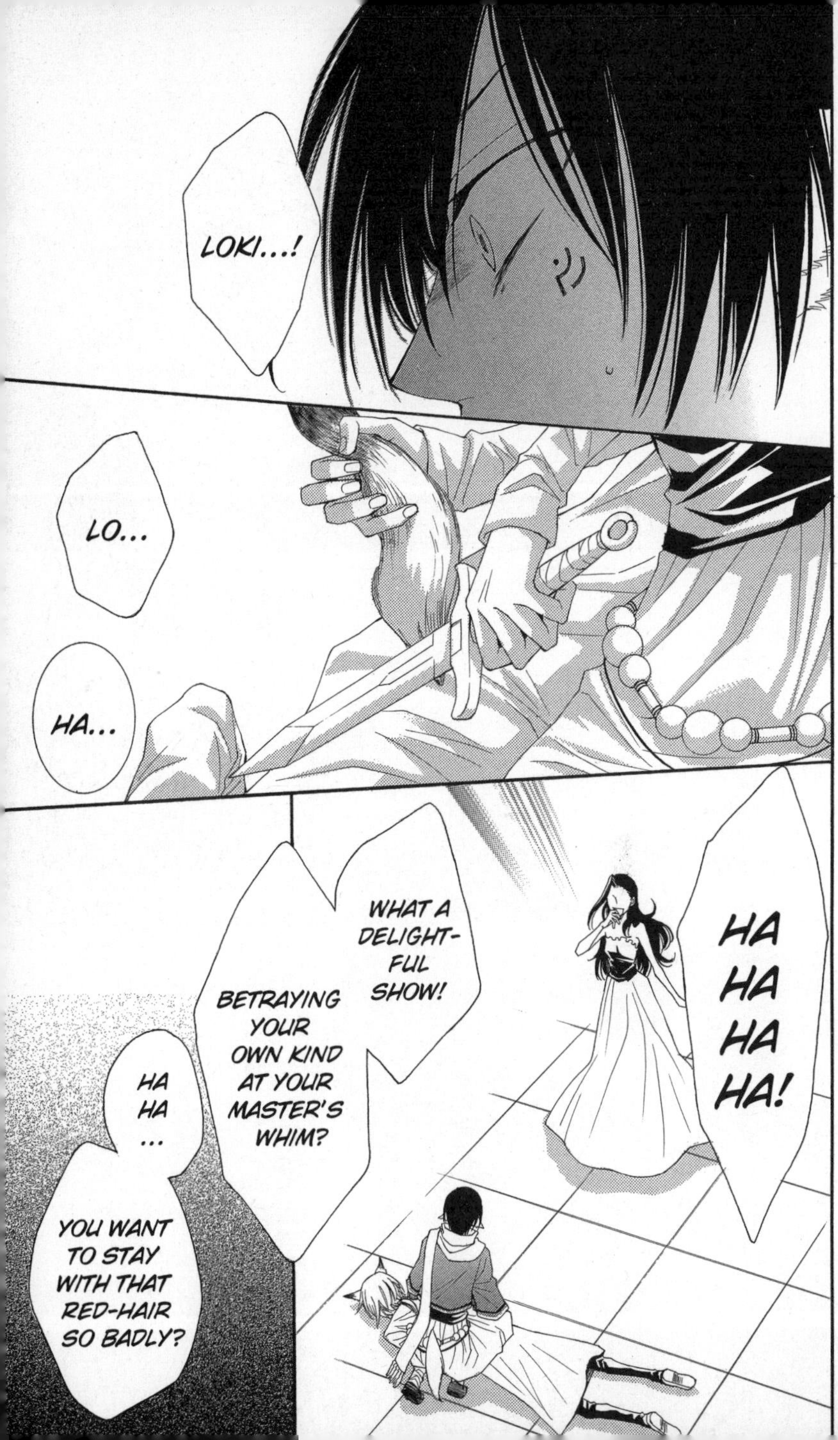
LOKI...!
LO...
HA...
HA HA HA HA!
WHAT A DELIGHT-FUL SHOW!
BETRAYING YOUR OWN KIND AT YOUR MASTER'S WHIM?
HA HA ...
YOU WANT TO STAY WITH THAT RED-HAIR SO BADLY?

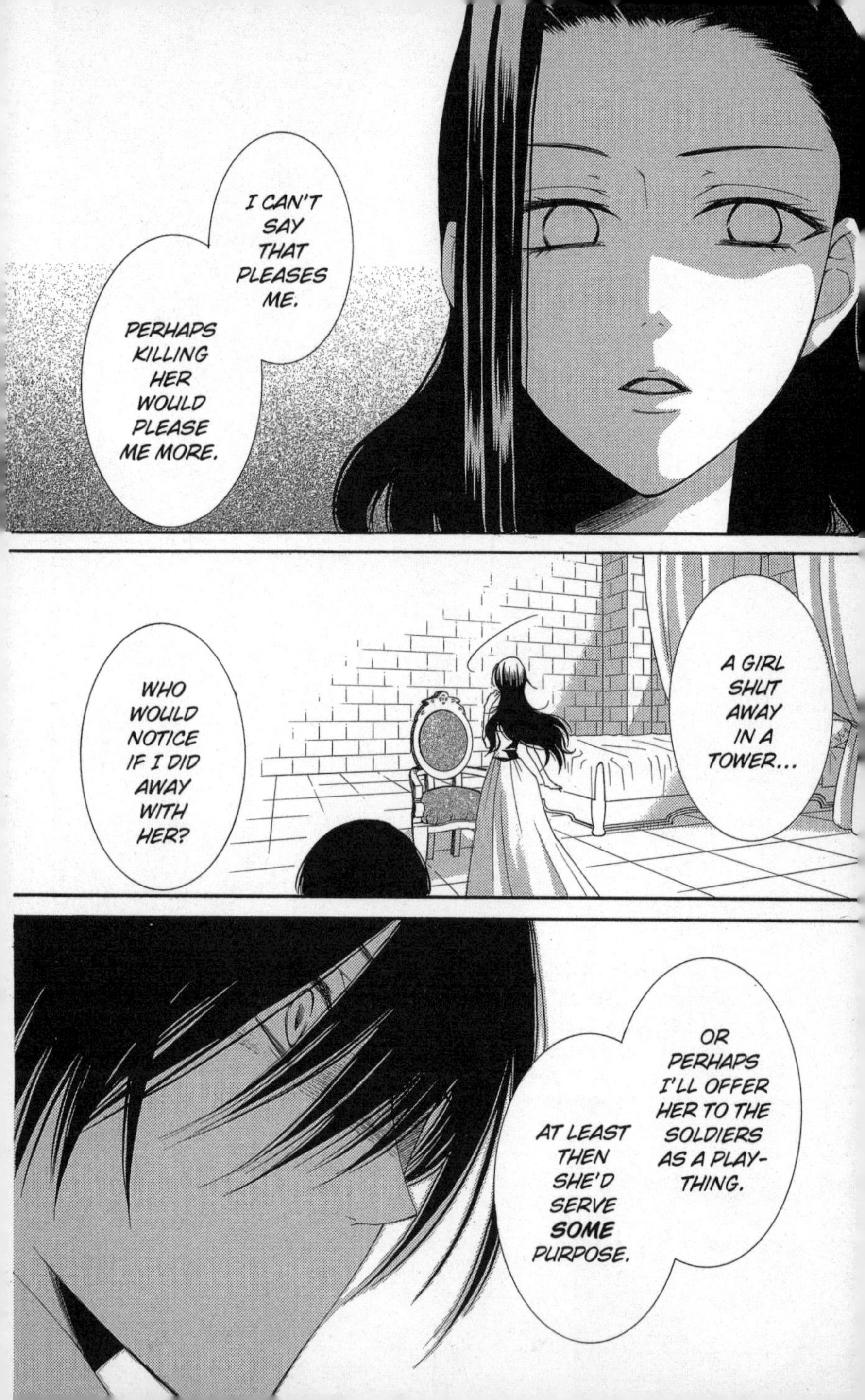
I CAN'T SAY THAT PLEASES ME.
PERHAPS KILLING HER WOULD PLEASE ME MORE.
A GIRL SHUT AWAY IN A TOWER...
WHO WOULD NOTICE IF I DID AWAY WITH HER?
OR PERHAPS I'LL OFFER HER TO THE SOLDIERS AS A PLAY-THING.
AT LEAST THEN SHE'D SERVE **SOME** PURPOSE.

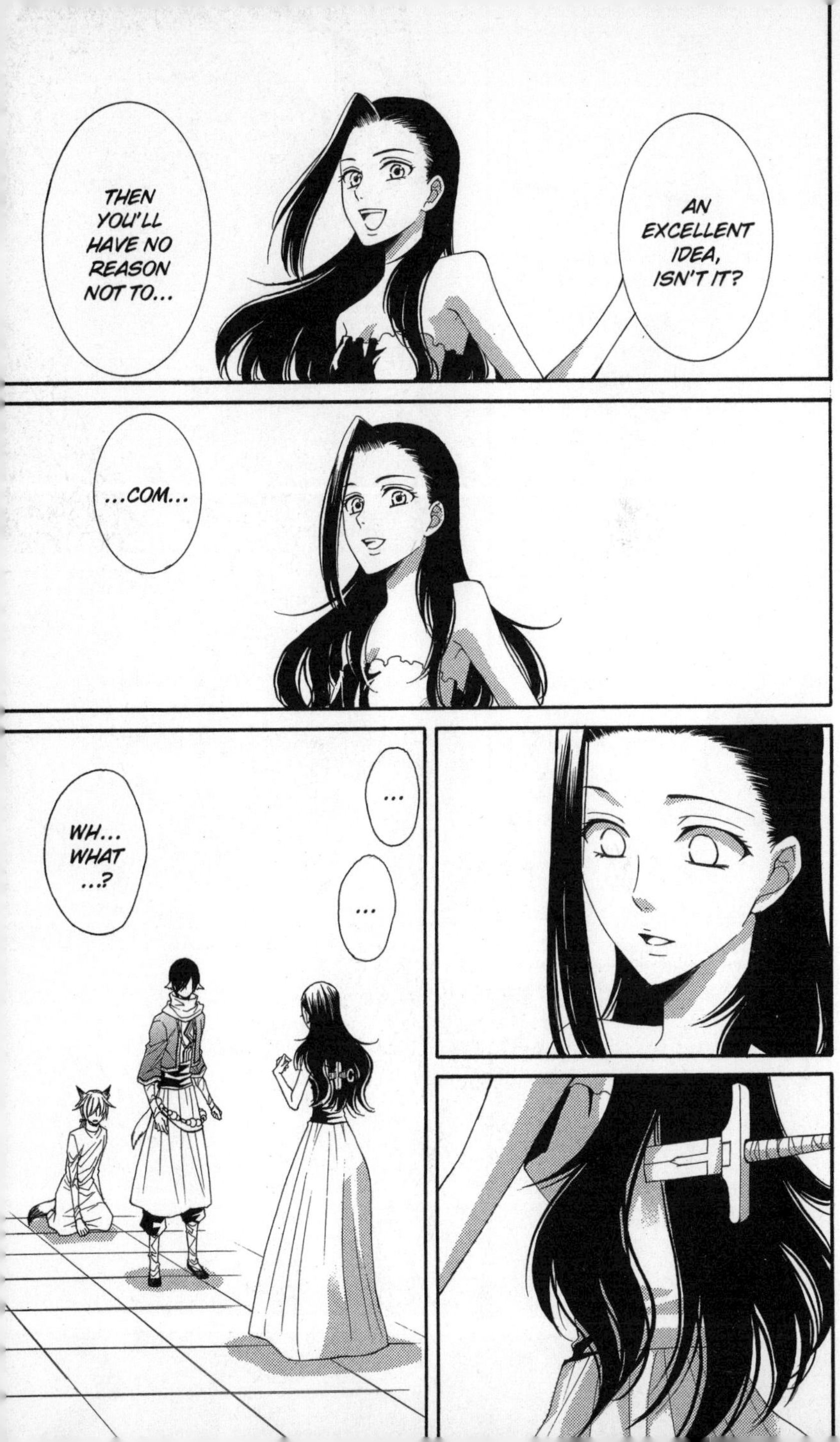
AN EXCELLENT IDEA, ISN'T IT?
THEN YOU'LL HAVE NO REASON NOT TO...
...COM...
...
...
WH... WHAT ...?

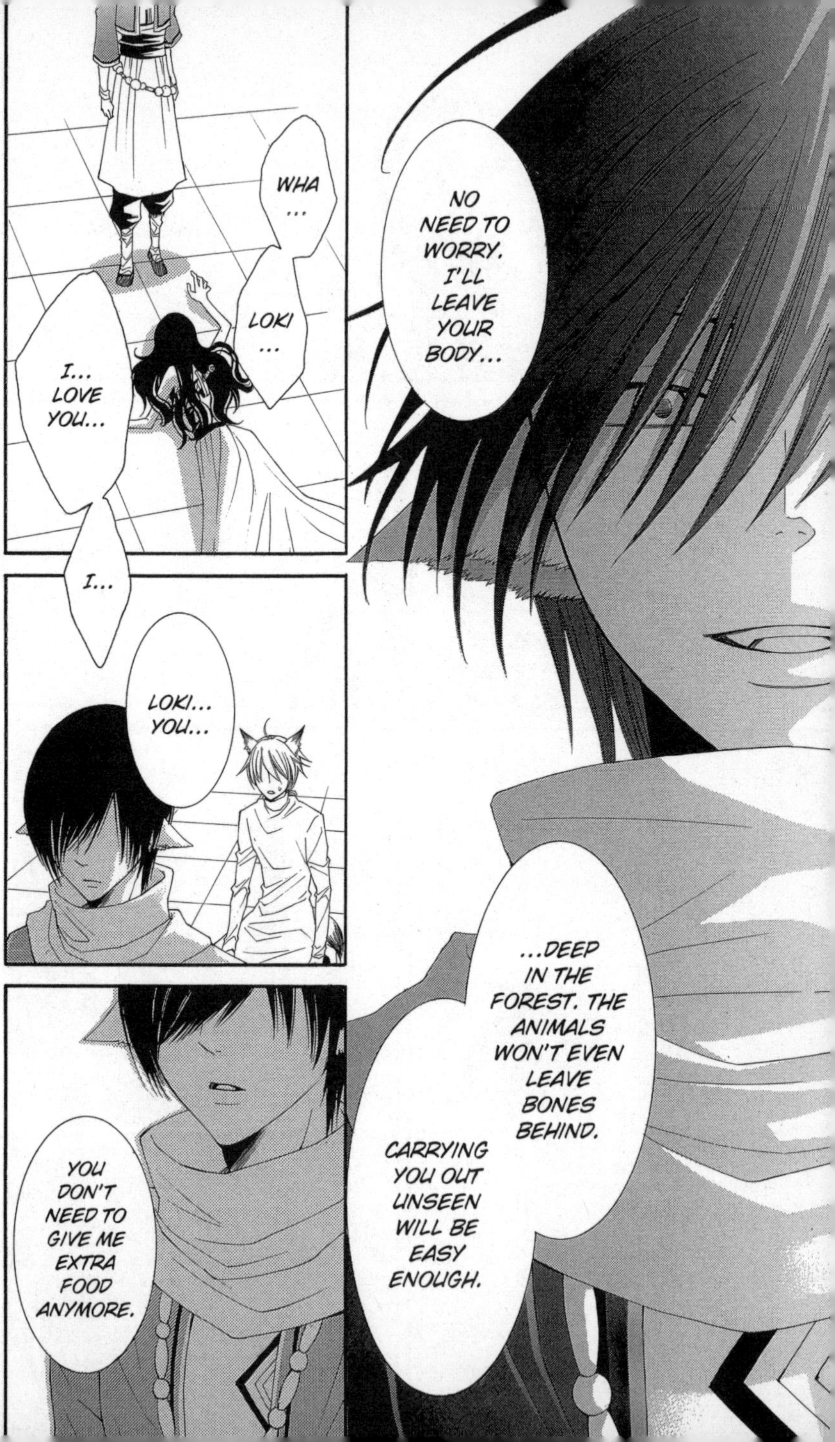
WHA...
LOKI...
I... LOVE YOU...
I...
LOKI... YOU...
YOU DON'T NEED TO GIVE ME EXTRA FOOD ANYMORE.
NO NEED TO WORRY. I'LL LEAVE YOUR BODY...
...DEEP IN THE FOREST. THE ANIMALS WON'T EVEN LEAVE BONES BEHIND.
CARRYING YOU OUT UNSEEN WILL BE EASY ENOUGH.

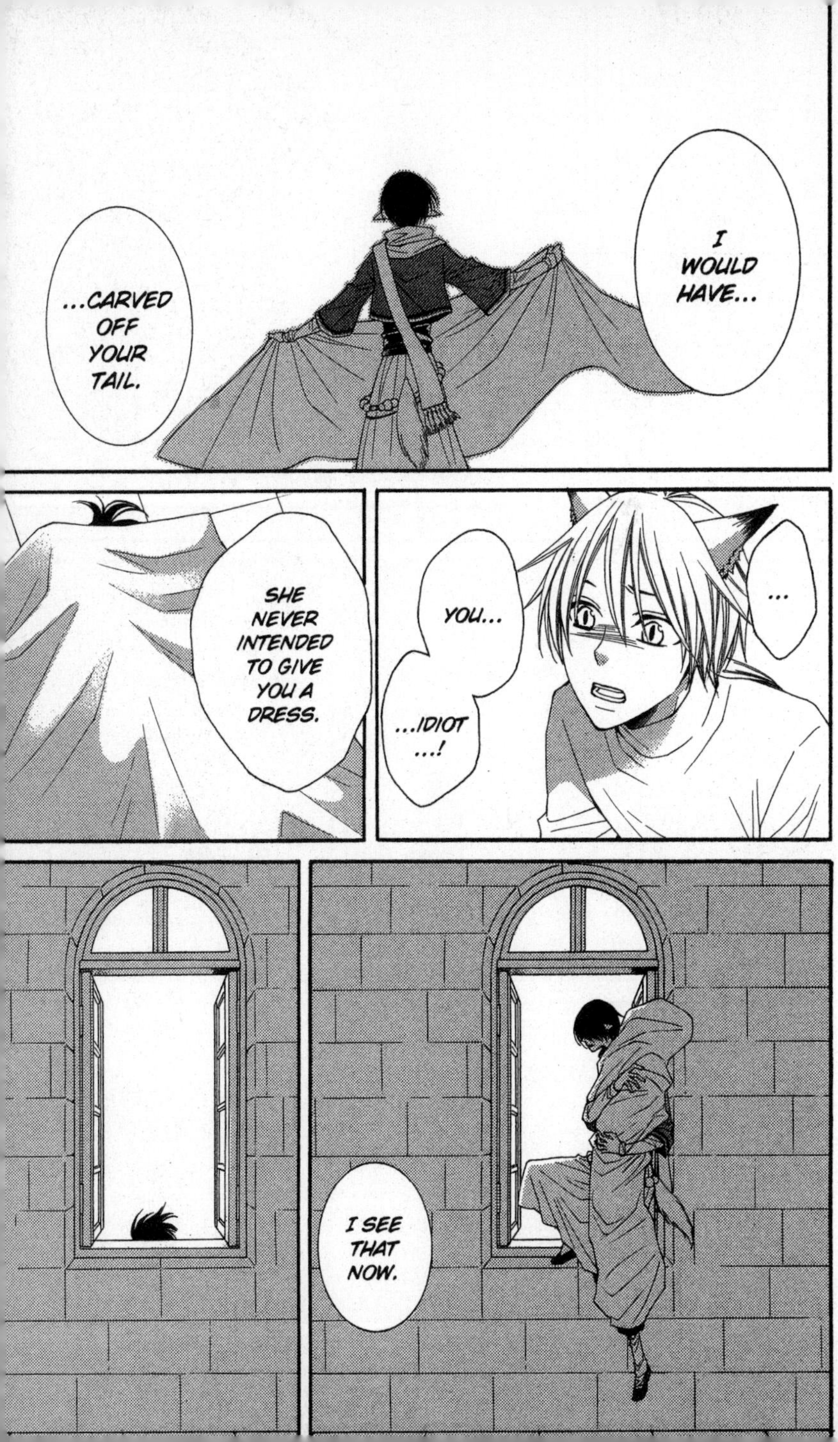
I WOULD HAVE...
...CARVED OFF YOUR TAIL.
...
YOU...
...IDIOT ...!
SHE NEVER INTENDED TO GIVE YOU A DRESS.
I SEE THAT NOW.

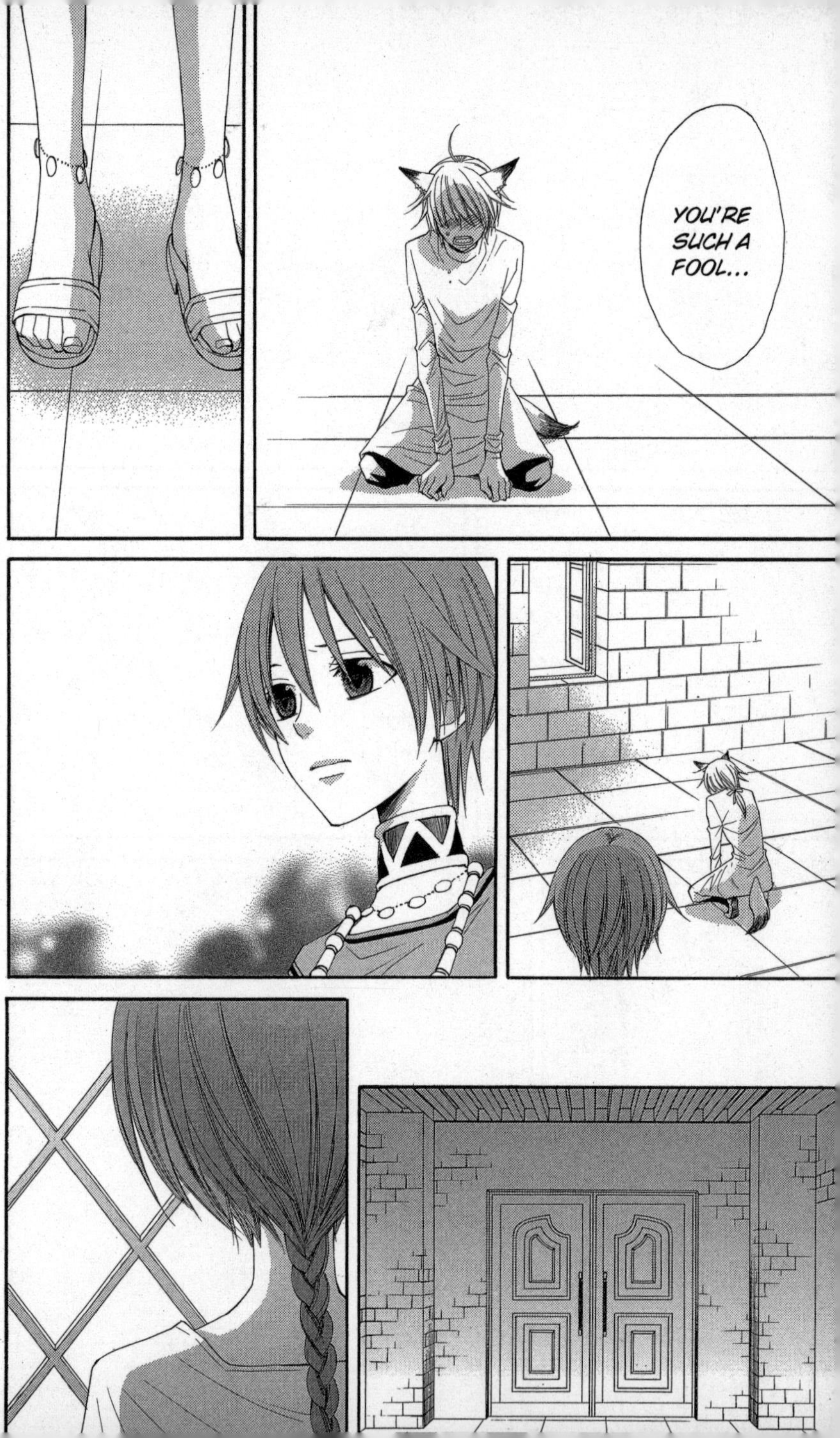
YOU'RE SUCH A FOOL...

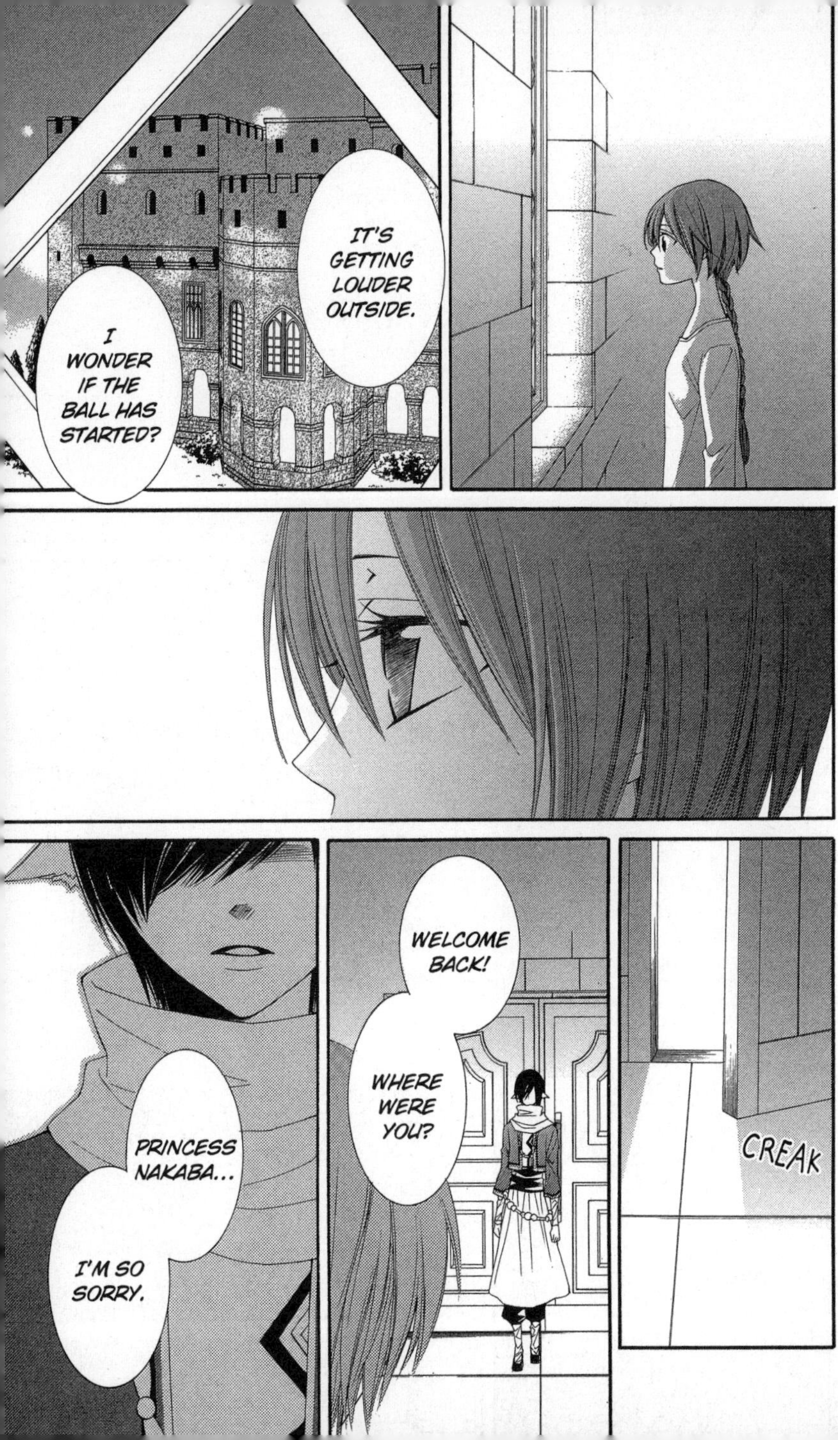
IT'S GETTING LOUDER OUTSIDE.
I WONDER IF THE BALL HAS STARTED?
CREAK
WELCOME BACK!
WHERE WERE YOU?
PRINCESS NAKABA...
I'M SO SORRY.

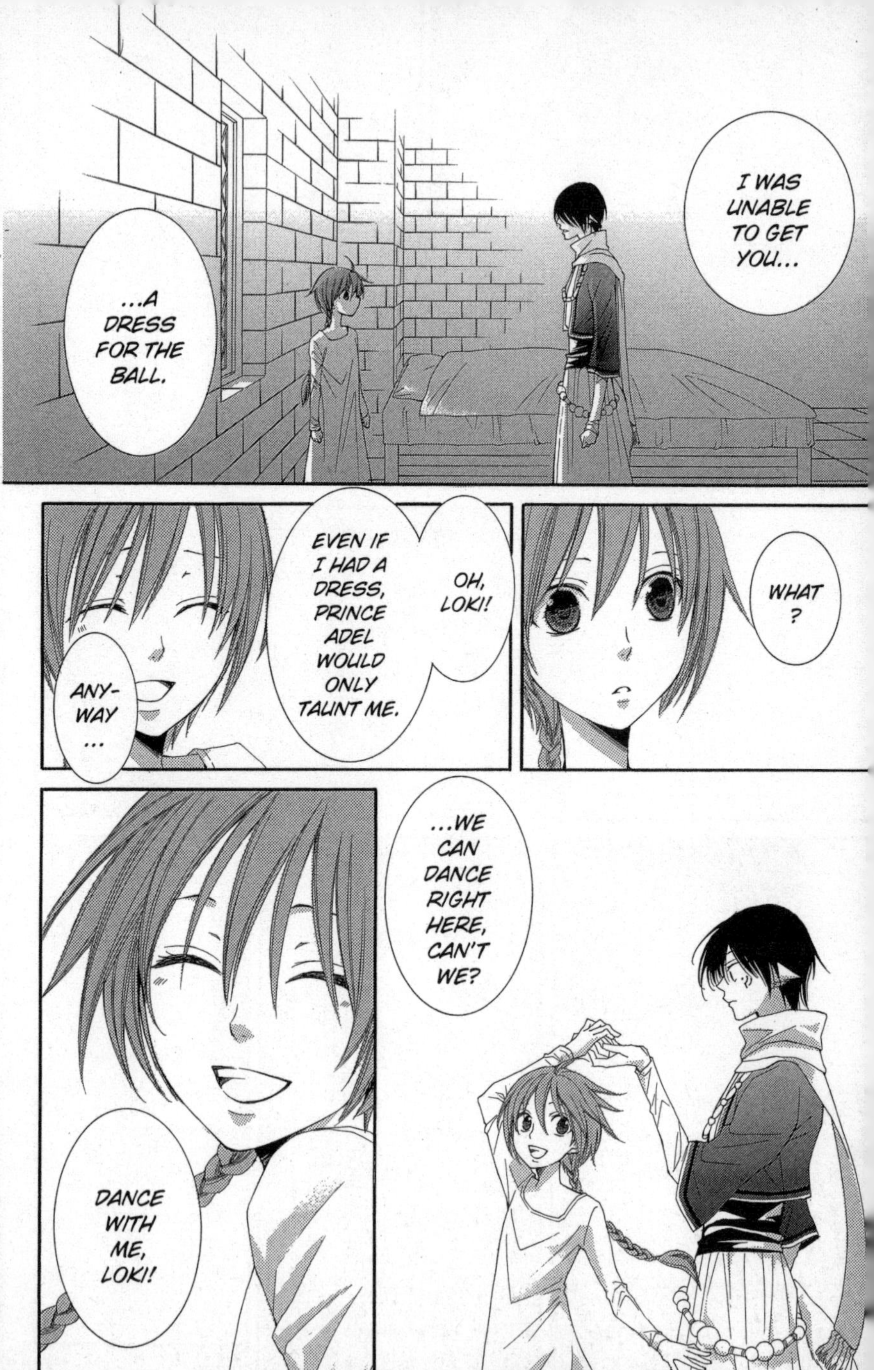
I WAS UNABLE TO GET YOU...
...A DRESS FOR THE BALL.
WHAT?
OH, LOKI!
EVEN IF I HAD A DRESS, PRINCE ADEL WOULD ONLY TAUNT ME.
ANY-WAY...
...WE CAN DANCE RIGHT HERE, CAN'T WE?
DANCE WITH ME, LOKI!

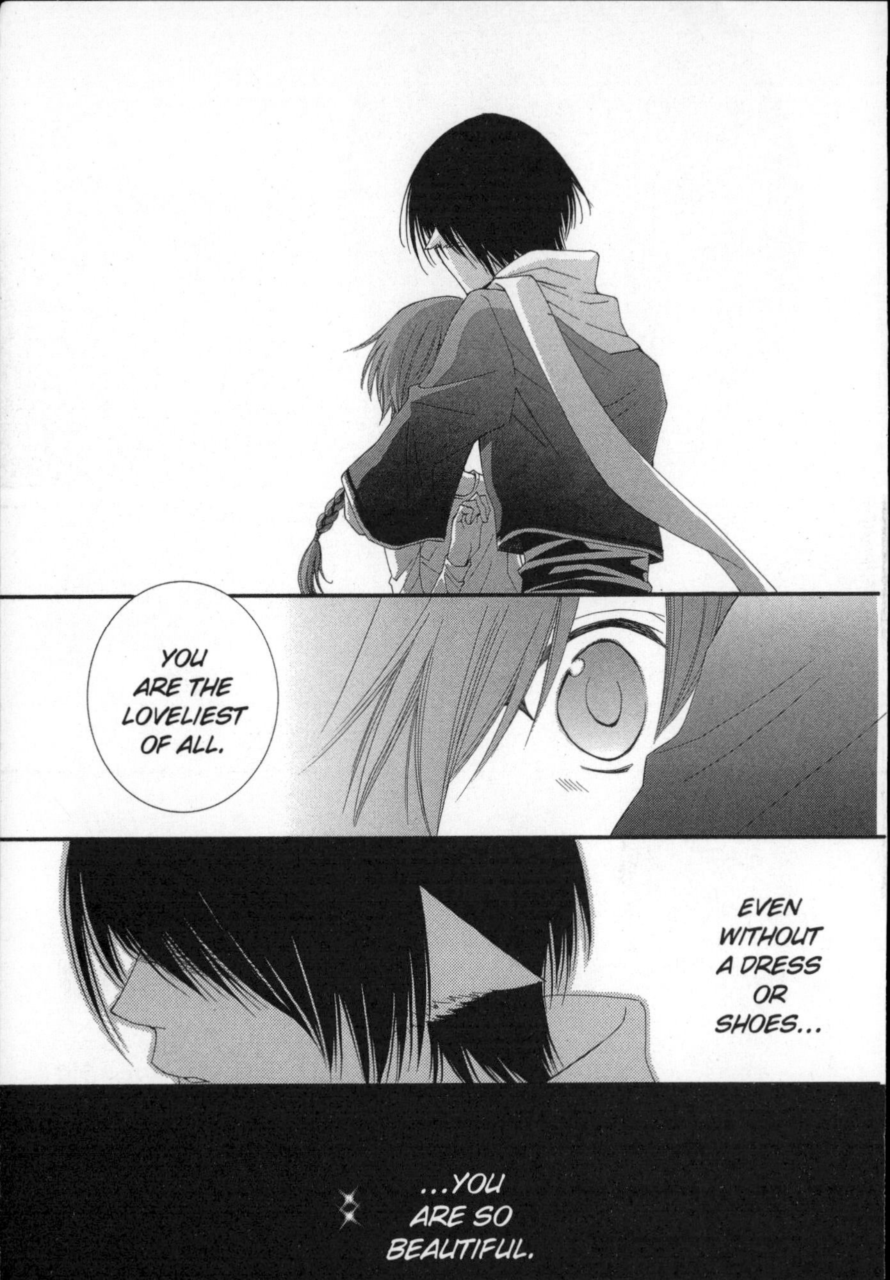
YOU ARE THE LOVELIEST OF ALL.
EVEN WITHOUT A DRESS OR SHOES...
...YOU ARE SO BEAUTIFUL.

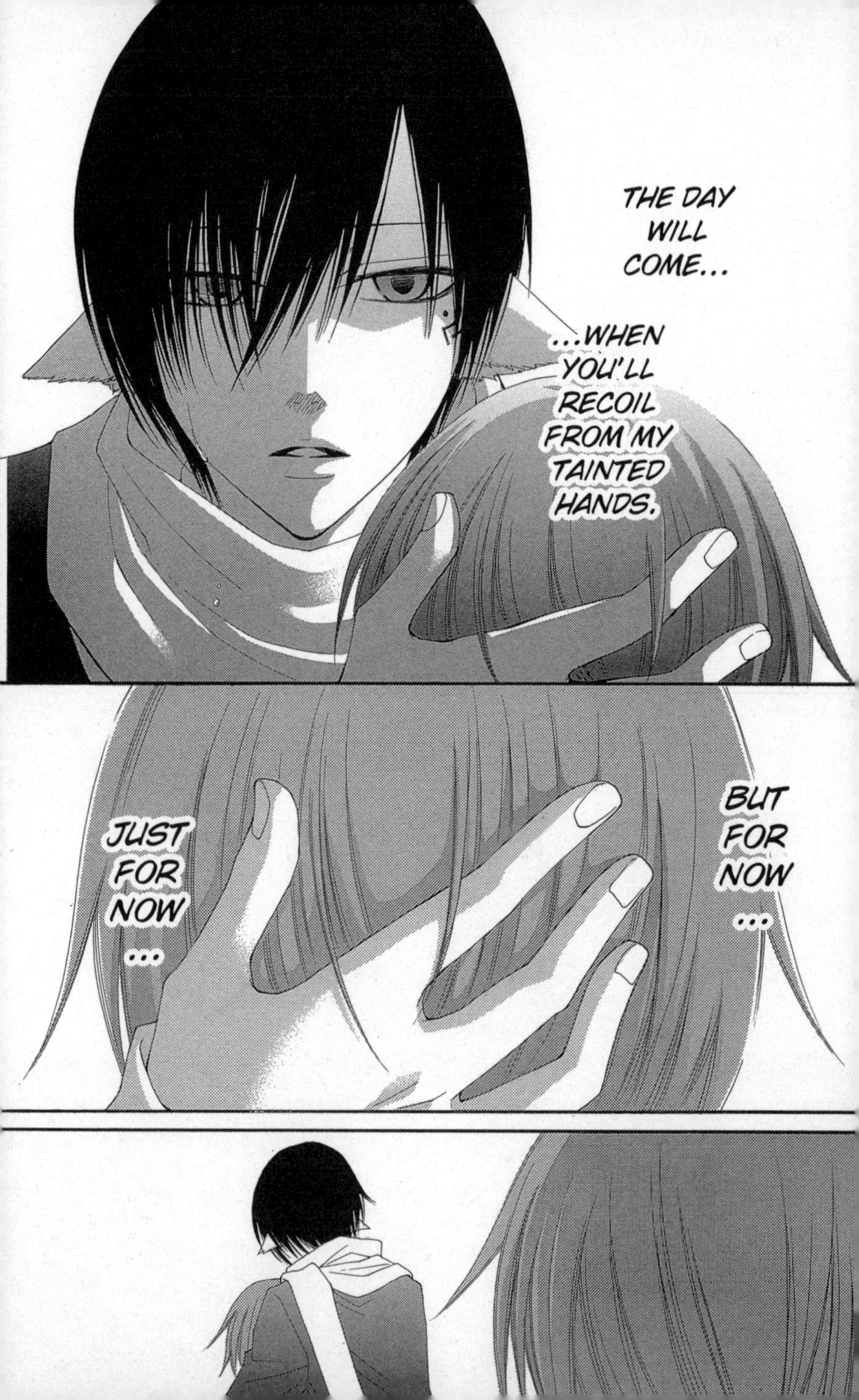
THE DAY WILL COME...
...WHEN YOU'LL RECOIL FROM MY TAINTED HANDS.
BUT FOR NOW ...
JUST FOR NOW ...

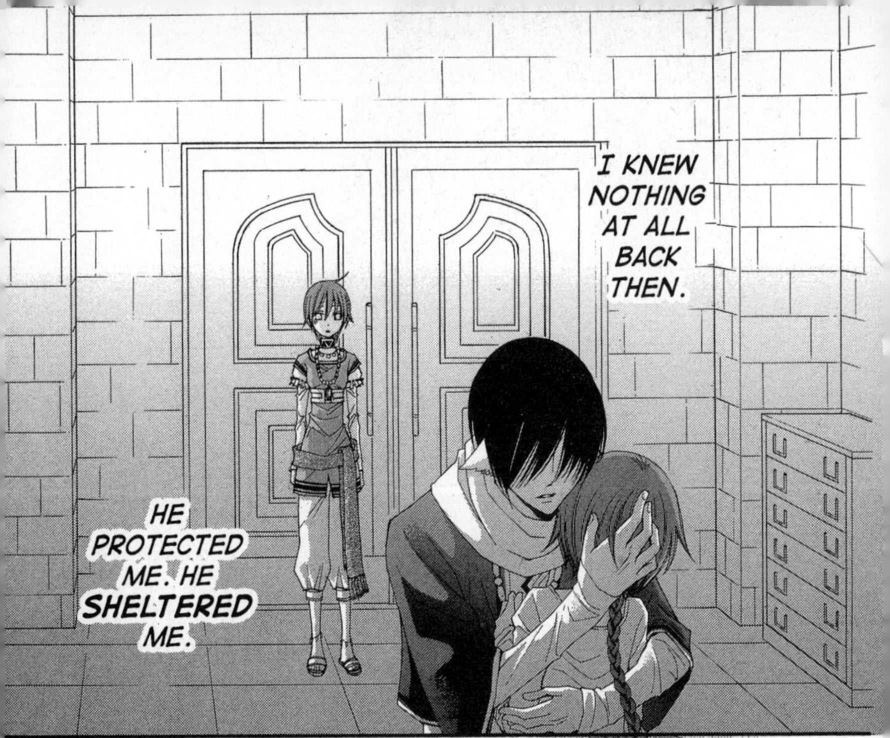
I KNEW NOTHING AT ALL BACK THEN.
HE PROTECTED ME. HE SHELTERED ME.
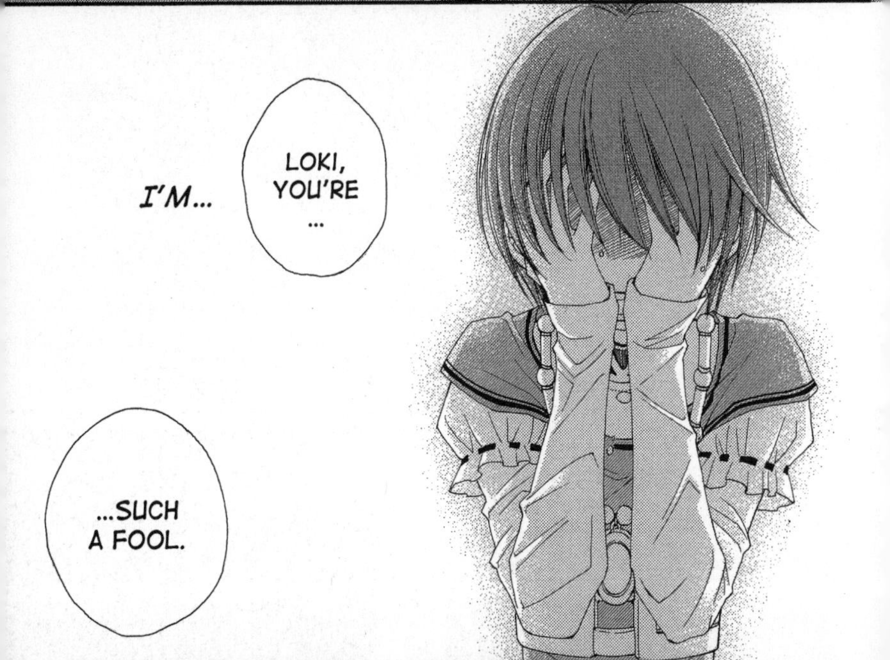
LOKI, YOU'RE ...
I'M...
...SUCH A FOOL.

DAWN OF THE ARCANA 8 (THE END)

As you can see, we've reached the end of
volume 8! Thank you for reading, everyone!

I really enjoy your letters! I'm so sorry I can't respond to them all...
Please let me know what you thought of this volume.

Send your fan mail to:
Rei Toma
C/O Dawn of the Arcana Editor
Viz Media
P.O. Box 77010
San Francisco, CA 94107

From here on out, it's going to be like this picture above. Oh, what'll I do? (*Ha ha*)

–Rei Toma

Rei Toma has been drawing since childhood, but she only began drawing manga because of her graduation project in design school. When she drew a short-story manga, *Help Me, Dentist*, for the first time, it attracted a publisher's attention and she made her debut right away. Her magnificent art style became popular, and after she debuted as a manga artist, she became known as an illustrator for novels and video game character designs. Her current manga series, *Dawn of the Arcana*, is her first long-running manga series, and it has been a hit in Japan, selling over a million copies.

DAWN OF THE ARCANA
VOLUME 8
Shojo Beat Edition

STORY AND ART BY
REI TOMA

© 2009 Rei TOMA/Shogakukan
All rights reserved.
Original Japanese edition "REIMEI NO ARCANA"
published by SHOGAKUKAN Inc.

English Adaptation/Ysabet MacFarlane
Translation/JN Productions
Touch-up Art & Lettering/Freeman Wong
Design/Yukiko Whitley
Editor/Amy Yu

Printed in the U.S.A.

Published by VIZ Media, LLC
P.O. Box 77010
San Francisco, CA 94107

10 9 8 7 6 5 4 3 2
First printing, February 2013
Second printing, June 2014

www.viz.com   www.shojobeat.com